The Theatre of Conor McPherson:

'Right beside the Beyond'

Editors

Lilian Chambers and Eamonn Jordan

Carysfort Press

A Carysfort Press Book
The Theatre of Conor McPherson:' Right beside the Beyond'
edited by Lilian Chambers and Eamonn Jordan

First published in Ireland in 2012 as a paperback original by
Carysfort Press, 58 Woodfield, Scholarstown Road
Dublin 16, Ireland
ISBN 978-1-904505-61-7

Typeset by Carysfort Press
Cover design by eprint limited

Printed and bound by eprint limited
Unit 35
Coolmine Industrial Estate
Dublin 15
Ireland

This book is published with the financial assistance of
The Arts Council (An Chomhairle Ealaíon) Dublin, Ireland

Table of contents

Acknowledgements   *ix*
Introduction   1

1 | **The Early Years**   21
      Anthony Roche

2 | **The Geography of Conor McPherson's**   31
      Plays: The City as Salvation or Hell?
      Sara Keating

3 | **The Art of Disclosure, the Ethics of**   43
      Monologue in Conor McPherson's Drama:
      ***St. Nicholas, This Lime Tree Bower* and**
      Port Authority
      Clare Wallace

4 | **Representing Sexual Violence in the Early**   61
      Plays of Conor McPherson
      Lisa Fitzpatrick

5 | **Conor McPherson's *St. Nicholas*: A Study**   77
      in Comic Anguish
      Susanne Colleary

6 | **'shame shame shame': Masculinity,**   89
      Intimacy and Narrative in Conor
      McPherson's *Shining City*
      Kevin Wallace

7 | **'This is what I need you to do to make it**   103
      right': Conor McPherson's *I Went Down*
      Emilie Pine

8 | **The Buoyancy of Conor McPherson's**   113
      Saltwater
      Kevin Kerrane

9 | **Issues of Narrative, Storytelling and**   127
      Performance in Conor McPherson's *The*
      Actors
      Carmen Szabo

10 | **Mysterium Tremens: Conor McPherson's**   137
        Dublin Carol
        Ian R. Walsh

11 | **The 'Sweet Smell' of the Celtic Tiger: Elegy**   151
        and Critique in Conor McPherson's *The*
        Weir
        P.J. Mathews

12 | **The Measure of a Pub Spirit in Conor**   165
        McPherson's *The Weir*
        Rhona Trench

13 | **'Stumbling around in the light': Conor**   183
        McPherson's partial eclipse
        Ashley Taggart

14 | **The Supernatural in Conor McPherson's**   197
        The Seafarer* and *The Birds
        Christopher Murray

15 | **The Gravity of Humour in Samuel**   215
        Beckett's *Endgame* and Conor
        McPherson's *The Seafarer*
        Eric Weitz

16 | **Conor McPherson's *The Seafarer*: Male**   231
        Pattern Blindness
        Audrey McNamara

17 | **Interview with Pál Göttinger**   241
        Mária Kurdi

18 | **Para-Normal Views/Para-Gothic Activities**   251
        in Conor McPherson's *The Veil*
        Eamonn Jordan

19 | **Interview with Conor McPherson**   275
        Noelia Ruiz

Biographical notes   291
Performances and Bibliography   297
Index   303

Acknowledgements

Special acknowledgement to Dan Farrelly for his significant and patient work on this project and for his substantial and ongoing commitment in his roles as Chairperson and General Editor of Carysfort Press. We would like to thank the Arts Council for their continued backing of publishers like Carysfort Press, as their support ensures that publications like this one can happen. *The Theatre of Conor McPherson* documents, contextualizes and critically evaluates the writing and performance of work by a world-renowned Irish writer and director of film and theatre.

All excerpts from plays and screenplays by Conor McPherson are strictly protected by copyright and are reproduced with the permission of McPherson's publisher, Nick Hern Books: www.nickhernbooks.co.uk

Thanks to the Gate Theatre for permission to reproduce the image from its production of *The Weir* in 2008, directed by Garry Hynes and designed by Francis O'Connor, with Genevieve O'Reilly and Seán McGinley playing Valerie and Jack respectively. We also wish to thank photographer Anthony Woods for providing us with the image. Thanks to all our contributors for the work that they have produced to make this collection of essays the substantial volume that it is.

Finally, many thanks to Conor McPherson for agreeing to be interviewed for this project, for the range, generosity, insights of his plays, for the keen articulations of his points of view in the media and other fora, and for his ongoing commitment to the processes of rehearsal and performance; and perhaps above all, for his interests in and respect for audiences around the world.

Introduction

Conor McPherson has produced an extraordinary body of work over the last two decades and more. Born in Dublin on 6 August 1971, McPherson has worked as an actor, screenwriter, film and theatre director and most of all as a playwright. He first came to prominence in the early 1990s at Dramsoc – University College Dublin's Drama Society.[1] Having graduated, McPherson's early work was produced by Fly By Night Theatre Company.[2] His major breakthrough came after two productions at the Bush Theatre in London. The Bush did a production of *This Lime Tree Bower* (a winner of the Stewart Parker Award) which opened on 3 July 1996, having been previously co-produced by Íomhá Ildánach/Fly by Night Theatre Company on 26 September 1995 at the Crypt Arts Centre, Dublin. Perhaps even more significantly, *St. Nicholas* opened at the Bush Theatre on 19 February 1997, with Brian Cox in the lead role, a work which McPherson wrote while he was attached to the theatre under the Pearson Television Theatre Writer's Scheme.[3] McPherson appears to have been making the most of the many opportunities that were coming his way at the time.

A commission from London's Royal Court Theatre led to the multi-award winning production of *The Weir*, which opened on 4 July 1997 at the Royal Court Theatre Upstairs. Directed by Ian Rickson and designed by Rae Smith, *The Weir* is the work which has established McPherson's international reputation. (*The Weir* transferred to the Royal Court Downstairs, St Martin's Lane, in London's West End, on 18 February 1998 where it ran for two years, with a number of cast changes throughout the run.)[4] *Dublin Carol*, also directed by Rickson and designed by Rae Smith, opened on 7 January 2000, and *Shining City* also premiered at Royal Court's Theatre Downstairs on 9 June 2004 with McPherson directing.[5]

More recently, *The Seafarer* (2006) opened at the National Theatre's Cottesloe auditorium in London on 28 September 2006, with McPherson again directing. When the play reached Broadway, with McPherson continuing to direct the work, it was nominated for Tony Awards in the category of Best Play and Best Director, having earlier received nominations for Best Play for both the Laurence Olivier and Evening Standard Awards. Further, Jim Norton won a Best Supporting Actor Olivier Award 2007 and a Tony Featured Best Actor Award in 2008 for his performances as Richard Harkin. His most recent play *The Veil* received its first production at London's National Theatre's Lyttleton auditorium on 4 October 2011, with McPherson directing.

McPherson's stage adaptation of Daphne du Maurier's short story *The Birds* received its American premiere on 29 February 2012 at the Dowling Studio of the Guthrie Theater, Minneapolis, directed by Henry Wishcamper, who had previously directed *Port Authority* for New York's Atlantic Theater Company in 2008. This adaptation of *The Birds* was first performed at the Gate Theatre in Dublin on 25 September 2009 during the Dublin Theatre Festival, with McPherson directing, and with Sinead Cusack and Ciarán Hinds in the lead roles.

At this stage of his career, one can see the broad range of theatre companies with which McPherson has worked in London, namely The Bush Theatre, The Royal Court and London's National Theatre and there is an obvious pattern of premiering work in London before transferring it elsewhere. Indeed, the Gate Theatre's production of *Port Authority* opened at the New Ambassadors on 22 February 2001 in London, before transferring to Dublin on 24 April 2001. (Normally, the tendency for an Irish writer is to open a play on the island and hope for a transfer to places like London.) At the Gate Theatre, McPherson has established a very good working relationship with Michael Colgan, the theatre's Artistic Director. *Shining City* also transferred there in September 2004. *Come on Over* was performed at the Gate from 2 October 2001 as part of an evening of three plays, alongside Neil Jordan's *White Horses* and Brian Friel's *The Yalta Game*. A production of *The Weir* which opened on 12 June 2008, also at the Gate, directed by Garry Hynes, was warmly received. The Gate had already staged a production of the play a decade earlier in 1999. Additionally, in 2000 McPherson directed *Endgame* for the *Beckett on Film* series, having already directed a production of *Endgame* at the Gate in April 1999.

McPherson also directed Billy Roche's *Poor Beast in the Rain* there in April 2005. Until more recently, McPherson's relationship with Dublin's Abbey Theatre has been somewhat less fruitful; a production of *The Seafarer* on the Abbey Theatre stage in 2008 was a homecoming of sorts. McPherson had directed Eugene O'Brien's *Eden* initially at the Abbey's Peacock Theatre in January 2001. This exceptionally successful play had national and international tours, and eventually played on the Abbey's main stage.

McPherson has the determination, confidence, skills and self-assurance to direct the premieres of many of his own plays. It is a task that most people would be encouraged not to do, as playwrights are generally seen to be too close to the work, or they are regarded generally as being less likely to be creatively interpretative of their own work and thus more prone to the construction of a limited or conservative *mise-en-scène*. In many respects McPherson is often quoted as seeing the directing of the work as a completion of the writing project, as there is ample opportunity to revise and re-configure the work during the rehearsal period.[6]

In the same year as *The Weir* garnered international acclaim, his film script for *I Went Down* (1997) was also well received critically. *I Went Down* got the Spanish Circle of Screenwriter's Award for Best Screenplay and the San Sebastian film festival award for Best Film. This was followed by *Saltwater* (2000), an adaptation of *This Lime Tree Bower*, which McPherson wrote and directed. *Saltwater* won the CICAE Award for Best Film at the Berlin Film Festival. In 2003 *The Actors* opened, which McPherson again wrote and directed. *The Eclipse*, directed by McPherson and co-written with Billy Roche, premiered at the Tribeca Film Festival in 2009, where Ciarán Hinds won Best Actor Award. Additionally, at the Irish Film and Television Academy Awards in 2010, *The Eclipse* won Best Film and Best Screenplay Awards and Aidan Quinn won Best Actor in a Supporting Role in a Film. The film also won the Méliès d'Argent Award for Best European Film at the Sitges, Catalonian International Film Festival in 2009.[7] In terms of film, McPherson made a cameo acting appearance in *I Went Down* and appeared briefly in *Inside I'm Dancing* (2004) and in the TV series *Paths to Freedom* (2000) and *Fergus's Wedding* (2002). He also wrote some of the music for *The Actors* and worked on the score for *The Eclipse*, with his wife, the painter and musician, Fionnuala Ni Chiosain.

An awareness of how plays impact on audiences comes through again and again in McPherson's comments on the writing for and directing of theatre. And of course, it is his consistently expressed admiration for actors and designers that comes across in almost all his reflections on the making of theatre.[8] Engagements with McPherson's strikingly rich body of work is aided considerably by his willingness to commit to interviews and give considered responses to detailed questions, to write opinion pieces, and to offer reflections on the art of playwriting. His engagement with emerging writers and directors at a number of University programmes in Ireland and America, including University College Dublin's Masters in Directing and Drama and Performance Programmes where he is currently Adjunct Professor, displays a willingness not only to encourage new work, but to contribute positively to the training environments of upcoming practitioners.

In this collection we have gathered an array of very interesting voices, who sometimes share common perspectives, but are also now and then at odds in their responses to the work. The reader is encouraged to negotiate with and between these opposing points of view. The approaches here vary from the explication of text to broad theorizing in relation to gender, from reflections on issues of morality to analysis of the monologue form, from the consideration of space to discussions on the supernatural and dramaturgical considerations of more complex consciousnesses beyond the real, and from reflections on comedy to considerations of approaches to direction and conditions of performance. (As many of the plays have been published in very different forms, page references are to the specific publications, as our contributors had used the published versions of plays that they had at their disposal.) As editors, we decided not to cover the very early plays, but even with these exclusions, and as with any edited book like this, there remain obvious gaps. Regardless, this collection marks over two decades of substantial, significant and landmark output, and interrogates critically work that has been produced around the world in a variety of ways and in many different contexts.

Anthony Roche captures the early career of McPherson during his time in University College Dublin (1988-93), where he studied English and Philosophy for his undergraduate degree, before going on to complete an MA in Philosophy. During this period, apart from his academic development, McPherson effectively achieved an unstructured, extensive and decisive early training in theatre and performance. Roche's reflections on the hot housing, informal and formative influences of academic and student life on McPherson are matched by his astute reading of McPherson's MA major thesis 'Logical Constraint and Practical Reasoning: On Attempted Refutations of Utilitarianism,' a work which is in the words of Roche 'a strong-minded and robust defence of the theory of utilitarianism, arguing that people undertake goals in life not because they are trying to be objectively moral but to satisfy their own wants and desires.' In many ways that academic thesis provides a philosophical backdrop to much of McPherson's work to date.

With the early successes of the monologues like *Rum and Vodka*, *The Good Thief* and *This Lime Tree Bower*, many in the theatre and academic communities wondered about the viability, even validity, of monologues as theatrical pieces, worried about the apparent closing down or erasure of character interaction and conflict. Additionally, the relationship between monologue and gender has raised a whole series of complicated questions that the works themselves do not set out to answer. In his Author's Note to *Three Plays*, McPherson says, 'The first problem for the actor performing these pieces is probably "Where am I"? "Where is the play set"? I've made up my mind about this. These plays are set "in a theatre." Why mess about? The character is on stage, perfectly aware that he is talking to a group of people... The temptation may be not to launch a one man "performance," to "act things out." But such a performance will never be as interesting as one where the actor trusts the story to do the work.'[9] As McPherson is always keen to suggest that the monologues are set in the theatre, this fact alone raises fundamental issues about the monologue form itself. In this volume of essays the monologue form comes under particular scrutiny.

Although regularly set in a theatre as McPherson suggests of the early monologues in particular, Dublin proves to be a significant marker not only in the early work, but almost throughout all of the plays and films. Given particular focus in the plays is Dublin's north side, in particular, areas close to Raheny where McPherson grew up. Places like Baldoyle, the Bull Wall, Clontarf, Dollymount Strand, Fairview, Howth, Kilbarrack, Killester, Malahide, Phibsboro, and Sutton are referenced. Numerous Dublin public houses, some landmark ones, are also mentioned in passing. Other familiar Dublin locations like Bachelor's Walk, Merrion Square, and Trinity College are thrown in as if the co-ordinates of the space give an initial spatial specificity that more often than not dissipates as the plays progress. Sara Keating identifies the evolution of McPherson's relationship with the fringes or borders of his home city, evident in his early monologues, a connection in Keating's words which moves 'to a deeper metaphysical engagement with a more provisional city in his later work.' Those senses of 'metaphysical engagement' and of a 'provisional city,' link in with many of the theories proposed by urban geographers and sociologists on issues of space, residuality, identities, marginality and the transgressions and mobility between and across spaces and boundaries. Keating suggests that the work has both contextual tendencies and equally its opposite, for through the defamiliarization of these spaces, and through the admission of the uncanny, the otherworldly, the 'habits and routines' of the everyday and the familiar are alienated, estranged or disenfranchised.

That sense of spatial disorientation or dislocation links in with issues of marginalized masculinities and femininities, which are subordinated in different ways, we may add, but persistently they are ones that are very much at odds with the dominant cultural imaginary. Sometimes the city is the space to be evaded or fled from as in *The Good Thief,* sometimes Dublin holds out the possibility of a homecoming of sorts as in the case of *St. Nicholas* and sometimes it is the place to be abandoned for an isolated west of Ireland as in *The Weir*. For Valerie, in this play, the west is a space of sanctuary and re-integration, fundamentally opposed to the city, which is aligned with decay, loss and dysfunction. For the male-centric monologues it is often sex that appears to be the siren call to a world elsewhere, which is often perceived 'as more sexually and socially liberated than their own,' as in *Rum and Vodka* and in *Port Authority*, as Keating instances.

If Keating's primary focus is on space and its significance in terms of character, mobility and boundaries, Clare Wallace examines in particular the relationship between the monologue form and the centrality of disclosure to questions of ethics in three of McPherson's monologues. Wallace highlights what she regards as 'the pivotal quality of ambivalence that might serve to distinguish modern monologue from its predecessors,' so that there are not clear distinctions between a revelatory, authentic truth and lies. The innate performativity of the monologue complicates matters further. What this achieves, Wallace notes, is 'narratological and by extension ontological provisionality, uncertainty, or even failure.' Wallace's impressively argued work also contends with issues of agency and the implications of the absence of moral clarity.

Susanne Colleary's consideration of *St. Nicholas* places emphasis less on ethics and morality and more on the 'comedy of entropy' and how this might be negotiated with an audience in performance. Colleary cleverly selects McPherson's comments on Martin Scorsese's *The King of Comedy* (1983) and identifies the relationship between these comments and his own work, particularly recognizing the need for delusion or a pipe dream to maintain lives, and a 'need to be able to laugh at the absurdity of it all.'[10] The irony of course is that the main character in *St. Nicholas* is a journalist and theatre critic, who joins a sect of vampires and agrees to procure victims for the group's blood lust.

Across the body of McPherson's work, male identities are shaped fundamentally by their experiences with women, but the regular lack of prominence given to women characters, even their absence is often regarded as one of the persistent features of the body of work. *This Lime Tree Bower* has three male characters and *Port Authority* likewise. *The Weir* has four men and one woman, *Shining City* has three male characters and one female one, *Dublin Carol* has two male and one female roles. *The Seafarer* has an all male cast. In *Come On Over* there is one male and one female character and in *The Veil* there are three male and five female roles.

In Lisa Fitzpatrick's article on the early work she looks at acts of violence perpetuated by men on women, but notes that these remain off stage; there is neither enactment of violence on stage nor are there graphic details of such violation. This feature makes the work very different to the work of Mark O'Rowe whose monologues *Howie the Rookie* (1999), *Crestfall* (2003) and *Terminus* (2007) contain lucid and lurid descriptions of rape and violence, and the rhythms of the language are informed to some extent by the way that these traumas are detailed.

Whether it is having sex with a sleeping wife Maria in *Rum and Vodka* or the rape of the child Patience by Matthew in *Come on Over*, Fitzpatrick considers both the patterns and dynamics of sexual violence in the work and also the invisibility or obscurity of women generally. Fitzpatrick links both the dramaturgy of the plays and the role of the spectator through Jill Dolan's work on subjectivities, ideologies and performance, and argues how ideology most commonly 'denies subjectivity to female characters and positions the male characters at the centre of the action as protagonists and antagonists, with the female characters in a range of supporting roles and, often, functioning as objects of transaction between the men.' In a way then the plays are tested against this type of ideological dispositioning. In *The Good Thief*, Greta is swapped, exchanged and transacted between a number of gangland figures, but it says less about the problems of dramaturgy and more about how, in this underworld, sex is particularly commodified, women are easily objectified and subjectivity and agency are seen primarily in terms of woman's exploitation of "erotic capital". Indeed Anna exchanges sex for the life of the narrator. In this instance, the trope of woman as sacrificial victim appears apt, but it moves well beyond that stereotype, because she also sexually betrays the narrator.

Kevin Wallace discusses issues of masculine shame in *Shining City*, noting the failures of communication, self-knowledge and self-reflection. Wallace argues: 'Every attempt at communication is hobbled by redundant, formulaic phrasing ('you know,' 'you too,' and 'good luck'),' something that McPherson picked up from David Mamet as much as from Anton Chekhov. Dramatically, interrupted expression, unfinished exchanges, the lack of desire to complete a negotiation are often far more potent in the theatre than clarity and closure. Wallace interrogates both the performance of confession and that of therapy, and evaluates notions of exchange, displacement and intimacy therein, using the work of Ariel Watson. A 'performance of intimacy' in view of strangers does not of course mean that the characters can benefit from the transactional qualities of play, which are less voyeuristic and safe, and more participative and potent. The therapist does not normally actively partake, whereas in play there is an expectation for all parties to be adequately versed and committed to such a performance. In much of the McPherson work the male characters seldom summon any spirit of play, or participate in any significant status shifting, as they are locked into modes of existence that are predominantly destructive.

As Wallace notes, sexual desire, heterosexual, homosexual, or both, is one of the forces that breach notions of moral probity, as does the inability of most characters either to sustain a relationship or to see through on their familial duties. The focus of the male characters seems to be on sex, motivated by desire, but linked to it is some loose aspirational quality that is very much ungrounded, unspecified, almost as if its vagueness serves not as something to chase down, but something on which to hang longing and unrealizable dreams. Sex is seldom about an embodied intimacy, as something relatively free from fear, power, control or anxiety. However, the potential for something more positive cannot compete with that fundamental sense of loss around that which has to be forfeited, the risks of trust and of intimacy in relationships. In *Shining City*, John equates his sexual infidelity with the death of his wife. It is not so much evidence of Newtonian causality, but more of the randomness of cause and effect – a chaos theory of sorts. Guilt is equated not so much with remorse, but with a sense of punishment and haunting.

Yet, if there is something almost innately negative or destructive about masculinity in the plays, the early films seem to be a counter to that. Emilie Pine demonstrates in her analysis of *I Went Down* (1997), a film directed by Paddy Breathnach and produced by Robert Walpole, how classic stereotypes of Irish male inarticulacy and stubbornness can be framed as touchingly redemptive. Part buddy film, part road movie, this gangster comedy seems inspired by comedy capers such as Martin Brest's *Midnight Run* (1988), which stars Robert De Niro and Charles Grodin. This Irish film finds itself not in the back alleys of say Martin Scorsese's New York, and not on the expansive highways of America, but in 'the industrialized bogs of the midlands and insalubrious north Dublin,' as Pine articulates. Pine distinguishes between the final edit of the film and McPherson's published screenplay, identifying in the former how it is the male-male homosocial relationship of Bunny (Brendan Gleeson) and Git (Peter McDonald) that is most emphasized, whereas, in the latter, Git's relationship with Sabrina Bradley (Antoine Byrne) is the more prominent. The scenes cut from the screenplay effectively relegate 'the male-female bond,' Pine suggests. While homosocial bonds are usually exercises in emphasizing and reinforcing heteronormativity, it is more problematic in this instance, as Bunny has had a relationship with a man while in prison, and this is used by French (Tony Doyle), the main gangland figure, to blackmail him. Bunny does not want his wife to know about this prison liaison, as he hopes to reconcile with her. As Pine claims, it is French's wife, who does not appear in the film, who cheats on French with his best friend Grogan (Peter Caffrey), and it is she who eventually double-crosses them both. And it is Sabrina, who also cheats with Git's friend Anto (David Wilmot).

If *I Went Down* has the sinister presence of French, played brilliantly by Doyle, both Git and Bunny, despite their connections to criminality, are comically out of their depth and trapped in this criminal underworld, Bunny by the previously mentioned blackmail and Git by indebtedness, after he blinded one of French's lieutenants while saving Anto from an assault. For Pine, 'What McPherson is keen to show, then, is how Git and Bunny attempt to play certain social roles – the dutiful son and best friend, the tough guy – but because these roles don't fit them, they fail at them or, worse, are failed by them.'

Kevin Kerrane's essay considers in great detail the approach of McPherson as he adapted for screen the 1995 play *This Lime Tree Bower* into *Saltwater* in 2000. McPherson was both screenwriter and first time film director on this project. Kerrane shows that a more upbeat, almost buoyant tone emerges in the adaptation, thus the work is not a simple re-working; more, it is a thorough re-conceptualization of the sensibility and tone of the play. The monologue format of the play has of necessity to be reworked to find interaction and verbal exchanges between the characters, and to engage with characters other than the three key roles found in the drama. Kerrane marks the continuities and significant differences between the drama and film and the implications of these in terms of character complication and mood. In particular, the introduction of additional characters broadens the story base. On the notorious vomiting scene in a crowded UCD lecture theatre Kerrane precisely notes:

> When narrated on stage, this episode was disgusting but abstract; seen on screen, it is as startling as the moment in *Alien* when the creature bursts out of John Hurt's body. In either case, it seems grotesquely funny, as if the vomiting expressed Ray's disgust at academic pretensions – including his own as he rises to ask a question that is supposed to show his intellectual superiority.

Status adjustment, role reversal, and the grotesque are comfortable bedfellows in this comic film.

The failure of the male characters to play or fulfil particular social roles is again very evident in *The Actors*. As Carmen Szabo notes, the conceit of the film is a simple one: 'two actors, not very good at their craft, plan to get hold of easy money by conning some mobsters.' These two characters Tom Quirk (Dylan Moran) and Tony O'Malley (Michael Caine) are even more out of their depth than Bunny and Git. Both actors are in a disastrous though surprisingly award winning production of *Richard III*. Caine's Tony maintains the wonderful fantasy of still being young enough to play

Hamlet, and his concept is to play the vowels only, in order to capture Hamlet's troubled or dis-consonant disposition. A little better at deception than at the stagecraft of acting the two actors begin to spin more and more lies in order to maintain their scam.[11]

As Szabo notes, 'Although it seems a light comedy, *The Actors* touches upon multiple layers of issues about theatricality, the illusion of reality and artistic manipulation.' Significantly she adds: *The Actors* 'becomes a film about acting and actors in a world that only appreciates superficiality.' In a way McPherson's work generally transgresses the real, by foregrounding theatricality and simulation. Yet it is that sense of creativity and contrivance in the dexterity of the actors to cover their tracks and to improvise, however close they veer towards incompetence, that informs McPherson's homage to the craft of the actor.[12] Yet, in contrast, the heightened theatricality of *The Actors* seems at odds with the types of performances that McPherson goes after when he directs monologues.

Across both the films and plays there is a fundamental awareness of theatricality, persistent attempts to undermine a quotidian reality through the consistent awarenesses of ghosts, other worlds, other dimensions or consciousnesses and how these impact on the circumstances of the characters in the work. There is an embrace of mystery and confusion, a celebration of incidental victories, and a comfortableness with chance, as notions of the heroic are isolated to a considerable degree.

Ian R. Walsh interrogates *Dublin Carol,* by deploying Elinor Fuchs' concept of the 'mysterium' in order to show how the work evades very easily the limits of naturalism. Walsh argues that this work has a good deal more to do with experimentation and with a not conservative dramaturgy that is often the reflexive response to work loosely framed by the traditions of realism/naturalism. So for Walsh, *Dublin Carol* 'could be considered a mysterium since it takes salvation as its subject but also as its dramaturgy rests not on the development of character but on the unfolding of a pattern.' Walsh argues that *Dublin Carol* 'would seem to take from the biblical cycle, in that the structure of the passion of Christ, his death and resurrection would seem to be a potential pattern.' Walsh continues that the conflation of the eternal and the temporal is very evident in this work. Equally, he proposes, citing Fuchs's work, that there is a persistent ironic dramaturgical undermining of the work's 'own cosmic pretensions.'

P.J. Mathews considers the relationship between the success of Irish theatre during the Celtic Tiger period and how 'Behind much of this criticism lies a suspicion that the achievement and high visibility of Irish culture globally during the Tiger years was enabled by the increasing capitulation of Irish artists to international taste, expectations and market forces.' Mathews adds that there is nothing new in that disposition and he highlights the negative reception of Thomas Moore's *Irish Melodies* and how even J.M. Synge was 'castigated in his own time for presenting Irish experience in terms of the passing fads of French decadence.' For Mathews, '*The Weir* now stands as an astute analysis of that transition in its exploration of a society caught between impulses of heroic isolation and willing submission to the forces of globalization.' Mathews identifies the manifestation of 'the creeping obsession with property and real estate' and the shifting economic order. The play indicates the shift from unoccupied and hard-to-sell haunted houses to the development of major housing projects in places like Sligo, Leitrim and Roscommon, some of which today remain unfinished or unsold and are now known, uncannily perhaps, as ghost estates. Additionally, Mathews notes:

> Ironically, at the very moment in which the rural Irish pub was being replicated in abundance around the world, the same globalizing forces that promoted its popularity abroad were threatening the original of the species at home.

Rhona Trench's essay on *The Weir* also deals with the interlocking of tradition and the Celtic Tiger period, but in ways that do not demonstrate 'their integration and co-existence, but rather their existence in parallel.' The fundamental journey of characters away from city living to rural retreats is vital to much of McPherson's writing, and such journeys become additionally complicated in *The Weir* for the character of Valerie who seeks sanctuary in an isolated, low-density community, amongst a group of males. As Trench confirms, this pub setting is of huge significance in that it accommodates in particular the uncanny and the supernatural. Indeed, across a range of the plays, some of the greatest dramaturgical and performance challenges that McPherson's work brings is its accommodation of the otherworldly, a facilitation of the world of spirit or of the unconscious in public, shared spaces. There is often the weaknesses of rationality or logic in the face of fear and instinct, the frailties of perceptions and understanding in the face of that which cannot be contained. The

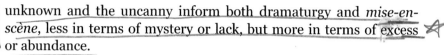

unknown and the uncanny inform both dramaturgy and *mise-en-scène*, less in terms of mystery or lack, but more in terms of excess or abundance.

In *The Weir* the ghost stories and the personal narratives suggest a persistent haunting, a past that cannot be let go of, as memories retard momentum into the present, and alongside this, grief, fear, stubbornness, cussedness, or other forebodings impact on the choices in the lives of the plays' characters. Using the work of Paul Ricoeur, Trench articulates how 'an excess of subjectivity bleeds outside of the pub space, outside of the narratives recounted and into worlds of 'otherness' in the play.' That sense of excess, of bleeding and blending with 'otherness', confronts other critical responses to this play that attempt to ground it only in a sort of naive naturalism. Clearly, naturalism/realism is not the default setting of Irish theatre generally, despite certain received wisdoms, and McPherson's work seems to be an absolute affirmation of that fact.

The Eclipsed (2009) is loosely based on a Billy Roche original short story, *Table Manners* from the collection *Tales From Rainwater Pond* (2006). The film has strong supernatural overtones, in contrast to the story which 'eschews all supernatural elements' as Ashley Taggart suggests. It is the 'melding of genres,' a term used by McPherson and reported by Taggart which not only complicates this film, but is also something which made some financial investors reluctant to back the project, as Taggart sees it. Taggart poses the question about the film: 'Is this a ghost story containing a love story, or a love story which happens to contain some ghosts?' The answer is to say that in many ways it is both. Further, during the film 'the themes of haunting and writing interweave and feed one another' and in such a manner, the work becomes a meditation on the act of writing itself as Taggart notes. (The figure of the writer of course returns again in *The Birds* (2009) and also most recently in *The Veil* (2011).) Equally, the presence of performers, either of actors in *The Actors* or storytellers in the likes of *The Weir* seems to suggest that one of the dominant themes of the full body of work is how the writing reflects on creativity, and on its relationship with memory, desire, trauma and the imagination. Creativity is as much an act of reflection as it is a transaction, exchange or negotiation, whereby failures of clarity or of consciousness are less about failures of representation, and more about the inadequacy of certain modes of representation. In response to *The Eclipse* Taggart argues: 'Faced with the ineffable, our faculty of reason will always show a comic deficit,' and in relation to *The Birds*, Christopher Murray argues that McPherson's adaptation of Daphne du Maurier's short story titled *The Birds* 'radically changed this 1950s existentialism to something much more vague, nightmarish, and postmodern.' Additionally, in the apocalyptic atmosphere of *The Birds*, the chaos of nature destroys humankind without anything like negative intent. In performance, that nightmarish quality, that sense of foreboding, had some spectators seeing the work as a refraction of the anticipated terrors from the fallout of the economic collapse of the Celtic Tiger.

Murray also offers a thorough analysis of the supernatural, evil, justice, morality and consciousness in McPherson's *The Seafarer*. Drawing on both McPherson's comments and on the epigraphs accompanying the work, Murray argues that in *The Seafarer*

> McPherson is concerned with two questions in the play: what is the role of consciousness in the presence of evil? And what is the responsibility of the artist in the face of ultimate moral breakdown?

Murray's work cogently demonstrates how 'McPherson thinks allusively and analogically,' and if stories structure a consciousness, they also establish communal networks and it becomes the responsibility of individuals, despite the awarenesses of death and despite the collapse of moral frameworks, to make choices, to make sense of their frailties and opportunities. A sense of humaneness is reliant in part on an acknowledgement of failings, but also in the celebration of possibility, because possibility fundamentally means facing up to the perils of living and not being cowed by death. Additionally, frailty and weakness trump a self-conscious evil, which takes the form of the Mr Lockhart figure.

Murray argues that Samuel Beckett's *Endgame* 'gave him the hint he needed to convert the folktale into a contemporary exploration of the nature of good and evil in an entertaining style'. Indeed Eric Weitz suggests that when McPherson directed *Endgame* for the *Beckett on Film* series, an alternative light can be shone 'upon his comic sensibilities as apprehended through another writer's text'. In his article Weitz notes that 'McPherson's *Endgame* demonstrates a sensibility for humorous effect driven by earnest investment in character and situation rather than bold outline of comic intent.' Weitz highlights particularly reflections of comic augmentation, arguing that 'This rocking between lightness and harshness of mood is, perhaps, embedded in Beckett's words, but is modulated by McPherson for a narrower range and richer depth of feeling.' In relation to *The Seafarer*, Weitz argues that 'much of the humour written into the play trades on a socio-cultural stereotype of grand-talking, do-nothing camaraderie, held together by the glue of alcohol dependency' and that the play demonstrates Conor McPherson's 'sure grasp of humour's affective nuances.'

Audrey McNamara's analysis of McPherson's own production of *The Seafarer* at the Abbey Theatre in 2009 illustrates such 'affective nuances.' McNamara forcefully demonstrates how Liam Carney as Sharky, Maeliosa Stafford as Richard, Don Wycherly as Ivan, and Phelim Drew as Nicky interrelate, as they are bonded by their need to consume alcohol, play cards and to obliterate so many of the pressures of their existences. In contrast, Nick Dunning's Mr Lockhart has no feel for such a sensibility. For McNamara, Paul O'Mahoney's basement space, decorated like a pub, captures the squalid conditions of Sharky's and Richard's home, which has become a sort of doss house of sorts, and its decrepitude expresses the destructive ways that the characters interact with and within the space. This production illustrates how the characters share, in McNamara's words, a sort of 'Ground Hog Day' situation and the setting of the play on Christmas Eve substantiates that as well, as the characters have their own traditions and rituals. McNamara notes that Carney's superb performance is driven in part by indifference, diffidence and in part by rage, and that it does not allow an audience either to be driven into a Christmas reverie, or to 'relax comfortably into the comedy of the play.' Ultimately McNamara argues that the superb acting 'ensured that the audience left with a feel-good factor; the comedy of the piece masked the dark underlay that protects against the knowledge that perhaps evil forces really are at work.'

Mária Kurdi's interview is with Pál Göttinger, who directed *The Seafarer* in Budapest, Hungary, based on László Upor's translation. This production is currently still playing at the Bárka Theatre. The work has entered the repertoire system since 2008, effectively, 'meaning that a performance is put on the programme two or three times a month,' as Göttinger explains, with about fifty productions of it performed over the last three years, making it a very different repetoire system to Ireland, or Britain for instance. Göttinger acknowledges that he 'did not borrow from another nation's style of acting or draw from the storehouse of their cultural meanings' and neither did he 'want to have the characters look like Irishmen, or parody the Irish.' Kurdi's question on the influence of Eugene O'Neill's *The Iceman Cometh* on the McPherson play draws an interesting insight from the director: 'I think that Lockhart's failure is comic, therefore people come to like him. It may sound strange, but this is the reaction we detected amongst the Hungarian audience. They see a lonely poseur in him, who tries to compensate for this by showing off his darkness of being and terrible secrets.' Göttinger tellingly adds, 'Either way, this tired man, who goes away empty-handed, does not at all look like Satan.' The audience experience of Lockhart as a comic failure speaks to many of the essays in this book.

Eamonn Jordan's article on the Gothic drama *The Veil* considers how McPherson's many public comments on his first history play, in advance of its opening, signal that this historical/supernatural piece is not only about the past, but also about the present and the future. If theatre has the potential to drag its audience into a 'deeper trance,' as the opening quote to this article suggests, then this play lifts the veil on Ireland's widespread trance-like fixation on property, possessions and conspicuous consumption during the Celtic Tiger period. The dispossession and the array of evictions facing many of the characters in the work, and the pressures to emigrate resonate very clearly with a Post-Tiger society, where economic sovereignty is effectively handed over to a Troika, comprising the International Monetary Fund, the European Commission and the European Central Bank. Despite these negatives, the play's ending focuses on resoluteness of the characters to face down seismic changes.

Noelia Ruiz's interview gives McPherson the space and opportunity to offer exceptionally insightful responses to her pertinent questions. A number of things stand out – for instance, in relation to performers McPherson admits: 'My most emotionally open and enthusiastic relationships are with the people I am working with.' Also McPherson's comment on audiences is especially insightful:

> as a group, collectively, in the dark, we all collude in suspending our disbelief together, willingly, to allow an illusion to unfold before us. In theatre you have to concentrate quite hard to maintain the illusion, but that collective effort deepens the experience and takes us into a kind of a trance. And when that happens I think it really concentrates the theatre's peculiar brand of magic which reflects the magic of being alive, the

magic of being conscious, the mystery and the miracle of that, the complete unknown aspect of all of that which is so necessary to live our lives.

For over twenty years now, McPherson has produced an exceptional body of challenging work that raises particular issues about identities, relationships, cultures and societies in which the work is set and performed, but not simply in the sense of mirroring specific cultural moments and the ideological realities therein, but more in relation to the struggles of his characters to face down the dilemmas, confusions, inequalities, opportunities and pleasures of living. Additionally, a simple understanding of theatre from a mimetic point of view only, fails to accommodate appropriately the supernatural as much as the ideological as they occur in his work.

Additionally, how characters negotiate with an apparent deficit rather than a lack of agency is crucial to any understanding of McPherson's work. Some critics have long argued that McPherson's representations of female characters are conservative to say the least, but to say so is often to miss the point. While women characters in the plays exist more in relation to the masculine homosocial bonds, they are not simply misrepresentations per se, more indicators of the psychological states of the male characters and their own concerns and fundamentally their disconnectedness. In the later plays, women have many of the same anxieties as their male counterparts. Some women characters are particularly decisive, for instance, Jack's girlfriend in *The Weir*, who will not indulge him over time, and Valerie, who is not afraid to articulate her anxieties and centralize herself in a predominantly male space. *The Veil* is probably McPherson's most wide-ranging response to gender and class politics.

And if monologues thankfully deprive male characters of active self-reflection and quality insight, then it is the spectator who might just carry that burden. That way, the characters are dislodged and dislocated from their own narratives. Words are inappropriate but estimated responses to the material and spiritual conditions that the characters find themselves in. This complex relationality is not so much empathy dependent, but reliant more on the capacity of the spectator to embrace the narrative, but also to read against the grain of that narrative not so much in search of anomalies, or to be judgmental and cosily objective, but to identify perhaps with parallel weaknesses, and insecurities and to critique their own needs for self-approval and self-assurance or patterns of denial and misjudgement. Temporarily perhaps, a more compassionate sense of inter-connection or inter-dependency evolves from the transaction. In all of this, there is always the sense that McPherson himself heeds the words of advice he regularly gives to young playwrights, 'you always need to be with and ahead of your audience.'

In McPherson's comment, also cited by Christopher Murray, 'Once the show starts, you have to keep the love flowing,'[13] there is a considerable disclosure by the playwright. Love, belonging, protection, despite a forbidding doom, are the aspects or dispositions that unnerve the characters in some of the work and also seem to be the markers of bonding and interconnection in plays like *The Weir*, *The Seafarer* and *The Veil*. McPherson associates Ireland's historical consciousness and its fringe, privileged location as the place 'right beside the beyond'. Grounded in such a consciousness, McPherson's work embraces the comic and the tragic, the gothic and the grotesque, the barbarous and the civil, and the terrors and opportunities of the periphery.

---

[1] Early plays by McPherson are *Taking Stock* (1989), *Michelle Pfeiffer* (1990) and *Scenes Federal* (1991).[1] The extraordinary *Rum and Vodka,* written in this university environment, and first performed on 27 November 1992, provided not only a substantial template for his own later monologues, but also, in some respects, this play proved to be an inspiration for a generation of writers who were curious about, comfortable with and keen about exploring the monologue form.

[2] *Radio Play* was first performed on 17 August 1992 at the International Bar, Wicklow Street, Dublin and *A Light in the Window of Industry* was produced in the same venue on 3 August 1993. *Inventing Fortune's Wheel* got its professional premiere on 3 March 1994 at The Firken Crane Centre, Cork, having previously been given a one-off performance on 12 February 1992 in Dramsoc. *The Good Thief* (first performed under the title of *The Light of Jesus*) opened on 18 April 1994 in the City Arts Centre, Dublin produced by Fly by Night Theatre Company and *The Stars Lose Their Glory* opened 1 August 1994 again in the International Bar. In this same year, on 30 August *Rum and Vodka* was performed at the City Arts Centre, Dublin. Based on this rough sketch alone, one can see the early impetus for McPherson's career as a playwright and the commitment of the Fly by Night Theatre Company to produce his work.

[3] After its successful London run, *St. Nicholas* transferred to Primary Stages in New York and opened on 17 March 1998.

4 The play won the Laurence Olivier Award for Best New Play 1999 (for the 1997-8 season), the Evening Standard Award, the George Devine Award and the London Critics' Circle Award.

5 McPherson also directed the Broadway premiere of *Dublin Carol* in 2003 at the Atlantic Theater Company. *Shining City* opened on Broadway in 2006, and was nominated in the Best Play category for the Tony Awards. See http://www.tonyawards.com/en_US/archive/-pastwinners/index.html [Accessed 10/1/12]

6 However, McPherson is less inclined to direct his work beyond a play's premiere; with some exceptions, such as the production of *The Seafarer* on Broadway in 2007 and at the Abbey in 2009, after Jimmy Fay had directed its first run in 2008. McPherson took on the task of directing *Dublin Carol* for the Atlantic Theater Company production in 2003, after Ian Rickson had initially directed it. McPherson follows a long tradition of Irish playwrights who have successfully directed their own work, including Brian Friel, Tom Murphy and Frank McGuinness, but none have done so with the regularity of McPherson.

7 Details on films are taken from Internet Movie Database. See http://www.imdb.com/title/tt1346961/ [Accessed 6/1/2012]

8 See Conor McPherson, 'Film or theatre, which is better? Conor McPherson, director of *The Actors*, says "it's all in the performance"', *The Guardian*, Friday 2 May 2003, http://www.guardian.co.uk/culture/2003/may/02/artsfeatures [Access 11/1/12]

9 Conor McPherson, *This Lime Tree Bower, Three Plays* (London: Nick Hern Books, 1996).

10 Sarah Donaldson, 'Film-makers on film: Conor McPherson talks to Sarah Donaldson about Martin Scorsese's *The King of Comedy* (1983),' *Telegraph*, 17 May 2003.

11 Gangland is the attraction not only for McPherson, but for Mark O'Rowe with *Intermission* (1999) and *Perrier's Bounty* (2009) and of course Martin McDonagh with *In Bruges* (2008). Actors, for example, like Peter McDonald, Brendan Gleeson, David Wilmot, and Michael McElhatton form a common pool utilized by McPherson, O'Rowe, McDonagh and his brother John Michael in *The Guard* (2011). In these works, the dominant concern seems to be less about criminality per se, and far more about comedy.

12 See Melvyn Bragg's *South Bank Show*. Special episode on Conor McPherson, London Weekend Television, May 18 2003.

13 Conor McPherson, 'Afterword.' *Plays Two*. London: Hern, 2004. 207-20: 220.

1 | The Early Years

Anthony Roche[*]

Irish playwright Conor McPherson, whose plays have been acclaimed on the stages of London, Dublin, New York and beyond, attended University College Dublin between 1988 and 1993, where he took a BA in English and Philosophy and an MA in Philosophy. In his final BA year, he ended up in one of my weekly Modern English tutorials. It was my first year as a Lecturer in English at UCD, so he had not requested that he be placed there. In the opening session, I asked the students what they did in their extra-curricular time, what college societies they were active in, what possible careers they might be considering for the life after their June exams. The young man with the close-cropped red hair and the direct look from behind the steel-framed glasses said: 'I write plays.' I asked what they were about, and in return he outlined a drama about a group of young men who gather to discuss a previous evening involving young women and a good deal of drink which had ended in a rape. As he spoke, I realized – and told him – that I had seen the play, staged some months earlier in Dramsoc. And what I hope and think I communicated was how impressed I was, by the focused intensity, the authenticity and the verbal concision of the writing.

This was my introduction to Conor McPherson. During this first year at UCD, I had resolved to see as many Dramsoc productions as possible, without quite realizing that this meant two shows a week, an hour at lunchtime, a full-length play in the evening: over forty for

---

*This essay was first published in *The UCD Aesthetic: Celebrating 150 Years of UCD Writers*, edited by Anthony Roche (Dublin: New Island. 2005).

the academic year. (At the university in the US where I had been teaching, the annual total had been five.) This attendance meant, among other things, that I saw a great deal of Conor's work. Not only was he writing plays but frequently directing them, both by himself and by the group of which he formed a part, subsequently named Fly By Night. One of these was by Coilin O'Connor, who was in the same tutorial group; his work was no less quirky and playful than Conor's but more overtly literary. And McPherson also turned his hand to acting. I recall his appearance in a Harold Pinter play, exuding just the right mixture of comedy and menace; and he managed quite a turn as the academic sociologist Dobbs in Brian Friel's *The Freedom of the City*, suggesting links with the philosophy lecturer Dr. Raymond Sullivan in his own later play, *This Lime Tree Bower* (1995). Both Pinter and Friel were to be important influences in Conor's own development, not least in their deployment of monologue as a profound dramatic resource, and they need to be set beside the (if anything) overstated emphasis on the influence of David Mamet. Certainly, Mamet's star ran high in Dramsoc in those days; his plays were frequently put on there, some of them directed by my colleague Dr John Barrett, who also lectured on Mamet's plays to the undergraduate English students. One of Conor's original plays was as close to an Irish translation of Mamet as it is possible to get. But I felt once he had made that homage, Conor had absorbed Mamet's idiom and rhythm and was free of any overt influence or indebtedness. The style Conor McPherson developed in those years was distinctly his own – dialogue-driven, displaying a great talent for storytelling, inducing frequent outbursts of laughter while remaining utterly serious in what his plays were pursuing, providing a real and recognizable x-ray of the young Irish male and his insecurities, mingling the profane and the sacred.

Both Conor McPherson and Coilin O'Connor attended our tutorials and wrote their essays while maintaining a high profile in Dramsoc, thus giving the lie to the widely held belief that the two activities are inimical and mutually exclusive. Where Coilin was more low key, Conor kept the rhetorical level of the tutorial high. If I said something was white, he would maintain it was black; or vice-versa. One of the plays he put on that year was entitled *Michelle Pfeiffer* and the posters for the production all over college featured a photo of the delectable Ms Pfeiffer. 'Conor,' I said during one of our sessions on feminism, 'your play entitled *Michele Pfeiffer* has not a single reference to her in the text. Is it not rather a device to use her in the poster and so objectify her as woman?' Conor retorted: 'You have a photo of Sinead O'Connor on your wall,' pointing at the *Rolling Stone* cover affixed to my filing cabinet. He was one of the very few students I have met who seemed clearly set on a path, looking ahead at something the rest of us could scarcely discern, while remaining true to the pragmatics of the present. There was a rare cast of honesty and outspokenness, always with the humorous edge, which made him stand out even then.

In the year after their graduation, Conor and Coilin joined with Peter McDonald, Valerie Spelman, Kevin Hely and others to form Fly By Night and stage plays in the International Bar. His first breakthrough play, *Rum and Vodka*, was staged that same year in 1992 in UCD and subsequently in a Fly By Night production in the City Arts Centre close by Tara Street train station. What has struck me when I have seen productions of Conor's subsequent plays in London at the Royal Court or in Dublin at the Gate is how true to the aesthetic of LG1 in Belfield his theatre has remained. One can call it a theatre of poverty (an economic necessity, no doubt) or a theatre of minimalism (if one wants to make an aesthetic virtue of necessity). But it has always relied on an openness of staging and a minimum of props. Increasingly, the mainstream Dublin theatres have had to learn to adapt from their proscenium origins to accommodate writers like Conor McPherson or companies like Galway's Druid Theatre Company and Dublin's Rough Magic who have found their way to a life in the theatre through the openness and experimentation of college drama societies. When you sit in LG1, you stare into a space of infinite possibility; when someone comes on and stands in the light, you are ready to trust them to take you on a journey. A great deal of Conor's preference for monologues and storytelling comes from working for five years in this space. It underwrites his frequently stated reply when asked 'Where am I?' 'Where is the play set?': 'These plays [of mine] are set in a theatre. Why mess about? The character is on stage, perfectly aware that he is talking to a group of people. I've always tried to reflect that simplicity in productions.'[1]

The recurrent criticism encountered in relation to McPherson's theatre is that the plays are mostly or are entirely made up of monologues. But McPherson's plays are a reminder that Irish drama arguably had its origins at least as much in the communal art of the oral storyteller performed in the home or in the pub as in a fourth wall drama performed on a proscenium stage. Brian Friel drew on monologue as the exclusive source of his 1979 drama *Faith Healer*, where three characters – the faith healer of the title, his wife Grace, and manager Teddy – appear in turn before the audience to tell their versions of the story they have all participated in. McPherson has clearly been influenced by *Faith Healer*, drawing on its four interlocking monologues for *This Lime Tree Bower*. And the visit by the traumatized Irishman to the disturbed psychiatrist in his 2004 play *Shining City* not only brings Tom Murphy's *Gigli Concert* (1983) to mind but stresses how central the monologue is to Murphy's achievement as a playwright. There are formal storytellers in the plays of Beckett and Pinter also, who frequently face their audiences with little more than their story to tell. All of these major twentieth-century playwrights constitute a resource for contemporary playwrights like McPherson, Sebastian Barry, Mark O'Rowe, Enda Walsh, and Eugene O'Brien.

In 2000, Conor directed O'Brien's debut play *Eden* at the Peacock. In a series of alternating monologues, a man and a woman in their early thirties from the Irish Midlands spoke of the difficulties their marriage was going through. In O'Brien's writing, McPherson's directing and the acting of Don Wycherly and Catherine Walsh, but most of all through the monologue form, the audience gained a more unmediated and intimate access to the two characters' thoughts and feelings. The play toured and transferred to the Abbey a year later. I met Conor while he was rehearsing *Eden* for the main stage. I asked if he foresaw any problems with this, and he said no, he did not. It was not just his characteristic lack of intimidation at the prospect of the large Abbey stage; it was also that he saw no reason to alter his theatrical methods from what he had learned in LG1.

Conor McPherson graduated from UCD in 1991 with a double First in English and Philosophy. The way was open for him to do an MA and in the end he chose to do it in Philosophy. In the main, the Belfield campus rarely makes it into a McPherson play. But an exception occurs in 1995's *This Lime Tree Bower*. One of the three characters is a philosophy lecturer and the play includes a description of the UCD Philosophy Department which can be identified by the fact that must strike anyone who goes there: it is the only department in the John Henry Newman building (or the Arts Block, as it is referred to by one and all) to occupy a 5th floor. As Ray puts it in one of his monologues:

My office was on a corner of the highest part of the college.
This tickled Tony Regan no end.
He said that the philosophy department was near heaven so
that when the questions became too unbearable we could lean
out the window and ask God.[2]

The Belfield bar, where Ray holes up much of the time, is only
too recognizable; and he gives his lectures in Theatre O. Ray himself
is hardly an advertisement for the academic profession. Filled with a
curious but credible mixture of pomposity and self-loathing, he
preys relentlessly on the more attractive of his female
undergraduate students. While the Belfield locations may be
recognizable, nobody in the Philosophy Department at UCD, so far
as I am aware, has been matched up with this archetypal character.
I've always wondered whether, if Conor had chosen to do his MA in
his other subject, the play's lecherous lecturer would have been a
member of the English Department. In *St. Nicholas* (1997), the sole
character is a drama critic who again preys on young women, in this
instance an actress from an Abbey Theatre production. But the play
is quite explicit that the man is not an academic but a theatre
reviewer who walks 'out of plays ten minutes before the end' and
'usually had reviews written before the play was finished.'[3] One
imagines that any young playwright trying to get a hearing in Dublin
would have a few scores to settle with the local critics. McPherson,
in the manner of Dante assigning appropriate fates in his
Purgatorio, has his theatre critic end up in the company of vampires
(or blood-sucking parasites, if you prefer.) Perhaps it's just as well
McPherson did not pursue an MA in English.

In 1993 he was awarded an MA in Philosophy for a major thesis
entitled: 'Logical Constraint and Practical Reasoning: On Attempted
Refutations of Utilitarianism.' Unlike many contemporary Irish
writers who suppress their academic qualifications for the sake of
'street cred', Conor gave the full title of his thesis in the Royal
Court/Gate Theatre programme for *Shining City*, as something of
which he is (justifiably) proud, as something which is part of the
record and as an avenue along which he might have continued, had
he not turned full-time to the world of theatre and (in more recent
years) film. The MA thesis makes for fascinating reading, not least
when taken in conjunction with the plays. It is a strong-minded and
robust defence of the theory of utilitarianism, arguing that people
undertake goals in life not because they are trying to be objectively
moral but to satisfy their own wants and desires. These latter can be

described as 'hedonistic,' particularly when one bears in mind the single-minded pursuit of alcohol and sex to which many of his theatrical creations are dedicated, but the term is expanded to include the entire range of those desires which a person wishes to fulfil. Nevertheless, McPherson is opposed to any hierarchical distinction between 'higher' and 'lower' pleasures, as he makes clear when he criticizes John Stuart Mill's classic study, *Utilitarianism.* Mill distinguishes between elementary pleasures which are 'fleeting' – eating, drinking, resting and so on – and pleasures of a more distinctively human achievement, which require more effort and which may last for perhaps a lifetime. But, McPherson counters: 'Can Mill say that pleasures involving our "higher" faculties are qualitatively "better" than rolling in the mud?' [4] In seeking to show that no argument for the objective nature of 'the good' can be sustained, McPherson devotes much of his thesis to going one-on-one with Alasdair MacIntyre and John Rawls, in particular the former. The ultimate object of attack is Aristotle and a 'tradition of enquiry' which locates human activity in a 'telos' or goal that every object moves towards. MacIntyre's conservatism sees the break with this objective goal as occurring in the eighteenth century, with the emergence of scepticism and the triumph of the individual. But McPherson keeps querying just where 'the good' is located, outside of the individual and their desires. Rhetorically, he seeks to demonstrate that MacIntyre is forced to rely on utilitarian arguments to prove his case, despite claims that he is doing the contrary. His repeated argument against MacIntyre and against Rawls with his concept of a socially agreed concept of justice is that it requires one person to point out 'the good' to another and then have them submit to it, that it is finally located in an invocation of 'authority.' I was reminded throughout of William Blake's dictum: 'I must create my own philosophy or be imprisoned by another man's.'

In *This Lime Tree Bower* Wolfgang Konigsberg, an eminent philosopher with an international reputation, is invited to UCD to give a series of lectures, held in Theatre L and beamed via 'a closed circuit system to the next theatre, where everyone could see him.'[5] There are traces of the 'utilitarianism' thesis strewn throughout the play: Dr. Ray Sullivan is teaching a 'third year utilitarianism group'[6] and one of his reported dreams features an enigmatic and otherwise unaccountable appearance by the philosopher John Rawls [who is not otherwise identified]: 'John Rawls came down from the mountains and his wife was choosy about what she ate.'[7] Ray longs for 'the chance of a question and answer session' with the visiting philosopher 'where we could discuss his ideas. I knew I could have this guy on the ropes if I had the opportunity to press him,'[8] – a boxing metaphor I have already employed to describe the pugilistic way McPherson takes on MacIntyre and Rawls in the thesis. After a great deal of argument, the famous philosopher finally agrees to take Ray's question. When the latter staggers to his feet, very much in the grip of a severe bout of delirium tremens, and opens his mouth, 'absolutely beyond my control, a long stream of orange puke shot out of my mouth.'[9] Finally, he speaks: 'I would like to ask Professor Konigsberg if, during his long and eminent career, he has ever seen anything like that.' By way of reply, the philosopher doesn't speak but finally, slowly, shakes his head. Ray thanks him politely and departs, revealing: 'I couldn't even remember what I wanted to say.'[10] In the play, the scene was entirely conveyed by means of Ray's monologue. In a case of life imitating art, when *This Lime Tree Bower* was filmed as *Saltwater* (2000), the scene was re-enacted under Conor McPherson's direction in a packed Theatre L. It would be tempting if Professor Konigsberg could be identified as either John Rawls or Alasdair MacIntyre. But the description Ray offers of the visitor's philosophy shows its concern to be with the death of language – 'he said that language was an organic thing [...] it was born, lived healthily for a while, making other little languages like its offspring, and then it died'[11] – and it in no wise resembles the philosophy of the two opponents of utilitarianism.

It is elsewhere in the play that one must look for the debate that is central to the thesis to be dramatized. For Ray's is only one of three strands that intertwine in the overall narrative. The primary location, as so often in McPherson, is Dublin's Northside, especially along the seafront – his young male protagonists are as drawn to this location as those in Neil Jordan's early fiction. The other two character are brothers, the seventeen-year-old Joe, who is still in school, and his twenty-two-year old brother, Frank, who works with his dad in the family chipper. Ray enters their lives through his liaison (yet another) with their sister, Carmel. The play's plot hinges around Frank's decision to rob the local bookie and loan shark, 'Simple' Simon McCurdy, who is putting pressure on their hard-working, harassed and widowed father to repay a loan. The title of another McPherson play, *The Good Thief* (1994), seems relevant to the discussion of what Frank proposes and undertakes in the play, and to the discussion of 'the good' in McPherson's MA thesis. In no conventional or Christian reading can the life of a thief be read as anything other than immoral (in the Christian reading, the 'good' thief is the one of the two crucified with Christ who repents and is promised redemption.) And there is the Romantic inversion of the Christian ethos which would see the 'bad' thief exuding attractive qualities of rebellion and independence, as in the American gangster films that influence the McPherson-scripted film, *I Went Down* (1997).

What is primarily at issue here are consequences and contingency, two key issues in the thesis and in McPherson's dramatic world. Again, a quote from Mill is relevant:

> Who ever said that it was necessary to foresee all the consequences of each individual, "as they go down into the countless ages of coming time"? Some of the consequences of an action are accidental; others are its natural result, according to the known laws of the universe. The former for the most part cannot be foreseen; but the whole cause of human life is founded on the fact that the latter can.[12]

In the plays, the distinction is not so clear-cut. When Frank has robbed McCurdy's and is about to be caught by a violent henchman, Ray appears in his car and saves him – not because he thinks he is performing a good deed but because he happens to see him. Pure contingency – the arbitrary point at which one narrative strand meets another. When Frank asks McCurdy to open the safe (not even knowing whether he has one), the haul escalates from thirty pounds to nearly thirty thousand. The police come to their house. But it turns out that Joe, the younger brother, has been accused of rape, something we know from his monologue to be untrue. It is his best friend Damien who is guilty and who has in turn shopped him. In the end, Frank emigrates and sends large sums of money back to his father – a 'good' thief, perhaps, because the consequences, though unseen, are just in terms of what he has sought to achieve. Damien is rightfully charged for the rape; but in seeking to shift the blame to Joe, he has betrayed their private personal relationship, the most important in young Joe's life since the death of his mother. And Ray? Well, he gets away with his philandering; but he stands accused by what comes out of his mouth when he opens it to speak.

At the end of *The Good Thief* the title character denies the epithet, not just to himself but to all of the characters in the play. He does so in terms of consequentialism: 'I knew nothing good could come out of what had happened because of everybody's stupidity.'[13]

In an interview in 2001 with Gerald C. Wood, Conor McPherson describes how his characters reject the maps they are given and asked to accept for the conduct of their future lives – 'go to school, leave school, work, get married, have children, pay a mortgage, go on holiday, your parents die, then you die.'[14] Instead, his characters break out and go to the extremes so vividly dramatized in his plays, just as his thesis tries out potential scenarios to illustrate and test philosophical positions. He generalizes that they 'always tend to find an innate sense of what's right and wrong [...] and usually come back to traditional moral law, which is basically utilitarian: if I don't treat other people well, I may not get treated well myself.' The fear with which they are left is 'the fear of not being loved. [...] And nobody can answer that for them; everybody learns different ways of dealing with it.' With no ready made answers, with each of his characters having to work out their own destiny, the number of potential scenarios is infinite. Conor McPherson the playwright, for all of his achievement, still has many stories to tell.

Works Cited

McPherson, Conor, 'Logical Constraint and Practical Reading: On Attempted Refutations of Utilitarianism'. MA thesis, Department of Philosophy, UCD. October 1993.

---, *This Lime Tree Bower: Three Plays* [*Rum and Vodka*; *The Good Thief*; *This Lime Tree Bower*] (Dublin: New Island Books; London: Nick Hern Books, in association with the Bush Theatre, 1996).

---, *St. Nicholas* and *The Weir: Two Plays* (Dublin: New Island Books; London: Nick Hern Books, in association with the Bush Theatre, 1997).

Wood, Gerald C., *Conor McPherson: Imagining Mischief*. Dublin: The Liffey Press/Contemporary Irish Writers series, 2003.

---

[1] Conor McPherson, *Rum and Vodka* in *McPherson: Four Plays* (London: Nick Hern Books, 1999): 37.

[2] Conor McPherson, *This Lime Tree Bower: Three Plays* [*Rum and Vodka*; *The Good Thief*; *This Lime Tree Bower*] (Dublin: New Island Books; London: Nick Hern Books, in association with the Bush Theatre, 1996):99.

[3] Conor McPherson, *St. Nicholas* and *The Weir: Two Plays* (Dublin: New Island Books; London: Nick Hern Books, in association with the Bush Theatre, 1997):6.

[4] Conor McPherson, Unpublished MA Thesis, 'Logical Constraint and Practical Reasoning: On Attempted Refutations of Utilitarianism': 48-9.

[5] McPherson, *This Lime Tree Bower, 114.*

[6] *ibid.* 88.

[7] *ibid.,* 89.

[8] *ibid.,* 99.

[9] *ibid.,* 117.

[10] *ibid.,* 119.

[11] McPherson, Unpublished MA Thesis: 113.

[12] McPherson, Unpublished MA Thesis: 40.

[13] McPherson, *The Good Thief* in *Three Plays* [*Rum and Vodka*; *The Good Thief*; *This Lime Tree Bower*] (Dublin: New Island Books; London: Nick Hern Books, in association with the Bush Theatre, 1996): 77.

[14] Gerald C. Wood, *Conor McPherson: Imagining Mischief.* (Dublin: Liffey /Contemporary Irish Writers series, 2003): 135.

2 | The Geography of Conor McPherson's plays: The City as Salvation or Hell?

Sara Keating

> 'The village is no longer the objective correlative for Ireland: the city is, or to be precise, *between* cities is. That space between. That's not to say that people don't live in the country anymore, or that rural life isn't "valuable"; it's that culturally it's played out. It no longer signifies. Mythologically, it doesn't resonate anymore.'[1]

In his influential essay '*Who The Hell Do We Still Think We Are?*,' playwright Declan Hughes questions the relationship between contemporary Irish drama and the cultural climate in which it is nurtured and produced. Where, he asks, is the influence of popular music, Hollywood film or American TV in our theatres? Why, he asks, is the Irish canon defined by the past? In attempting to revise and modernize our understanding of Irish identity and Irish theatre, Hughes posits a new provisional space in which they might be reinvented: the city, 'or to be precise, *between* cities... That space between.'

In this essay I will examine how this idea of the city as a 'space between' helps us to see a distinct evolution in the work of Conor McPherson, beginning with an imagined geographical journey around the fringes of contemporary Dublin in his early monologue plays, and moving to a deeper metaphysical engagement with a more provisional city in his later work. In particular it allows us to examine the tension between the abstracted theatrical space of the physical journeys in plays like *This Lime Tree Bower, Rum and Vodka, The Good Thief* and *Port Authority,* and the abstract spiritual dimension represented through the more realistic theatrical spaces of *Dublin Carol, Shining City,* and *The Seafarer.*

Conor McPherson's earliest plays are plays for single voices. Taking their cue from the confessional, the monologues are, as McPherson explains, 'set "in a theatre." Why mess about? The character is on stage. Perfectly aware that he is talking to a group of people...'[2]

Much has been written about the significance of the Irish monologue play; its limited dramaturgy and one-dimensional perspective; its tendency to eschew rather than embrace the social context informing its characters' world-views. And yet the very form of these plays embodies the increasingly individualistic reality of late-capitalist Celtic Tiger Ireland, a society where traditional communities had been shattered by urban migration and the swell of social housing on Ireland's cities' outskirts. The monologue form expressed a fundamental dis-ease with a society where the governing structures of Church and State had entirely fallen away. The monologue *embodied* the legacy of these failures rather than debated the consequences.

However, while the writer's self-conscious awareness of the form's directness appears to set aside a particular socio-political context by setting the play in the theatre, it might also be argued that the monologue establishes an immediate intimacy with that world through the specific context of the character's own particular milieu as it is evoked for the audience. The characters' naming of the familiar landmarks of their daily lives – the pubs they drink in, supermarkets they shop in, bookies they bet in – allows us to imagine them as part of, and yet separate to, a specific geographical landscape and social structure. Indeed, the abstracted form of the monologue recreates the city in a limitless way that does not depend on the recreation of geography in any literal sense, as realism does. Furthermore, their particular descriptions indicate to us not merely the characters' habits and routines, but how they see their world, and thus how they see their place within it. As much as naturalism suggests that environment determines character, so the characters' relationship with the city is expressed by the form of the monologue, and how it throws into relief the narrated conflict between the speaker and the social world he inhabits.

If Irish drama from the 1960s onwards had been concerned with expressing a fracture between tradition and modernity in Irish society, the monologue form 'closed down that dialectic,'[3] leaving us with the split subjectivity of a single protagonist instead. Most of the early monologue plays by McPherson, Mark O'Rowe and Enda Walsh, most significantly, enacted this through the marginality of almost exclusively male characters disenfranchised from the city they occupy. In Sebastian Barry's monologue play *The Pride of Parnell Street,* recovering heroin-addict Joe expresses the condition powerfully: 'The fucking inner city they call it, like it was something inside something, something hidden inside, or safe inside, I don't fucking know. But the place where I come from is all raw in the wind, *outside* with fucking knobs on, nothing fucking inner about it, it's as out as you can get, like the North pole.'[4] As Eamonn Jordan has commented it is 'dislocation rather than location'[5] that is the defining condition for the male characters in the monologue plays of McPherson et al, and yet this dislocation undeniably expresses a specific type of urban environment from which the idea of belonging is constantly denied.

Instead of a unified Irish society, in their monologue plays McPherson and his generation of writers depict for us a diffuse and permeable culture that has no single voice. What is being presented, to borrow a phrase from Mark O'Rowe's 2002 film *Intermission,* is the idea of the 'little big city';[6] the monologue play is not a composite portrait, but a multiplicity of individual voices that reflects the diversity of the singular lives encompassed within it. And by and large it is alienation, an inability to connect with others, a search for something more substantial, that defines the condition of living in this world. Through the first-person narration that the monologue offers, we are brought on an odyssey that expresses this alienation; a series of adventures or escapades from the periphery of the city to the centre and back to the fringes again, as the characters introduce us to the landmarks that mark out the different stages of their existential crises.

In McPherson's monologue plays, the voices we hear are exclusively male, and much of the action revolves around the consumption of alcohol as a means of escaping what seems like a pre-determined fate. *Rum and Vodka* narrates an epic binge-drinking 'boozerama,'[7] in which the unnamed narrator attempts to stave off the mundanity of married life and mortgage payments by indulging in a conscience-obliterating excess of sex and alcohol. Of the three characters in *This Lime Tree Bower,* teenager Joe has his first encounter with alcohol, his older brother Frank is a seasoned ritual social drinker, and lecturer Ray is so debauched that he disgraces himself professionally when he vomits over some of those gathered in a lecture theatre to hear a visiting professor. In *Port Authority* three generations of men use drinking as a social crutch: Kevin to woo the woman he lives with; Dermot to convince his peers of his aptitude; and Joe to alleviate his unspoken loneliness after the early death of his wife.

Despite the abstracted nature of the dramaturgical space, each of these characters presents to us a vividly imagined urban landscape, which provides us with the concrete locational reference in which their cultural dislocation becomes relatable and, more importantly, authentic or believable. For the narrator of *Rum and Vodka,* for example, the 'thrill of having your own house'[8] is qualified by its location: Raheny, a Northside suburb he associates with stifling domestic obligations and working class ennui. The environment he inhabits reflects his state of mind; or, rather, his perception of his environment reflects his mental anguish. His friends live in 'disgraceful kip[s].'[9] From his work-desk he looks out onto an overcast city, 'the buildings on Bachelor's Walk, all falling down and filthy.'[10] The city's dilapidation gives him 'all the righteous indignation of an innocent victim'[11] being oppressed by the social world he is forced to inhabit. The sites of his debauchery are made more intimate for the audience by the fact that they are named – real pubs and places evocative of a seedy Dublin.

All of this contrasts with the bohemian glamour of the world he enters when he meets Myfanwy, to whom he looks to save him from the inevitability of the future offered by his social standing. Myfanwy represents a different type of city which he has no access to; a city of en-suite bathrooms and Jacuzzis and film students and actors, where people have their own cars, no shortage of disposable income and no responsibilities. Again real places are named to contrast with the degradation of the squalid life he is seeking to escape from. In contrast to the grubbiness of the quays, we have the grandeur of Merrion Square and Trinity College. Even the pubs Myfanwy frequents are different: historic pubs with literary associations like Davy Byrnes.

The specific places and the awareness of the Northside/Southside divide might be exclusive to a Dublin audience, but the class anxiety experienced by the narrator as he moves towards catharsis is a more universal one, and in *Port Authority* class anxiety is also a significant factor in the characters' alienation and dis-ease in the city, as each of the men strives to escape a fate he feels thrust upon

him: by the circumstances of his upbringing in Kevin's case, by
marriage in Dermot's case, or by personality (the timid Joe). Their
monologues describe their desire and various attempts to transform
themselves; like the narrator in *Rum and Vodka*, to escape into a
world which they perceive as more sexually and socially liberated
than their own. Again this more privileged world is evoked through
the specific naming of real places and the contrasts suggested: in
Dermot's case, for example, the sea-view at Sutton, where his boss
O'Hagan lives, and his own dreary suburban existence.

The crisis for each of the men in *Port Authority* and in *Rum and
Vodka*, however, ultimately leads them towards recognition of the
mutual spiritual poverty of both social worlds. In *Rum and Vodka*
the narrator becomes the victim of infidelity himself, when he
witnesses Myfanwy engaged in a sexual encounter with another
man, and it is this betrayal – his realization that behind the
trappings their worlds are not so different – that drives him back
home to his wife and children. In *Port Authority*, meanwhile, the
men are denied the opportunity to consummate their fantasies. For
Dermot humiliation becomes the cathartic force for his acceptance
of his own reality, but for Kevin and Joe it is a less painful process of
self-recognition, albeit one defined by regret; for Kevin that means
accepting his new girlfriend as she is, for Joe a posthumous
reconciliation with the woman he loved. Eventually the three
characters settle back into their lives. They may feel that they are
alone, but the existential anxiety that Joe expresses – 'I've no idea
about myself. I don't even know if I'm happy or sad!'[12] – is revealed
as a universal feeling, and there is consolation for the men in that
sober fact.

The resonance of hope for the characters in the monologue plays,
then, comes from the characters' retreat from the city that seems to
offer escape into their individualized social units again as they seek
solace in the domestic. In *Rum and Vodka*, the narrator creeps into
his daughters' bedroom to watch them sleeping, observing 'Their
fair hair and white cotton pyjamas. Their little white hands. I
couldn't bear it.'[13] Their fragility is a sobering reminder of what is at
stake for him. In *Port Authority*, Kevin settles down with a different
girl, while a defeated Dermot returns to the wife he has derided for
comfort. He is 'a hunched figure,' dependent on her to put him
together again; 'My face falling slowly into her lap.'[14] Joe,
meanwhile, nearing the end of his life, enjoys a moment of peace,
his regrets finally exorcized, and his closing lines leave a resounding

sense of spiritual peace for the audience: 'I did what any Christian would do. I turned out the light and went to sleep.'[15]

In *This Lime Tree Bower,* however, McPherson offers a more concrete representation of men overcoming the social injustice they see encoded in the city. The young men get away with their crime: Frank goes to Chicago, Joe goes to college, and Ray publishes a philosophy book that no-one will read, but 'that was the point. So in the end it was like things started off good, and just got better.'[16] The disenfranchised finally claim victory over those who hold the power.

McPherson's later plays break out of the formal monologue mould, although the naturalistic framework of plays like *Dublin Carol* and *Shining City* are still structured by the single-voice confessional. Important moments of self-revelation are delivered by the protagonists as a story prompted by an interlocutor (*Dublin Carol*) or more self-consciously, as in the case of *Shining City*, as part of a therapy session. Just as in the earlier plays, the central characters are men at the peak of some existential crisis, which they attempt to solve through the emotional crutch of alcohol. However, in contrast to the earlier monologues, these plays are set in concrete locations represented literally on stage. The imagined city thus fades to a more abstracted space that the characters do not engage with in any particular meaningful way during the plays which are confined to a single-room setting. And yet through an established symbolic resonance, the city is suggested as a symbol of hope for the characters: a site imbued with the possibility of potential spiritual redemption.

Dublin Carol is set in an office, realistically rendered by 'old wooden desks, carpet, comfortable chairs, filing cabinets, tasteful paintings, elaborate lamps ... etc.'[17] and a few meagre Christmas decorations hung in recognition of the season. As in McPherson's 2006 play, *The Seafarer,* the symbolic resonance of the play's setting on Christmas Eve establishes an important spiritual tone for the play, as John, estranged from his wife and grown children for many years, comes to terms with the damage he has done to his family by his drinking and his eventual abandonment of them.

The action takes place on 'the Northside of Dublin, around Fairview or the North Strand Road'[18]; a location that places the action just outside the main city. This peripheral location seems deliberate. For undertaker John, the city is a lonely place, and yet it is also a place of sudden intimacies and connections: with the mourners he comforts; with his casual assistant Mark, who seeks out his advice on Christmas Eve; and with his equally isolated bachelor boss Noel, who will be spending Christmas in hospital. Dealing with death daily, however, John is aware of his own mortality and the unlikely possibility of his own salvation: 'I've seen enough funerals where people have been genuinely heartbroken for me to expect people to be, you know, mourning me and all this. I just want to slip away, you know? Under the cover of darkness.'[19]

As John comes to terms with his past, the spectre of the city itself emerges in symbolic context throughout the play. At first he suggests it is a site of temptation: 'I'm a Dublin man. Sometimes I wish maybe if I'd lived out in the country, what the hell would I've been like.'[20] But that familiar association between the innocence of the country and the corrupting threat of the city is immediately dismissed: 'Probably the same. A bullshit artist.'[21] John's journey in *Dublin Carol* is not, unlike the spiritual journeys of the young narrators in the monologue plays, one of self-deception but of self-acceptance. Being called upon to bury the wife that he betrayed allows him to make this transition; he will conduct the funeral, a concrete act of contrition for the wrongs he has visited upon his family. The ringing out of the bells in final moments of *Dublin Carol*, as John adjusts the advent calendar and decorations in a quiet domestic manner, suggest the optimistic tone of new beginnings.

In *Shining City,* which premiered at the Royal Court Theatre in London in 2004, the office in which the play is set is characterized by the centrality of its location close to the city's centre. Perhaps because the play debuted abroad, McPherson meticulously defines the type of area in which the office is located as 'an old part of the city which, while it retains a sense of history, is not a salubrious area … It doesn't feel like a suburb, if anything it feels like a less commercial part of the city centre.'[22] Just as in *Dublin Carol,* where the sound of church bells chiming has symbolic resonance so the 'one or two church spires' visible 'from [Ian's] elevated position at the back of the building,'[23] and whose ringing punctuates the beginning of the play, will become particularly significant for the redemptive aspects of the story; their absence at the end indicative of the central character's final inability to face himself.

In *Shining City* McPherson again conceives of an intricately imagined realist space where the protagonist, ex-priest and psychotherapist Ian, holds sessions with his troubled clients and is currently sleeping at night time. The unfinished haphazard arrangement of the furnishings echoes Ian's transitional life state: 'He is a man who has struggled with many personal fears in his life and has had some victories, some defeats ... He is a gentle man, but sometimes his desire to get to the lifeboats, to feel safe, drives him in ways that even he himself doesn't fully understand.'[24]

As in *Dublin Carol*, Ian's interaction with the city is also characterized as a set of discrete and fleeting encounters. Indeed the three male characters, who do not have any relationship beyond a professional one, are all seeking some sort of intimacy or comfort. Ian, for example, has left the priesthood and the woman who has born his child in order to understand himself better. As he says to his fiancée Neasa: 'the fucking huge mistake I made was thinking that [leaving the priesthood] was the end of the journey for me.'[25] He has fled the stability of his relationship with her for the solace of anonymous encounters in which he can freely experiment with his sexuality. As the play progresses, he confronts his fears in a liaison with another of the city's lost-souls, Laurence, a drug-addict and rent-boy, whose only means of survival is selling his body.

John, Ian's only patient, is haunted by the dead wife whom he betrayed. He has moved out of the family home because he keeps seeing her ghost everywhere, a reminder of his infidelity. He decamps to a local Bed & Breakfast, because he 'just didn't want to be on my own like,'[26] and he soon falls into a routine with the owner who becomes a surrogate wife. For him the city is an accumulation of journeys – to the sea at the Bull Wall, the local pub at Dollymount Strand – and the details of these expeditions are important because they set up the most vital journey that he tells Ian about in his final confession: the journey he made to the far side of the city to betray his wife, and the endless wanderings that followed as he found himself unable to return to the quiet domesticity she offered. When his wife died, John's exile was complete; even with her death he cannot forgive himself.

In *Shining City,* however, the beacon of hope offered by the intimacy with strangers that McPherson explores is ultimately a false hope. John's exorcism is only partial: the real result of his therapy is transference. With his own betrayal of Neasa, Ian inherits John's guilt, and the haunting that John has spoken about is revealed as literal in the final moments of the play. Where John's exile was from the family home, Ian is exiled from the city itself, and he retreats from Dublin altogether – 'Dublin's ... you know ... it's a tough town'[27] he offers. The bells of the church spires visible from his window do not ring out in celebration, but remain silent, as if in admonition. Ian seems no closer to spiritual redemption than he was at the beginning of the play. This assumption of Ian's continued self-exile is borne out by the way in which the countryside to which he retreats with Neasa is configured in two other of McPherson's plays: *The Good Thief* and *Rum and Vodka*.

In *The Good Thief,* the real geography of Dublin stands in as shorthand for the type of city the character inhabits: a wild, dangerous and crime-ridden place, where even the sanctity of family-life is an illusion. However, *The Good Thief* plays with traditional constructs of the city in modern Irish culture: the typical dialectic between the city as a site of corruption and amorality, and the spiritual purity offered by rural life. In *The Good Thief,* the narrator flees the city-site of his sins to the countryside for safety and redemption. However, the countryside proves no sanctuary. The idea of refuge is literally razed to the ground in the monologue's final narrated scenes, as the criminal gang the eponymous anti-hero is hiding from follow him to ensure he receives his just punishment.

Similarly, when the characters of *This Lime Tree Bower* abscond from the scene of the robbery they have just committed (Frank) or been accessory to (Ray and Joe), it is to the countryside they flee as well. McPherson again reverses traditional characterizations by making the countryside a place of anonymity. In contrast, the city is a small-world site of recognition where everybody knows your business. And yet their rural retreat is not characterized by rustic simplicity either, but by five-star hotels, consumption and excess. The mythology of rural Ireland that Hughes contests in his essay '*Who the Hell Do We Still Think We Are?*' is thoroughly depleted.

Hughes idea of 'between cities' is a valuable frame for looking at the imagination of place in McPherson's work. It suggests the provisional nature of a rapidly changing geography but also the provisional nature of the characters' relationship to it, as they traverse the city searching for salvation. It also echoes the transitional psychological state for the characters, embodied extra-textually by their confinement in the purgatorial form of the monologue plays, or in the realist plays by their peripheral position to the wider city culture.

In McPherson's most recent original play, *The Seafarer*, this idea of the liminal is pushed towards supernatural realization, with the arrival of a stranger, Mr Lockhart, to the house of the protagonist, Sharky, on Christmas Eve; a stranger who later reveals himself to be the devil. Mr Lockhart's characterization of hell echoes the ambiguous characterization of the city in Conor McPherson's work: the attractions it offers for losing oneself, but also its inevitable alienating force.

> **Lockhart**: What's Hell? (*He gives a little laugh*) Hell is ... (*He stares gloomily*) Well you know Sharky when you're walking round and round the city and the street lights have all come on and it's cold. Or you're standing outside a shop where you were hanging around reading the magazines, pretending to buy one 'cause you've no money and nowhere to go and your feet are like blocks of ice in those stupid little slip-on shoes you bought for chauffeuring. And you see all the people who seem to live in another world all snuggled up together in the warmth of a tavern or a cosy little house, and you just walk and walk and walk and you're on your own and nobody knows who you are. And you're hoping you *won't* meet anyone you know because of the blistering shame that rises up in your face and you have to turn away because you know you can't even deal with the thought that someone might love you, because of all the pain you always cause. Well that's a fraction of the self-loathing you feel in Hell, except it's worse. Because there truly is no-one to love you.[28]

Works Cited

Barry, Sebastian, *The Pride of Parnell Street* (London: Faber and Faber, 2008).

Hughes, Declan, 'Who The Hell Do We Still Think We Are? Reflections on Irish Theatre and Identity in *Theatre Stuff: Critical Essays on Contemporary Irish Theatre,* ed. Eamonn Jordan (Dublin: Carysfort Press, 2000).

Jordan, Eamonn, 'Look Who's Talking Too: The Narrative Myth of Naïve Duplicity,' in Clare Wallace ed, *Monologues: Theatre, Performance, Subjectivity* (Litteraria Pragenzia: Prague, 2006), 125-156.

Singleton, Brian, 'Am I Talking to Myself? Men, Masculinities and the Monologue in Contemporary Irish Theatre' in Clare Wallace ed. *Monologues: Theatre, Performance, Subjectivity* (Litteraria Pragenzia: Prague, 2006), 260-77.

---

[1] Declan Hughes, 'Who The Hell Do We Still Think We Are? Reflections on Irish Theatre and Identity in *Theatre Stuff: Critical Essays on Contemporary Irish Theatre* ed. Eamonn Jordan (Dublin: Carysfort Press, 2000): 12.

[2] Conor Mc Pherson, *Rum and Vodka* in *McPherson: Four Plays* (London: Nick Hern Books, 1999):37.

[3] Brian Singleton, 'Am I Talking to Myself? Men, Masculinities and the Monologue in Contemporary Irish Theatre' in Clare Wallace ed. *Monologues: Theatre, Performance, Subjectivity* (Litteraria Pragenzia: Prague, 2006): 263.

[4] Sebastian Barry, *The Pride of Parnell Street* (London: Faber and Faber, 2008): 18.

[5] Eamonn Jordan, 'Look Who's Talking Too: The Narrative Myth of Naïve Duplicity,' in Wallace ed., 153.

[6] Mark O'Rowe, *Intermission,* (Unpublished Screenplay)

[7] Mc Pherson, *Rum and Vodka* in *McPherson: Four Plays,* 37.

[8] *ibid.,* 12.

[9] *ibid.,*14.

[10] *ibid.,* 16.

[11] *ibid.,*17.

[12] Conor McPherson, *Port Authority* in *Plays: Two* (London: Nick Hern Books, 2004): 51.

[13] McPherson, *Rum and Vodka,* 47.

[14] McPherson, *Port Authority,* 182.

[15] *ibid.,* 186.

[16] McPherson, *This Lime Tree Bower* in *McPherson: Four Plays,* 133.

[17] McPherson, *Dublin Carol* in *Plays: Two,* 79.

[18] *ibid.,* 78.

[19] *ibid.,*88.

[20] *ibid.,*93.

[21] *ibid.,* 93.

[22] Conor McPherson, *Shining City* (London: Nick Hern Books, 2004):5.

[23] McPherson, *Shining City,* 5.

[24] *ibid.,*7.

[25] *ibid.* 22.

[26] *ibid.,*13.

[27] *ibid.,* 56.

[28] Conor McPherson, *The Seafarer* (London: Nick Hern Books, 2007): 64.

3 | The Art of Disclosure, the Ethics of Monologue in Conor McPherson's Drama: *St. Nicholas, This Lime Tree Bower* and *Port Authority*

Clare Wallace

No appraisal of Conor McPherson's work for theatre can completely sidestep his extensive use of the monologue. More than half of his plays to date use the device. Although many of his contemporaries in the 1990s and 2000s such as Sarah Kane, Neil LaBute, Eugene O'Brien, Mark O'Rowe, Enda Walsh or Mark Ravenhill have intermittently turned their hands to stage monologue, none has seemed quite so engaged with the form as McPherson. *Rum and Vodka, The Good Thief, This Lime Tree Bower, St. Nicholas, Port Authority* and *Come On Over* all involve actors addressing the audience. Indubitably McPherson has demonstrated his skill with dialogue too in *The Weir, Dublin Carol, Shining City*, and *The Seafarer*, yet these plays are also structurally dependent on narrative. Over the years McPherson's work has showcased the naturalistic portrayal of character and an ear for the cadences of everyday speech. Dramaturgically, he has remained faithful to a vision of the stage as a space where 'ordinary human emotions are expressed very simply.'[1] Consequently his plays are rarely underpinned by abstract, mythical or epic structures; instead they unfold the ways in which ordinary people attempt to make sense of their lives and their decisions.[2] Indeed in a note published with the text of *St. Nicholas* McPherson comments directly on his belief in a universal human need to seek meaning and the responsibility reason bequeaths us.[3]

Monologue drama and performance encompass a very wide spectrum of projects, some traditional, some experimental, some autobiographical, making generalizations about the genre difficult to sustain. Nevertheless, what is fascinating about monologue theatre in all its diversity is its potential to 'solicit ... questions about the very nature of theatre itself, about the nature of performance and audience response, truth and illusion, narrative and experience.'[4] Although McPherson's drama is firmly planted at the conventional end of this spectrum, these issues still resonate strongly in the work. Such questions also point to monologue theatre's often divisive character. Playwright Marina Carr is not alone in her contention that 'there is something intrinsically un-dramatic about the monologue ... You can indulge your "literary sensibility" ... but finally, that is not what theatre is about. It is about the spoken word and conflict.'[5] By contrast McPherson has stated that the monologue form permitted him 'to tell smaller stories in a bigger way.'[6] Despite the threatened diminution of mimesis by diegesis, when successful, monologue theatre not only releases the vital potential of narrative performance, but also has the power to stimulate spectators to consider their role in the performance situation and to respond in unforeseen ways. McPherson's work with monologue reveals his acute consciousness of both these dimensions to the form.

Acts of disclosure in McPherson's drama are complemented by an acknowledgement, in interviews, of his interest in the collusive and mischievous aspects of the theatre experience. Perhaps paradoxically, simultaneous with the recognition of this sense of playfulness is a certain critical consensus that McPherson is, as reviewer Patrick Brennan recently put it, 'a deeply moral playwright.'[7] So how do these elements interact? In what follows I shall explore the implications of the monologue form, and trace the contours of relations between monologous disclosure and the question of ethics in McPherson's three most significant monologue plays: *St. Nicholas*, *This Lime Tree Bower* and *Port Authority*.

Monologue, Meaning, and Morality

The malleability of the monologue, its tendency to deconstruct the fourth wall of the stage, and to map out a space of performative subjectivity are certainly among the factors that have led to its popularity on the contemporary stage. And in its challenge to the theatre of dramatic illusion, monologue points toward the ways in which reality and identity are discursively constructed.[8]

Contemporary monologue spans the poles of elevated, often confessional authenticity, and ambivalent or possibly false communication, as can be observed to some degree even within McPherson's own work. It is precisely the pivotal quality of ambivalence that might serve to distinguish modern monologue from its predecessors. As Deborah Geis has elaborated, contemporary monologues rarely serve a solely revelatory purpose, as for instance a soliloquy might; rather they tend to foreground their own theatricality and possible trickery.[9] While McPherson's theatre shuns direct autobiographical reference common to some of the theatre work Geis examines, his monologues subtly unfold the ambiguities of narrative as a means of knowing and communicating, thereby suggesting narratological and by extension ontological provisionality and uncertainty.

Such concerns, initially at least, seem Beckettian in character. Beckett's experiments with the limits of stage monologue, the failure of narrative and the self alienated in language from *Krapp's Last Tape* (1958) through to *Ohio Impromptu* (1981), can scarcely escape any Irish playwright working with the form. Yet if Beckett's approach is existential and modernist, McPherson's is essentially different in focus and effect. Language itself is not problematized, narrative is not abandoned. Thus McPherson's use of monologue is much more readily associated with the dramatic models provided in the Irish context by Brian Friel, Tom Murphy or Frank McGuinness, or Billy Roche as reviewers and critics have remarked.

As cultural cliché would have it the Irish have a genetic predisposition towards storytelling. It is little wonder then that in 1997 McPherson's London break-though with *The Weir* was greeted as evidence of a continuing tradition of native Irish narrative talent. At the very moment when many young British playwrights were provocatively staging the outcomes of a postmodern consumer culture, the young Irish playwright was popularly perceived as a voice of cultural authenticity and traditional dramatic craftsmanship. *The Weir* was welcomed by reviewers as a genuine instance of 'the Irish love of fable ... [and] pure theatrical poetry.'[10] However, *The Weir* was actually McPherson's third play staged in London.

This Lime Tree Bower and *St. Nicholas* had been produced by the Bush Theatre in late 1996 and early 1997 respectively. Notably all three plays make extensive use of narrative monologue but to apparently vastly differing ends. In *The Weir*, a realist fourth-wall drama, the device was widely understood as a vehicle for authenticity (emotional and cultural). The same device as it is used in *This Lime Tree Bower* and *St. Nicholas*, both of which break the illusion of the fourth-wall, seems to direct interpretion away from a celebration of types of authenticity and towards states of ethical ambivalence.

As noted above, McPherson was not alone at this time in turning to the monologue format. Unsurprisingly critics have subsequently sought to explain the significance of the proliferation of monologue theatre of Irish provenance in the 1990s and early 2000s in various ways. One convincing interpretation advanced by Brian Singleton is that monologue served as a space for the articulation of contemporary Irish masculinities in crisis.[11] Eamonn Jordan partially concurs with this analysis, but further elucidates the connotations of monologue specifically in terms of 'narrative as identity formation,' 'licence and embellishment,' 'the notion of naivety' and the role of audience.[12] Both these readings of the meaning of monologue in Irish theatre might be usefully conjoined, as I have argued elsewhere, with Jean François Lyotard's theory of the changing status of narrative in *The Postmodern Condition* (1979).[13] Lyotard asserts that the predominant characteristic of knowledge under postmodernity is an 'incredulity towards metanarratives.'[14] Grand narratives or belief systems 'such as the dialectics of the Spirit, the hermeneutics of meaning, the emancipation of the rational or working subject, or the creation of wealth'[15] have been undermined and depleted. In a specifically Irish context, the authority of the Catholic Church, nationalist ideology, the primacy of rural experience and traditional notions of family constitute metanarratives that over the course of the last thirty years have splintered. Such metanarrative mechanisms, in Lyotard's terms, are substituted by a multiplicity of language games and micro narratives that can only exist and function provisionally.[16]

It is pertinent then how character in McPherson's work is a function of narrative. Read through Lyotard this might be understood as indicative of the doubtful, yet habitual, condition of identity in postmodernity and its particular inflection in Celtic Tiger Ireland. Monologue theatre in this context is remarkable as a site of narrative contestation and the performance of ambivalence. Without substantial onstage action, how characters speak, their vocabularies and the rhetorical devices that they employ constitute their identities. Thus in the telling of their stories, in effect, they talk themselves into existence (in contrast, it might be argued, to Beckett's characters who seem to talk themselves out of existence). As Scott T. Cummings remarks 'I have a story, therefore I am' might be considered the motto of McPherson's drama to date.'[17] Or, as McPherson himself rather controversially puts it, it is the words which are to do the work rather than the spectacle of the stage design or the characters' actions.[18] Notably too, in the productions of the plays directed by McPherson, he insists on a diminution of physical action, a voicing rather than an acting out of story. Even considering the work produced since the publication of his essay, Cummings' assertion that the plays 'all hinge on personal narratives, public confessions of private sins which provide first an entertaining evening and then, upon reflection, an investigation into the nature and function of story itself'[19] remains valid. The result is not an unequivocal affirmation of the truth of story. Throughout the narratives and anecdotes, doubt and dissensus are inherent to the performance of telling and this sense of doubt inevitably rebounds on our sense of character. As already mentioned, the intrinsically mischievous dimension to his work has been pointed out by both McPherson himself, and his commentators.[20] Though initially apparently ordinary and familiar, his staged stories 'take advantage of the listener's initial trust ... [often] going to implausible extremes.'[21] Repeatedly this involves the small-scale story, legitimated only in the act of telling which is itself multi-layered and dubious.

As has often been observed, Lyotard's theory of micronarratives encounters an impasse with regard to a system of justice, which requires some generally agreed set of values rather than a profusion of equally valid narrative possibilities. The implications of a micronarrative imperative where self is performative rather than predetermined, and where codes of morality may prove to be just as provisional and contingent, fundamentally challenge notions of moral or ontological stability. Evidently McPherson's monologues are not apologues; they do not propose a moral course of action to be imbibed by audiences. So where can the assertion that McPherson is a moral playwright figure in this account? Gerald C. Wood argues with some confidence that 'McPherson's theatre of mischief is designed to stimulate the moral imagination of his audience, without endorsing any specific morality itself' and that the 'plays invite audiences to practise compassion and, hopefully, imagine their own reasonable conclusions.'[22] For Jordan such practice is not so much a matter of compassion but of resistance; he suggests that 'If society offers no resonating myth, the final authority might be the myth of self through 'story' ... the myth of self is an elemental contestation of the demise of metanarratives or master narratives. The struggle to constitute is a defiance of the postmodernist impulse to unhinge subjectivity, and thus of identity in free fall.'[23] Monologue from this angle embodies 'the spectacle of naivety' that is 'about accountability and not complicity.'[24] Singleton, too, points to a rupture of myths, specifically of notions of hegemonic or authentic masculinity. Through monologue alternative constructions of masculinity are voiced, but contrary to Jordan, Singleton highlights the 'toxicity' of the identities performed and the disturbing ways in which monologue arrests the possibilities for interaction or transformation.[25]

Each of these conclusions returns by a different route to the question of morality or, more accurately, ethics, in McPherson's work and how revelation and judgement interact. In an attempt to take the debate in a somewhat different direction I would argue that McPherson's drama, in which form and content are woven from various narrative games, tacitly demonstrates some of the principle characteristics of the narrative forms Lyotard describes, and inscribes their troubling implications, even when understood to be acts of resistance. In other words, monologue in McPherson's plays functions in micronarrative terms, raising questions about narrative ethics, ambivalence and subjectivity as spectacle.

Revelation and (Ir)Responsibility

As Adam Zachary Newton notes in *Narrative Ethics*,

> Circumstances of narrative disclosure, their motives and their consequence, conduce ... to a set of ethical questions.[26] These derive from a recognition of narrative as a performative act and as 'a participatory act ... part 'Said' ... and part 'Saying,' the latter ... being the site of surplus, of the unforeseen, of self-exposure.[27]

Narrative ethics in this frame encompasses the intersubjective relations between text and audience in fiction and between performers, text and audience in theatre. In each of the monologue orientated works I have selected these relations are enacted differently.

The dynamics of narrative, questions of perspective and the construction of discursive reality are presented overtly and provocatively by *St. Nicholas*. The play explicitly engages the audience in a game of suspension of disbelief, related by an increasingly dubious narrator. The fact that the speaker is anonymous and appears to break out of character at several points sharpens McPherson's challenge to stage illusion and the established safe distance between audience and performer. The speaker literally tells a story of how he found 'his' story – a type of self legitimating micronarrative. A cynical theatre critic, he marshals an armoury of rhetorical devices to secure credibility for an unlikely disclosure that turns out to be a road to Damascus type tale about an encounter with vampires. He accosts the audience directly and aggressively, employing a variety of strategies to tell the story including description, nostalgic appeals, humour, insults, self-deprecation, boasting, argument and direct refutation of disbelief. Moreover, the narrator's disdain and acerbic commentary are turned not only on the subjects of his story, but also on the audience. As a result, the audience is never fully allowed to get caught up in the current of the narrative, but is repeatedly reminded of their own role.

The speaker describes how, as a cultural arbitrator, he can take advantage of 'the best of everything. [He] could stand there with the cast and ruin their evening. And get paid for it.'[28] Ironically, in his current role he has even replaced the cast. As Cummings explains, the narrator as critic feeds, like the vampire, upon others – upon their artistic endeavours, and upon their fear of his power. Moreover, his role as storyteller may be equated to the procurer role he fulfils for the vampire household – drawing in victims / listeners, exploiting their sympathy and feeding upon their credulity.[29] The narrator also plays upon the construction of identity through storytelling and the arbitrariness of such micronarratives that function not because they reveal a profound or universal truth, but as a process of self-performance; as he suggests early in the monologue, 'we all need a purpose in life, even if we've got to make it up.'[30]

McPherson's interest in questions of credulity and theatricality are indicated in his prefacing the play with an anecdote which highlights the contexts in which 'lies' are acceptable. People do not 'expect complete strangers to lie' to them in a pub for instance, but in the theatre invented stories are expected. He goes on to stress how, in a monologue, the character on stage is in fact a guide 'telling us about somewhere outside the theatre, not trying to recreate it indoors. The theatre is simply where we meet him.' This relationship, however, is far from 'simple' and involves the audience's collusion with the actor and ultimately participation in a 'type of playing.'[31]

Such playing is primarily concerned with states of ambiguity that efface the boundaries between fact and fiction and implicitly those between responsibility and irresponsibility. As if to highlight this matter, the speaker in *St. Nicholas* opens with a childhood reminiscence – 'When I was a boy ...'[32] to introduce the subject to vampires. He addresses what might be the audience's immediate assumptions or associations, appealing to common knowledge of superstition and fiction and by using the second person plural – 'like all of us' – or the ideas 'we get in books.'[33] Then he begins to challenge them with the assertion that vampires materially exist, they are 'Matter of fact,' 'casual' and 'ordinary.' As such, 'practical things' must be learned in order to deal with them. Later, he more forcefully interrupts his own story in a collusive manoeuvre, appearing to drop the pretence of character to refute audience scepticism:

> Mm. There's always going to be a smugness about you listening to this. As we all take part in this convention. And you will say, "These vampires are not very believable, are they"? And you are entitled. This convention. These restrictions, these rules, they give us that freedom. I have the freedom to tell you this unhindered, while you can sit there assured that no one is going to get hurt.[34]

Casting convention aside, he then goes on to criticize the audience's reliance on 'the lazy notions foisted upon you by others in the effort to make you buy more popcorn.'[35] While 'we' think we can apprehend the world through science, in fact we understand it very little in practice. To illustrate his point he notes, 'We may know that the earth goes round the sun. And we may know that this is due to "gravity". But not one of us knows why there is gravity. So don't sit there and cast judgement on the credibility of what I say, when you don't even know why you aren't floating off your seats.'[36] In making disbelief the focus of attention, McPherson's play self-consciously folds theatricality and the mechanics of storytelling back upon themselves but at the expense of the audience.

At one level then, the core of the play is a *narrative* crisis – the speaker's self-confessed problem is a deficit of innovation. He is plagued by what is a highly postmodern dilemma – he feels doomed to process, respond to, and recycle others' artistic products. 'I had no ideas. No ideas for a story. [...] Nothing ever came. I could only write about what there was already.'[37] His frustration is colourfully expressed:

> Tried to convey the feelings I had. That I genuinely fucking had – for people. I loved people. I loved the stupid bastards ... I wanted to let my compassion seep out across the stage. Handicapped people in love. Queers and lesbians absolving each other. A liberal, fucking, all encompassing ... you know.[38]

The first and most obvious irony is that as the rest of his story amply testifies the narrator is a hardened misanthrope. Even when trying to claim compassion for humanity, language betrays him. Without doubt the effect is comic, yet the inclusivity of the final 'you know' also presumes a certain audience complicity with the sentiments expressed which are, upon closer scrutiny, none too complimentary. Narrative desire here is exploitative and self-serving.

At the end of the play the narrator boasts how he now has a story. But what is that story? His tale is one of self-destruction, in which the protagonist must reach a nadir in order to re-evaluate his life – a familiar narrative trajectory. It is also one in which a wayward protagonist encounters vampires, but manages to live to tell the tale – again, an old favourite with multiple variations in literature and film. It might be argued, with considerable evidence, that in spite of the concluding bravado, the narrator still 'only write[s] about what there was already.'[39] Recognition of this cliché may figure in the game the monologue plays with its audiences.

Recalling Newton's notion of narrative as a participatory process, the 'type of playing' undertaken by *St. Nicholas* implies that this ludic monologue comes at the price of ethics. The storymaking staged in *St. Nicholas* is clever, but coercive. Although McPherson emphasizes the human quality of interpretation and the responsibility of reason, the structure of the monologue affords the audience little space to exercise such capabilities. As already noted stage illusion is undermined through direct address, yet the audience's role is strongly predetermined by this mode of address. They are interpellated aggressively as passive auditors, their values and judgements are assumed, and, without the option of reply, they are berated for these assumed values and judgements.

This Lime Tree Bower unfolds without such overt self-reflexivity; monologue here is the vehicle for a cluster pseudo-confession. As I have suggested elsewhere, the play 'can be seen in part to return to the alcohol-soaked, yet curiously lucid, narrators of [McPherson's] earlier plays and a core set of moral dilemmas, but both these elements are realized in a theatrically richer fashion ... the ensemble monologue structure facilitates multiple points of view [and] gives rise to a mosaic of observations and stories that ultimately fit together as a coherent whole.'[40] The three speakers – Joe, a teenage schoolboy, Frank, his brother who works at the family chip shop and Ray, a philosophy lecturer who is their sister's boyfriend – each tells stories of their recent past to the audience, and apart from one exception, they ignore each other on stage.

Each speaker's monologue deals with acts of transgression and their responses to transgression fashion our view of their characters, thus questions of narrative and ethics are embedded from the outset. McPherson establishes a sense of structure and movement with the arrangement of the acts of disclosure, achieved through a fixed rhythm of turn-taking, but also within each character's monologue via speech patterns. What results is a narrative performance composed of three distinct modes of perception – naivety, cynicism and pragmatism – plaited together around three associated ethical predicaments – the witnessing of a rape, a robbery and professional misconduct.

Joe's naivety is conveyed by both the thematic foci of his monologue but also by the guileless mode of expression. His concerns are juvenile, his vocabulary simple. Self-doubt limits his perspective on the events he relates and the conclusions he draws. He oscillates in a confused manner between his adoration of Damien, the new boy in school, masturbatory fantasies about the girls he sees in the park, and another girl, 'Deborah Something,' he claims to be really interested in, but has ironically 'only ever seen from the side.'[41] Joe's analytic horizons are comically suggested by his preference for his brother's 'thrillers and westerns':

> I liked his books because the sentences were always short. The writers gave you the facts. In school we did books where nobody said what they meant and you had to work out what everybody wanted. [In contrast] [t]hese books knew how to be read.[42]

McPherson balances this artlessness with a nascent adolescent self-consciousness that links narrative self exposure with the development of a sense of judgement. Repeatedly Joe's monologue indicates the problem of knowing who to believe, or how to act, as he puts it, in a 'town full of spoofers.'[43] He instinctively responds negatively to Damien's apparently flirtatious relationship with his own mother, and he is unable to dissimulate when he knows he is 'being false.'[44] Yet, when he witnesses his friend rape a drunken girl although he feels physically sick, he fails to intervene. Naïve moral response is clearly not wedded to action.

Ray, in stark contrast, is a misanthropic and purportedly amoral opportunist. The character provides a prime example of what Singleton has described as toxic masculinity: self-destructive, and implicitly, if not actually, violent.[45] His bravado and disingenuousness are evident from the beginning of his first speech when he describes waking up in bed with one of his students but pretends amnesia with regard to her identity – 'What was her name? I can't remember.'[46] Ray's narrative bristles with swearwords, sarcastic retorts, harsh judgements and smoulders with aggression. He drinks in the student bar because '[he] hate[s] academics'; he despises the students who buy him drinks; he refers to the student he has slept with as 'a stupid fat bitch'; the Head of the Philosophy Department is a 'terrible gobshite'; even his girlfriend 'annoy[s] the fuck out of [him]' because he suspects her of superior intelligence.[47] Accordingly, the character's ethics are described less by his reported actions than by the ways in which they are enunciated.

Ray's specialization in philosophy and, in particular, utilitarianism lends his toxic narrative an additional twist. Having petitioned for the right to question the visiting eminent Professor Konigsberg (who ironically prefers monologue to dialogue), his intervention is substantively non-verbal – he vomits dramatically before the auditorium and over part of the audience. The fantastically disgusting story functions as a punctuation mark in the play. Not only does it incorporate the disbelief of the spectators at the lecture, it seems designed to inspire scepticism among the play's audience or readers and finally, it also provokes the play's only lines of dialogue:

> **FRANK:** (*To Ray*): I never heard that.
> **RAY**: I've been saving it.[48]

This moment might be understood as an acknowledgement of 'shared discourse' that serves to fix 'the narrative of the monologue in a shared reality.'[49] Frank's reflection upon Ray's storytelling and the stage direction that the characters are aware of each other emphasize the performative dimension to all the monologues and, therefore, the blurring of distinctions between collusion, concealment, truth and falsehood. Why does Ray save this part of his story? If the characters are performing for each other then what is the status of Joe's naivety? Is it too a performance? What is the space they occupy from which they relate their stories and how is the audience to understand their role in this space? These are dilemmas raised by the play which remain unresolved.

The denotative mode of the third speaker balances the extremes of his co-monologists. Frank represents a realistic approach both in narrative and ethical terms. He meets his father's weaknesses for storytelling and alcohol with tolerance and solves the problem of his father's debt to a loan shark by robbing the loan shark. Frank's reasoning is founded on the assertion that 'principles will only fuck you up, because no one else is ever moral,'[50] a conclusion he has reached through the example of his own blighted father. Thus, if Joe is naïvely moralistic and Ray is cynically amoral, then Frank, in recognizing his father's rightness and his own wrongdoing, is pragmatically immoral.

At the play's conclusion Joe introduces a key question that brings us back to the relations between narrative disclosure and ethics – 'So in the end it was like things started off good, and just got better. Is that cheating? I don't know. It's hard to say.'[51] Joe expresses surprise at their story's happy ending, thus indirectly suggesting that they have managed to trick their way out of the fates they deserve. Indeed, despite the speakers' differing modes of perception, it is important that none take the consequences of their reported actions. Their evasion is served as entertainment, ethical dilemmas are side-lined, and the audience is left with amusement and equivocation.

The combination of acts of disclosure with the ensemble monologue format recurs in *Port Authority* with different emphasis. Again the stage functions as an abstract space where the spoken word prevails, yet in contrast with *This Lime Tree Bower* the impression produced by the three monologues is of paralysis rather than movement. Gone is the cynical, laddish bravado and humour of the earlier play. What is offered by *Port Authority* is a spectacle of sincerity and regret. This performance is composed of monologue blocks – contiguous but discrete – delivered in stage limbo. As it gradually becomes clear, although they share references to Dublin locations, they refer to different times and are not chronologically arranged and, as Jordan observes, 'the connections between the three characters initially appear incidental at best.' Admittedly the layering of the speeches intimates a more 'complicated perspective,'[52] but the ultimate effect is an emphasis on selves in isolation, tentatively, even apologetically, attempting to make sense of experiences of failure.

While the play lacks any religious superstructure it is sprinkled with subtle religious references that complement its confessional tendency. The ringing of a bell before each character speaks gestures toward ritual perhaps vaguely recalling the Angelus bell. Just as the Angelus prayer is directed to the Virgin Mary, here the bell prompts stories anchored in responses to women, perceived by the speakers to be untouchable, unobtainable or superior in some way. We meet these characters in a temporally and spatially unspecified place – 'in the theatre' as the sparse stage directions indicate – as they relate accounts of 'transitional moment[s]'[53] in their lives. Kevin, an unemployed young man in his twenties, has just moved out of home to share a house with some friends, one of whom he has a crush on. They both begin relationships with other people despite being strongly drawn to each other. Dermot, an unsuccessful middle-aged salesman and covert alcoholic, is offered a desirable new job and momentarily basks in the prospect of success amongst his affluent new colleagues. However, during a heady excursion to Los Angeles with his future colleagues and boss it is discovered that he was employed on the basis of mistaken identity. He returns home to his wife and son in humiliation, a casulty of crony capitalism and a victim of his own insecurities and weaknesses. Joe, a retired widower who lives in an old people's home, receives a photograph in the post that takes him back to the past and a moment when he found himself attracted to his next-door neighbour.

Each narrative outlines an emotional journey in which the narrator confronts a moment of choice and its consequences. Once more the responsibility of agency is pondered in micronarrative monologue form. Joe, confronted with desire for another woman, is deeply perturbed. He does his best to extinguish his feelings, to behave morally according to Christian principles, but believes that despite his efforts God has seen him. Now that both women have died he finds himself with mementos of them both, attempting to reconcile himself with his decision and his lingering emotions. Dermot, when faced with the prospect of a new career, spirals into drunkenness and deceives his wife. Afterwards he describes himself ironically as 'one of those figures you see in the religious paintings where God is pointing for them all to go to Hell. And they're all looking up at him, very much feeling the reality of their situation.'[54] In spite of his faults his wife, Mary, welcomes him home with forgiveness, reminding him that it was she who chose him and of her commitment to care for him. Kevin's passivity runs so deep that he allows himself to be claimed by the girl he is less interested in. Following the death of his grandmother he wonders whether perhaps 'there isn't a soul for every person in the world ... Maybe lots of us just share a soul. So there's no judgement, because there's no point.'[55]

Unlike the mixed signals emitted in *This Lime Tree Bower*, *Port Authority* adheres consistently to a confessional mood. It is difficult to ignore the conclusion drawn by Singleton, that the monologues in *Port Authority* stage a 'self-confessed lack of agency in the world and ... complicity with that lack.'[56] Monologue as it is deployed here positions the audience as witnesses to acts of flawed expiation, observers of human paralysis or failure, and invites empathy. What is interesting about the operation of monologue here is the way in which each speaker comes to a point in their narrative where they view themselves externally as a character in their own drama. This is most explicit in Dermot's confession:

> And it was like I was looking at the three of us there in the
> garden from high above [...]
> I could see me and Mary sitting there at the table.
> Her hand was on the back of my head.
> And I was like a hunched figure.
> My face falling slowly into her lap.[57]

If the effect of confessional sincerity is to give the impression of an apotheosis of authenticity that collapses space for critical response, then it is in moments like these that the game of narrative self-performance is perceptible.

With the exception of *Come On Over* in 2001, McPherson has not returned to a full scale monologue play, perhaps signalling the end of this phrase in his work, perhaps signalling that the transitional cultural moment of which they seemed a part has passed. What is for certain, as these plays illustrate, is that monologue for McPherson stages a complex interaction between the performance of disclosure, acts of transgression, questions of narrative ethics, and the ambivalent male self, and this nexus is irreducible to singular interpretation or straightforward moral coding.

Works Cited

Adams, Tim, an interview with Conor McPherson, 'So There's These Three Irishmen ...,' *Observer* 4 February 2001 [online].

Brennan, Patrick, Review of *The Good Thief* by Conor McPherson, *Irish Theatre Magazine* 21 April 2010 [online].

Cummings, Scott T., 'Homo Fabulator: The Narrative Imperative in Conor McPherson's Plays.' *Theatre Stuff: Critical Essays on Contemporary Irish Theatre*, ed. Eamonn Jordan (Dublin: Carysfort, 2000): 303-312.

Geis, Deborah, *Postmodern Theatric(k)s: Monologue in Contemporary American Drama* (Michigan: U of Michigan P, 1993).

Hutcheon, Linda, *A Poetics of Postmodernism. History, Theory, Fiction* (London and New York: Routledge, 1988).

Jordan, Eamonn, "Look Who's Talking, Too: The Duplicitous Myth of Naïve Narrative." *Monologues: Theatre, Performance, Subjectivity*, ed. Clare Wallace (Prague: Litteraria Pragensia, 2006): 125-156.

Lyotard, Jean-François, *The Postmodern Condition: A Report on Knowledge*, 1979. Trans. Geoff Bennington and Brian Massumi. Foreword Fredric Jameson. Theory and History of Literature, Vol. 10 (Manchester: Manchester UP, 1984).

'Marina Carr in Conversation with Melissa Sihra,' *Theatre Talk: Voices of Irish Theatre Practitioners*, eds Lilian Chambers, Ger FitzGibbon and Eamonn Jordan (Dublin: Carysfort, 2001): 55-63.

McPherson, Conor, *Plays: Two* (London: Nick Hern, 2004).

McPherson, Conor, *The Weir and Other Plays* (New York: Theater Communications Group, 1999).

Newton, Adam Zachary, *Narrative Ethics* (Cambridge MA: Harvard UP, 1995).

Singleton, Brian, '"Am I Talking to Myself?" Men, Masculinities and the Monologue in Contemporary Irish Theatre,' *Monologues: Theatre, Performance, Subjectivity*, ed. Clare Wallace (Prague: Litteraria Pragensia, 2006): 260-277.

Wallace, Clare, 'Monologue Theatre, Solo Performance and Self as Spectacle,' *Monologues: Theatre, Performance, Subjectivity*, ed. Clare Wallace (Prague: Litteraria Pragensia, 2006): 1-16.

---, 'Conor McPherson,' *The Methuen Drama Guide to Contemporary Irish Playwrights*, ed. Martin Middeke and Peter Paul Schnierer (London: Methuen, 2010): 271-289.

---, *Suspect Cultures: Narrative, Identity and Citation in 1990s New Drama* (Prague: Litteraria Pragensia, 2006).

Wood, Gerald C., *Conor McPherson: Imagining Mischief* (Dublin: Liffey, 2003).

---

[1] Gerald C. Wood, 'An Interview with Conor McPherson,' in *Conor McPherson: Imagining Mischief* (Dublin: Liffey, 2003): 134.

² The exception here is the Faustian reference in *The Seafarer*.

³ Conor McPherson, *The Weir and Other Plays*, (New York: Theater Communications Group, 1999): 75-76.

⁴ Clare Wallace, 'Monologue Theatre, Solo Performance and Self as Spectacle,' *Monologues: Theatre, Performance, Subjectivity*, ed Clare Wallace (Prague: Litteraria Pragensia, 2006): 2.

⁵ See 'Marina Carr in Conversation with Melissa Sihra,' *Theatre Talk: Voices of Irish Theatre Practitioners*, eds. Lilian Chambers, Ger FitzGibbon and Eamonn Jordan (Dublin: Carysfort, 2001): 61.

⁶ Gerald C. Wood, 128.

⁷ Review of *The Good Thief* by Patrick Brennan, *Irish Theatre Magazine* 21 April 2010 [online].

⁸ Linda Hutcheon, *A Poetics of Postmodernism: History, Theory, Fiction* (New York and London: Routledge, 1988): 4-7.

⁹ Deborah Geis, *Postmodern Theatric(k)s: Monologue in Contemporary American Drama* (Michigan: U of Michigan P, 1993).

¹⁰ Michael Billington's comments from the *Guardian* are posted at <http://www.albemarle-london.com/weir.html>.

¹¹ Brian Singleton, 'Am I Talking to Myself? Men, Masculinities and the Monologue in Contemporary Irish Theatre,' *Monologues: Theatre, Performance, Subjectivity*, ed. Clare Wallace (Prague: Litteraria Pragensia, 2006): 260-277.

¹² Eamonn Jordan, 'Look Who's Talking, Too: The Duplicitous Myth of Naïve Narrative,' *Monologues: Theatre, Performance, Subjectivity*, ed Clare Wallace (Prague: Litteraria Pragensia, 2006): 134.

¹³ I discuss McPherson's work at length in terms of micronarratives in *Suspect Cultures: Narrative, Identity and Citation in 1990s New Drama* (Prague: Litteraria Pragensia, 2006): 39-84.

¹⁴ Jean-François Lyotard, *The Postmodern Condition*, trans. Geoff Bennington and Brian Massumi (1979; Manchester UP, 1984): xxiv.

¹⁵ Lyotard, xxiii.

¹⁶ Lyotard, xxiv.

¹⁷ Scott T. Cummings, 'Homo Fabulator: The Narrative Imperative in Conor McPherson's Plays,' *Theatre Stuff: Critical Essays on Contemporary Irish Theatre*, ed. Eamonn Jordan (Dublin: Carysfort, 2000): 303.

¹⁸ Tim Adams 'So There's These Three Irishmen ...,' *Observer* 4 February 2001 [online].

¹⁹ Cummings, 303.

²⁰ See McPherson's note to *St. Nicholas* in *The Weir and Other Plays* 75-76, Cummings, 'Homo Fabulator' and Wood, *Conor McPherson: Imagining Mischief*.

²¹ Cummings, 305.

²² Wood, 118, 119.

23 Jordan, 155.

24 Jordan, 156.

25 Singleton, 277.

26 Adam Zachary Newton, *Narrative Ethics* (Cambridge MA: Harvard UP, 1995): 27.

27 Newton, 3.

28 McPherson, *The Weir and Other Plays*, 87.

29 Cummings, 308.

30 McPherson, *The Weir and Other Plays*, 99.

31 *ibid.*, 75-76.

32 *ibid.*,79.

33 *ibid.*, 79.

34 *ibid.*,108.

35 *ibid.*,108.

36 *ibid.*,109.

37 *ibid.*, 81.

38 *ibid.*,80-81.

39 *ibid.*,81.

40 Clare Wallace, 'Conor McPherson,' *The Methuen Drama Guide to Contemporary Irish Playwrights* ed. Martin Middeke and Peter Paul Schnierer (London: Methuen, 2010): 274.

41 McPherson, *The Weir and Other Plays*, 143.

42*ibid.*, 156-57.

43 *ibid.*,155.

44 *ibid.*,141, 142.

45 Singleton, 270.

46 McPherson, *The Weir and Other Plays*, 143.

47 *ibid.*,144, 147, 161, 159-60.

48 *ibid.*,185.

49 Singleton, 271.

50 McPherson, *The Weir and Other Plays*, 186.

51 *ibid.*, 193.

52 Jordan, 128.

53 Singleton, 272.

54 Conor McPherson, *Plays: Two* (London: Nick Hern, 2004): 180.

55 *ibid.*, 179.

56 Brian Singleton, 272.

57 McPherson, *Plays: Two*, 182.

4 | Representing Sexual Violence in the Early Plays of Conor McPherson

Lisa Fitzpatrick

Conor McPherson's plays frequently evoke a sense of sexual violence and threat. The violence is not enacted on stage or expressed in violent dialogue, but rather is usually spoken by one character as a past-tense, reflective narrative, that functions to reveal something significant about the characters, their emotional states, or transitional events in their biographies. This essay aims to examine four of McPherson's early plays to explore the representation of sexual violence and its dramatic function.

McPherson's broadly naturalistic aesthetic stages stories of haunted characters – sometimes literally haunted – who are seeking some kind of redemption through the confession of their fears and sins. These confessions often include acts of violence that the character either perpetrated or was complicit in; and the form that violence takes is reflective of issues that were occupying public discourses with increasing urgency in the years when the plays were written – rape, and particularly the sexual abuse of children. *Rum and Vodka* (1992) *This Lime Tree Bower (1993)* and *The Good Thief* (1994) all incorporate narrated acts of sexual violence against women, while *The Weir* and *Come On Over* make reference to the sexual abuse of young girls. In *The Weir* the violence is in the stories told by Jim and Valerie, while *Come On Over* has the character of the priest narrate an event that implicitly reveals his abuse of a girl in an unnamed African country.

The Weir is the play that brought McPherson international recognition as a dramatist. First staged at the Royal Court Theatre

Upstairs in 1997, it transferred to the Royal Court's main space the following February and played for two years, touring overseas. The play is a collection of ghost stories told by a group of men in a rural pub to Valerie, a woman from Dublin who has a terrible story of her own. These stories are modern versions of the traditional country ghost stories told around the fire: tales of fairies and ghostly apparitions. But Jim's story tells of the ghost of a paedophile searching in the churchyard for the grave of a young girl: 'And he wanted to go down in the grave with the ... little girl. Even after they were gone. It didn't bear ... thinking about.'[1] The ellipses in Jim's speech mark moments when something is either implied, or is expressed in opaque or euphemistic terms: 'The fella who'd died had a bit of a reputation for em ... being a pervert.'[2] These brief pauses prompt the audience to fill in the gaps and to imagine what it is that 'doesn't bear ... thinking about.' Valerie responds with the story of her small daughter's death by drowning. In the days after the funeral, she believes she has a phone call from her dead child begging her to come and rescue her. The child is frightened by 'the man standing across the road, and he was looking up and he was going to cross the road,'[3] a night-time terror that the child had repeatedly expressed during her short life. These scenes evoke a particular moment in Irish society and culture when such stories were becoming public knowledge, so that the imagination of the audience is engaged with what is not said, but implied: that the man means harm to the child, and that that harm is likely to involve sexual abuse. Outside of that cultural context, the lines are innocuous, the man's intentions neutral or even possibly benign. The sense of threat is evoked by the child's fear and by the audience's readiness to make that imaginative leap.

However, in his earlier plays McPherson creates narrator figures who speak the action to the audience; there is very little mimetic representation other than perhaps brief personifications of the unseen others that the narrator encounters. *Rum and Vodka* and *The Good Thief* are both solo performances in which the male narrator leads the audience through a series of significant events in his life. In *Rum and Vodka*, the unnamed narrator quits his job after a violent, drunken attack on his supervisor; he returns home drunk and has sex with his wife, but leaves her and their two small children the following morning for a weekend of drinking. He sleeps with a girl called Myfanwy, fights with some people at a party, steals twenty pounds from Myfanwy's wallet and at the end of the play returns home, seemingly sadder and more resigned than when he left. The scene under discussion, however, takes place when the narrator returns home drunk after he has quit his job, and gets into bed beside his sleeping wife:

> I wished I could wake her up and talk but I was too tired to think.
> And then the curse of any tender moment, an erection.
> I suddenly wanted her more than ever.
> And drink'll do that to you.
> And all this ... aggression.
> 'This is my house.
> I'm in bed with my wife.
> And I'm going to fuck her now.'
> I rolled over and felt her tits
> She was warm and soft.
> I pulled the front of her nightie up and felt between her legs.
> She was fast asleep.
> I waited til she was ready, then I held myself above her like I was going to do press ups, and I slid inside her.

He wakes late in the morning:

> And then I remembered ...
> Everything came flooding back and my stomach leapt.
> This was very serious.
> I could go to jail[...]
> I mean, that's pretty close to rape.[4]

As in *The Weir*, the references to rape and violence are largely incidental within the overall plot, and function mainly to create place and character. The narrator's anxiety seems misplaced: his actions may have been 'pretty close to rape,' and he notes at the time that his feelings of aggression rapidly become feelings of lust for his sleeping wife, but there is no suggestion of brutality on his part or resistance on the part of his wife. Since marital rape was criminalized in Ireland in 1990, only one man has been tried and convicted for the offense;[5] the narrator's anxiety however reflects the public discussions in the years before the play was written, when the legislation on rape was under review and feminist analyses of the crime were becoming more audible in Irish culture and society. The narrator's drunken behaviour and his subsequent shame and fear serve to characterize him as a well-meaning and decent individual who nonetheless makes significant and damaging decisions while drunk, which have potentially profound consequences for his life. He cheated on his loved girlfriend with his wife Maria when he was drunk; Maria became pregnant and they married; he quit his job when drunk, and he is drunk when he sleeps with Myfanwy. That the consequences for others may be equally profound – his wife must also contend with an early marriage and motherhood, and a reckless and immature husband besides; he has two small daughters that he can hardly support – seems not to occur to the narrator until, possibly, the last lines of the play when he sits with his sleeping children 'and listened to their breathing [...] I couldn't bear it.'[6] Eamonn Jordan describes the play as 'in part about inappropriate attempts to validate the self – the masculinity astray model,' and notes 'a pattern of acknowledgement and almost simultaneous denial' in many of the characters' monologues[7]. In this scene, for example, the narrator's 'aggression' and decision to 'fuck her now' sits oddly against his self-justifying 'I waited 'til she was ready' (though unconscious) and his fear on waking 'I wanted to crawl under the quilt and hide like a kid.'[8] In fact, he repeatedly attempts to evade Maria's wrath; he does so again in the supermarket when he delays telling her that he does not have the money for the groceries.

The narrator's description of his assault on his wife functions mainly to establish character, but also to mark a particular temporal moment in a play that is geographically firmly located in Dublin. The narrator traces his journey across the city, sometimes giving specific directions, sometimes making references to public buildings such as Crazy Prices in Kilbarrack where he shops with his wife, or Davy Byrne's pub where he drinks with Myfanwy. But the landscape and moment is that of the late 1980s and early 1990s, identifiable by details of characterization and location: the topics of conversation of Myfanwy and their friends; his surprise that Myfanwy has a car (a mini); he does not have a car but has a mortgage and earns, he tells us, 'hundred and eight quid a week.'[9] Alongside these details, and congruous with them, is the narrator's reckless drunken sex with the sleeping Maria and his fear of prosecution when sober: the assumed awareness on the part of the spectators that such a prosecution is possible, coupled with a clear sense of authorial disapproval of the character's behaviour.

The Good Thief, first performed in 1994 at the City Arts Centre in Dublin, is again a one-man-show spoken by an unnamed narrator, the eponymous Good Thief. The title recalls the story of the Crucifixion and the thief who repents on the cross,[10] and the show was first performed under the title *The Light of Jesus*.[11] Unlike the narrator in *Rum and Vodka*, who appears to narrate from more or less the dramatic present, the narrator in *The Good Thief* is reflecting on a past series of life-changing events. The opening description of what he had been doing at the time these events began to unfold paints a picture of a deeply violent person with little or no compassion for others. He was working as a paid thug for a local villain named Joe Murray, had been beating up his girlfriend Greta who had just left him, and his description of some of the things he has seen – such as Joe Murray 'putting it up girls' arses'[12] outlines a brutal social context for his actions. In the opening scenes Murray gives the narrator a hundred pounds to frighten a man named Mitchell who has not been paying his protection money. Two of Murray's other thugs – Vinnie Rourke 'an old time vicious bastard' and Seamus Parker 'a little fucker who followed him everywhere' – overhear the instructions.[13] The job goes badly wrong, and when Vinnie and Parker arrive the narrator realizes he has been set up and goes on the run, taking Mitchell's wife Anna (whom he refers to as Mrs Mitchell) and her child Niamh 'a little girl of about three or four' with him.[14]

The sense of sexual threat builds from the opening scenes. The narrator's description of his girlfriend's promiscuity and her relationships with violent men, his comment that he had seen Murray 'putting it up girls' arses' (his presence suggests that this was an act of violence rather than a private consensual act, as does his later request to Murray not to do that to Greta), and Vinnie Rourke's comment in the chaos of Mitchell's house that he 'likes' the witnesses (Anna and her child), all establish a social context where women are vulnerable to the violent whims of a pack of gangsters. Vinnie's phrase is sufficiently ambiguous to suggest both a sarcastic comment that the narrator has been incompetent enough to leave witnesses, and a more chilling comment that he has a sexual interest in Anna and possibly her child. Later, when Vinnie and his gang find them, the narrator expresses briefly and obliquely what happens:

> I knew he'd break my neck if he kept kicking me. I was passing out.
> I saw Greta and Mrs Mitchell leading me up some stairs in newly painted flats beside a river. There was a war and they were looking after me.
> Then I was drenched on the floor [...]
> 'And I suppose you want to know about flat chest Mitchell and the sprog' said Murray and the way he said it told me everything.

> When I was out cold, they'd had a party.
> Maybe the dream I'd had of her when I was getting that kicking
> was her soul and she had met me while things were still
> happening to her body. I still like to think that.[15]

The building of a sense of sexual threat from small moments, choices of words, and the characterization of Vinnie and his comrades engages the spectator's worst imaginings. Vinnie is not entirely credible: from being only 'an old time vicious bastard who'd done fifteen years for armed robbery' and 'a psycho ... a real pro'[16] in the opening scenes, over the course of a short drama and no more than two days he has murdered Mitchell, a family of five, and Anna and her child. Nonetheless, in a reflection of the *In-Yer-Face* aesthetic that was in the ascendancy in 1990s Britain, in Vinnie McPherson creates a character who acts without conscience. For the narrator figure, the final scene of the play relates his long prison sentence and his present isolation and regretful reflections.

In all of these instances, the focus is very much on the narrator and the effect of the events on him (or her, in the case of Valerie); the victim in each case is obscured – unconscious or dead. The solo form that McPherson uses for *Rum and Vodka* and *The Good Thief* (and *This Lime Tree Bower*, discussed below) draws the audience into an intimate relationship with the narrator who appears to share his private thoughts with us. The performer addresses the audience directly, starting either with a confession 'I think my overall fucked-upness is my impatience'[17] or with a story 'Let's begin with an incident.'[18] In each case, the audience's curiosity is aroused and the performer works to establish a sympathetic or empathetic connection. The characters' awareness of their faults and admission of their own wrong-doing gives them a vulnerability that seeks to draw the audience into a kind of complicity: the Good Thief is a criminal, but as spectators we are positioned in sympathy with him and against those who are chasing him; he is less bad than the men who catch him and kill his hostages. The narrator is also careful to explain that Anna is not particularly distressed at being held at gunpoint, tied up and kidnapped – she seems unmoved in a way that he repeatedly puzzles over. It is he, therefore, who retains the main focus for the audience's sympathy and his behaviour seems less reprehensible since he is not taking her against her will. Rather similarly, the narrator in *Rum and Vodka* retains the focus of our sympathy while he assaults his wife – largely because he does so without violence and while expressing concern for her 'I waited 'til she was ready' – and because of his subsequent remorse. Since his wife does not wake up and is not physically harmed, the act has no consequences.

Jill Dolan discusses the concept of feminist spectatorship as a process that 'analyzes a performance's meaning by reading against the grain of stereotypes and resisting the manipulation of both the performance text and the cultural text that it helps to shape.'[19] While these early plays by McPherson, written in the first half of the 1990s, reflect a set of cultural texts and anxieties about violence against women and children and the rapidly changing social and cultural landscape of late twentieth century Ireland, the work also intervenes to add its weight to the range of representational strategies available. Dolan reads performance as always ideologically positioned and argues that 'representation offers or denies subjectivity by manipulating the terms of its discourse, images, and myths through ideology.'[20] Most commonly it denies subjectivity to female characters and positions the male characters at the centre of the action as protagonists and antagonists, with the female characters in a range of supporting roles and, often, functioning as objects of transaction between the men.

In *The Good Thief*, Greta and Anna function mainly as objects of transaction. According to the narrator, Greta is sleeping with a number of men, including Murray, and this is why he beats her. In the final lines of the play, he remarks on seeing her getting out of a big car with a man twice her age. He notes that he thinks of her sometimes, and that he owes her his life because, though she betrayed him to Murray, she did so on condition that he not be killed. Her relationships seem to make her physically vulnerable as she is passed or (according to the narrator) gives herself to a number of men who are all part of a criminal underworld. Greta seems to narrowly avoid the fate that befalls the other off-stage female characters, Anna and her child and the mother of the family murdered by Vinnie and his thugs, only because Murray is in love with her and because she is willing to trade sex for protection ('Power attracts women,'[21] the narrator notes in his opening lines). But Greta has no existence outside the narrator's memories, and the audience's access to what she thinks and feels is minimal. Unlike a number of the other unseen characters – Murray, Vinnie and his gang – Greta does not drive the action. She serves rather as an object that is passed within the group, depending on who is in the ascendancy at any given time.

The characters of Anna and the child Niamh are equally marginal to the action and take their meaning from the role and interpretation delivered by the narrator. Even their fate is only tentatively established by Vinnie's oblique comment and the narrator's interpretation of it from 'the way he said it,'[22] information that the spectators are not party to since Vinnie is not present on stage. Their bodies are never found. But the audience do get a sense of Anna as a figure, as she appears in the narrator's story. Her primary function appears to be to motivate his remorse and reformation, as the unseen and unheard rape victim in *The Lime Tree Bower* will do for Joe. To express the action in terms from Victorian melodrama, by her death Anna saves the narrator's soul; her death is thus readable as a sacrifice. She is by no means a conventionally saintly figure: though married to Mitchell she doesn't love him and her child is not his. The narrator, upon learning this, feels he understands her lack of grief at Mitchell's violent death, though in fact her lack of feeling strikes the spectator as odd as well. Yet the interpretation we are finally given for her behaviour is structured around stereotypical cultural conceptions of female behaviour and psychology: her lack of attachment to Mitchell is explained by her attachment to another man, and her indifference to her husband's death is explained by a singular (monogamous) love for someone else. She doesn't sleep with Mitchell, she explains, but the man she loves cannot settle down and support them because his career as a journalist means that he travels constantly.

The construction of Anna's situation is both unobtrusive and dramatically credible – it fits with other conventional models of behaviour for female dramatic characters – and reiterates tired stereotypes that are almost comical: she lives in celibacy with her husband for four or five years after giving birth to her lover's child, because her lover values his career over her and, apparently, she must live with someone and be supported by him. Although her strange, dissociated behaviour is referred to in the monologue, her explanation for it is not equally problematized, so that gender stereotypes are reiterated without being interrogated. Similarly, Greta's only intervention into the action – when she asks for the narrator's life to be spared – is an appeal to the active, male agents. Dolan comments that the feminist spectator

> sees women ... relegated to supporting roles that enable the more important action of the male protagonist ... While the men are generally active and involved, the women seem

marginal and curiously irrelevant, except as a tacit support system or as decoration that enhances and directs the pleasure of the male spectator's gaze.[23]

In this monologue form, the women are further marginalized by the presence of the single, male body on the stage; their erasure seems complete.[24]

A feminist analysis of McPherson's next publicly performed work, *This Lime Tree Bower*, which was staged in the Crypt Arts Centre in Dublin in 1995, opens this issue for further discussion. In this play, three performers play Joe, Ray and Frank. There is very little dialogue – only two lines – and the characters tell their stories in overlapping monologues. The stage directions note that 'All remain on stage throughout, and are certainly aware of each other,'[25] but there are no other directions given; there are points in the play where the characters could signal their awareness or engagement in each other's stories, but these are at the discretion of the director. For example, the 2010 production at the CoHo Theatre in Portland has the characters at a distance from each other 'in a triangle of plain wooden chairs on a plain wood-plank floor, with nothing else around but that bare, willowy tree pushing up through the floorboards behind them.'[26] The 1996 production at Primary Stages in New York City has the characters 'come on stage after an off-stage drink (behind a scrim which is never alluded to or used again in the performance) and begin speaking, one after the other. Rapidly. Looking straight at the audience and speaking directly to the audience about themselves and about one another';[27] and the 2005 production at Theatre 503 in London set the play in 'a bare sandy space, furnished with benches and coat hooks.'[28] In these productions, the characters do not interact or speak to each other, apart from one exchange between Ray and Frank.

Typically for McPherson's work, the characterization is deft and witty and achieved entirely through the spoken word, and some of the scenes are very funny. Joe is seventeen; his brother Frank is in his twenties and both live at home with their widowed father. Ray is their sister's boyfriend and is a philosophy lecturer.

The first monologue is spoken by Joe, and it is his story that will be the main focus here. Joe begins by describing a new boy in his school, Damien – a boy that Joe idolizes. Damien seems different from the other boys, and is more daring than Joe. When he suggests that they 'bonk off school' (play truant) one day, Joe says yes, needing to seem as rebellious as his friend. Joe's teenage anxiety about sex is reflected in his fears and dreams about girls and women; his embarrassment when Damien claims he can tell if someone is a virgin just by looking at them, and his masochistic fantasy of 'Miss Brosnan, our biology teacher' who has 'huge tits.' He says, 'I was imagining her catching me on the mitch and making me fuck her as a punishment.'[29] In contrast, Damien's speech – as reported by Joe – is sexually aggressive. One weekend he suggests that they go to a local disco in a bar that is known for its fights, promising Joe 'that if I didn't get my end away, he'd give me a hundred quid.'[30] Though intrigued, Joe is disappointed and disgusted by what he sees: 'It was a shithole. Everyone behaved like animals. I had quite a lot of principles.'[31] Eventually Damien wants to leave, bringing with them a thin, drunken girl with dyed blonde hair, who is 'getting off' with Damien and who wants them to walk her home to the Grange 'where all the knackers lived.' But as they walk to the Grange, Damien takes the nearly unconscious girl into a graveyard and after a few minutes Joe follows:

> I saw something moving on a grave.
> I nearly shit myself because I thought it was something
> crawling out of the grave.
> But it was worse.
> Damien had his trousers down and the girl's legs were on either
> side of him, like they were broken.
> Her neck was on the low rail around the grave and her head
> hung over the gravel.
> Damien was pushing into her like he wanted to put her in the
> ground.
> I ran straight back to my bike and cycled home.
> I said goodnight and got sick in the bathroom.
> I wondered if the girl knew what was happening to her. I
> wanted to hop on my bike and go back.
> [...]
> I wanted [Damien] to tell me that the girl had a great time and
> he saw her home.
> I didn't want to hear anything else.'[32]

This Lime Tree Bower approaches the subplot of the rape from the perspective of the teenaged narrator, who not unnaturally sees it as something that has happened to him. He is frightened by the violence of what he has witnessed, and is unsure how to interpret his friend's behaviour. He wants to intervene to help the girl, and since he doesn't – 'it was too late' – he hopes that Damien will reassure him that everything was fine. Although his distress is sincere, his physical response is ambivalent: 'The horrible thing was that what I saw made me sick to my stomach, but at the same time it was really turning me on.'[33] Later, Frank recounts how Joe tried to tell him a story about 'some eejit from his school having it off with a knacker from the Grange. It had really upset him. But I couldn't see the big deal and I didn't know what to say to him.'[34] In the final scenes Joe narrates how the girl made a report to the police, naming Damien as the rapist, and Damien denied it and named Joe. Joe is quickly cleared, however, by a blood test and the fact that his testimony matches the girl's.

In this story of Joe's loss of innocence[35] the violence enacted on the young girl is unseen and her voice is unheard. The only thing she is reported as saying is that she wants the boys to see her home.[36] The absence of any mimetic representation means that the violence is expressed through language, suggested in the connotations of the words used. Referring to the unnamed girl Joe uses the word 'broken,' the proximity of the adjective to the nouns 'legs' and 'neck' suggesting injury, the comfortless atmosphere suggested by the harsh consonant sounds in graves and gravel, and the violence suggested in the phrase 'pushing into her like he wanted to put her in the ground.' While the violence characterizes Damien and Joe, contrasting the corruption of one and the innocence of the other, its dramatic function is not entirely clear. The other act of violence is Frank's armed robbery of Simple Simon's betting office, in which no one is physically hurt though Simon is humiliated and forced to strip. McPherson, like the playwrights of the *In-Yer-Face* movement, uses violence to create dramatic worlds where ordinary people are confronted with their capacity for harm and brutality, and sexual violence is a recurring motif in that body of work.[37] In some ways, this is attributable to the especial abhorrence with which most people respond to rape and sexual violence. Yet these acts also subtly reiterate stereotypes of gender and the tendency noted by Dolan for female characters to exist only in relation to the male protagonists. Where the female characters are completely erased, as in this monologue form, they become even more identified with and through the male characters. Thus Ray's girlfriend, Joe and Frank's sister, never appears on stage; she is characterized solely through what is said about her. The brothers' mother is dead; Damien's mother is seen only through Joe's eyes, and the raped girl is also seen only through Joe's words, Frank's characterization of her as 'a knacker from the Grange,' and Joe's imagined conversation with

Damien. The girl is thus dismissed from the audience's attention until the very end, when Joe explains that everything has ended well but adds, 'I can still see the girl.'[38]

It is not the purpose of this essay to argue that rape can only be represented in a particular way, or that every play should have female speaking roles. However, male-narrated sexual violence is a motif in McPherson's early work, as is the absence of female characters (until *The Weir*, which has one out of a cast of five). And the absence of female characters from the stage does not mark a performed fluidity of gender in which the male narrator might impersonate or demonstrate the female characters, but seems rather to reiterate the iconicity of gender in naturalistic performance. The male characters, represented on stage through the physical male bodies of the actors, re-inscribe gender conventions visually as well as dramaturgically – their gendered bodies reflect the conventions that the dramatic plots express. In this as in the other monodramas, the girl exists only in relation to Joe and Damien.

In its portrayal of the rape, the play identifies what Hanley, Healy and Scriver describe as the typical rape scenario in Ireland: both parties have consumed alcohol; they know each other, and they go consensually to a private place together. However, the aggressor then insists upon having sex which the victim resists, but minimal violence is used. The rape is reported more than twenty-four hours later. Hanley at al conclude 'The chances are good that this rape will not be prosecuted.'[39] Yet the suggestion in the play is that the rape is prosecuted, and Joe tells us that Damien will be charged with the crime. Like the narrator in *Rum and Vodka* worried that he will be prosecuted for raping his wife, *This Lime Tree Bower* suggests that rape is investigated, prosecuted and punished far more commonly than statistics support.

The final play discussed here is the later short two-hander, *Come On Over*, which was first performed at the Gate Theatre in Dublin in 2001. The characters are hooded, an artistic choice that was criticized in the reviews at the time. They are Margaret and Matthew, two former lovers who are reunited late in life when Matthew, a priest, returns to Ireland, badly injured, after spending time as a missionary in an unnamed part of Africa. He narrates how he accused another expatriate, 'the Englishman,' of abusing a local girl named Patience, and was so distressed by this interview that he got a migraine. As he lay in bed, Patience approached and stabbed him repeatedly in the face. Though the priest never admits explicitly what he has done, his description of the events, coupled with the audience's extra-theatrical knowledge of events in the 'actual' world, opens two possible readings: one in which both the priest and the Englishman are abusing the child and she takes revenge upon Matthew for his hypocrisy, and one in which Matthew, driven by his jealousy and lust for the child, falsely accuses the Englishman.

As in the other plays, Patience is known to the audience only through Matthew's testimony. And like the other female victims in these plays, she is described in terms that re-inscribe gender conventions: she 'seems older' than eleven, 'she looked like a woman. I mean a small grown woman'[40] and she helps the nurse inoculate the babies. This alignment of Patience with women's work and maternity helps to position her within Matthew's monologue as a potential sexual partner, and allows him to overlook the fact that she is a child. The female character on stage, Margaret, seems not to hear this confession. In her own monologues, she narrates her unrequited love for Matthew and the story of her marriage, but little else; there is no real sense of who the hooded figure is, other than in relation to the male protagonist whose story drives the plot. The story of the abuse of the child, to which Margaret scarcely reacts, is a plot device to drive Matthew back to Dublin and to the case of a possible saint, a young girl whose body has not decomposed in the grave. Indeed, this might recall *The Weir* and Jim's story of the dead paedophile, still searching for the little girl's grave.

Sexual violence, a motif in McPherson's early work, functions mainly as a plot device and to establish character in these monodramas written between 1992 and 2001. The monologues are spoken in the present of the near or distant past, and their reflective tone is more evocative of a sense of threat or dread than of the immediacy of enacted violence. This past-ness of the violence has the potential to engage the audience's imaginations while the inexorability of the unfolding events heightens their unease. This is particularly true of *The Good Thief*, where the vividly spun context of extreme, comic-book gangster violence foregrounds the vulnerability of the women, and even the opening lines refer to the narrator beating up his girlfriend. Yet the insistent focus on the male narrator or narrators, whose bodies are the only ones visible on stage, erases the voices, bodies, and experiences of these off-stage female characters. Girlfriends, wives, and children, they are defined almost entirely in terms of the male characters. The plays thus seem to re-inscribe gender stereotypes conventional to naturalistic performance, in which the male protagonists drive the action and the female characters play supporting roles. In performance, there is no record of these pieces being used to interrogate gender as a performative or to explore the fluidity of gender identity. Rather, the violence is framed as something in the life of the male protagonist, and its effect on him becomes the focus of the drama. This aspect of the work, I would argue, reflects social and cultural debates and anxieties in Ireland during the 1990s around violence against women and the role and status of women in society, in a society that was still deeply conservative and patriarchal in its attitudes to gender.

Works Cited

Bal, M. *Reading Rembrandt* (Cambridge: Cambridge University Press, 1991)

Burke, J. 'Marital Rape ... a crime with no punishment for sixteen years' *Sunday Tribune* 30/01/2011. Available online at http://www.tribune.ie. [Accessed 29/07/11]

Cummings, Scott, T. 'Homo Fabulator: The Narrative Imperative in Conor McPherson's Plays,' *Theatre Stuff* ed. Eamonn Jordan (Dublin: Carysfort Press, 2000): 303-312.

Dolan, Jill. *The Feminist Spectator as Critic* (Ann Arbor: University of Michigan Press, 1991)

Hanley, C., D. Healy, S. Scriver *Rape and Justice in Ireland* (Dublin: The Liffey Press, 2010)

Hughley, M. '*This Lime Tree Bower* talks the talk at CoHo Theater' *The Oregonian* 10/05/2010. Available online at www.oregonlive.com. [Accessed 29/07/2011].

Jordan, Eamonn, *Dissident Dramaturgies* (Dublin: Irish Academic Press, 2010)

Lehmann, H.T. *Postdramatic Theatre* Trans. Karen Jürs-Munby (London & New York: Routledge, 2006).

McPherson, Conor, *Plays: Two* (London: Nick Hern Books, 2004).

---,*This Lime Tree Bower: Three Plays* (London: Nick Hern Books; Dublin: New Island Books, 1996)

Pfister, Manfred. *Theory and Analysis of Drama* (Cambridge: Cambridge University Press, 1988)

Roberts, D. 'This Lime Tree Bower' *Theatre Reviews Ltd* 13/05/1999. Available online at www.theatrereviews.com. [Accessed 29/07/2011].

Thaxter, J. 'This Lime Tree Bower' *The Stage* 17/02/2005. Available online at www.thestage.co.uk. [Accessed 29/07/2011].

Wallace, Clare. 'Conor McPherson' *Contemporary Irish Playwrights* ed. M. Middeke & P.P. Schnierer. (London: Methuen, 2010): 271-289.

[1] McPherson, *The Weir* in *Plays: Two* (London: Nick Hern Books, 2004):51.

[2] *ibid.*, 51.

[3] *ibid.*, 53.

[4] McPherson, *Rum and Vodka* in *This Lime Tree Bower: Three Plays* (London: Nick Hern Books, 1996):18-19.

[5] John Burke, 'Marital Rape ... a crime with no punishment for sixteen years' *Sunday Tribune* (30th January 2011). Available online at http://www.tribune.ie/.

[6] McPherson, *Rum and Vodka*, 45.

[7] Eamonn Jordan, *Dissident Dramaturgies* (Dublin: Irish Academic Press, 2010): 223.

[8] McPherson, *Rum and Vodka*, 18-19.

[9] *ibid.*, 11.

[10] The Gospel according to Luke, 23:39-43.

[11] Noted in *This Lime Tree Bower: Three Plays* (London: Nick Hern Books, 1996):48.

[12] McPherson, *The Good Thief*, 51.

[13] *ibid.*, 52.

[14] *ibid.*, 54.

[15] *ibid.*, 74-75.

[16] *ibid.*, 52.

[17] McPherson, *Rum and Vodka*, 9.

[18] McPherson, *The Good Thief*, 49.

[19] Jill Dolan, *The Feminist Spectator as Critic* (Ann Arbor: University of Michigan Press, 1991): 2.

[20] Dolan, 16.

[21] McPherson, *The Good Thief*, 49.

[22] *ibid.*,75.

[23] Dolan, 2.

[24] There are not many Irish-authored monodramas for women. Published examples include those of Beckett (*Rockaby* and *Footfalls*), Dermot Bolger's *The Holy Ground*, Maggie Cronin's *A Most Notorious Woman*, Geraldine Aron's *My Brilliant Divorce* and Frank McGuinness's *Baglady*. Compared to the number of monodramas for male actors, however, they are few in number.

[25] McPherson, *This Lime Tree Bower*, 80.

[26] Marty Hughley, '*This Lime Tree Bower* talks the talk at CoHo Theater' *The Oregonian* (May 10, 2010). Available online at www.oregonlive.com.

[27]David Roberts, 'This Lime Tree Bower' *Theatre Reviews Ltd.* (May 13, 1999). Available online at www.theatreviews.com.

[28] John Thaxter, 'This Lime Tree Bower' *The Stage* (17 February 2005). Available online at www.thestage.co.uk.

[29] McPherson, *This Lime Tree Bower*, 83.

[30] *ibid.*, 107.

[31] *ibid.*,109.

[32] *ibid.*, 109-110.

[33] *ibid.*,110.

[34] *ibid.*, 119.

[35] Jordan, 2010, p.85.

[36] McPherson, *This Lime Tree Bower*, 109.

[37] For example, in the work of Sarah Kane or Mark Ravenhill, or in the monodramas of Mark O'Rowe.

[38] McPherson, *This Lime Tree Bower*, 124.

[39] C. Hanley, D. Healy & S. Scriver *Rape and Justice in Ireland* (Dublin: Liffey, 2010):360.

[40] McPherson, *Plays: Two*, 199.

5 | Conor McPherson's *St. Nicholas* – A Study in Comic Anguish

Susanne Colleary

Comic Impulse

Conor McPherson wrote *St. Nicholas* while he was the writer-in-residence at the Bush Theatre in London in 1997. A one man play written for a man in his fifties, McPherson realized that casting the part was going to be difficult. In an 'Afterword' to the published edition of *Four Plays*, McPherson observed, 'we knew it needed someone with a strong presence who could give us a bleak devastation and make it funny.'[1] McPherson admits to 'grinning [like an] idiot,'[2] when the Olivier award winning actor Brian Cox agreed to take on the role of the immoral, cynical and anonymous (the character is unnamed in the play) theatre critic from Dublin. McPherson recounts something of the worry he possessed about staging a play which openly derides theatre critics and their ilk. He described opening night at the Bush Theatre:

> We opened. Press night had about twenty-five critics. I sat waiting for the moment when Brian says, "Mmm. I was a bollocks to all the other critics. And I'll tell you why, because it was this: they were all cunts." I could remember writing that line ... my mischievous self-satisfaction thinking what a great fellow I was altogether. And now here it was ringing out over a roomful of critics. There was a silence like someone had pressed the detonator and nothing happened. And then bang, the place erupted. We were all playing.[3]

St. Nicholas has received consistently good reviews in the years since opening in 1997. Paul Taylor, writing for *The Independent* described *St. Nicholas* as the story of 'a jaded Dublin theatre critic, lost in hard drinking hack hell, [who] goes through a form of emotional breakdown ... brilliantly performed by Brian Cox.'[4] Taylor goes on to praise the production for the same vibrant qualities evident in McPherson's previous play, *The Lime Tree Bower*, at the same address. For Taylor, storytelling and comedy are central to the two plays, and as with *The Lime Tree Bower*, Taylor praises *St. Nicholas* for the power of its 'narrative grip and laconic comedy.'[5]

After its London run, *St. Nicholas* played at the Primary Stages in New York, where Ben Brantley reviewed the production for the *New York Times*. Brantley described the production as 'a delectably droll celebration of storytelling as striptease, [and of Cox's performance, as that which] radiates tart pleasure as the man playing Rod Sterling to *The Twilight Zone* of his own life.'[6] Bearing these ideas in mind, this article looks at how ideas of black humour or the comedy of entropy functions in *St. Nicholas*. Specifically, I want to look at how the humour of entropy fuels the theatre critic's perceptions of himself, his relationships with others and his world view. I also want to look at how the comedy of entropy functions, as it acts as a mode of connection and communication between the theatre critic and the audience. Finally, I wish to connect the comedy of entropy with what can be described as an entropic attitude, and how that attitude can inform and underpin contemporary perceptions of experience in everyday life.

The Comedy of Entropy at Play

Conor McPherson's own comic views are expressed in an interview with Nev Pierce about McPherson's film *The Actors* in 2003. During that discussion, McPherson observes:

> The thing about comedy is that it's really, really hard; it's really really difficult to do. If it's a horror film, you can go, 'What we need now is a big shock', and you can work that out and do it ... whereas with comedy you go, 'Well, what happens now is we've got to make everybody laugh'. And it's like, 'How the **** are we going to do that'?[7]

McPherson has also, on many occasions, expressed his admiration for Martin Scorsese's cult classic film *The King of Comedy* (1983). While discussing the deluded central character of Pupkin, brilliantly played by Robert De Niro he observed:

> The impetus for me to write something ... comes from the
> thinking that the world is an insane and horrible place, that
> this is a kind of hellish existence. We all require a necessary
> amount of delusion just to get through our lives. And we need
> to be able to laugh at the absurdity of it all.[8]

The twin concepts of delusion and absurdity are central to the
mechanics of *St. Nicholas*. The story that makes up *St. Nicholas* is
narrated to the audience by an anonymous theatre critic over two
acts. In ninety minutes or so, the critic regales the audience with his
story. In what can be described as the 'monologue form [understood
as] essential storytelling, [as] a stripping away of dramatic illusion,'[9]
and with a bare stage as backdrop, the critic tells the audience of his
selfish and debauched life as a journalist and theatre critic in
Dublin. He paints a verbal picture of dysfunction in his domestic
life, of his loveless marriage and his failure as a husband and a
father. He speaks of his artistic failures and of having no ideas of his
own for a story. He describes his growing infatuation with a young
actress named Helen, who is playing the part of *Salomé* in a
mediocre production at the Abbey Theatre. Smitten, he follows her
and the production to London. Soon after his arrival, very drunk and
very late, and in a bizarre attempt to see Helen, he disrupts the
household of actors and proceeds to tell the cast a series of feeble
and unconvincing lies. Their response is incredulous and
disbelieving, and so, having exposed himself as a failed liar, the
critic wanders in a drunken haze until he passes out in Crystal
Palace Park.

Here he meets William, and readily complies when William
suggests that the critic come and stay at William's house. What the
critic soon discovers is that William is the leader of a sect of
vampires and, having taken up residence in the house, the critic
agrees to procure fresh victims for the sect from the pub and club
scenes in London. This arrangement seems to work for a time;
however, the critic eventually comes to loathe his hosts. He decides
on a particular night that it will be his last; however, the last
consignment of victims includes Helen, the object of his recent
obsession. On returning to the house and despite the critic's feeble
efforts, they are both bitten by the vampires. Leaving Helen in the
house, the critic decides that it is finally time to return to Dublin and
to his old life in possession of that which he had previously yearned
for and sorely lacked, finally, in possession of a story.

The surrealist André Breton coined the term 'humour noir' in his *Anthologie de l'humour noir*, first published in 1939. Breton has variously described the condition of black humour as 'subversive, disruptive of accepted values and systems ... an aggressive weapon ... in others a defence strategy ... containing a strongly satirical element, [with] subject matter which would normally be considered taboo.'[10] Patrick O'Neill suggests that black humour may evoke in the reader (or in the terms of this discussion, the spectator) 'a bitter, ironic or sardonic laughter or amusement, in other cases it is of a more extreme type, which produces less amusement than horror or disgust.'[11] O'Neill's development of a model for black humour in literary criticism builds on Breton's (among others) conceptualization which in crystallized form is described as the comedy of entropy. O'Neill argues that the condition of black humour contrasts with other modes of humorous expression:

> Benign humour is warm, tolerant, sympathetic ... the humour in a word, of unthreatened norms, while derisive humour is cold, intolerant, unsympathetic, the humour of rejection or correction, the humour of defended norms ... Black humour on the other hand contrasts with both of these, in that it is the humour of lost norms, lost confidence, the humour of disorientation ... Physicists express the tendency of closed systems to move from a state of order into one of total disorder in terms of the systems entropy: black humour, to coin a phrase, is the comedy of entropy.[12]

There are rich veins of entropic comedy running through *St. Nicholas*. In the first act, the theatre critic paints a darkly comic picture of his journalistic cronies as drunken hacks. He describes them and ironically, himself as, 'drunken pig-headedness being passed off as authority ... that was the world I was in. Fuck. You think I was going to surround myself with people who were succeeding?'[13] This in effect mirrors the critic's own lack of journalistic professionalism and manifests the frustration he clearly feels about the fact that he had 'no ideas for a story ... [and that despite his efforts], nothing came.'[14] He tells the audience that he has fundamentally let his wife and children down, of a miserable home life, where once there was hope of better things, 'I loved her once when we were young ... all we had to do was keep holding hands. And I couldn't even do that.'[15] Yet his description of her is acutely satirical, a 'fat tracksuit wife. She didn't want anything. She was happy enough to get a half bottle of gin into her. And the days just slipped through her thick fingers.'[16] His infatuation for the attractive young actress Helen causes him to consider physical desire and beauty, 'what if you woke up in the morning and you were the physical specimen you always wanted to be. Wouldn't that make you happy? Of course it would ... Because now your smile would beam confidence.'[17] Before long however, the critic's self-loathing reappears, as he maliciously satirizes his own physical shortcomings. On arriving in London in search of Helen, he decides to get 'some natty duds. Impress the ladies. Changing in a little cubicle. Caught myself in the mirror. Belly like a mountain. Little tits and everything ... got a linen jacket. And I went drinking.'[18] Toward the end of the first act and after his shambolic and drunken failure to impress Helen, the critic does experience a transitory moment of clarity, albeit it through a visionary flood of alcohol, in Crystal Palace Park:

> I'd made a total fool of myself. I couldn't understand how I'd been so stupid as to think anything would have come of this. And I'd fucked myself up as far as Dublin was concerned. Everywhere I went people would laugh. I must have looked like a lunatic. I was bollixed.[19]

This moment of self realization is a brief one, as the critic is taken over by a series of alcohol infused disorientating and nightmarish hallucinations before passing out cold. This episode is quickly followed by the critic's first encounter with William, who, incredibly, is the leader of a sect of vampires, and the audience are catapulted into a story which takes on a distinctly 'tales of the unexpected' glow.

The critic's story now moves abruptly from the realm of the credulous into that of the incredulous. However, very early into the second act, not long into his story about living with and working for Williams's sect of vampires, the critic ambushes his own narrative. He breaks abruptly out of character in order to directly address and to make a series of satirical verbal assaults on the audience:

> Mm. There's always going to be a smugness about you listening to this. As we all take part in this convention. And you will say, these vampires are not very believable, are they ... if they were vampires, why don't their victims become vampires? And you are, of course, relying on the lazy notions foisted upon you by others in the effort to make you buy more popcorn.[20]

The narrator ridicules the audience for what in his view is their misguided belief and faith in science and the rational world over and above nature or magic or superstition:

> We may know that the earth goes around the sun. And we may know that this is due to gravity. But not one of us knows why there is gravity. So don't sit there and cast judgement on the credibility of what I say, when you don't even know why you aren't floating off your seats.[21]

And this is a very interesting dramatic strategy in the play, because the theatre critic has stepped outside the bounds of conventional theatre to speak directly to the audience, which simultaneously acts to abolish any dramatic illusion as well as casting doubt into the minds of the audience as to the veracity of his story. This act also breaks down any presumed or traditional perceptions of safe distance between the spectators and the performer. Additionally, by stepping outside of the character and challenging the audience's alleged rationalistic world view, the critic actively attempts to disorient the audience. This act of audience sabotage mischievously transposes that sense of disorientation and uncertainty that the character is experiencing directly onto the audience as the play progresses.

Comic Arbitration

Deploying the tactics of direct address, satirical sabotage and disorientation techniques on the audience foregrounds the importance of the performer-audience exchange at work in *St. Nicholas*. Up to this point in the discussion I have been attempting to look at how the comedy of entropy works as a characteristic mode of expression in *St. Nicholas*. For the moment, I would like to look at how an audience may respond and react to the comedy of entropy running through the play. The audience may well question the reliability of both the narrator and the narrated, and as Scott T. Cummings has noted, 'Casting judgement on the credibility of what his narrator says is precisely what McPherson wants his audiences to do because it necessitates a more general judgement of the narrator's character.'[22] And this is an interesting point, as the ideas of an audience's judgement can, I believe, constitute elements of comic arbitration. The audience can respond with sardonic or scornful amusement to the critic's descriptions of himself brimming as they are with a mixture of arrogance, self loathing and satirical contempt both for himself and those around him. The audience can also respond with a certain comic bitterness or hostility, as when the critic berates and directly challenges them for what he perceives as their disbelief at the supernatural turns of his story. The scornful or bitter amusement of the audience can also be tinged with disgust at the grotesqueries of the critic's continued downward spiral into alcoholism. An instance which perhaps best describes the tipping point between comic repulsion and real horror and disgust on the part of the audience comes again in the closing moments of the first act. On waking in the actors' house, his clothes drenched in spilled whiskey, the critic barely finds his way to the bathroom, where he vomits up raw whiskey and finds something hidden behind the sink, 'I pulled it out. It was a porno mag. *Readers' Wives*. They were in bits. On their living room sofas, legs spread. Arses in the air ... and I wanted Helen that way.'[23] And for a moment the audience are moved from the comic grotesqueries of alcoholic behaviour, into the realm of real horror as the critic contemplates an act of sexual violence on Helen. He manages to stop himself from carrying out the act because 'reason had crept into the room behind me and caressed my neck. I was thinking about my girl you see? I was thinking of something real.'[24] There is also something of the ludicrous in the critic's assertions of a new found sexual potency, 'And I knew. I knew I'd been filled with charm. I'd been made attractive,' gifts made to him by William in order to lure victims back to the house, which can also certainly be read sardonically by an audience as a sort of a middle-aged crisis of masculinity. Additionally, the cynical humour of the critic as he glibly procures his victims on that first night is clear, he tells the audience that he held those first victims:

> enthralled with my brutal wit. And then I had an 'idea.' Let's all go back to my house, for God's sake. And I have to admit it. I was curious. I didn't like them. I was looking forward to seeing what was going to happen to them. I think you'd call that, having a streak in you.[25]

The glibness with which the critic procures those victims allows an audience to respond with feelings of scornful amusement mingled with mild repulsion at the critic's complete disregard for the welfare of his victims, those 'young people with that shine off them.'[26] Near the end of the play, the critic has another 'moment of clarity' and resolves 'that this was the last night I was doing this. This was the last batch of idiots I was bringing back.' That last batch turns out to be a group of actors, among which is Helen, the critics recent object of obsession. Although somewhat concerned for her safety, the critic has little compunction in enticing them back to the house, and describes with some glee his satisfaction as:

> this was the first time I'd been surrounded by artists and actually felt in charge. This was the ideal last batch. In the morning, none of them would remember what had happened. And I would know. And they'd be fools in my eyes forever. I had the power now.[27]

This again, I would argue, places the audience in a position of comic disdain as the theatre critic, despite his experiences, is unchanged; he remains deeply flawed, cynical, selfish, and cruel, as he continues to wallow in self pity, jealousy and spite.

An Entropic Attitude

As *St. Nicholas* reaches its final moments, both Helen and the critic have been bitten by the vampires. The critic pulls Helen away from William's grasp; nonetheless, he leaves her asleep with her friends and exits the house. Earlier in the evening William recounted a Grimm's fairy tale style of story to the critic but was unable to account for its moral. In another moment of clarity, the critic realizes that the vampires have no ability for self reflection and no conscience. This realization allows the critic to break the spell he had been labouring under and he makes his decision to return to his old life. He speaks with smug glee:

> about the fuss people were going to make of me. The potential it gave me to bully sympathy out of everybody ... Talking to My Wife. Giving My Children My Advice. I had my health. I had resolve. But most important. I had a story.[28]

The storytelling aspects in the works of Conor McPherson have been much discussed and debated in recent years. Ben Brantley has described *St. Nicholas* as exemplary of many forms of storytelling from 'extended self serving lies born of drunkenness to a proper Brothers Grimm like fable ... [and that] the effect of all this is to suggest how stories give the chaos of life form and shading and how everyone to some extent makes use of this artistic process.'[29] So too, Mic Moroney applauds Mc Pherson's aptitude for monologues, which are more often than not male centred, and which reveal the stories of his characters with 'a grimly philosophical tinge ... [McPherson exposes] their hard-wired, anti-social desires, and [offers] little antidote other than black humour.'[30] McPherson's theatre critic recounts a story about how he acquired his story, but the journey in search of that story does not redeem the character in any way. It is clear that the critic at the end of this play is just as selfish, cruel, repulsive, and defined through his resentment and disdain for everyone around him, as he was when first we encountered him. Moroney rightly argues that McPherson offers the audience little in the way of redemption for his characters with only laconic black humour as antidote. However, there is I believe, something more to be said for the significance of black humour as remedy in *St. Nicholas*. McPherson's theatre critic may not be for saving; however, McPherson's use of black humour is deeply embedded in the theatre critic's character and the stories that he tells. What I am suggesting here is that in *St. Nicholas*, McPherson deploys the tactics of entropic humour, as a dramatic device, yes, but which is also deeply embedded in what can be also described as an entropic attitude. McPherson's brand of black humour constitutes a fundamental philosophical attitude which acknowledges and recognizes black humour as the humour of acute uncertainty and doubt, as the best means through which to carry the bleak devastation that beats at the heart of the play. For me the critic is defined by an entropic attitude, it colours and informs his self perceptions, his self hatred and his overwhelming feelings of inadequacy; it speaks to the depths of his uncertainty and doubt. An audience may respond by making the critic the subject of their comic judgement, but I would argue that that judgement is not coming from a place of derision or rejection, nor of correction, it holds a deeper resonance than that. I would argue that it comes from a shared understanding and recognition of the value of black humour as an entropic attitude.

In a world, as O'Neill notes, where contemporary society has 'seen a loss of belief in our selves, in our societies and in our gods,'[31] an entropic attitude rests on a fundamental incongruence; it treats serious material comically in order to articulate profound feelings of disorientation. Perhaps then in the end there is something to be said for the theatre critic's redeeming features. The deployment of an entropic attitude allows the character to negotiate his life through black humour, as a defence strategy, as a coping mechanism and perhaps even as a wry acknowledgement of his imploded and impotent self. And if this is the case, I suggest that the audience also have the power to recognize and share in that entropic attitude, the deployment of which can operate in a myriad of ways, but which can function as a valuable tool through which to negotiate and mediate the experiential depths of contemporary everyday existence. As Eugené Ionesco once observed, 'to become conscious of what is horrifying and to laugh at it, is to become master of that which is horrifying.'[32] In the end, and for my part, that's an attitude well worth having.

Works Cited

Brantley, Ben, 'Theater Review: A Most Dramatic Drama Critic,' *New York Times*, 18 March 1998, <http//theater.nytimes.com/mem/theater/treview.html>

Cummings, Scott T., 'Homo Fabulator: The Narrative Imperative in Conor McPherson's Plays,' in *Theatre Stuff: Critical Essays on Contemporary Irish Theatre*, ed. Eamonn Jordan (Dublin: Carysfort Press, 2000): 303-312.

Donaldson, Sarah, 'Film-makers on film: Conor McPherson: Conor McPherson talks to Sarah Donaldson about Martin Scorsese's *The King of Comedy* (1983),' *Telegraph*, 17 May 2003, <http://www.telegraph.co.uk/culture/film/3594723/film-makers-on-film-conor-mcpherson.html>

McPherson, Conor, *Four Plays* (London: Nick Hern Books, 1999)

Moroney, Mic, 'The Twisted Mirror: Landscapes, Mindscapes, Politics and Language on the Irish Stage,' *Druids, Dudes and Beauty Queens: The Changing Face of Irish Literature* ed. Dermot Bolger (Dublin: New Island, 2001): 250-275.

O'Neill, Patrick, 'The Comedy of Entropy: The Contexts of Black Humour,' *Canadian Review of Comparative Literature*, 10:2 (1983): 145-166.

Pierce, Nev, 'Conor McPherson: The Actors,' [n.d.] October 2003, <http://www.bbc.co.uk/films/2003/05/09/conor_mcpherson_the_actors_interview_shtml>

Taylor, Paul, 'Don't make a drama out of a critic: Theatre; *St. Nicholas*, The Bush Theatre, London,' *Independent*, 24 February 1997, <http://www.independent.co.uk/arts-entertainment/don't-make-a-drama-out-of-a-critic-1280430.html>

Wallace, Clare, 'Monologue Theatre, Solo Performance and Self as Spectacle, in *Monologues: Theatre, Performance, Subjectivity*, ed. Clare Wallace (Prague: Litteraria Pragensia, 2006): 1-16.

---

[1] Conor McPherson, *Four Plays* (London: Nick Hern Books, 1999): 188.

[2] *ibid.*, 188.

[3] *ibid.*, 190-191.

4 Paul Taylor, 'Don't make a drama out of a critic: Theatre; *St Nicholas*, The Bush Theatre, London,' *Independent*, 24 February 1997, <http://www.independent.co.uk/arts-entertainment/don't-make-a-drama-out-of-a-critic-1280430.html> [Accessed 25 June 2011]

5 Taylor, 'Don't make a drama out of a critic'

6 Ben Brantley, 'Theater Review: A Most Dramatic Drama Critic,' *New York Times*, 18 March 1998, <http//theater.nytimes.com/mem/theater/treview.html> [Accessed 25 June 2011]

7 Nev Pierce, 'Conor McPherson: The Actors,' [n.d.] October 2003, <http://www.bbc.co.uk/films/2003/05/09/conor_mcpherson_the_actors_interview_shtml> [Accessed 14 June 2011]

8 Sarah Donaldson, 'Film-makers on film: Conor McPherson: Conor McPherson talks to Sarah Donaldson about Martin Scorsese's The King of Comedy (1983),' *Telegraph*, 17 May 2003, <http://www.telegraph.co.uk/culture/film/3594723/film-makers-on-film-conor-mcpherson.html> [Accessed 14 June 2011]

9 Clare Wallace, 'Monologue Theatre, Solo Performance and Self as Spectacle,' *Monologues: Theatre, Performance, Subjectivity*, ed. Clare Wallace (Prague: Litteraria Pragensia, 2006): 6.

10 Patrick O Neill, 'The Comedy of Entropy: The Contexts of Black Humour,' *Canadian Review of Comparative Literature*, 10:2 (1983): 149.

11 O'Neill, 149.

12 O'Neill, 154.

13 McPherson, *Four Plays*, 141.

14 *ibid.*, 138.

15 *ibid.*, 140.

16 *ibid.*, 139.

17 *ibid.*, 147.

18 *ibid.*, 149.

19 *ibid.*, 156.

20 *ibid.*, 160.

21 *ibid.*, 160-1.

22 Scott T. Cummings, 'Homo Fabulator: The Narrative Imperative in Conor McPherson's Plays,' *Theatre Stuff: Critical Essays on Contemporary Irish Theatre*, ed. Eamonn Jordan (Dublin: Carysfort Press, 2000): 307.

23 McPherson, *Four Plays*, 154.

24 *ibid.*, 155.

25 *ibid.*, 164.

26 *ibid.*, 163.

27 *ibid.*, 173.

[28] *ibid.,* 177.

[29] Ben Brantley, 'Theater Review: A Most Dramatic Drama Critic.'

[30] Mic Moroney, 'The Twisted Mirror: Landscapes, Mindscapes, Politics and Language on the Irish Stage,' *Druids, Dudes and Beauty Queens: The Changing Face of Irish Literature* ed. Dermot Bolger (Dublin: New Island, 2001): 269.

[31] O'Neill, 'The Comedy of Entropy,'165.

[32] O'Neill, 165-166.

6 | 'shame shame shame': Masculinity, Intimacy and Narrative in Conor McPherson's *Shining City*

Kevin Wallace

'Shame shame shame.
Drown in your fucking shame.'[1]
Sarah Kane, *4.48 Psychosis*

Shining City is Conor McPherson's ninth play and was first performed at the Royal Court Theatre, London, in June 2004, before transferring to the Gate Theatre, Dublin, and later to the Biltmore Theater, New York, in May 2006. The play tells the story of two men and the feelings of guilt and shame that haunt them. Ian is a counsellor and former Catholic priest; he left the priesthood and has a child with Neasa. In scene two the audience discovers that Ian is about to end his relationship with Neasa, because he 'doesn't want … [it] anymore.'[2] The reasons he gives for this break-up are evasive and inarticulate, but in scene four it is revealed that Ian is a closet homosexual (when he brings a male prostitute back to his office). John, Ian's patient, is recently widowed and haunted, both by his wife's ghost and by the guilt he has over her death. John blames himself for her presence in the fatal car accident and believes that he had pushed her away emotionally after he committed a sexless act of infidelity.

The sexual element, and associated shame, in both men's stories is very important as it illustrates how both are haunted by their desires and their failed human relationships, and both men are haunted by their deviation from the social roles that they believe they should be playing as men. In short Ian and John are ashamed of their difference, and in response to this shame John uses his story and the space of the counsellor's office to absolve himself of this guilt and shame by story-telling. This article will tease out the interconnections between masculinity, narrative, and shame in *Shining City*.

Like McPherson's other plays *Shining City* retains a unity of place so that its five scenes are all staged in Ian's office in Dublin, a space that is (at the start of the play) serving both as his living quarters and his place of business. The sets for the first productions used an almost empty stage. In her work Ariel Watson argues that the staging in these productions was 'defined by its normalcy, a setting that, in its bland utility, serves as a blank slate for the projections and associations of the audience.'[3] Yet these projections and associations are all played with by the playwright. This empty space becomes haunted because John's story creates a ghost that, while for most of the play lives in the imagination of the characters and the audience, becomes real in the final moment of the play.

Shining City brings together a number of devices and themes common to the rest of McPherson's oeuvre. Like *Rum and Vodka* (1992), *Port Authority* (2001), and *The Weir* (1997), *Shining City* is structured around story-telling and is impelled by both the playwright's and the actors' ability to construct a tense and affective narrative. Like *The Weir* and *The Seafarer* (2006), this play takes the form of a supernatural thriller where, as in *The Seafarer*, Christianity and superstition loom large. The use of the Devil (in *The Seafarer*) and the concept of the haunting frame life in a contemporary Dublin setting within the structure of a fable. In line with this, both plays have a cautionary or parable element and introduce gothic or supernatural elements to upset the more comfortable story-telling atmosphere created on-stage. The play does nothing to confirm or deny John's story of his wife's ghost until the final scene when she appears on stage to haunt Ian. Up to that point the audience has a safe distance from John's distress, the haunting can be dismissed as a figment of his imagination, but the equilibrium created by the story's apparently happy ending is upset when Mari appears '*looking at IAN just as JOHN described her; she wears her red coat, which is filthy, her hair is wet. She looks beaten-up. She looks terrifying.*' There is no exorcism, as the ghost has merely left John in order to haunt Ian.

However, there is more to this play than just a straightforward ghost story. Mari's appearance at the end underlines the falseness of Ian's resolution to marry Neasa and move to Limerick. It underlines his inability to reflect on his own life and to be true to his own desires rather than the social pressures he feels. Indeed Ian's work as a counsellor reinforces his own past failures. His role in the play is less as a psychologist and more of a priest in a pseudo-confessional, listening too, and in the process figuratively absolving John of his guilt. Indeed the ghost's appearance at the end of the play can be seen both as a literal haunting and as a metaphorical one.

Intimacy and Shame

Shining City plays with levels of failure: failure of communication, failure in relationships, and the failure of self-knowledge or self-examination. Both of the male characters are inarticulate in the face of their dilemmas, John cannot express his fears or desires about Mari without punctuating almost every sentence with the refrain '... you know ....' This appeal to Ian's empathy is at once an emotional plea for help and simultaneously an attempt to circumvent communication. He is constantly looking for a method to avoid or shut-down intimacy. Ian is no less incommunicative when confronted by Neasa in scene two. Indeed the distance between them is written into the stage directions as well as the halting dialogue: '*Perhaps she sits on the clients' couch. Maybe at the beginning it looks like a therapy session.*' Their relationship is broken by a failure to communicate honestly. Ian cannot explain to Neasa why he wants to leave her or what form exactly their relationship, or his relationship with their child, will take after he does so. The majority of Ian's phrases in this scene are broken by hiatus, almost as if he is censoring himself or double-thinking.[4]

All in all, the men in *Shining City* are crippled by their inability to express themselves. At the end of the play when John's ghosts have been exorcized and it seems Ian has got his life and relationship with Neasa on track (moving to Limerick to set-up a practice there with Neasa as his *fiancé*),[5] neither John nor Ian can truly express the friendship that has grown between them over the course of multiple therapeutic sessions.

> **JOHN:** Do you know what I mean?
> **IAN:** I do. I know.

Pause

> **JOHN:** Look, I'll love you and leave you. Good luck with
> everything, alright?
> **IAN:** Well, you too and thanks, for the present. It really is so
> thoughtful ...
> **JOHN:** (*Interrupting*). Ah it's nothing, good luck.[6]

Every attempt at communication is hobbled by redundant, formulaic phrasing ('you know,' 'you too,' and 'good luck') and when Ian wants to thank John with a personal comment he is interrupted. It is as if now that John has told his story and been exorcized that he can return to 'normal.' Meaningful communication between the two men (other than John's story of the haunting) has become almost taboo.

Watson argues that counselling and therapy are 'often cited as the inadequate successor to support networks of family and friends. As with so many other quintessential contemporary encounters, it is a performance of intimacy before strangers.'[7] Both Ian and John are unable to be honest with their partners about their relationships, their sexual needs and desires. Both men have taken flight from their homes in order to physically hide from the reminders of this repression and shame. John is afraid to go home to the house he shared with Mari, because he believes her ghost is haunting it; Ian has left home because he seems to be afraid of his sexuality and cannot continue in his relationship with Neasa. Both men feel that they have failed their partners, and for this reason both have chosen to run away. Rather than confront the absence of real intimacy in their homes, John hides in a Bed & Breakfast, and Ian hides in his office. Indeed even in the final scene rather than both men being 'cured' by the play's events the audience is given a glimpse of two men who cannot talk to one another, and in the closing moment Ian is visited by Mari's ghost. Michael Billington argues that:

> beneath the everyday Dublin world of business meetings and
> fumbling adulteries lurks a powerful sense of loneliness; and
> McPherson implies the Irish obsession with the dead is not just
> a religious hangover but a consequence of failure to achieve
> proper contact in life.[8]

The men substitute connection for treatment; they replace intimacy with a commercial relationship. *Shining City* stands out from McPherson's work for its lack of pastoral or nostalgic references. This play shows Dublin in its commercialized state in the 2000s, a point signalled in the opening stage direction which places the office in an area that '*doesn't feel like a suburb, if anything it feels like a less commercial part of the city centre.*'⁹ Unlike *The Weir* or *The Seafarer*, the setting is not a friendly environment; it is almost a space built around an absence of prior knowledge or friendship, a neutral location, all of which is reflected in the first production's Spartan staging.

Another way of looking at this is to consider that Ian and John substitute real intimacy with the space of the pseudo-confessional. As Watson suggests the 'confessional mode of priesthood overlays [Ian's] impassive demeanour.'¹⁰ The Dublin locale is figured in *Shining City* in contradictory terms, dominated by Church spires but at the same time a commercial district: '*It has a Victorian feel, lots of redbrick terraced houses dominated by the Mater Hospital, Mountjoy Prison and the church spires of Phibsboro Church and the church at Berkeley Road.*'¹¹

Ian's work is literally and figuratively overshadowed by Catholicism and in his office, '*one or two church spires loom outside.*'¹² Indeed, the play's title is a biblical allusion to Matthew 5:13-16 in which Jesus tells the people: 'You are the salt of the earth. ... You are the light of the world. A city that is set on a hill cannot be hidden ... let your light shine before men, that they may see your good deeds';¹³ and one that directly echoes Ronald Reagan's usage of that biblical image in his inauguration speech as President of the United States: 'I've spoken of the shining city all my political life.' What this play attempts to do is contrast a profound Christian idea of community, openness and connection with a contemporary sense of isolation, alienation and ambivalence towards the Catholic Church in Ireland. In such a reading the term 'shining city' becomes a cynical note on life in Dublin in the 2000s, shining with commercial light but darkened by the loneliness and disconnection of its inhabitants.

Apart from the emotional distress that Ian has suffered in relation to his social role, he was also a priest who decided to leave in order to pursue a life outside the church and to have a sexual relationship with Neasa. He is a father and ends the play as Neasa's *fiancé*. However, Ian is sexually attracted to men and seems to be ashamed of, or in denial about this. As such I would contend that his character's greatest conflict is his repression of these desires.

Ian begins the play wanting to end his relationship with Neasa, in a conversation that reveals he is a failed Catholic priest and is struggling to build a career as a counsellor (Ian is not earning enough even to rent an apartment for them and has Neasa and their child living in the spare room of his brother's house).[14] On the one hand this plays into a stereotype of Irish male homosexuality and the Catholic Church, on the other it reveals a series of instances in which Ian has attempted to perform a normative, heterosexual masculine role and has failed to do so. Ian seems to be unable to reconcile his homosexuality with his role as a father, and the play's narrative arc reinforces this socially conservative view. This leaves him haunted at the end of the play, unable to express his needs and desires, and perhaps ashamed of them. Part of this may be the Catholic Church's ideology regarding homosexuality as 'sinful.' Another part may be the pressure Ian feels to bring up his child in a heterosexual nuclear family, which could be seen as another aspect of the Catholic ideology but I would contend is part of a socially conservative image of masculinity (as father and provider of a nuclear family). However, what is clear at the end of the play is that Ian is haunted by the repression of his sexuality and the feelings of guilt and shame due to that.

Mari's ghost haunts John because he cannot reconcile his act of infidelity with his marriage – he cannot come to terms with his sexual desire and blames that for his wife's death. In a similar way, Ian comes to be haunted by Mari after he has failed, again, to reconcile himself with his sexuality. John on the other hand has finally moved on and is starting a relationship with a younger woman. However, as Ian tells John: 'you felt maybe you couldn't move on without being ... punished somehow,'[15] which is precisely what happens to Ian at the end of the play.

Masculinity and Narrative

Ian feels, in his own words, that he needs to be punished, that he is paralyzed, cannot express his sexuality. He is trapped by normative concepts of masculinity, trapped by his own shame at being something different, at being Other. In Richard Dyer's book *White* he explores the cultural motifs and discourses of whiteness and white masculinity. One recurrent idea in his work is the notion of the masculine mind's power over its body. He notes that this is particularly to be seen in body building images where the bodies have become symbols of 'the spirit reigning over the flesh.'[16] Masculinity for Dyer is surrounded by concepts and discourses of control and self-fashioning, and I would suggest that narrative functions in this way for McPherson's male characters. Telling stories about themselves seems to give these men a sense of control, a power over their place in the world, their history and their identity.

Karen Fricker argues that McPherson's *Port Authority*, while seeming to critique notions of masculinity in crisis in Ireland, is in fact limited by how discourses 'of masculinity and femininity have been historically, and problematically, linked to national identity.'[17] She argues that: 'what is communicated most clearly in McPherson's work is a sense of gender roles being a trap of which the characters may become aware but from which they cannot escape.'[18] This is what is at stake in McPherson's representation of masculinity and femininity in *Shining City*, *Rum and Vodka*, and *The Seafarer*, as evidenced in the stories that the men tell. It is important to note that the women in these plays are often less than characters, they function only to reinforce the men's sense of failed masculinity and to exemplify their desires, or fears.

In *Shining City* Neasa nags Ian for not being able to provide for her and their baby, and tries to convince him to continue a nuclear family arrangement by perpetuating their relationship. All in all, she is present in order to reinforce norms for gender and society; norms of fatherhood, heterosexual relationships and career success, norms for masculinity. She becomes a ghost of what is expected of Ian. In this way her function is exactly the same as Mari's in underscoring her male partner's 'failure'. They both function as absences in the play, and even when they are present on-stage they are not active characters, they cannot effect change, other than stir feelings of horror, repulsion or shame on the part of the men.

Karen Fricker argues that 'Irish culture is still caught in binary and essentialist definitions of gender roles that discourse in many other cultures around the world has left behind.'[19] She goes further stating that McPherson's portrayal of gender roles is 'remarkable in [its] conservatism.'[20] I would agree and suggest that the play's use of an almost fairytale structure allows it to blur the boundary between realism and fantasy because of the audience's familiarity with that structure. Indeed the narrative arc of Ian's relationship to the supernatural is reminiscent to a ghost story told in McPherson's *The Weir*, wherein Maura Nealon, who liked to play practical jokes, claimed to hear the fairies until eventually she is actually haunted by them.[21] Furthermore in *Dissident Dramaturgies* (2010), Eamonn Jordan notes McPherson's use of apparently 'simplistic' narrative structuring devices. He contends that the narration of an apparently personal story (a single narrative that explains the person telling it), is a sleight-of-hand that plays with notions of authenticity. He points out that in *The Weir* the 'pastoral lives' of the male characters are 'relatively unsullied by the compromises of first-world capitalism,'[22] whereas *Shining City* reveals something very different, both Jack and Ian are indeed compromised by 'first-world' living. Also, whereas in *The Weir* ghost stories (even very personal ones, as told by that play's Jack) are articulate and free-flowing in the rural economy of *The Weir*, John's story is halting and awkward. In the urban, commercial, anonymous environment he cannot express himself.

While the differences between these representations of men are interesting, the similarities are equally revealing. As Fricker notes, McPherson's male characters are paralyzed, incapable of action, whose overriding emotion is of guilt. She argues that 'McPherson's men all share an inability to act effectively or forcefully on their true desires,'[23] and that McPherson's use of monologue in *Port Authority* is delivered as a kind of confession. In *Shining City* this confessional mode is all the more pronounced with the failed priest, Ian, listening to John explain how his sexual infidelity (or perhaps the guilt over it) resulted in the death of his wife. In McPherson's plays confession and guilt are intertwined with masculinity. Fricker notes that McPherson's depiction of masculinity is of men who 'have screwed up, and their compulsion to talk about their transgressions becomes the theatrical act ... and there is a sense in McPherson's earlier plays that the speaker gains a measure of redemption through the act of telling his story.'[24]

In *Shining City* John is healed, or absolved, by his encounter with Ian, but Ian, who does not express himself, and does not articulate his feelings of guilt (feelings that are obvious to the audience in scene two when he tries to leave Neasa and in his encounter with the prostitute Laurence in scene four) becomes haunted by the same ghost that haunted John. As Fricker has argued, Ian is aware of, and trapped by, his notions of masculinity. Fricker links McPherson's work to issues of 'masculinity in crisis' (the collapse of patriarchy and of the attendant 'traditional' gender roles for both men and women),[25] a state of uncertainty for men, due to the growth of equality for women and an end of discrimination against homosexuals.[26] However the *growth of equality* is not at all what is at issue in many of McPherson's plays.

The roles for women in *The Seafarer* and *Shining City* are very conservative or stereotypical (Mari and Neasa are both dependent on their partners, neither have a job, and both are depicted as victims of their partners' failings). Structurally speaking women do not have an active role in the play except as ghosts. The crisis of masculinity at work in his theatre is not due to the obsolescence of 'traditional' gender roles but rather the inability of these men to fulfil those same gender roles. Indeed as Fricker suggests, McPherson's theatre tells 'the stories of men trapped by their own self awareness, too weak to be good in their lives but smart enough to know how bad they are.'[27]

Ian in particular is haunted by his relationship with the Catholic Church and haunted by his relationship with Neasa. His is a conflict between ideology and desire, between religion and sexuality. This crisis is as a result of his self-awareness of the conflict but his inability to resolve it. John on the other hand has the ability to transform his failure into narrative giving him a sense of its resolution.

In Watson's reading of the play, therapy 'becomes a way of coming to terms with the most profound of interruptions, grief,'[28] I would point out, however, that this view overstates the counselling aspect of Ian's role and I would argue instead that what happens in Ian's office is more consistent with the confessional and more broadly the use of story in McPherson's plays. In a sense, and rather than it being therapy that helps John, it is the act of story-telling. In *On Stories* (2002), Richard Kearney argues that narrative is a profound attempt at reconciling the individual with their sense of loss. Storytelling becomes an effort to recover what is gone from one's life. Kearney argues that it is 'through the *quasi*-experience of loss, which fiction solicits, that we may even ... reconnect with truths from which we are protected in everyday existence.'[29]

In McPherson's work stories are powerful, in *The Seafarer* Mr Lockhart (the Devil in human form) is powerful because he knows the secret stories of the men in that play. These men, Sharky and Ivan, have both separately made deals with the Devil after their actions led to other people's deaths. The title character, Sharky, killed a vagrant in a pub brawl, and Ivan caused a fire in a hotel that led to the death of two families.[30] The facts of both men's guilt are kept secret, wrapped up in these stories that only the devil knows, and kept out of the men's thoughts by excessive drinking. During the card game that is the major plot twist of the drama, Lockhart reminds Ivan of his guilt while the rest of the men try to distract him, try to keep him away from that part of his memory. In *The Seafarer* narrative effectively holds power over life and death, because stories are the Devil's greatest trick. I would argue that something similar can be said about *Shining City*. Narrative is the sole form of meaningful communication in the play. The rest of the dialogue is redundant, halting or *cliché*. Richard Kearney argues that narrative is an attempt to create and share an identity and build a community.[31] However, as I've argued above, in McPherson's work narrative is a source of power; the story-teller is in control because they shape the world that the other characters inhabit.

In their stories these men create a role for themselves that is denied to them by the reality in which they live. Storytelling and the space of storytelling become a haven for 'traditional' discourses of masculinity and femininity. As Fricker contends, McPherson's theatre becomes a space where the deep unresolved anxieties 'about identity and gender in contemporary Ireland' are expressed.[32] While again I would broadly agree, it should be noted that it is also possible to read the representation of masculinity in *Shining City* as a criticism of Irish society where gender equality is growing, but where the culture and specifically the way stories are narrated has not moved on. Thus it could be argued that the men in McPherson's plays are broken because the modes of expression that they use reinforce their incapacity for intimacy and a conservative, or 'traditional', discourse on gender and identity in Irish society. Particularly in *Shining City* the play creates a space in which the repression of emotion, social alienation, and the absence of true dialogue are explicitly criticized.

Sameness and Difference

Eamonn Jordan argues that McPherson's plays are based upon a 'myth of self,'[33] a narrative of personal identity, constructed in traditional forms, that situates the individual in a context that replaces the collapsed (or collapsing) meta-narratives of Religion, Nationality, Capitalism and Citizenship. A grand narrative for the alienated individual that gives the illusion of depth, context, and purpose, where in fact there is none. That said, McPherson's use of these 'myths of self' allows his theatre to intersect subtly with issues from other ideologies and discourses: for example in *The Seafarer* these are fairytales and discourses about Irish drinking habits, in *St. Nicholas* (1997) these are folktales about Vampires and issues around date-rape; and in *Shining City* these are parables and issues of Catholicism, shame, and sexuality. The personal narrative allows McPherson's theatre to walk a tight-rope between fairytale and naturalism.

Nicholas Grene has argued, in relation to McPherson's *Port Authority*, that what is created are 'stories in shallow space: deeper structures, echoes and resonances are deliberately denied.[34] Jordan contradicts this position by contending that the depth is '"not so much denied" as significantly inaccessible to contemporary dramaturgy.'[35]

Conor McPherson does not write *agit-prop* nor does his work take the form of national drama, but this does not make his work apolitical. McPherson's theatre is smaller, telling personal stories, using very conventional forms and structures of dramaturgy. His is, theatrically speaking, a conservative aesthetic that relies on modes and spaces of story-telling (monologues, pub conversations, and therapy sessions or confessions), as well as highly codified and traditional narrative genres (ghost stories, fairytales, and fables). Within these structures, with their pre-existing roles for men and women, it is very difficult for a piece to do anything other than, as Karen Fricker argues, reinforce 'essentialist' and/or 'conservative' gender roles.[36] However I would contest the claim that all of these stereotypes are unchallenged. McPherson's plays offer the possibility of critique by depiction. The representations of both John and Ian in *Shining City* are not only un-idealized, but I would argue criticized. The burdens of shame that these men carry, and their attitudes to them, are at the heart of McPherson's cautionary tale; the end of the play underlines that neither shame nor desire can be repressed, or run-away from. It is necessary for Ian to come to terms with his own sexuality rather than to deny it. He must break-out of the socially conservative role or story that he has constructed for himself or he will remain haunted by repressing his desires.

Whether in *Shining City*, *The Seafarer*, *Port Authority*, *The Weir*, *Rum and Vodka*, or *St. Nicholas*, McPherson's male characters deal with difference and shame through story-telling. Their stories mythologize themselves in order to give them an illusory sense of control over their identity. This, at least temporarily, absolves them of their failures, relieves them of their sense of shame, and functions as a substitute for intimacy in an alienated society. These stories give these men a sense of context, a sense of sameness that through the process of story-telling erases that difference. Perhaps this is actually the most problematic aspect of McPherson's representation of masculinity, but it is also potentially the most innovative.

These men long to be the same, to be homogenous, but whether McPherson is reinforcing or criticizing that urge by depicting it is up for debate. As Jordan has noted, the current dramaturgy used in the production of McPherson's work prejudices it towards a reinforcement of what Fricker describes as 'essentialist' representations of gender,[37] and what Jordan calls pastoral representations of Ireland.[38] If, as Nicholas Grene argues, there is a lack of depth in the stories told by McPherson's male characters,[39] it is because productions may not be successfully communicating the instability and contradictions in these stories. Indeed, in *Shining City* all of the duplicity, fabrication, and sleight-of-hand inherent in the theatricality of story-telling is on show, and has as its palimpsest the model of the Catholic sacrament of confession. *Shining City* has the potential to be revolutionary in its portrayal of masculinity, by exposing this duplicity and sleight-of-hand. However, it simultaneously has the potential to be deeply conservative due to its portrayal (and marginalization) of femininity and homosexuality as a source of horror and shame. This tension cannot be resolved until characters are brought into dialogue, either aesthetically or textually. For as long as McPherson's men are circumventing intimacy with redundant phrases, or telling stories *at* one another, rather than talking with each other, their horror at the idea of difference will continue to haunt them.

Works Cited

Billington, Michael, '*Shining City*, Royal Court, London,' *The Guardian*, 10 June 2004 <http://www.guardian.co.uk/stage/2004/-jun/10/theatre>

Dyer, Richard, *White* (London: Routledge, 2004).

Fricker, Karen, 'Same Old Show: The Performance of Masculinity in Conor McPherson's *Port Authority* and Mark O'Rowe's *Made in China*,' *The Irish Review* 29 (Autumn, 2002): 84-94.

Grene, Nicholas, 'Stories in Shallow Space: *Port Authority*,' *Irish Review* 29 (2002): 70-83.

Jordan, Eamonn, *Dissident Dramaturgies: Contemporary Irish Theatre* (Dublin: Irish Academic Press, 2010).

Kane, Sarah, *4.48 Psychosis* in *The Complete Plays* (London: Methuen, 2001)

Kearney, Richard, *On Stories* (London: Routledge, 2002).

Conor McPherson, *This Lime Tree Bower: Three Plays* (London: Nick Hern Books, 1996).

---, *St. Nicholas & The Weir* (London: Nick Hern Books, 1997).

---, *Four Plays* (London: Nick Hern Books, 1999).

---, *The Weir* (London: Nick Hern Books, 2000).

---, *Plays: Two*, Vol. 2 (London: Nick Hern Books, 2004).

---, *Port Authority*, (London: Nick Hern Books, 2005)

---, *The Seafarer*, (London: Nick Hern Books, 2006).

---, *Shining City* (London: Nick Hern Books, 2010).

Watson, Ariel, 'Cries of Fire: Psychotherapy in Contemporary Drama,' *Modern Drama* 51.2 (Summer 2008): 188-210.

---

[1] Sarah Kane, *4.48 Psychosis* in *The Complete Plays* (London: Methuen, 2001): 209.

[2] Conor McPherson, *Shining City* (London: Nick Hern Books, 2010): 19

[3] Ariel Watson, 'Cries of Fire: Psychotherapy in Contemporary Drama,' *Modern Drama* 51.2 (Summer 2008): 203.

[4] McPherson, *Shining City*, 19-23.

[5] *ibid.*, 55-57.

[6] *ibid.*, 64.

[7] Watson, 205.

[8] Michael Billington, '*Shining City*, Royal Court, London,' *The Guardian*, 10 June 2004 <http://www.guardian.co.uk/stage/2004/jun/10/theatre>

[9] McPherson, *Shining City*, 5.

[10] Watson, 205.

[11] McPherson, *Shining City*, 5.

[12] *ibid.*, 5.

[13] Matthew 5:13-16.

[14] McPherson, *Shining City*, 18.

[15] *ibid.*, 63.

[16] Richard Dyer, *White* (London: Routledge, 2004): 155.

[17] Karen Fricker, 'Same Old Show: The Performance of Masculinity in Conor McPherson's *Port Authority* and Mark O'Rowe's *Made in China*,' *The Irish Review* 29 (Autumn, 2002): 84-85.

[18] Fricker, 89.

[19] *ibid.*, 85.

[20] *ibid.*, 86.

[21] Conor McPherson, *The Weir* (London: Nick Hern Books, 2000): 20-22.

[22] Eamonn Jordan, *Dissident Dramaturgies: Contemporary Irish Theatre* (Dublin: Irish Academic Press, 2010): 119.

[23] Fricker, 87.

[24] *ibid.*, 88-89.

[25] *ibid.*, 84-87.

[26] *ibid.*, 85-86.

[27] *ibid.*, 89.

[28] Watson, 206.

[29] Richard Kearney, *On Stories* (London: Routledge, 2002): 26.

[30] Conor McPherson, *The Seafarer*, (London: Nick Hern Books, 2007)

[31] Kearney, 4-5.

[32] Fricker, 94.

[33] Jordan, 235-236.

[34] Nicholas Grene, 'Stories in Shallow Space: Port Authority,' *Irish Review* 29 (2002): 82.

[35] Jordan, 235.

[36] Fricker, 85-86.

[37] *ibid.*, 85-86.

[38] Jordan, 116-133.

[39] Grene, 82.

7 | 'This is what I need you to do to make it right': Conor McPherson's *I Went Down*

Emilie Pine

Conor McPherson's first film project, *I Went Down* (1997), is all about screwing it up, then making it right. The film follows the fortunes of two hapless and somewhat accidental gangsters as they careen around the Irish countryside in a series of stolen cars desperately seeking a fugitive and a set of forged dollar printing-plates. McPherson's characters are familiar types: inarticulate Irish men trapped in narrow identities because of their inability to change. Yet what makes *I Went Down* a successful black comedy is the way McPherson's screenplay, and the finished film, modulate these character types with a genial humanity that is, in the end, redemptive.

McPherson was commissioned to write the script for *I Went Down* by director Paddy Breathnach and producer Robert Walpole, after they saw his play *The Good Thief* (1994). The resulting film showcases all three men's interest in exploring genre in an Irish context, as well as bearing the hallmark of McPherson's abiding interest in the complex relationships within all-male communities. *I Went Down* hybridizes the male-dominated genres of the buddy road movie and the gangster flick; instead of the wide horizons of California highways or the gritty streets of New York, the film is set against a background of small Irish country roads, the industrialized bogs of the midlands, and insalubrious north Dublin. While the film is thus inflected by American film culture, it is undeniably Irish, not only due to its physical landscape but also its social and cultural landscape in which men struggle to be heroes.

I Went Down is the story of Git Hynes (Peter McDonald) and Bunny Kelly (Brendan Gleeson). Git has been in prison for eight months, in the process losing his girlfriend Sabrina (Antoine Byrne) to his best friend Anto (David Wilmot). On his release, Git goes to see Anto and becomes embroiled in a fight between Anto and two tough guys. Git defends Anto but in the process blinds Johnner (Michael McElhatton), the henchman of local gangster Tom French (Tony Doyle). French demands Git repay the debt by taking on a job for him. The job involves joining forces with Bunny to track down French's missing associate Frank Grogan (Peter Caffrey). Predictably, the job does not go as planned and Bunny and Git end up kidnapping Grogan after French employs a hitman to kill him. Grogan tries to escape but he is brought eventually to French. It transpires that French and Grogan were former accomplices on a forgery job twenty years earlier that went fatally wrong. Though the two men appear to have reconciled themselves, French double-crosses Grogan and kills him, then shoots at Bunny. Git shoots French, saving Bunny, and the two of them bury the dead men and take the forged dollar printing-plates. The end of the film sees Git and Bunny leaving their disastrous personal lives behind them and travelling together to America.

The plot of the film follows the schema of a crime thriller, as the relatively innocent Git becomes increasingly involved in an underworld of guns and gangs. There are frequent double-crosses and missed opportunities. These plot machinations serve to make the two central male characters dependent on one another; though they were strangers at the beginning of the film, by the end a strong friendship has been established. Though each of the men has a significant female other, and both also have sexual encounters with women during the film, they exist within an almost exclusively male community of fellow gangsters and friends, and their relationship, which is unquestioningly a straight friendship, is defining in this context, in which masculine identity is connoted or granted by your connections with a significant male figure.

Git is defined by a series of relationships with men. He 'went down' for a crime that his father committed, in order to spare him the hardship of prison. As a result of his prison sentence, Sabrina switched her affections to Anto. While we might expect Git to fight for Sabrina, in fact it is Anto that he fights for, saving him from a punishment beating for unpaid gambling debts. In this scene, in the backroom of a bar, Git is revealed as a hard fighter, easily knocking down the first aggressor and then taking on Johnner who is wielding a broken bottle. Though Git is normally quiet, polite and calm, this early scene suggests he is capable of real violence and ruthless behaviour in defence of a man he has been close to 'since I was six years old.' The final edit of the film emphasizes this relationship and the sense of an all-male community even more than McPherson's screenplay does, as it cuts several scenes between Sabrina and Git, thus prioritizing the male-male bond over the male-female bond.

Once French has bullied Git into taking on the task of finding Grogan, he is paired with Bunny. Initially, Bunny is introduced as a hard-man, capable of hurting even his own grandfather. He is older than Git and seeks to dominate the younger man, insisting that they follow his plan, and literally being in the driving seat of the car. Yet this assumed authority is undercut from early on, when Bunny is shown imploring his wife Theresa to let him into his own house after she changed the locks, and when he bungles an attempt to get petrol. Unbeknownst to Git, they are driving in a stolen car, meaning that when they stop for petrol, Bunny has to force the petrol cap, alerting the pump attendant to them as thieves. In response, Bunny ties up the attendant and robs the till. Git's disgust at Bunny's actions is given weight by the film when the two men are forced to dump the stolen car in a field just as a heavy downpour begins. Bunny then compounds this failure by stealing a second car which backfires loudly as they drive off and then breaks down. All of these car-related incidents mean that the two men are late to meet their liaison and, as a result, have failed in their first task.

The initial expectation then that Bunny and Git will fall into a Father/Son binary is complicated from the outset by Git's obviously superior logic and ability to operate as an intelligent gangster, as against Bunny's 'act first, think later' approach. However, Bunny's aggressive approach is later endorsed in several situations that call for force, such as the kidnapping of Grogan and the confrontation with the hitman. In the hitman scene, Git's compassionate approach and tendency to reason rather than act are out of place and result in him almost losing his life, until Bunny unexpectedly appears and saves Git's life (which Git will later reciprocate). This moment signals a shift in their relationship as the two men begin to function as a team, illustrated when they simultaneously pull their guns on the hitman as he tries to escape. When Git says 'All everybody's been doing is lying to us. But we hang onto him. Do this on our terms. We can walk away ... I say let's stop fucking around and *use* this bastard,' he not only stops empathizing with Grogan, but realizes that as a team he and Bunny have bargaining power that they don't have as individuals.[1] The moral here is clear: both men must learn from each other in order to survive and, in the end, to succeed. Bunny and Git's alliance thus becomes an interdependent relationship, in which they successfully shift between dominant and subject, teacher and pupil, aggressor and protector.

Bunny is also defined by significant male relationships, as we learn in a pub scene where he confesses 'a terrible secret' to Git, which is that while in prison for armed robbery he had a homosexual relationship with his cell mate. Though Bunny is attempting to reconcile with his wife, Tom French is threatening to tell her the secret, thus forcing Bunny to work for him. Bunny is not able to define himself as he is subject both to his wife's refusal to talk to him and, most importantly, to French's blackmail. Bunny's limbo is not because his sexuality is in question, but because he is unable to set his own self-defining boundaries. Indeed, Bunny insists that he is 'not a queer' and hence the primary function of his confession to Git is not as a revelation about Bunny's character but as a representation of their (straight) male bonding. The film further shies away from the suggestion of Bunny as queer, and the potential of two men as romantic partners when, immediately following Bunny's confession, Git catches sight of two attractive women and Bunny leads him over to chat them up. Though the film concentrates on Git's night of passion with 'the Girl,' it is also keen to confirm Bunny's heterosexual status, showing him waking up the next morning next to a naked woman. Neither woman is named, indicating their roles as plot devices to illustrate the male characters' virility, which the screenplay doubly emphasizes with the Girl's exclamation over Git's physical endowment, and the two men's discussion of the women's 'big tits' (though both these bits of dialogue are cut from the film's final edit).

The homosocial bonds of the gangster world, and the adjunct-status of women, are further reinforced in the extended references to Tom French's wedding, at which Frank Grogan was best-man. During a flashback to the wedding day, French is shown not with his new wife, but with her uncle, the gangster Sonny Mulligan, whom it is revealed Grogan murdered.

French's wife never appears in the film, but she is often referred to because she has had an affair with Grogan. Like Sabrina, she appears to be a pawn between two men. This is hilariously undercut when it becomes apparent that Mrs French has absconded with the money she was meant to give to Grogan on behalf of French. As Bunny says, 'I'm fucking delighted. She did yous both,' in a rare instance of female self-determination. [2]

The focus on men over women is not exclusive to *I Went Down* but is typical of McPherson's work in general, as profoundly seen, for example, in his play *The Seafarer* (2006), which focuses exclusively on a group of male characters, using women as plot devices in the men's personal dramas. Though wives and girlfriends are referred to, they never appear onstage. When female characters do appear, as Valerie in *The Weir* (1997) or Mari in *Shining City* (2004), they are more than a match for the male characters. And in *Port Authority* (2001), though again it is an exclusively male play, the three characters see their relationships with women as ways of defining themselves. Yet time and again women are more absent than present in McPherson's drama and films. In his early monologue play *This Lime Tree Bower* (1995), later adapted and directed by McPherson as the film *Saltwater* (2000), the family at the centre of the plot consists of a father, two sons and one daughter. Both play and film are only really interested in the male characters: Carmel, the daughter, does not appear in the stage version, while in the film she is given very little screen time. In fact, her boyfriend Ray is a far more developed and important character (in the play he is one of the three monologists, the other two being Carmel's brothers Joe and Frank). Though McPherson's films have larger casts than his plays, this focus on the male characters remains constant, as in *The Eclipse* (2009) in which a man fears he is being haunted by his dead wife, yet the central conflict is gradually revealed as being between him and his father-in-law. While women can be empowered, as in the seduction of Git by a confident and sexually predatory young woman, in general McPherson is more interested in exploring meaningful relationships between his male characters as a way of illustrating the struggles for self-definition within the tribes of Irish masculinity.

In *I Went Down* there are several male archetypes: the powerful bully, the dutiful son, the loyal best friend, and the errant husband. Each of these is complicated, either because Git as the loyal son and best friend is continually let down by both his father and Anto, or because Bunny's extra-marital affair while serving six and a half years for armed robbery was an event which has done at least equal damage to his marriage as the sexual relationship with his cell-mate.

Masculinity as a performance is pointed up also by certain culturally specific archetypes, from the American-style gangster to the cowboy. Tom French aspires to be a big crime boss to the extent that he speaks with a slight American accent. Yet his small-time operations are far from the glamour and power associated with a crime lord. Likewise, though Bunny avidly reads a cowboy novel, his attempts at charisma are hapless at best, as illustrated by his appalling sartorial choice in cowboy-style footwear.

What McPherson is keen to show, then, is how Git and Bunny attempt to play certain social roles – the dutiful son and best-friend, the tough guy – but because these roles don't fit them, they fail at them or, worse, are failed by them. There is a certain degree of self-conscious awareness of these performances, as when Bunny bullies Git into following his plan by saying 'Stay here and be a boy then. The men are getting in the car.'[3] In forging a friendship, what each of these men learns is not merely a different perspective, but to see that they no longer fit the roles they earlier performed. Ironically, leaving these roles behind involves them being selfish and ignoring others' needs, but this is something the film inevitably champions as, in rejecting these roles, they achieve something closer to independence and self-actualization.

What these archetypes, and Git and Bunny's failure to fit into them, ultimately illustrate is the limited models of masculinity and, in particular, the limits of traditional conceptions of the male hero. In *I Went Down* traditional heroic roles tend to go wrong, so that when Git saves his best friend from a beating, he ends up in an even more morally compromised position. And, instead of instilling ethics in Git, Bunny-as-father-figure teaches him how to load a gun and use it to intimidate 'fucking culchies.'[4] There is thus no moment in which male heroism is not either impossible or corrupted by its context and consequences. The quandary for Git and Bunny is how to behave as a result, and what the film eventually endorses is not acting true to type but forging their own terms.

The ending of the film illustrates this shift in values as Git and Bunny, with Grogan and French dead, become the gangsters themselves. They decide not to stay in Dublin, however, travelling together, presumably to America, changing the narrative and continuing the buddy road trip. Their attitude to America is filtered through pop culture rather than experience, as shown by this exchange:

BUNNY: The States is brilliant.
GIT: You been there?
BUNNY: Yeah. Nah, I mean just on the telly and that ...'[5]

America is both a known quantity and an unknown space, representing the promise of a new life and wider horizons. Of course, the promise and the reality are frequently very different, and since the masculinities performed on 'the telly' are not any more liberating than those functioning in a Dublin gangster community, there is a strong likelihood that Git and Bunny will be just as hapless and unsuccessful in America as they have been in Dublin.

There is an echo here of an earlier play that also tackles the narrow limits of masculine identity, Brian Friel's *Philadelphia, Here I Come!* (1964). In Friel's play, the schoolmaster Boyle tells Gar on the eve of his emigration that America is 'a vast restless place that doesn't give a curse about the past' and again Boyle is gaining this information from the idea of America, rather than any direct experience of it.[6] Gar turns to emigration in part because of the limited economic opportunities available to him in Donegal, but mostly because of the paucity of emotional possibilities open to him as a young man. He dreams that in America he will be freed of both kinds of constraint and he aspires to the American freedom of expression and lifestyle that Bunny also does. In the thirty years since the first production of *Philadelphia* some things have not changed, in particular the idea of Ireland as antithetical to the full development of masculine identity. What has changed, however, is the ability of two men to bond as a way of overcoming the constraints they feel. In Friel's play, the central male relationship is within Gar himself, between his public persona and his private self. This relationship is created out of necessity because of the absence of emotional support in other areas of Gar's life, due to his mother's death, his father's emotional distance, and the inability of his male friends to be honest with one another. However, the honesty of the relationship between Git and Bunny and the challenge that each poses to the other, offers a different model, in which male collaboration can effect positive change, as Bunny says, 'the benefit of the doubt can even save your life. I'm learning that.'[7]

If Git represents the emotional evolution of Gar, then there are plenty of other ways in which McPherson's screenplay – and indeed his stage plays – embody the lack of development in the Irish male's ability to articulate himself. Bunny, in particular, struggles to speak meaningfully, constantly repeating himself, breaking off in the middle of sentences, and making abstract statements which he is then unable to explain. Git, in contrast, measures his words, speaks infrequently but is clear and logical. As argued above, Git learns the importance of action over words from Bunny, but we might say that Bunny learns the reverse too. In the final scene between Bunny and Sabrina, he is much more measured and calm and he says what he means. In this scene too, Bunny is much more stylishly dressed and well groomed, and both his language and his appearance indicate his advancement in the male hierarchy. In contrast, the most loquacious character in *I Went Down* is Grogan whose constant stream of words and stories results in him being gagged, shut in the boot of the car and, eventually, killed. Whereas the Irish theatrical model of Christy Mahon in J.M. Synge's *The Playboy of the Western World* (1907) is to envision the Irish male as coming into full existence through the performative power of narrative, in McPherson the less said, the better.

McPherson is not the only Irish playwright turned successful film-maker, as Martin McDonagh's *In Bruges* (2008) demonstrates. McDonagh's film has striking similarities to *I Went Down*, partly because it adheres to some of the same generic conventions of gangsters involved in a plot gone wrong. The central concept is that hit men Ray (Colin Farrell) and Ken (Brendan Gleeson) are hiding out in the Belgian medieval city of Bruges after Ray accidentally kills a child during a hit. The relationship between Ray and Ken is remarkably similar to that between Git and Bunny, not least because of the consistency of Brendan Gleeson's presence and levity. In this scenario, Ken takes a more obviously fatherly role to Ray, consoling him for his mistake and looking after his wellbeing. The echoes here are more than simply an older man caring for a younger protégé, however, as Ken also learns from Ray, analogously to Bunny and Git's relationship.

Unbeknownst to Ray, Ken is under orders from their gangster boss Harry (Ralph Fiennes) to kill Ray for his mistake in shooting the child. Ken fails to do this, however, choosing instead to give Ray a second chance. When Harry travels to Bruges to carry out the killing himself, Ken sacrifices his own life in order to save Ray. In an interview about the film, Gleeson says of his character that 'the interaction with Ray allows him to see that it is possible to think in another way, because he'd begun to believe that the only way was Harry's way ... Ray allows him to see a sense of hope, and in turn that liberates himself to begin to hope again ... and there is redemption of some nature.'[8] This change in Ken's character mirrors the effect Git has on Bunny in *I Went Down* and again illustrates the ways a supportive masculine community can effectively act as a counter to the oppressive male archetypes that these men, partly because of their criminal occupation, and partly because of their identity as Irish, struggle with.

In both *I Went Down* and *In Bruges*, the capacity to change is the most hopeful aspect of the plot, and this is something which is strikingly absent in each writer's plays. In McDonagh's Leenane and Aran trilogies, and McPherson's *The Seafarer, Port Authority* and *Dublin Carol*, the male characters all seem permanently isolated within their individual contexts and thus also within their limited identities. However, on film the men are able, despite still being very limited characters, to overcome a sense of resignation and oppression in order to be a little more self-realized. When Ken dies in order to save Ray, the soundtrack of *In Bruges* plays The Dubliner's song 'Raglan Road.' This romantic and tragic song becomes a ballad of Ken's life, suggesting the wife he lost but still loves (he still wears his wedding ring) and his willingness to 'lose his wings' at the end of the day. Neither McPherson nor McDonagh would make the case that their male characters are angels, but in their mutually supportive humanity these comic-tragic men achieve something close to heroic nonetheless.

The failed male hero is a central feature of Conor McPherson's work on both the stage and the screen. In this, McPherson follows a tradition within Irish culture of representing tortured and torturous male characters, a tradition so longstanding that the trope has become entirely normalized in plays and films from Samuel Beckett to Jim Sheridan.[9] In *I Went Down* McPherson generates humour from the constant cock-ups and madcap recoveries of Git and Bunny as performers out of their depth, yet he also generates emotional resonance with his creation of characters adeptly given life by Peter McDonald and Brendan Gleeson, who try, come what may, to make it right.

Works Cited

Breathnach, Paddy, *I Went Down* (Treasure Films, 1997).

Friel, Brian, *Philadelphia, Here I Come!* in *Plays: One* (London: Faber & Faber, 2001).

McDonagh, Martin, *In Bruges* (Blueprint Pictures, 2008).

McPherson, Conor, *I Went Down: The Shooting Script* (London: Nick Hern Books, 1997).

McPherson, Conor, *Saltwater* (Treasure Films, 2000).

---

[1] Conor McPherson, *I Went Down: The Shooting Script* (London: Nick Hern Books, 1997): 60.

[2] McPherson, *I Went Down*, 97.

[3] *ibid.*, 25.

[4] *ibid.*, 37.

[5] *ibid.*, 67.

[6] Brian Friel, *Philadelphia, Here I Come!* in *Plays: One* (London: Faber & Faber, 2001): 52.

[7] McPherson, *I Went Down*, 103.

[8] Brendan Gleeson, 'When in Bruges,' Bonus Material, *In Bruges* DVD (2008).

[9] Indeed, McPherson paid homage to this tradition by directing Beckett's *Endgame* for the 'Beckett on Film' series in 2001.

8 | The Buoyancy of Conor McPherson's *Saltwater**

Kevin Kerrane

When Conor McPherson adapted his play *This Lime Tree Bower* (1995) into the film *Saltwater* (2000), he did not simply rewrite the story: he reconceived it. In his debut as a film director, McPherson was able to reframe the play visually through panoramic shots, close-ups, and montage – and psychologically through subtle shifts in characterization and tone. He established a more upbeat mood (literally upbeat because of the music he chose to heighten key scenes), smoothed away some of the play's rough edges, and gave more latitude to its central figures. The result was a film that maintained the general outlines of the original story while highlighting its most redemptive or buoyant qualities.

Radical revision would have been necessary in any case, because the original play has no scenes. *This Lime Tree Bower* unfolds as a series of monologues addressed directly to the audience, without benefit of sets, sound effects, or even dialogue.[1] The monologues, ten in all, are delivered by three male characters: Joe, a schoolboy of seventeen; Frank, his older brother; and Ray, their sister's boyfriend, a university lecturer. These narrators report plenty of action – including a rape, an armed robbery, and an outrageous incident of projectile vomiting in a crowded academic amphitheatre – but all of that is left to the audience to imagine. Instead of seeing such incidents represented on stage, the audience hears them

---

* For many helpful editorial suggestions, and for specific insights into the use of music in *Saltwater*, I am very grateful to Maya Bouvier-Lyons and Kelli Shermeyer.

recounted by one or another storyteller. To turn this kind of drama into a film, McPherson needed to visualize the action through an objective lens rather than filtering it through a particular character's point of view. He had to substitute dialogue for monologue, and to flesh out characters who had been only mentioned in the stage version. Fortunately, the story already possessed cinematic momentum because *This Lime Tree Bower* does not question any narrator's reliability. Unlike Brian Friel's *Faith Healer*, in which three narrators offer conflicting accounts, McPherson's play presents monologues that dovetail, each confirming the others as it impels the action forward.[2] But when he envisioned his story as a movie, McPherson decided that it must avoid direct narration, even to clarify moments of ambiguity: 'I didn't want anything which would keep it bound to its theatrical beginnings. So there's no voiceovers or monologues in the film.'[3]

Monologue plays, especially those with multiple narrators, seem naturally resistant to cinematic adaptation, and to date no producer has been brave enough to underwrite film adaptations of Friel's *Faith Healer* or *Molly Sweeney*, Mark O'Rowe's *Howie the Rookie* or *Crestfall*, Abbie Spallen's *Pumpgirl*, or McPherson's own *Port Authority*. One exception is *Eden* (2008), directed by Declan Ricks, with a script by Eugene O'Brien based on his play of the same title. (When the drama premiered at the Abbey Theatre in 2001, it was directed by Conor McPherson.) Like *Saltwater*, the movie version of *Eden* shows that the very process of adapting a monologue play for the screen necessarily makes it less stark: instead of standing alone as islands of consciousness, the narrators are now conversing, and are interacting directly with other characters, within a setting that has been opened up visually.[4] The sparse aesthetic underlying the theatrical success of a monologue play could not sustain a commercial venture aimed at a wider audience, or a storytelling medium hospitable to what François Truffaut called 'privileged moments.' Gerald C. Wood identifies such moments in the 'small but resonant' scenes of *Saltwater* that slow the action in order to explore character or to reveal the subtleties of a relationship.[5]

In terms of structure rather than texture, *Saltwater* follows *This Lime Tree Bower* by maintaining three distinct plot lines, each leading toward a climactic incident. (a) At school the naïve Joe Beneventi befriends a new student, Damien, who is cool, defiant, and sexually experienced. When the two boys leave a disco with a drunk girl, presumably to help her home, Damien leads her into a graveyard, tells Joe to wait outside, and then rapes her. As soon as Joe glimpses the act, he flees in confusion. (b) At the Beneventi chip shop, Frank helps his widowed father, who owes over £2,000 to a piratical bookie named Simple Simon. On the day following the rape (which he knows nothing about), Frank dons a disguise and holds up Simple Simon's betting shop. As he runs away, his pockets stuffed with cash, he is about to be caught by Simon's nephew when Ray miraculously drives around a corner and rescues him. (c) At his university Ray is a philandering philosopher who gets drunk with students and sleeps with one of them, while still professing deep affection for Carmel, the boys' sister. His academic ambitions focus on proving his own brilliance by 'taking down' a distinguished visiting philosopher in a public forum – but he prepares for this intellectual confrontation by getting drunk and sleeping with his student, waking up groggy and dehydrated, and chugging a carton of orange juice. At the end of the visiting philosopher's lecture, Ray rises to ask a question – and then vomits violently over several rows of attendees.

In both the play and the film, these plot lines converge as all three characters, feeling the need to 'get away' after their intense experiences, use a bit of the stolen money (about £30,000 in all) to drive off together for a weekend at a fancy hotel in Cork. When they return, they find a squad car outside the chip shop. The characters (and the audience) assume that the police are there to arrest Frank for the robbery, but the crime in question is actually the rape, which Joe has been accused – by Damien – of committing. Once that false charge is sorted out, the story concludes with Frank's departure for America, which will make it possible for him to send money home without arousing suspicion. In this respect, both the play and the film offer a qualified happy ending, but each tries in a different way to foreground Joe as the character most affected by events.

On stage Joe delivers the opening and closing monologues, bookending the play as a story of his belated movement toward maturity. The only woman is Joe's life is Carmel, his older sister; his mother died a few years earlier – and late in the play Joe mentions her illness, and his inability to visit her in the hospital when she no longer knew who he was,[6] 'I was glad when she died ... I didn't talk about her and I didn't like thinking about her. It scared me.' Although Joe's sexual fantasies focus on females (particularly a schoolgirl he knows only as 'Deborah Something'), much of his early narration fixates on Damien as a handsome rebel, and this preoccupation leads Frank to tease him about being gay. Joe says that when he tried to tell his brother about the new boy at school, 'he called me a poofter and told me to go asleep.'[7] Even after witnessing Damien having sex with an unconscious girl in the graveyard, Joe seems painfully immature. The next day he is upset to find Damien absent from school: 'I needed to see him. I wanted him to tell me the girl had a great time and he saw her home. I didn't want to hear anything else.'[8] Only when Joe learns that Damien has accused *him* of the rape is he freed of his obsession. After being cleared by the police, Joe celebrates as part of a family 'shindig' and goes on to explain how well things worked out for everyone. Then he utters a haunting final line that suggests the burden of responsibility he now carries: 'I can still see the girl.'[9]

On screen Joe has few speeches, and most of them are short. As portrayed by Laurence Kinlan, Joe seems serious, soulful, and young for his age. (Kinlan was 16 at the time of filming.) *Saltwater* omits the exposition about Joe's mother provided in the play, relying instead on subjective images as if the audience had access to fragments of memory in Joe's mind.[10] The film's one concession to the interiority of the play is a visual motif that accompanies several scenes of Joe waking up: as he blinks himself out of sleep, he sees bright but blurry images of a woman wearing a red dress, turning in slow motion by the sea. This dreamscape changes during a sequence shortly after the rape: Joe sees the woman's face replaced for a split second by the face of the victim, and the woman's pirouette is juxtaposed to an image of Damien on top of the girl. Jerking awake, Joe reaches for a photo of his mother with him as a baby, and then holds it to his heart as he lies in bed with eyes wide open.

The play, using words instead of images, works toward a resolution of Joe's inner conflicts when, near the end, he recovers a happy memory of his mother: 'Dad was teaching me how to skim stones on the beach. And Mum was trying to do it and she couldn't. It was summer and she had a red dress on. Dad was slagging her and she was laughing at herself. And I felt safe and the safe feeling stayed'.[11] In the film this feeling of safety – and of family wholeness, just before Frank's departure for America – comes neither from narration nor subjective images, but from dialogue: a new scene between Joe and his father, George (Brian Cox). George tells his son a kind of bedtime story: that after the death of Joe's mother a tiny tooth was discovered lodged in one ear, apparently a tooth she had placed under her pillow as a child, which explained why she had been hard of hearing on one side. George claims to have saved the tooth as a memento, but now discovers that the paper it was wrapped in is empty: 'I think I'm after losing the fucking thing.' The scene ends in laughter as Joe asks: 'Dad, were you always a bit mad?' Rolling his eyes in a lunatic grimace, George replies: 'A bit. Always. You'll go mad too. Sleep tight.'

In his *Shooting Script* McPherson commented on the 'unusual effect' of this father-son connection:

> Without really resolving anything it just has an atmosphere of resolution. There's a gentle winding down and the tooth disappearing is an unexpected laugh where we mightn't have felt there was a place for one. I'm really pleased with this work but I'm not sure I can explain its effect. Perhaps it's like a tiny connection to the spirit world for Joe and George, a suggestion of their mortality which binds them to Maria finally even though they've been anxious to avoid talking about her before. I think this scene somehow provides a sense of perspective.[12]

Two other changes provide comparable perspectives. First, Joe's attraction to Damien remains unexplained in the film, and consequently seems less intense. No longer presented from Joe's private viewpoint, Damien (David O'Rourke) is seen from the start as more obviously crass, manipulative, and violent. In a scene of foreshadowing, he makes a crude sexual drawing in his notebook, and is berated by his teacher: 'Is that how you see women?' Later he and Joe sit outside the school, watching from a distance as the same teacher helps another man retrieve a sliotar caught in a tree branch. 'Do you want to see a good aim?' Damien asks Joe – and then throws a rock that hits his teacher in the head. As both men fall to the ground, the boys jump on their bikes and pedal away – and Joe's instinctive, desperate flight may also foreshadow his reaction to the rape.

A second change involves the victim of that crime. The play gives her a name, Sarah Comisky, but no real characterization. In the film she is renamed Tara, and in fact she is the same girl Joe has been admiring from afar: the one he calls 'Deborah Something' in the play. Early in *Saltwater* Tara (Caroline O'Boyle) is shown from Joe's perspective, standing and smoking a cigarette as he bicycles past her to school. At the disco, amid the din and the strobing lights, she approaches Joe to ask for help: 'Someone's after taking my bag.' As Joe heads toward the door to see if the bag might have been turned in, Tara takes his hand. A moment later both of them have been pushed outside, where they are confronted by older boys who taunt them. Joe answers meekly, but Tara stands her ground and punches Joe's antagonist in the nose. When she is knocked down, Joe tries to pull her attacker away, but both he and Tara are beaten and kicked until the bullies leave of their own accord.

In his *Shooting Script* McPherson described this sequence as one of his favourites because it 'feels very real to me,' thanks to the technical skill of Cian de Buitléar, who was using a hand-held camera.[13] In the next scene Joe and Tara sit checking their wounds. As Joe notices a cut near her mouth, Tara asks: 'Are you going to kiss it better?' – but he is too shy to respond to this cue. 'I want to go asleep', Tara says as she rests her head on his shoulder. Just as Joe puts his arm around her, Damien appears and the three young people begin their fateful walk.

McPherson's decision to make Tara a fuller character, and the object of Joe's romantic longing, intensifies the drama and provides the basis for a smart ending. In the film's final sequence Joe is cycling home from school when he sees Tara standing in her usual spot looking at him. He goes over to her and the two simply stand staring at each other for a long moment as a group of schoolgirls walks past. McPherson recalls that this scene was filmed by a new cameraman who did not understand its point. Told that the tableau of Joe and Tara would be the last shot in the movie, he asked: 'Should they not be smiling?' The cameraman was not alone in his puzzlement over this 'wide-open ending.' According to McPherson, 'The financiers were like "I don't get it. What's the hidden meaning?" And there was no hidden meaning. He's going to see this girl, take responsibility, which means everything.'[14] In searching for a cinematic analogy to the pensive line that gave closure to the play ('I can still see the girl'), the writer-director found a more hopeful emphasis. Joe is *literally* seeing the girl – and she is looking right back at him. Even if they never become a romantic couple, each of them is now thinking as an adult, and is regarding the other in that light.

In the play the only wrinkle in forward action is a shift in chronology. Act 1 ends with Frank's narration of the robbery he committed on a Monday morning, but before heading for Simple Simon's he noticed that Joe 'was in a funny mood.'[15] At the beginning of Act 2 the audience learns the reason for that mood when Joe tells of the rape he witnessed on Sunday night. *Saltwater* irons out this wrinkle by putting the two crimes in correct chronology, dramatizing the rape the night before the robbery, which encourages the audience to see Frank's action as less morally problematic.

In both versions the inspiration for the robbery comes from Frank's witnessing his father being humiliated by Simple Simon, who pretends that he is just being helpful even when he is most predatory – but in the film Simon is more provocative (he proposes becoming a partner in the chip shop), and Frank takes longer to work up his nerve.[16] The antagonism on screen is deepened by the performances of Peter McDonald as Frank and Brendan Gleeson as Simon. In *I Went Down*, the previous film scripted by McPherson, these two actors had been generic buddies (rookie and veteran, clam and chatterbox) in a story about inept criminality. In *Saltwater* they play off against each other with such ease that the robbery is presented as more of a caper than a crime.

The film lays the groundwork for this comic tone in Frank's preparations. When he tries to secure a gun, Frank does not approach a hard man, as in the play, but a 'headbanger' named John (Michael McElhatton), who is celebrating his release from jail by drinking a pint of cider at every pub in town. And instead of giving Frank a real sawed-off shotgun, John helps him fashion a fake one. A subsequent scene shows Frank in his bedroom, wearing a bobble hat with eyeholes cut out, wielding the 'gun' as he practices his entrance: 'Everybody on the fucking floor. Nobody fucking move. I'll blow your fucking heads off.' His sister knocks on the door to see what's happening, and Frank claims to have been listening to the radio – then gestures helplessly when Carmel points out that there is no radio in the room. When he finally robs Simple Simon's, only a few minutes in screen time after the episode of Tara's rape, the effect is comic relief.

Saltwater complicates Frank's storyline through the creation of a new character, Sergeant Duggan, a female detective played by Gina Moxley. When she appears early in *Saltwater* as a customer in the chipper, she tells Frank that he should consider joining the Guards – but behind that invitation is another: that he might want to accompany her some evening to 'that new place out in Lusk.' In this scene Frank becomes as flustered as in his later conversation with Carmel about the nonexistent radio, and Duggan interrupts his lame excuses: 'Don't have a heart attack. And forget I asked.'

Gerald C. Wood describes Duggan as 'a sensitive and bright policewoman' who 'intuits both the innocence of Joe and the guilt of

Frank.'[17] In her conversations with Frank after the robbery, she obviously knows that he's hiding something, and he knows that she knows. In their last encounter, at the police station after Joe has been cleared, Duggan starts to question Frank again but then gives up. After a long close-up look, she sighs 'Oh Frank' – and the source of her utter disappointment appears to be romantic as well as ethical.

Unlike the other two main characters, Frank evinces no particular interest in female companionship, either in the play or the film. At one point in *Saltwater*, he sits looking at a topless photo in *News of the World* (Duggan teases him about it), but with real women he seems just as shy as Joe. A brief scene at the posh hotel in Cork shows Frank sitting alone in a Jacuzzi: when a beautiful bikini-clad girl gets in, he says an awkward hello, starts whistling, and looks in every direction but hers.

By contrast, Ray seems insatiable. Conor Mullen, who played Ray in the original production of *This Lime Tree Bower*, reprises this role on screen, and his character still oscillates between Carmel, the woman he claims to care for, and a 21-year-old student he treats as a sexual diversion. In the play the student was given no name: Ray claimed not to remember it, and referred to her as 'a stupid fat bitch.'[18] As played by Eva Birthistle in the film, she is certainly attractive and now has a name, Deborah McCeever, but she remains fairly stereotypical – as does Carmel (Valerie Spelman).

Both women may exist on screen mainly to illustrate Ray's confusion or indecision: he is a philosopher who can't make up his mind. In one pub scene he apologizes to Carmel for not thinking about her enough. 'Are you trying to confess something to me?' she asks, and Ray responds: 'I'm not that sorry.' In a later pub scene he explains to Deborah that they must stop seeing each other, and then drunkenly asks her for a hug – which leads to another night in her bed. The difference is that Carmel seems to see through Ray, perhaps in the way that Sergeant Duggan sees through Frank.

Ray's most memorable scene, of course, is his vomiting in a crowded UCD auditorium. When narrated on stage, this episode was disgusting but abstract; seen on screen, it is as startling as the moment in *Alien* when the creature bursts out of John Hurt's body. In either case, it seems grotesquely funny, as if the vomiting expressed Ray's disgust at academic pretensions – including his own, as he rises to ask a question that is supposed to show his intellectual superiority.

After the deluge, Ray calmly asks an ironic question ('I would like to ask Professor Konigsberg if, during his long and eminent career, he has ever seen anything quite like that'), and then departs as the befuddled moderator asks the bespattered audience: 'Are there any further questions?' The camera next shows Ray outside the Beneventi home contemplatively smoking a cigarette, looking as though he is taking stock of priorities before heading off for the weekend with Frank and Joe.

The best example of the movie's softer focus comes in this implication that Ray is ready and able to change. In the play Joe was the only character journeying to maturity, and the earnest teen was a worthy foil to the errant ethicist. The film hints that the two characters are moving along similar arcs – and that Ray might become a mentor to Joe or, conversely, that he might be inspired by Joe's sincerity. At the beginning of the weekend in Cork, as Joe is still trying to sort out the significance of what he witnessed in the graveyard, he sits in a sauna with Ray and asks a general question about how to treat women. Ray, seen in a prolonged close-up, becomes meditative:

> I think the thing about things like that is . . . just don't be a bollocks. Isn't it? But sometimes, you know, you just can't fucking see past yourself, and you just go on and be a bollocks anyway and you know that you are. And then that might get you annoyed and you keep going. . . . But I'll tell you this much: I wish I'd respected women more in my life. Because nothing's worth ending up on your own for, Joe. Nothing.[19]

The attempt to deepen Ray's character continues in the next scene, set in the hotel disco. What had been a brief reference in the play becomes another 'privileged moment' in the film: Ray talks a pretty girl (Nuala O'Neill) into dancing with Joe, and the two teens proceed to share a moment of affection set to music: 'Pieholden Suite' by the American alternative-rock band Wilco. The audience hears romantic lyrics as Joe and the girl slow-dance, kiss, and then hug – and Joe's eyes remain closed as though he were being healed by the simplicity of a woman's touch.[20] As lyrics give way to melody (amplified through an electronic keyboard and stronger percussion), the camera then dwells on Ray and Frank watching wistfully, as if envious of a youthful innocence they no longer possess. Before the film's final cut, this sequence had led directly to a scene of Ray phoning Carmel in the middle of the night and asking her to live with him: 'I want you to stay with me for ages ... and I won't let you down.'

McPherson says in his post-production notes that several scenes in this part of the film had to be cut simply to maintain pace, but Ray's telephone call may have looked particularly expendable because his sudden conversion appears so unlikely.[21] This wolf seems to be most himself in his last scene, when Frank is about to leave for the airport. As Ray stands next to Carmel, Frank shakes his hand affectionately. 'Keep your nose clean', he says. And Ray replies, with a half-shrug: 'You know me.'

To the extent that *Saltwater* is a family drama, however, Ray remains an integral character, even if the film shows him spending more time with Frank and Joe than with Carmel. In the opening scene Ray is included in the literal family circle of a penny-ante poker game at the Beneventi home. This sequence was cut and reshaped many times in the editing process, but McPherson says that it always remained essential: 'as we struggled with the first half hour of the film and dropped more and more scenes, we increasingly felt the card game gave a coherence to the characters – they had a relationship.'[22] That relationship is defined quickly when Ray goes to the kitchen for a beer, and the four Beneventis begin trading cards and stacking the hands. Returning to find that he has three jacks, Ray talks boldly, and then is astonished by George's three queens and Frank's three kings. Seeing the others laughing, Ray says: 'What's the point of playing cards, you know, if you're going to cheat? It's just ... stupid.' As Joe deals a new hand, George comments casually: 'We're Italian, Ray.'

George's Italian heritage is not really a major element of his portrayal in either the play or the movie.[23] In *This Lime Tree Bower* Frank characterizes his father more pointedly as a steady drinker who, after losing his wife, also lost the will to contend with the likes of Simple Simon. But when McPherson filled out George's role for the film, he once again accentuated the positive, taking advantage of Brian Cox's gift for warm humour (in the 'tooth scene', for example) and cutting two sequences that show George drinking whiskey: 'We felt that heavy drinking might negate the character. It might feel like he's in trouble *because* he drinks rather than the other way round. We decided to make him a more together person so as to make Simon's takeover appear more aggressive.'[24]

Business at George's chip shop is supposed to be slow because it's off-season in this seaside area, and the film's panoramic shots often convey a sense of emptiness in showing individuals against the backdrop of the ocean and a vacant beach. McPherson told Gerald C. Wood that the seascape provided the logic for the title of *Saltwater*, especially in relation to Joe's characterization at the end of the film: 'It's all played out against an environment we can't live in, which is the sea. So it's also about reaching a limit. There is nowhere else to go; he has to come back and live or die. It's about tears and taking responsibility.'[25]

McPherson's film opens up the story aurally as well as visually. In addition to diegetic music, such as the romantic song by Wilco in the hotel disco, *Saltwater* relies on original background music by The Plague Monkeys, a Dublin band noted for what some fans have called 'ethereal pop.'[26] McPherson says that he was attracted by the 'gentle percussive feeling' of their songs, by the beautiful voice of lead singer Carol Keogh, and by 'bells and sounds you really couldn't identify which were samples from everyday ambience.'[27] In some scenes this music may be most important as a substitute for narration, particularly by Joe.

On screen Joe obviously has less to say than he did on stage, and less to do than the other principal characters in the film. (His total time on camera consists less of action than reaction.) Laurence Kinlan's performance is wonderfully subtle, but the dreamy harmonies of The Plague Monkeys also suggest the yearnings that Joe does not articulate. In general, non-diegetic music in *Saltwater* enriches moods. Sometimes it simply lightens them: when Ray, Frank, and Joe are on the road to Cork, for example, the background instrumentals convey a jauntiness that contrasts with the characters' sombre expressions. Such music is particularly helpful in linking montages, starting with the opening of the film. After the poker game, 'Unsung' by The Plague Monkeys plays on the soundtrack while the credits are projected against shots of the empty beach, of the exterior of Beneventis' shop, and then of each family member inside fast asleep. (Ray, next to Carmel, lies wide awake and thoughtful.) From Joe's dreaming perspective, just before he wakes, the audience sees blurry images of the woman on the beach – later understood to be a memory of his mother – and hears the refrain sung by Carol Keogh: 'And it always seems to me, I'm winning.' At the very end of the movie, this same song plays underneath the tableau of Joe and Tara looking deeply at each other. As the lyrics fade away, the sound is mellow but not sad, and its effect is to bring the story full circle while evoking a sense of new possibility.

Saltwater was made for a mere £2 million, with no significant budget for advertising. When it premiered at the 2000 Berlin Film Festival, it won a Best Film award given by the International Confederation of Art House Cinemas, but it did not cross over from art houses to multiplexes in Europe – and it was never released theatrically in the United States. *I Went Down*, the 1997 film scripted by McPherson and directed by Paddy Breathnach, had succeeded partly because it was easier to categorize (road movie, buddy movie, crime comedy), whereas *Saltwater* seemed to fall between genres. But according to Robert Walpole, a producer for both films, *Saltwater* was meant to be 'warmer, more human, more embedded in a set of real characters to whom real stuff is happening.'[28] Looking back on his first directorial effort, McPherson expressed most satisfaction with its tonal complexity: 'Where executives for a studio may try to shore up what they see as holes in the plot, we were able to actively try to create holes and make some space and hopefully allow the audience to make up their own minds as to aspects of the story.'[29]

The play had compartmentalized the characters, who conveyed the action in the past tense of narrative. The film moves them through a series of present moments – many of them 'privileged' either as pauses for solitary thought or as scenes of subtle interaction. In this light, Ray appears less swaggering, Frank less impulsive, and Joe less credulous. Ultimately, what makes *Saltwater* most buoyant is not that it tries to put a happy face on dark material, but that it gives its characters room to develop and finds fresh cinematic approaches to the portrayal of their relationships.

Works Cited

McPherson, Conor, *This Lime Tree Bower: Three Plays* (London: Nick Hern Books, 1996).
---, *Saltwater: The Shooting Script* (London: Nick Hern Books, 2001)
Wood, Gerald C., *Conor McPherson: Imagining Mischief* (Dublin: Liffey Press, 2003).

----

[1] The one exception comes in the moment after Ray narrates an episode about vomiting. When Frank says 'I never heard that', Ray responds: 'I've been saving it.' The script notes that all three characters 'remain on stage throughout, and are certainly aware of each other.' See Conor McPherson, *This Lime Tree Bower: Three Plays* (London: Nick Hern Books, 1996): 80 and 118.

[2] In this regard, the play offers a neat analogy to the books that Frank keeps by his bed-thrillers and westerns noteworthy for their rapid pace: 'These books', Joe says (97), 'knew how to be read.'

[3] Quoted by Gerald C. Wood, *Conor McPherson: Imagining Mischief* (Dublin: Liffey Press, 2003): 142.

[4] In the play version of *Eden*, Billy and Breda (the only two characters) speak to the audience but never to each other. In the film version their lack of communication is dramatized by showing conversations in which they avoid the issues bothering them most – until the end, when both are crying after a night of humiliation and infidelity. Whereas the play ends with Billy lying in a stupor on the floor of his daughters' room, the film ends with Billy and Breda tearfully embracing, apparently with the intention of trying to salvage their marriage.

[5] Wood, *Conor McPherson: Imagining Mischief*: 72.

[6] McPherson, *This Lime Tree Bower*, 105.

[7] *ibid.*, 81.

[8] *ibid.*, 101.

[9] *ibid.*, 124.

[10] McPherson filmed, and later eliminated, a scene in which Frank argues with Joe about visiting their mother's grave. Here Joe, 'almost in tears', repeats a line from the play: that when his mother was in the hospital, 'she didn't even know who I was.' *Saltwater: The Shooting Script* (London: Nick Hern Books, 2001): 112-113.

[11] McPherson, This Lime Tree Bower, 123.

[12] McPherson, *Saltwater: The Shooting Script*, 139-140.

[13] *ibid.*, 132.

[14] Quoted by Gerald C. Wood: 142.

[15] McPherson, *This Lime Tree Bower,* 102.

[16] In the play Frank quickly formulates his 'mad plan' and tells Joe about it beforehand. In the film several montage segments show Frank alone looking out to sea, or looking at himself in the bathroom mirror, looking into the darkness instead of sleeping – as if thinking through his scheme, or screwing up his courage.

[17] *Conor McPherson: Imagining Mischief*: 71

[18] McPherson, *This Lime Tree Bower,* 90.

[19] Ray's meditation echoes a speech near the end of McPherson's *The Weir*, when Jack concludes his story of regret for a love he threw away. After an inspiring encounter with a barman in Dublin, Jack says, 'I was properly ashamed of myself. There was a humility I've tried to find since. But goodness wears off. And it just gets easier to be a contrary bollocks.' See Conor McPherson, *The Weir* (London: Nick Hern Books, 1998): 47.

[20] Jeff Tweedy wrote the music for the suite. Jay Bennett wrote the lyrics, which are most audible in the third verse, matching the actions

of Joe and the girl: 'In the beginning/ We closed our eyes/ Whenever we kissed/ We were surprised/ To find so much inside.' At the end of the film, the lively instrumental conclusion of the suite plays as the credits begin to roll.

[21] McPherson, *Saltwater: The Shooting Script,* 138.

[22] *ibid.,* 124.

[23] In *This Lime Tree Bower* Joe mentions his father's nationality in reference to conflicting local legends about a sunken ship: 'Dad said he wouldn't get involved in the dispute because he was from Italy and it was none of his business. He said that Irish people would rather make something up and if that's what they liked to do then he had no problem with it' (96). In the film Brian Cox plays Joe's father with an Irish accent and occasionally uses Gaelic words such as *leaba* (bed). At school Joe's teacher refers to him sarcastically as 'the Mafia man', and Frank calls him 'Joe-seppi' when he says good-bye near the end of the film.

[24] McPherson, *Saltwater: The Shooting Script,* 126.

[25] Quoted by Gerald C. Wood: 142-43.

[26] McPherson, *Saltwater: The Shooting Script,* 129.

[27] The Plague Monkeys broke up in 2000. In 2002 two band members, Carol Keogh (vocals) and Donal O'Mahony (guitar, mandolin, keyboards), reunited as part of The Tycho Brahe, which later became Tychonaut.

[28] Saltwater Press Release, quoted by Gerald C. Wood: 68-69.

[29] McPherson, Saltwater: *The Shooting Script,* 123.

9 | Issues of Narrative, Storytelling and Performance in Conor McPherson's *The Actors*

Carmen Szabo

Following a theatrical tradition based almost exclusively on the dramatic power of text and narrative, Conor McPherson has established himself as arguably the pre-eminent narrative dramatist of his generation. Starting from his first notable play, *This Lime Tree Bower*, and continuing with worldwide successes like *The Weir* or *Port Authority*, McPherson has produced a series of extraordinarily haunting tales about life in general and Irish life in particular. His strong belief in telling life stories through theatre was apparent from as early as *This Lime Tree Bower* which was accompanied by a mini-manifesto, a quote from the Romantic poet Samuel Taylor Coleridge's poem *This Lime Tree Bower My Prison*: 'No sound is dissonant which tells of life.'[1] And McPherson's narrative voices and dissonant sounds tend to capture just that, the essence of life, not only in its everyday practice but also in its philosophy.

A postgraduate in ethics at University College Dublin, he has always been inspired by his studies in moral philosophy and, as he notes in an interview with Tim Adams for *The Observer*, philosophy made him realize 'that I didn't know much about anything, and that none of us do.'[2] Thus, his plays became tools to probe, to explore the realities of life, of existence and in some sense the fragility of communication between human beings. McPherson's characters do a lot of soul searching but they also project their scrutiny outwards and attempt to connect with others in order to avoid a constant feeling of isolation that is present in his plays. McPherson believes that his childhood experience of visiting his grandfather in County Leitrim has had a determining influence on the way he writes. The remoteness of his grandfather's house made him think about loneliness and the stories created to alleviate it: 'My grandfather was there on his own. I was fairly quiet when I was a teenager, and I liked the way you could go down there and sit, you know, and not talk, really, and look at the fire with him. And then he might say something. Or he might not. Sometimes he might tell me a story. But it would always come out of this sense of absolute isolation and silence, and I guess just the atmosphere of that stayed with me, struck me as something important, I suppose.'[3] The silences he experienced between the stories told by his grandfather also marked the ways in which he uses silences in his plays and films. McPherson regards the issue of pace and the right use of silences as determining in the full understanding and theatrical realization of his plays.

In good Irish tradition, he also acknowledges the literary and theatrical influence of Samuel Beckett, which is at the forefront of McPherson's article for *The Guardian* on the importance of Beckett's 'hymns of nothingness' for the development of world theatre.[4] He was asked by Michael Colgan to direct the film version of Beckett's *Endgame* for the epic venture to film all of Beckett's work. The experience brought him not only extraordinary satisfaction as a director but it also made him give a much closer consideration to Beckett's plays and the methodology of his theatre making. McPherson's relationship with Beckett is as strained as that of many contemporary Irish playwrights. The Beckett legacy plays an important role in determining the position a playwright has in the mainstream of Irish theatre and that makes contemporary playwrights wary. McPherson, together with London based Martin McDonagh, has been acclaimed as a natural heir to the great Irish theatrical tradition and although he does not mind the labelling, he hopes that his plays speak for themselves rather than representing a continuation of a long tradition: 'If people want to say there's a renaissance in this or that, that's great I guess, because it helps theatres to market plays in London. But as a writer, you're not aware of it, and without it, anyway, I'd like to think my plays would find an audience ...'[5]

Directing Beckett's *Endgame* was not the only film offer that came McPherson's way. The huge success of *The Weir* prompted an inevitable series of offers from Hollywood for original screenplays and directing opportunities. Steven Spielberg's film company

Dreamworks got in touch with the offer to write a script for a film idea put forward by Neil Jordan. It would have been a comedy set in Dublin, about 'a pair of two bad actors who get themselves into trouble and have to use their crap skills to get out of it. It's kind of like an old Ealing comedy ...'[6] For about a year, McPherson was in high demand in Hollywood and it seemed as if the film was moving in the right direction. But eventually the politics of Hollywood got in the way and the playwright refused to continue the collaboration. The project collapsed due to a disagreement over casting. If McPherson wanted to cast European, and more specifically Irish actors given the setting of the film, the American studios wanted American actors who would put on Irish accents. McPherson declined to go ahead with the project and eventually got his script back from the American studio. Neil Jordan decided to refinance the project which became McPherson's first full-length feature film as a director after finishing *Endgame*.

Based on an early Neil Jordan story and then adapted by McPherson, *The Actors* (2003) is a light comedy that plays on issues of storytelling and pretence. As with most of his work, the film highlights the various possibilities of plot and narrative and the fundamental fascination that McPherson has with telling and incidentally making up stories. It is useful at this point to observe some of the theoretical frameworks that narrative has to offer any reader or spectator and which can aid any analysis of McPherson's films. Although narrative structures are at the basis of human communication and thus are relatively familiar, the theoretical underpinnings of any narrative theory provide a strong analytical support for any analysis of narrative in fiction, drama and film. According to Gerard Genette, in his seminal work *Narrative Discourse: An Essay in Method*, narrative refers to how a text is written and communicated. Developing on Genette's use of the term 'text' one might infer that 'text' is an extremely multifaceted notion and it can cover much more than the written text which usually constitutes the main analytical focus of narrative theorists. The frameworks that support communication enable a large variety of structures to become texts, regardless of the nature of their production. At its very basic, a text is a coherent set of symbols that transmits a certain message. Starting with Structuralist criticism however, any 'object' that can be read, regardless of the fact that it is a film, a series of photographs, a street sign or the architectural arrangement of a city block becomes a 'text' and it can be read and interpreted accordingly. The issue of interpretation is vital in any discussion of narrative and it implies a very strong connection between the text, its producer and the receiver, the reader, the viewer, the spectator.

In order to encapsulate both production and interpretation in one analytical construct, Peter Brooks uses the term 'plot' as 'the dynamic shaping force of the narrative discourse.'[7] For Brooks, 'plot' refers not only to how a text is constructed but also points towards the relationship between 'textual form and content and the reader's vital role in the understanding of narrative.'[8] In the case of the filmic text, the relationship between text and 'reader' becomes even more complex given the multifaceted form of the text. Although the central concepts of narrative: time, space and causality still appear within the filmic text, the most important aspect of the filmic experience for the viewer becomes the visual/visualizing force of the cinematic text. Narrative sequences determine the way we communicate in everyday life and these sequences come to life, become visible through filmic devices. Various theories of narrative in fiction and film have been discussed at length by theorists, considering the similarities and differences between the ways in which the narrative discourse is represented in fiction and film and interpreted by readers/spectators. The ways in which the central concepts of narrative – time, space and causality – are perceived by the film spectators differ substantially from those experienced by readers of fictional texts. The visual power of film creates a portal into a world which seems real to the point of confusion. The cinematic narrative constructs a copy of the real world, a simulacrum that at times seems more real than the original. The spectators are free to peep into this world without having to participate, without having real contact with the actors, without any element of chance that could alter the course of the narrative.

Postmodern theorist Fredric Jameson considered that film is 'essentially pornographic'[9] (original emphasis) in nature as the viewer's experience is based on watching but not being able to interact with or participate in the action. Thus, the visuality of film renders it pleasurable but safe. The freedom of interpretation, a determining factor in reception theories regarding written text, also experiences a fundamental change when connected to film. This occurs because of the crucial difference between verbal language and filmic language. If verbal language, although extremely multifaceted, represents a fixed system, filmic language is rather fluid and based on very different communication codes put forward not only by the director but also by the editor, cameraman, director of photography, actors, etc. Thus, the film narrative does not allow as much interpretive freedom as the fictional text, because the visual component fixes the story to be presented in much more solid frames. The viewer is still free to use his/her imagination but the limits of that imagination are much better determined than in the case of literary fiction. This problematic relationship between film and narrative is mainly due to the fact that viewers continuously reconstruct the film's narrative rather than 'constructing' it.

According to Jakob Lothe, 'much of the challenge to the film author lies in presenting the various elements that together form the film narrator in such a way that the viewer experiences them as necessary and thematically productive.'[10] This visual fixity of film is challenged by Conor McPherson in *The Actors*, as the script plays around with issues and the rules of storytelling and character construction. The film, as stated earlier, while based on an earlier story by Neil Jordan, is reworked by McPherson. In the film he allows the main actors, Michael Caine and Dylan Moran, to explore not only giving life to a plethora of characters, but he also allows them the false impression that they are actively manipulating the narrative. The premise of the film is a rather simple one: two actors, not very good at their craft, plan to get hold of easy money by conning some mobsters and following their dreams of Hollywood success. Although lacking in acting skills, Tom Quirk (Moran) and Tony O'Malley (Caine) strongly believe that by injecting some 'reality' into their art they would be able not only to mislead the mobsters but also to actually improve their craft. However, simple stories usually get complicated and the actors are forced to continue their story by playing a continuously increasing number of characters. The irony of the situation is that they seem to be much better at lying to people and putting on a show in a 'real' situation than on stage in front of theatre audiences. What McPherson plays with here is the difference between a knowledgeable, institutionalized audience who are going to the theatre to see Shakespeare's *Richard III*, and the mobsters, who become unknowing spectators in a show of deceit.

Although it seems a light comedy, *The Actors* touches upon multiple layers of issues about theatricality, the illusion of reality and artistic manipulation. The film opens with a panning image of Dublin and closes in on a classroom setting, where Tom's niece,

Mary, is writing a play in five acts, much like the Shakespearean play in which her uncle has a minor role. The film will be punctuated by the girl's narrative voiceover and by the titles of each act, corresponding to the various chapters in the film. Shakespeare becomes an important element in the film, underlining his position as the epitome of playwriting in the English speaking world and as creator of roles that Tom Quirk aspires to. The comedy of the narrative is enhanced by small scenes that comment on the situation of the actor in a world ruled by advertising and celebrity culture. Tom prepares the opening speech of *Richard III* for an audition for a sausage advert and is deemed by the director (played by Michael Colgan) 'not real' enough for his audience, while Tom O'Malley, by now an old actor who has known a certain level of success in the theatre, is dreaming of the financial perks that come with film roles in Hollywood. Having in mind the initial drama of the film's production and the refusal by *Dreamworks* to cast European actors, the director manages to insert a visual comment in the film by making Michael Caine's character wear a cap with the inscription *Far and Away*, the 1992 film starring Tom Cruise and Nicole Kidman, about a young Irish couple emigrating to America. Ron Howard's film has since become one of the most infamous examples of misjudged casting, for giving roles to American and Australian star actors who put on bad Irish accents. But the fame brought about by this type of film is what Tony O'Malley longs for, and not artistic quality. He craves stardom and realizes that playing Shakespearean roles in small Irish theatres to a handful of spectators is not what he has dreamed of when he started his acting career. He even puts forward the idea of playing the title role in *Hamlet*, and making it more groundbreaking by speaking only the vowels of the classical text.

The viewers are subtly introduced to a story that lies underneath the narrative of deceit that forms the basic plot of the film. *The Actors* becomes a film about acting and actors in a world that only appreciates superficiality. It is a film about simulation and performativity. Tom and Tony inhabit a world that encourages the creation of a multiplicity of stories. The world is a story. The world is a stage. And in this case, the stage itself, represented by the Olympia theatre in Dublin and the production of *Richard III* becomes the only snippet of reality that appears in the film. The rules of theatricality are turned upside down and the drama develops outside the limits of the theatre. Even the actors develop better acting skills when they are outside the theatre. Tom, for example, who is considered and who considers himself to be a 'bad' actor in the play, becomes the best impersonator of various characters in the conning story. However, his haplessness on stage saves his life when faced with the English mobsters. Magnani and her company arrive from London to recover their lost £50,000 and are told that Tom was the main culprit in the deceit. Seeing Tom on stage as a spear-carrier in *Richard III* (a production which parodies in its style the famous 1995 film of the play, directed by Richard Loncraine and starring Ian McKellen), they come to the conclusion that he is such a bad actor that it would be impossible for him to fool anybody. His real-life character is critiqued based on his role on stage. This blurring between real life and acting happens from the very beginning of the film. This is a Dublin story told by a nine-year old girl for a school project, in the form of a five-act play. The titles of the acts mirror the real life theatrics of the two actors. Act Two (*The Actor Prepares*) and Act Four (*Method Acting*) clearly allude to Stanislavsky's method of actor training and its further development in the United States. The titles are also ironic references to the ways in which both Tom and Tony prepare for their roles. While trying hard to find his 'motivation' for playing the role of a spear carrier in *Richard III*, Tom seems to have no problem putting on various roles in the conning plot: Clive, the useless mobster, Barreller, the Irish interloper or the Scottish hitman sent by Magnani to recover the money. Tony, on the other hand, takes the interpretation of the title role in *Richard III* very seriously, prepares for it like a method actor by researching 'real life villains' in Dublin's seedy bars, and acts like the undoubted star of the production. However, he is challenged when he has to act in real life to aid the completion of the plot he himself proposed.

The Actors also responds, in structure and plot, to the main theoretical requirements of postmodern philosophy. The film is a pastiche of stories, expected and unexpected, that keeps growing through layers and layers of narrative. McPherson manages to combine issues of parody and pastiche, which according to Fredric Jameson is 'parody that has lost its sense of humour.'[11] The characters seem compelled to create more and more stories in order to construct their own lives, their existence depends on the length of the story they are creating. The trigger for this deluge of stories is the real Barreller's made up story about his career as professional mobster. Played by Michael Gambon, Barreller confesses to Tom that he might have exaggerated the stories he told Tony as part of his research for the part of Richard III, but that he was star struck when he heard that Tony was a professional actor and he wanted to impress. After a lengthy 'comedy of errors,' the film and incidentally the five-act play, ends with yet another cliché connected to the world of film and theatre: the awards ceremony. Although the production of *Richard III* barely had any paying audience, Tony O'Malley is shortlisted as the best actor and he eventually gets the award. The 'Grand Finale' of Act Five ensures that Tom gets the girl, Dolores (Lena Headey), and Tony gets his prize, thus confirming the superficiality of the narrative.

Although its director called it a light 'Ealing comedy,' *The Actors* turns out to be much more than that. It is a film that through comedy, slapstick and witty dialogue manages to expose a contemporary world based on superficiality and consumer culture while highlighting the humanity that exists in every character and every story. These are characters that gain their personality, their individuality through acting and storytelling. But after all, isn't this what life is truly about?

Works Cited

Adams, Tim, an interview with Conor McPherson, 'So There's These Three Irishmen…', *The Observer*, Sunday 4 February, 2001

Brooks, Peter, *Reading For the Plot: Design and Intention in Narrative* (Harvard: Harvard University Press, 1984)

Genette, Gerard, *Narrative Discourse: An Essay in Method* (Cornell University Press, 1980)

Jameson, Fredric, *Signatures of the Visible*, (London: Routledge, 1992)

Jameson, Fredric, 'Postmodernism and Consumer Society' in Peter Brooker (ed.), *Modernism/Postmodernism* (London: Longman, 1992): 163-179

Lothe, Jakob, *Narrative in Fiction and Film* (Oxford: Oxford University Press, 2000)

McPherson, Conor, 'Chronicles of the Human Heart,' *The Guardian*, Wednesday 1 March, 2006

McPherson, Conor, *Four Plays* (London: Nick Hern Books, 1999)

Vincent, Sally, an interview with Conor McPherson and Dylan Moran, 'Funny, peculiar', *The Guardian*, Saturday 13 July, 2002

---

[1] Conor McPherson, *Four Plays* (London: Nick Hern Books, 1999): 3.

[2] Tim Adams, an interview with Conor McPherson, 'So There's These Three Irishmen …' *The Observer*, Sunday 4 February, 2001

[3] *ibid.*

[4] Conor McPherson, 'Chronicles of the Human Heart,' *The Guardian*, Wednesday 1 March, 2006.

[5] Tim Adams, an interview with Conor McPherson,

[6] 'Funny, peculiar' an interview with Sally Vincent, *The Guardian*, Saturday 13 July, 2002 .

[7] Peter Brooks, *Reading For the Plot: Design and Intention in Narrative* (Harvard: Harvard University Press, 1984): 13.

[8] *ibid.*, 7.

[9] Fredric Jameson, *Signatures of the Visible* (London: Routledge, 1992): 1.

[10] Jakob Lothe, *Narrative in Fiction and Film*, 30.

[11] Fredric Jameson, 'Postmodernism and Consumer Society' in Peter Brooker (ed.), *Modernism/Postmodernism* (London: Longman, 1992): 167.

10 | Mysterium Tremens: Conor McPherson's *Dublin Carol*

Ian R. Walsh

> I'm always looking for ways to go beyond the material world. I want to go somewhere totally new in theatre, to really transport the audience, to take them inside themselves and back out. [1]

> That whole play [Dublin Carol] is a hangover. When you have a really bad hangover like that, that's your mindset. It's gloomy, guilty, scary. [2]

Dickens in the opening passage of *A Christmas Carol* spends some time clarifying that 'Old Marley was dead.' [3] He explains that nothing 'wonderful can come of the story' he is about to relate unless this fact is clearly understood and goes on to employ a theatrical analogy to make his point:

> If we were not perfectly convinced that Hamlet's Father died before the play began, there would be nothing more remarkable in his taking a stroll at night, in an easterly wind upon his own ramparts, than there would be in any other middle-aged gentleman rashly turning out after dark in a breezy spot ... literally to astonish his son's weak mind.' [4]

Conor McPherson in his dramas would seem to turn Dickens's logic on its head. In his plays we are repeatedly presented with unremarkable people, particularly 'middle-aged gentlemen' who exist in extraordinary worlds where the boundaries between the living and the dead are never certain. In *St. Nicholas* a disgruntled drama critic is promised eternal life by a pack of vampires; in *The Weir* three middle-aged men try to spook a woman with their ghost stories only for her to tell them a haunting tale that scares them and in *The Seafarer* a group of Christmas Eve revellers end up playing a high-stakes game of cards with the Devil. Where Dickens readers are asked to make a distinction between the wonderful and the mundane in order to understand the fantastical tale of Scrooge's redemption, the audiences of McPherson's plays are asked to wonder at the fantastical notion of truth itself; they are unsure what to believe and are left in a state of wonder. Ben Brantley in his review of *The Weir* sums up the value of McPherson's playwriting: 'if the disturbing mysteries of existence haven't been given explanations, they have been given form, and that in itself is a victory.'5 It is the intention of this article to examine *Dublin Carol* in terms of form, in particular how it can be situated in relation to a specific established tradition of theatrical experimentation with modes of representation that has been designated by Elinor Fuchs as the 'mysterium.'6

An essay entitled 'Struggling Toward a Future: Irish Theater Today' published in the *New Hibernia Review* in 2001 manages to bring most of the prejudices against McPherson's drama together in their comments on *Dublin Carol*. For the authors of this piece (Paul Haughey, Cormac O'Brien and Josh Tobiessen) McPherson has 'not emerged from the shadow of past writers,' the play is 'rooted in the structure and language of Irish stage realism'7 and McPherson is characterized as a writer of plays that are not theatrical and are dependent on literary monologue:

> Admittedly, he does make more use of the one monologue than customary. Three quarters of a *Dublin Carol* is spoken by the lead character, often to himself. John tells his own story as much as enacts one devised by the playwright. McPherson's plays are linear in narrative and movement in a way that seems better suited to the novel than the stage.8

In my examination of *Dublin Carol* in relation to the mysterium I concentrate in particular on how two elements of dramatic form, time and character function in the piece. I do this in order to situate McPherson's work in relation to theatrical modes of analysis firmly establishing the theatrical rather than the literary nature of his plays. Identifying *Dublin Carol* in terms of the mysterium positions this play within a European tradition of experimentation with form (that includes Irish dramatists such as Yeats and Beckett) and challenges the assumption that McPherson's play adheres to a 'traditional naturalism.'9 It is hoped that this investigation will offer a different perspective on this play separate from (but still related to) the debates over language, narrative and Irishness that have dominated much of the criticism of McPherson's drama.[10] In one such analysis Clare Wallace examines how McPherson disrupts realistic representation in his dramas through his specific use of the monologue form. She views McPherson's brand of monologue play as being anti-illusionistic 'deriving many of its effects through recourse to stage techniques that are Brechtian,'[11] concluding that these self-reflexive techniques create a drama 'where self is performative, rather than predetermined, and where morality may be just provisional and contingent.'[12] Although Wallace states that her study 'raises issues that are pertinent to readings of all his [McPherson's] work' she dismisses McPherson's later plays, (including *Dublin Carol*) for their 'subsequent retreat into naturalistic forms.'[13] It is hoped that this examination will build on the foundations made by Wallace's arguments but using the alternative framework of the mysterium that is found to be more apt in an analysis of *Dublin Carol*.

In *The Death of Character* Elinor Fuchs identifies the shift from character towards 'pattern' as the fundamental innovation and transformation evident in contemporary theatre. She terms this the death of character, playing on the title of Roland Barthes's seminal essay entitled, 'The Death of the Author.' Fuchs identifies this shift from character to 'pattern' as beginning with symbolist dramatists of the late nineteenth century and their experimental revision of the medieval theatre. The symbolists reacted against naturalism's scientific approach to theatre that examined characters' psychology and behaviour in given circumstances. Interested in the occult and the mystical rather than logic and explanation, the symbolists and their inheritors found the allegorical methods of medieval theatre offered them a dramatic model that allowed for the mysterious. Fuchs labels this theatrical form, 'the mysterium' writing:

> The decline of interest in the psychological depth and substantiality of character toward the end of the nineteenth century made room for the emergence of dramaturgies that were not character-generated ... The question is not whether there are living creatures on the stage, but what it is we are following when we engage with them. Inwardness and its attendant conflicts, so important to the post-Shakespearean development of modern character, especially to the Romantics and Hegel, have been eclipsed by an abstract teleological patterning. What we follow in the mysterium, its true agent, is

the unfolding of the pattern (or as in *Waiting for Godot,*) its
failure to unfold.[14]

Dublin Carol could be considered a mysterium since it takes
salvation as its subject but also as its dramaturgy rests not on the
development of character but on the unfolding of a pattern. But for
Fuchs what makes the mysterium a distinctively modern genre is its
'ironic self-undermining ... often expressed as a structural
subversion by the dramaturgy of its own cosmic pretensions.'[15] Such
undermining is found in McPherson's play where the patterns
suggested change as they unfold. A wealth of patterns are clearly
alluded to in the text – the staves of *A Christmas Carol,* the
structure of a passion play, the progression of Advent and an
alcoholic's journey through the horrors of a hangover – but the play
does not follow any one pattern absolutely. Patterns are promised
but never delivered. In this way McPherson follows Beckett's
Waiting for Godot and its structure of the 'failure of a pattern to
unfold' but McPherson's world is never as abstract as Beckett's. It
deliberately situates itself in a reliable image of reality, the stage
directions read: '*The action takes place in an office on the Northside
of Dublin, around Fairview or the North Strand Road.*'[16] Here the
play sets itself in a knowable reality that can be located on a map.
The importance of the Dublin setting is highlighted in the title of the
play. McPherson undermines any 'cosmic pretensions' by clearly
setting his play in a gritty Dublin reality. The play would also seem
to follow the pattern of a well-made naturalistic drama: we are
presented with a diurnal progression divided into three distinct
parts of the developing day – '*Part One,* late morning,' *Part Two,*
early afternoon,' '*Part Three,* late afternoon'. Mapped onto these
three time divisions there is a three part dramatic structure with a
central character wherein we are presented with a crisis in the
second part which should be resolved by the close of the play – but
this pattern like all the others is also never fulfilled. A naturalistic
play is promised but never delivered.

Dublin Carol comprises of three duologues that take place in an
'old and musty' undertaker's office: the first is between hung-over
alcoholic undertaker John and a young assistant Mark after they
have just laid someone to rest on the morning of Christmas Eve;
next John is confronted in the early afternoon by his estranged
daughter who tells him that the wife he deserted is dying and that
she has requested to see him one final time; lastly Mark, drunk and
feeling guilty after dumping his girlfriend returns to the office for his

pay but instead receives more stories of John's ugly past as well as some poor advice. From one scene to the other there is little progression in terms of action. In the second part of the play John is confronted with a decision by Mary – she tells him that she will pick him up by five o'clock to visit her mother and thus a conflict is set up whether John will decide to go or not in part three. But McPherson does not offer a resolution. Instead the play ends on the static image of John alone on a chair fixing decorations on a tree while the bells chime the hour. We end uncertain if John will stay or go. Fuchs writes:

> The mysterium arrays itself against what realistic drama portrays as natural causality. In realistic drama, characters control, or hope to control, events. In the mysterium characters are guided, chastened, and surprised by cosmic interventions; the dramatic events, over which the characters have little or no control, are the medium by which these forces manifest. The spatial-temporal world of the mysterium subsumes its characters in an overall design that in effect designs them.[17]

McPherson's comments on working with Rae Smith, who designed the set for *Dublin Carol* when it was first produced by the Royal Court, would seem to visually reflect this desire to create a theatrical experience whereby the world of the play 'subsumes its characters in an overall design' through her effective use of darkness on stage:

> I like her designs because there's very little there – I don't like sets with walls. I don't like to have a room. I like there to be a lot of darkness around the image, the idea of the infinite spreading out from the story. It's more mysterious.[18]

When Benedict Nightingale in his review for *The Times* describes the set for the Royal Court production we are made aware that McPherson's preference was met by Smith: 'Dublin Carol is set amid the dimly lit mix of doleful furniture and festive decorations that is Rae Smith's idea of a Dublin undertaker's office on Christmas Eve.'[19] While Susannah Clapp in *The Observer* found:

> As the lights go down between scenes on Rae Smith's set, the ghostly sigh of chimes is heard and an amber glow on the back wall makes the silhouettes of everyday objects look like the jagged battlements of a gothic castle. The familiar rumble of the Tube sounds like a tip-off from Hades.[20]

Smith's set responds to and furthers the 'mysterious' aspects of McPherson's apparently naturalistic play. So affected by these aspects Clapp goes so far as to begin to imagine the world outside the theatre ('the familiar rumble of the Tube') in fantastical terms (Hades).

In the play John describes the hospital room of his dying friend Noel in terms that reflect the stage image created by Smith and the sense of otherworldliness such a design provoked in Clapp. He tells Mark: 'It was all kind of blue, and just the light coming off the telly, (*ominously*) on the shiny floor. Aw, it's a different world. You're very helpless.'[21] This sense of helplessness is to be found in the characters of the play who are all depicted either as being lost and without purpose or powerless. John's life is a wreckage of pain and loss that is charted through the play; Mark is described as 'kicking around a bit'[22] unable to commit to an occupation or indeed his decisions as is evident in the remorse he feels after breaking up with his girlfriend; Mary describes herself as alone, 'weird'[23] and disliked, she yearns for a connection with her father and mother which is not easily made. Those characters mentioned in the dialogue would seem to be as lost as the figures presented to us onstage. Noel, whose name and actions (he is the man who gave John the job as an undertaker and saved him from destroying himself entirely with alcohol) would seem to cast him as the 'Spirit of Christmas,' is reduced to a pathetic figure with 'sad eyes'[24] who is disgusted that he has lost control of his bowels. While Carol, another character from John's past, again with a name that points to Dickens's festive tale, is depicted as a false redeemer, a widow so overcome by loneliness that she becomes John's 'drink-angel'[25] who will not only put up with but support all his antics, just to have someone to love. John's wife and Mark's girlfriend are similarly painted as tragic in their love for these unworthy men who reject them. Paul, John's son, seems fated to follow his father as we learn from Mary that he drinks heavily and hides from his girlfriend rather than having to confront her.

There is no cosmic intervention in *A Dublin Carol* or an overall divine design or pattern that is followed through as in Fuchs's conception of the mysterium. Instead there is a yearning for such an intervention and the charting of repeated failure of patterns to unfold. John could be considered as a secular version of the allegorical Everyman figure who questions the notion of salvation as it occurs in the medieval morality play. Indeed, McPherson teases that John may die after Christmas and would thus have to face judgement just as in the famous medieval text. He has John describe how he would like to die and what he would like his funeral to be in part one, and then toward the end of the play in part three John speaks the ominous lines: 'Yeah there's some poor bastard out there. Looking forward to the old Xmas, not knowing he'll be under this roof on Monday waiting to be buried.'[26] But as already outlined the play does not offer a resolution to the question of John's deliverance – we are unsure if he is saved from drinking and reconciled with his wife and children by the end of the drama. In terms of the medieval mystery play *Dublin Carol* would seem to take from the biblical cycle, in that the structure of the passion of Christ, his death and resurrection would seem to be a potential pattern. This is set up by the naming of the play as a carol: a song that takes man's salvation as its theme sung most commonly during the seasonal celebration of the birth of Christ. John would seem to be a character dead-in-life that is in need of resurrection but no cosmic force intervenes and no Christmas miracle occurs for this to come to pass. Both medieval forms of theatre pattern time as divided between the eternal and the temporal. McPherson conflates the two time sequences: he represents temporal time – the progression of a day from morning to evening – but also hints at the divine by setting his play on Christmas Eve – a time bound up with ideas of resurrection and eternal presence. Also as his drama has no resolution – its progression is not teleological which further breaks down a division between the temporal that must end in death and the eternal which is endless.

The one consistent force that seems to exist is that of fear. All the characters are fearful and fear governs their actions: Mark fears commitment and so is 'kicking around' and breaking up with his girlfriend; Mary fears herself and meets with her father in the hope that if she comes to know him she may come to know herself; while John clearly cites fear as his reason for drinking. He speaks of living in a state of fear, anxiety and tension as for him 'the world was a bad place' and he felt too cowardly to protect his family from it. In the same way that he was too cowardly to protect his mother from being beaten by his father when he was a boy. This is why he drank in order to deliberately let his family down just to get their inevitable disappointment in him over with. Drinking is also a means of assuaging fear for John. In his lengthy description of a hangover John makes clear how fear possesses and structures his alcoholic's life:

And that special alcoholic's hangover. I pray you never get one. It's a fucking beaut. It's after a couple of days on the serious piss. What happens is, day one, for whatever reason you've started early and basically polluted yourself. It's a form of poisoning. And so, on day two, you are in the absolute horrors. I don't mean what most people feel after the Christmas party, sick tummy and a headache. This is a raging dose of the creaming paranoid shits. You're shit scared. Just to walk down the street you think you're going to be beaten up. And there's a sickening disgust with yourself to boot and there's only one thing you can do to stop it.[27]

Mark gives John the inevitable answer 'More Drink' and John proceeds to describe day three of the hangover that is full of drowsiness, where you have 'terrifying dreams and wake up crying and all that. Day four you won't be so bad. But it won't be long before day one rolls around again.'[28] Here, character is 'eclipsed by an abstract teleological patterning.' The hangover leads to an endless cycle that is driven by the need to assuage a self-perpetuating paranoia and fear. John is consumed by this cycle and is rendered as an object only given meaning in terms of a pattern. He claims 'There's nothing worse than decorations after Christmas. That's the way I'd sometimes used to feel putting my clothes on in the morning.'[29] But John ends the play decorating the Christmas tree with the decorations that were earlier taken down. In this he would seem to be accepting himself as an object that does not quite fit within the scheme of things. This image offers a moment of hope but not redemption for John or indeed real closure for the audience. In reply to Mark, questioning what he would like his own funeral to be, John says 'I just want to slip away, you know? Very quiet. Under cover of darkness.'[30] McPherson gives him his wish at the close of the play as the theatrical character who only exists for the duration of the play dies in those closing moments. Mark comments on John's idea of slipping away as the 'great escape' and indeed John as a character does escape the audience. The promotional photographs by Geraint Lewis of the Royal Court production are redolent of the chiaroscuro of Caravaggio where Brian Cox, playing John, cuts a luminous ghostly figure about to be snuffed out by an overwhelming darkness.[31]

But he is made a ghostly presence in the play text too – he would seem to stand-in for absence rather than confirming being. He has been an absent father but it seems as though he was absent even before he departed the company of his family – a ghost haunting them. This is indicated by Mary telling of their dog to which he replies, 'What dog?'[32] He then later speaks of one time taking Carol's dead husband's clothes after destroying his own with vomit. He dresses in these clothes to return to his wife and plea for reconciliation. But when he comes to the house his wife is not home and he leaves to go on a bender in the dead man's clothes. He literally walks in the shoes of the dead. And then his salvation by Noel is to give him the job of undertaker in which he finds some meaning in dealing with the dead rather than the living. Mark asks if the job has led to him becoming more religious as ritual has become such 'a part of his life' to which John replies that he is '*around* it' rather than part of it.[33] He is present but not partaking. Mark then later opens the door on the Advent calendar to reveal a picture of angels. John comments: 'A feast of heavenly angels, is it? No it's a host of heavenly angels. "A Feast." I'm losing my marbles entirely at this stage.'[34] John's confusion perhaps points to his treatment of his guiding angels Noel and Carol who have both played 'host' to John only for him to parasitically 'feast' upon them. He lives off others consuming them as he goes, leaving them to death and despair. He confesses to Mary how he feels disgust for Noel in his sickness. The 'good man' he thought to be so strong is shown to be weak before death. Carol is repulsive for loving the worst in him. He is a black hole, an absence that creates more absences by sucking in anything in its path. Fuchs's identifies:

> a tendency present in the mysterium from the beginning, the emptying of psychological character into the archaic sense of character as inscription, the making of, or merging with, a sign ... The world of the mysterium is a world of absent presences; represented by the mysterious signatures they leave on time, space, and all relationships.[35]

John becomes associated with two signs by the end of the drama – the Advent calendar and the decorations. When he is taking the decorations down with Mark towards the end of the play he says that 'They should have one of these with all year on it' and later adding,

> With little words of wisdom. Little cautionary words of advice. The second of July. A word of caution. Fourth of August, a word to the wise. You know? November, 'you're being a spa, cop on to yourself', you know?[36]

John longs for structure in his life, for a pattern he can follow that will save him. In his description of himself as being like decorations after Christmas and his final act of putting up the Advent calendar on the wall and redecorating the tree he is 'merged' with a sign (decorations) in relation to a pattern (Advent Calendar). He becomes his own inscription. The transformative act of the drama is not that of a flawed hero who changes after a moment of insight but the reconciliation of a character with his own created image. Scrooge's life is made a spectacle of by the spirits of Christmas who show him images of what he was, is and will be in Dickens's *A Christmas Carol*. He is terrified by the images and changes his behaviour. In a *Dublin Carol* John is never shown images of himself; he instead presents images of himself through his stories to the audience and finally identifies himself with one of those images through his final actions. The image of John as being like the decorations left after Christmas is transformed in its staging – as John begins to place decorations on the tree the stage image no longer evokes sadness and detachment as when it was first mentioned in the dialogue but instead represents defiance. If John dies as a theatrical character in the closing moments of the play slipping into darkness – it would seem that he is not going quietly as he earlier wished but leaves to the sound of 'music and bells' in a defiant image that would seem to rage against the dying of the light. Such a reading would seem to concur with McPherson's own comments on the play:

> The play [*Dublin Carol*] is about saying, 'I can't live here,' and anyone understands that. In a play we don't see the next day, so the feeling we're left with is hope. There is potential. I like to leave audiences with that feeling.'[37]

McPherson ultimately makes the spectator the interpreter of the patterns he has set up. He hopes to engender feeling (hope) but does not offer meaning or resolution. In a *Dublin Carol* he gives the sense that 'a witnessed reality is nevertheless not immediately knowable'[38] through his dissolution of character and deliberate frustration of teleological patterns.

The play does not offer a pattern to live your life by as the Christian morality and mystery plays of the Medieval theatre did. Instead as a modern mysterium *Dublin Carol* suggests that the world is a mysterious place full of many patterns but we are free to chose, reject or remake the pattern of our lives. In its creation of a theatre that rejects fated psychological character and dramatic resolution *Dublin Carol* depicts an essentially possible world, full of potential. In this the play would seems less a carol on the subject of redemption than an ode to the transformative power of performance.

Works Cited

Brantley, Ben, 'Dark Yarns Casting Light, *New York Times*, April 2, 1999.

Clapp, Susannah, Review of *Dublin Carol, The Observer*, February 23.

Csencsitz, Cassandra, 'Conor McPherson Lifts the Veil,' *American Theatre*, 24, (2007) 36-83.

Cummings, Scott. T, 'Homo Fabulator; The Narrative Imperative in Conor McPherson's Plays,' in *Theatre Stuff: Critical Essays on Contemporary Irish Theatre*, ed. Eamonn Jordan (Dublin: Carysfort Press, 2000): 303-312.

Dickens, Charles, *A Christmas Carol,* (London: Penguin, 1994).

Fuchs, Elinor, *The Death of Character: Perspectives on Theater after Modernism* (Bloomington: Indiana University Press, 1996).

Grene, Nicholas, 'Ireland in Two Minds; Martin McDonagh and Conor McPherson,' in *The Theatre of Martin McDonagh*, eds Lilian Chambers and Eamonn Jordan (Dublin: Carysfort Press, 2006): 42-59.

Haughey, Paul, Cormac O'Brien and Josh Tobiessen, 'Struggling Toward a Future; Irish Theater Today,' *New Hibernia Review,* 5.2, (2001) 126-133.

Jordan, Eamonn, 'Pastoral Exhibits: Narrating Authenticities in Conor McPherson's "The Weir",' *Irish University Press*, 34 (2004): 351-368.

Nightingale, Benedict, Review of *Dublin Carol, The Times*, 24 February 2000.

Singleton, Brian, 'Am I Talking to Myself? Men, Masculinities and the Monologue in Contemporary Irish Theatre,' in *Monologue: Theatre, Performance, Subjectivity*, ed. Clare Wallace (Prague: Litteraria Pragnesia, 2006): 260-277.

Wallace, Clare, 'A Micronarrative Imperative,' *Irish Studies Review*, 14 (2006): 1-10.

---

[1] Cassandra Csencsitz, 'Conor McPherson Lifts the Veil,' *American Theatre*, 24, (2007): 36-83:39.

[2] *ibid.*, 82.

[3] Charles Dickens, *A Christmas Carol,* (London: Penguin, 1994) p.1

[4] Charles Dickens, 1.

[5] Ben Brantley, 'Dark Yarns Casting Light, *New York Times*, April 2, 1999, p.1

[6] Elinor Fuchs, *The Death of Character: Perspectives on Theater after Modernism* (Bloomington: Indiana University Press, 1996): 49.

7 Paul Haughey, Cormac O'Brien and Josh Tobiessen, 'Struggling Toward a Future; Irish Theater Today,' *New Hibernia Review*, 5.2, (2001): 128.

8 *ibid.*, 128.

9 Clare Wallace writes that The *Weir, Dublin Carol* and *Shining City* 'formally return to a traditional naturalism.' Clare Wallace, 'A Micronarrative Imperative,' *Irish Studies Review*, 14 (2006): 10.

10 See Nicholas Grene, 'Ireland in Two Minds; Martin McDonagh and Conor McPherson,' in *The Theatre of Martin McDonagh*, eds Lilian Chambers and Eamonn Jordan, (Dublin: Carysfort Press, 2006): 42-59; Scott. T Cummings, 'Homo Fabulator; The Narrative Imperative in Conor McPherson's Plays,' in *Theatre Stuff: Critical Essays on Contemporary Irish Theatre*, ed. Eamonn Jordan, (Dublin: Carysfort Press, 2000): 303-312; Clare Wallace, 'A Micronarrative Imperative,' *Irish Studies Review*, 14 (2006): 10; Eamonn Jordan, 'Pastoral Exhibits: Narrating Authenticities in Conor McPherson's "The Weir",' *Irish University Press*, 34 (2004): 351-368; Brian Singleton, 'Am I Talking to Myself? Men, Masculinities and the Monologue in Contemporary Irish Theatre,' in *Monologue: Theatre, Performance, Subjectivity*, ed. Clare Wallace (Prague, Litteraria Pragnesia, 2006): 260-277.

11 Wallace, 'A Micronarrative Imperative,' 3.

12 *ibid.*, 8.

13 *ibid.*, 8.

14 Fuchs, *The Death of Character*, 49.

15 *ibid.*, 49.

16 Conor McPherson, *Dublin Carol*, (London: Nick Hern Books, 2000) .

17 Fuchs, *The Death of Character*, 49.

18 Cassandra Csencsitz, 'Conor McPherson Lifts the Veil,' 39.

19 Benedict Nightingale, Review of *Dublin Carol, The Times*, February. 24 2000.

20 Susannah Clapp, Review of *Dublin Carol, The Observer*, February 23 2000.

21 McPherson, *Dublin Carol*, 10.

22 *ibid.*, 11.

23 *ibid.*, 34.

24 *ibid.*, 11.

25 *ibid.*, 44.

26 *ibid.*, 51.

27 *ibid.*, 48.

28 *ibid.*, 49.

29 *ibid.*, 48.

30 *ibid.*, 12.

[31]Lewis, Geraint, *'Dublin Carol* Image Gallery', 9 June 2011, <http://geraint-lewis.photoshelter.com/gallery/DUBLIN-CAROL/G00009WlwbBTA7fs/>

[32] McPherson, *Dublin Carol*, 34.

[33] *ibid.*, 8.

[34] *ibid.*, 10.

[35] Fuchs, *The Death of Character*, 50.

[36] McPherson, *Dublin Carol*, 50.

[37] Csencsitz, 'Conor McPherson Lifts the Veil,' 82.

[38] Fuchs, *The Death of Character*, 51.

11 | The 'Sweet Smell' of the Celtic Tiger: Elegy and Critique in Conor McPherson's *The Weir*

P.J. Mathews

Recent criticism of contemporary Irish drama, especially that of the Celtic Tiger period, has thrown up a concern with the influence of globalizing forces on the production and reception of Irish theatre during the boom years. Fintan O'Toole has repeatedly drawn attention to the fact that, as he sees it, many of the most successful playwrights of the period enjoyed a level of popular acclaim that was inversely proportional to their direct engagement with the pressing issues of contemporary Irish life. 'If Ireland in general became more Americanized during the boom,' wrote O'Toole, 'Irish theatre shared in this condition. Big social drama became almost as rare here as it was in New York.'[1] Recent work by Patrick Lonergan also expresses concern that in the era of globalization many of Ireland's leading playwrights have become insensitive to local concerns in their themes and subject matter.[2] Catherine Rees, too, argues that contemporary Irish drama 'turned toward the global – not just in "content", but also in distribution – as Irish studies became a popular subject around the world, and international theatres began to perform and indeed premiere Irish plays.'[3] One of the plays often referred to in the course of this analysis is Conor McPherson's *The Weir*, with many commentators drawing attention to the fact that this highly regarded Irish play was actually first produced by the Royal Court Theatre in London.

Behind much of this criticism lies a suspicion that the achievement and high visibility of Irish culture globally during the Tiger years was enabled by the increasing capitulation of Irish artists to international taste, expectations and market forces. Such concerns about Irish cultural success, however, are not new and might be traced as far back as William Hazlitt's offhand dismissal of Thomas Moore's *Irish Melodies*.[4] Even the great founding figure of modern Irish theatre, J. M. Synge, was castigated in his own time for presenting Irish experience in terms of the passing fads of French decadence.[5] Rather than dwelling on the circumstances of *The Weir's* first production or the reasons behind its international appeal, the aim here is to look in some detail at the nature of the play's thematic engagement with its Irish locale. In many interesting ways, I would suggest, *The Weir* can be seen as part of a tradition of Irish plays which explore threshold moments of fundamental cultural and political shift at key historical junctures. Broadly speaking these plays reflect on the dynamics of Irish cultural change from a vestigial vantage point at a moment when a new dispensation is about to take hold. The play which inaugurates this tradition, is, of course, Synge's *Riders to the Sea* (1904).

In *Riders* Synge offers a view of Aran which is strikingly poised between a mood of elegy for the passing of a distinctive way of life and a sharp critique of the internal failings of that society which were hastening its demise. Far from providing a purely sentimental portrait of island life *Riders to the Sea* presents a sobering exposé of the atrophying influence of tradition, where youthful ambition is discouraged out of a pathological need to preserve old ways. At a time when cultural nationalists were heavily invested in proposing simplified idealizations of rural living as the basis of a conservative Irish identity, Synge delivered a necessary corrective to that narrative. His account of Aran life is astutely double-focused. In the first instance it performs an important decolonizing role in its detailed portrait of an autonomous pre-colonial culture of complexity and integrity. Crucially, though, it also levels a significant degree of auto-critique by pointing out the inherent weaknesses in that cultural formation in the face of the pressures of modernity. Writing from the perspective of the beleaguered vestige, Synge registers the tectonic movements taking place in Irish culture and society as they are happening. The full implications of these profound cultural shifts only become apparent after his death, yet much of his genius lies in his prescience and in a consciousness acutely tuned to the subterranean tremors of social change at a moment when Irish life was being transformed by the embrace of the modes of industrial capitalism.

The decaying vestige crops up again in Irish theatre with Brian Friel's *Translations* (1980). Just as in *Riders to the Sea*, Friel offers a portrait of Gaelic Ireland on the brink of collapse. In a programme note to the original production of the play Friel wrote: 'the main characters, English and Irish, stand at a moment of cultural transition, and the play explores their response to this crisis in their personal lives and in the historical life of the community.' *Translations*, then, is set as Ireland moves across the threshold into Anglicization, three decades after the Act of Union joined Great Britain and Ireland politically, integrating Ireland more fully into the Empire, and at a time when the cultural aftershock is beginning to hit. In this instance a waning Hedge School provides the setting from which unfolding events are witnessed. Like Synge, Friel offers an imaginative retrieval of a lost Gaelic perspective as a compensation for the absence of written accounts of that encounter and, simultaneously, in the character of Manus, a critique of a Gaelic mindset which refuses to engage with the forces of change and which sees the westward retreat as the only possible salvation.

It is tempting to read *The Weir* in this tradition, offering as it does a snapshot of pre-Celtic Tiger Irish life on the eve of its eclipse. First performed in July 1997, the play was written at a time when the phrase 'Celtic Tiger' was beginning to gain currency as a term to describe the unprecedented economic boom in the Irish economy that began in the mid-1990s and would last until the crash of 2007. During that heady period Ireland's anomalous position within the Western capitalist order as a politically neutral postcolonial State became regularized. Through the process of increasing European political cohesion and by virtue of the warmer embrace of the Irish State by the Anglo-American world in the wake of the Peace Process and the signing of the Good Friday Agreement in 1998, the Irish economy became more fully integrated into the mechanisms of global capitalism. One of the most obvious expressions of Celtic Tiger success was the greater visibility of Irish culture on a global scale. Indeed during these years Ireland was steadily 'transformed from a relatively impoverished backwater on the periphery of Europe, whose national culture was seen to be threatened by the homogenizing influences of mass global culture, into a prosperous economy whose culture was rapidly recruited to the global capitalist enterprise.[6] *The Weir* now stands as an astute analysis of that transition in its exploration of a society caught between impulses of heroic isolation and willing submission to the forces of globalization.

In this tale of storytelling in 'a small rural bar' in 'a rural part of Ireland, Northwest Leitrim or Sligo,'[7] McPherson revisits a place of family significance[8] and, in the process, registers some of the economic shockwaves that are beginning to make a mark on the social and cultural landscape. One of the notable side effects of the Celtic Tiger was the undermining of small-scale and local networks of economic activity that characterized life in rural Ireland up to that point. The building and property boom of the late 1990s led to a relative decline both in small-scale farming activity and in the ancillary services dependent upon it. It also brought about an unprecedented increase in construction and property development in the cities and larger towns that eventually spread to previously undeveloped tourist regions, including rural Leitrim and Sligo.

In the course of the play there are many hints of fundamental change in the air as the creeping obsession with property and real estate begins to manifest itself. In the same way as the 'sweet smell' of the potato blight forebodes the disaster of the Famine in Friel's *Translations* there are signs of the advance of the coming economic order.[9] Early on, Brendan discloses that his sisters have been putting pressure on him to sell part of the farm and bemoans their lack of attachment to place.[10] Finbar, the local boy made good, makes a rare visit to the pub in the company of a client to whom he has just sold a house. He is an hotelier and property developer who brags about having 'bought the whole town' and who enjoys goading the others with tales of his business acumen and 'eye for the gap.'[11] The house in question, it turns out, has been on the market for four or five years but has now been snapped up by Valerie who is happy to disclose the fact that property prices are relatively cheap in this part of the West. 'It's very reasonable all around here,'[12] she confides, making an implicit comparison with soaring real estate prices in Dublin. As it turned out, Leitrim and Sligo would subsequently experience huge levels of property speculation and development at the peak of the Celtic Tiger boom. Indeed, there is a dark irony, given the centrality of haunted houses in *The Weir*, that this region would inherit the unenviable title of 'ghost estates' capital of Ireland in the post-boom period.[13]

Hand in hand with the re-tooling of the Irish economy in the 1990s went a fundamental re-ordering of Irish social and cultural life. Patterns of settlement began to favour commuter towns in proximity to the larger urban centres and this inevitably led to a decline in remote rural towns and villages. One of the most visible manifestations of these fundamental societal shifts during the boom years was the decline of the civic infrastructure of rural Ireland as a consequence of the gradual withdrawal of state services such as post offices and Garda stations, and further, the demise of the small, independent, rural pub as the hub of Irish social life. From the mid-1990s onwards thousands of pubs across Ireland closed down.[14] This was not reflective of a general decline in alcohol consumption rates but of a greater tendency towards urban living and of changing patterns of social interaction. Ironically, at the very moment in which the rural Irish pub was being replicated in abundance around the world, the same globalizing forces that promoted its popularity abroad were threatening the original of the species at home.

Much of the potency of *The Weir* can be attributed to the prescience with which McPherson offers an insight into the shifting dynamics of rural Ireland on the eve of such fundamental change. Three of the lead characters, Brendan, Jack and Jim, dwell within the well-established, yet fading, rhythms of a pre-Celtic Tiger rural economy. Brendan, who has inherited the family farm and attached pub, has all but opted out of farming and struggles to make a living from the bar's diminishing clientele. Jack is a self-employed mechanic who survives on small jobs and the good will of the local community. Jim has no obvious regular means of income and seems to divide his time between odd jobs, caring for his elderly mother and betting on the horses. As the play proceeds this trio demonstrates the operations of the fragile and mutually dependent subsistence economy in which they partake. In the opening scene, Jack helps himself to a beer in the absence of the barman, Brendan. However, as the stage directions dictate, he is careful to pay for his drink:

> He turns to the till which he opens with practiced, if uncertain, ease. He takes a list of prices from beside the till and holds a pair of spectacles up to his face while he examines it. He puts money in the till and takes his change. [15]

Local economic interactions have their correlative in a heightened culture of communal solidarity which is a crucial feature in this play of manners. McPherson seems to foreground a particular form of social relations which values mutual concern over individualism and self-regard. The pub in this play functions as a kind of intermediate or 'third space' between the public and private which allows a unique kind of meaningful interaction to take place. This is emphasized by the opening stage directions which specify that 'the bar is part of a house and the house is part of a farm.' [16] In many respects, therefore, *The Weir* celebrates the gentle and unspoken civilities of local life at a time when these attributes are perceived, in wider Irish society, to be under threat by the brash, consumerist ethos of the Celtic Tiger. This is a world of easy-going decency and respect where idiosyncrasies are tolerated and where neighbours seem at ease with well-worn conversations, and with the silences between them.

Much of the power of the play lies in the simplicity and intensity with which it deploys the art of storytelling. In the course of the evening each character (Brendan excepted) tells a story and participates in a narrative exchange which ranges from the presentation of local history and folklore to the disclosure of personal regrets and anxieties. A central theme that emerges is the idea that a community's sanity and civility can be gauged by the extent to which it provides a warm, courteous space for people to tell their stories without fear of being judged or ridiculed. Yet there is never a total surrender to the redeeming potentials of pastoral in this play. As an audience we may be impressed by the warmth, openness, and richness of each character in story-telling mode but we are equally aware of the material and emotional poverty that underwrites these exchanges.

If anything, the play can be read as an exposé of a disintegrating rural community in which youthful ambition is stunted by a pathological attachment to place. Jack describes the condition very well towards the end of the play:

> **JACK.** I'm down in the garage. And the fucking tin roof on the thing. On my own on the country road. You see it was bypassed by the main road into Carrick. ... And there you'll be, the only car stopping in be someone that knows the area real well. Ah, you'd definitely feel it, like. [17]

Jim, the least well off of the three, lives out a life of confined possibilities as the primary carer of his aging mother, while Brendan is presented as a male version of Synge's Nora Burke grudgingly carrying out his duties and fighting off depression brought on by domestic incarceration. In the closing stages, he describes his own version of *The Shadow of the Glen* (1903):

> ... and nothing for me to do except pull a few pints and watch the shadow from the Knock moving along the floor, with the sun going down. I'm like some fucking mentler, I do be watching it! Watching it creeping up on the Germans. And they

don't even notice it. I must be cracking up if that's my entertainment of an evening.[18]

Unlike Nora Burke, however, Brendan shows no inclination to escape the condition of his own torment.

Brendan, Jack and Jim, single and childless, endure as the last representatives of a once-vibrant rural community. The snippets of local history dispersed across a number of the monologues create a picture of a spirited population in former days. The current torpor, in fact, is in striking contrast to the livelier times enjoyed by their immediate progenitors, commemorated in a photo taken at the time the weir was built in 1951 to generate electricity for the surrounding hinterland. Significantly, as Brendan and Jim recall, the local area has a history of some distinction: in the sixteenth century it functioned as an important centre of ecclesiastical activity in the wider region.

> **BRENDAN.** Oh, back in oh, fifteen something, there was a synod of bishop all came and met there for ... like ... eh.
> **JIM.** This townland used to be quite important back a few hundred years ago, Valerie. This was like the capital of the, the county, it would have been. [19]

In terms of this wider historical perspective, therefore, the present moment betrays evidence of a worrying dynamic of social disintegration. In a reversal of the pattern established in *Riders to the Sea* it is the men who are left behind as the vestigial remains of a once sustainable community.

As we find out in the course of the play, Jack, in particular, has missed out on life's opportunities. In a frank and moving monologue towards the end he recounts the chances he missed out on and offers a raw analysis of his own failings. In effect he diagnoses his own dysfunctional masculinity which is based on a false sense of self-sufficiency and an over-developed attachment to place. But this is also accompanied by a clear disdain for the settled orthodoxies of middle Ireland and the forces of centralization which are symbolized for Jack by a world in which nurses marry gardaí and live happily ever after. 'Enjoy your big gorilla,' he thinks to himself as his former girlfriend marries a policeman, 'cause the future's all ahead of me.' [20] Jack's story is a cautionary tale for Brendan who seems equally invested in delusional ideas of male self-sufficiency. Despite Jack's encouragement he shows no interest in selling the pub or in developing the tourist potential of the property. He, too, is incurious about the world outside the parish and, like Jack, has no desire to integrate into a wider network of economic relations. Catering to the 'Germans' is a compromise that he is unwilling to make.

Indeed, one of the most striking aspects of this play, which is so heavily invested in hospitality and the decorum of social interaction, is the distinctly incurious and unwelcoming attitudes of Brendan, Jim and Jack towards the not inconsiderable number of European visitors who frequent the pub and the local area. Significantly, during the early years of the Celtic Tiger, Ireland experienced a marked increase in the number of tourists visiting the country annually. Related to this, and in keeping with the high visibility of Irish popular culture globally at the turn of the Millennium, is the rise of the 'Irish pub' as a global phenomenon. As Cian Molloy pointed out in 2002:

> you can now order a traditional Irish pub from firms such as the Guinness-owned Irish Pub Company and the Irish Pub Design and Development Company, who will assemble your pub for you wherever you require. The second company offers six 'stylistic' choices: the cottage pub, the old brewing house, the shop pub, the Gaelic pub, the Victorian pub and the 'contemporary' pub.[21]

In this context it is possible to regard the frosty reception accorded by the locals to 'the Germans' as an act of resistance against an encroaching, vapid, globalized Irishness, synonymous with faux cultural exuberance and ostentatious conviviality. The extent of local indifference can be gauged by the fact that Brendan, Jack, and Jim dismissively refer to all non-English-speaking visitors as 'Germans.' Much to Brendan's annoyance his two regular customers vacate his premises at the height of the tourist season. What they find particularly galling is the fact that the visitors re-import the generic Irish pub concept into *their* local, effectively transforming their 'third space' into a venue of purely economic transaction. As Brendan puts it:

> The two of yous leaving me standing behind that bar with my arms folded, picking my hole and not knowing what the hell is going on. And them playing all old sixties songs on their guitars. And they don't even know the words.[22]

In this scenario Brendan's bar functions in the same manner as the thousands of generic Irish pubs across the globe – a convenient site for spurious if convivial 'folk' indulgence. His dismissal can be seen as a reaction against the hordes of pushy tourists with stereotyped notions of Ireland who expect interaction on their own terms. Finbar, on the other hand, is happy to play up to these expectations. Earlier in the play as Jack is about to tell the story of the fairy road running through Maura Nealon's house he discloses to Valerie that, 'The Germans do love all this.'[23] A willingness to relent to tourist expectations is surely important to his success as a businessman and hotelier. From another perspective, however, the studied avoidance of the tourists in Brendan's bar betrays a worrying xenophobia, particularly at a time when inward migration was becoming a visible feature of the Irish cultural landscape. Once again it is notable that the central virtue of hospitality celebrated in the play is not extended to foreigners. Jack resents feeling usurped on his own patch and grumbles that 'you don't know what they do be saying or anything.'[24]

In contrast, when Valerie, in her inaugural visit to the pub, enters with Finbar she is warmly received. Brendan extends the courtesy of offering her a first drink on the house. He is keen to meet her request for a glass of white wine and insists on retrieving a bottle from the house. In fact, even before she enters the pub at all Brendan voices concern that she be entertained in a mannerly way by Finbar:

> **BRENDAN**. Well it's, you know. If it's courtesy, which is one thing, and a business ... act or whatever, you know, you have to say, well okay and ... But if it's all messy, I'm trapped in here behind this fucking thing. And you wish he'd stop acting the mess. [25]

Significantly there is no attempt to curtail the robust verbal exchanges routinely indulged in by the men. Thus, there is no appreciable change in the tone of the conversation when she arrives, and no studied deference to perceived 'female' mores. Finbar, for example, in an early exchange jibes the others for staying 'out here on the bog picking their holes.'[26] Jack responds in kind by highlighting Finbar's opportunism in buying 'half the fucking town.'[27] Nor is there ever a sense that Valerie is offended by the coarseness of these exchanges. Further, as the outsider among the locals she functions as the catalyst who triggers the extended bout of storytelling over the course of the evening. Throughout the evening it is Valerie who sanctions the telling of the stories. 'No I'd like to hear it ... I'm interested in it,'[28] she confides, before Jack tells the tale about Maura Nealon's house. As the story ends she responds with the view that 'there's probably something in them [the fairy stories].'[29] At the close of Jim's particularly creepy story about the burial of the pervert she immediately engages the teller with the question 'Do you think it was a, an hallucination Jim?'[30]

Far from being upset by the tales she hears, Valerie is empowered by them and is encouraged to tell her own eerie and emotionally-charged story of the loss of her child. Hers is a deeply personal account of the circumstances that led to the death of her five year old daughter, Niamh, and the breakup of her marriage shortly afterwards. On the surface Valerie and her husband enjoy the prosperity and opportunities of Celtic Tiger Dublin – both work at Dublin City University. Yet in the aftermath of Niamh's tragic death the limitations of their advanced lifestyle become readily apparent. In this story of the drowning of a child which, again, recalls Synge's *Riders to the Sea*, the responses of Valerie's husband and mother-in-law to her profound grief are presented as hopelessly inadequate, deeply insensitive and utterly repressive. As Valerie relates:

> Daniel's mother got a doctor and I ... slept for a day or two. But it was ... Daniel felt that I ... needed to face up to Niamh being gone. But I just thought that he should face up to what happened to me. He was insisting I get some treatment, and then ... everything would be okay.[31]

Valerie's story culminates, therefore, in a robust critique of the atomized world of Celtic Tiger 'progress' in which complete investment in the potentials of scientific rationalism has become utterly repressive. Her exasperation with the containment and commodification of her grief through medication and 'treatment' is clear.

When she arrives in the pub for the first time Valerie enters as someone who has been estranged from the intimacy of others. She is introduced to Brendan, Jack and Jim who, in turn, have cut themselves off from the nourishment of human exchange and who face bleak futures of frustration and isolation. In the encounter, new possibilities arise for her as she experiences a deep sense of catharsis in the telling of her story, and in the non-judgmental reception of it by the men. Her presence, too, is transformative for them and offers a way out of their cultural stasis. In her proposed role as intermediary between the locals and 'the Germans' in Brendan's bar, Valerie offers a way out of the downward spiral of social disintegration which may also challenge the patronizing attitudes of the visitors. As the play ends Jack draws courage from Valerie's example:

JACK. If Valerie's willing to come in and brave the Germans, then I'm sure me and Jim'll come in and keep yous company, how's that now?[32]

Valerie's willingness to 'brave the Germans,' is a pledge of solidarity with Brendan, Jack and Jim; her suggestion, however, that she 'might even learn some German'[33] opens up the possibility that Brendan's bar may, once again, become a site of mutual cultural exchange. The play ends, therefore, by holding out the prospect of renewal engendered by her visit. As Brendan turns off the light and exits, the suggestion lingers that both the flippant xenophobic attitudes that he and Jack exhibit, and the bland globalized assumptions of the visiting tourists will be interrogated by Valerie's enabling presence, to the enrichment of all concerned.

Works Cited

Hazlitt, William, *The Spirit of the Age* (1825; London; J.M. Dent and Sons, 1932).

Jordan, Eamonn, (ed.), *Theatre Stuff: Critical Essays on Contemporary Irish Theatre* (Dublin: Carysfort Press, 2000).

Lonergan, Patrick, *Theatre and Globalization: Irish Drama in the Celtic Tiger Era* (Palgrave, 2009).

McPherson, Conor, *The Weir* (London: Nick Hern, 1998).

Mathews, P.J., 'In Praise of "Hibernocentricism": Republicanism, Globalization and Irish Culture,' *The Republic*, 4 (2005): 5-14.

Molloy, Cian, *The Story of the Irish Pub* (Dublin: Liffey, 2002).

O'Toole, Fintan, 'Can Irish dramatists tackle the big questions again?,' *The Irish Times*, 7 June 2011.

Rees, Catherine, 'How to Stage Globalization? Martin McDonagh: An Irishman on TV, *Contemporary Theatre Review* 16:01, (2005): 114-22.

---

[1] Fintan O'Toole, 'Can Irish dramatists tackle the big questions again?,' *The Irish Times*, 7 June 2011. This argument was further elaborated by O'Toole in the television documentary, 'Power Plays' RTE Arts Lives series, 7 June 2011.

[2] 'A problem arising from reflexivity and mobility is that local audiences are losing opportunities to generate meanings about their own localities. ... if productions are conceived with one eye on the mass market, then issues of specifically local importance can only be presented implicitly, if they are presented at all.' Patrick Lonergan, *Theatre and Globalization: Irish Drama in the Celtic Tiger Era* (Palgrave, 2009): 218.

[3] Catherine Rees, 'How to Stage Globalization? Martin McDonagh: An Irishman on TV,' *Contemporary Theatre Review* 16:01 (2005): 115.

[4] In 1825 Hazlitt damned Moore's verses for draining the radical energy out of his Irish subject matter: 'Mr. Moore converts the wild harp of Erin into a musical snuff-box!' William Hazlitt, *The Spirit of the Age* (1825; London; J.M. Dent and Sons, 1932) 174.

[5] Arthur Griffith famously attacked Synge's *Shadow of the Glen* on the grounds that the play was characteristic of 'the decadent cynicism that passes current in the Latin Quarter and the London Salon.' *United Irishman*, 17 October 1903, p.1.

[6] See P.J. Mathews, 'In Praise of "Hibernocentricism": Republicanism, Globalization and Irish Culture,' *The Republic*, 4 (2005), 5-14.

[7] Conor McPherson, *The Weir* (London: Nick Hern, 1998):1.

[8] 'The play takes place in a rundown pub in rural Leitrim, one inspired by places McPherson visited with his grandfather, whose death, according to the playwright, casts an influential shadow over the play's creation.' Scott T. Cummings, 'Homo Fabulator: The Narrative Imperative in Conor McPherson's Plays,' in Eamonn Jordan (ed.) *Theatre Stuff: Critical Essays on Contemporary Irish Theatre* (Dublin: Carysfort Press, 2000): 308.

[9] Unlike Friel, though, McPherson is writing *in medias res* and without the benefit of historical retrospection.

[10] Conor McPherson, *The Weir*, 5.

[11] *ibid.*, 14.

[12] *ibid.*, 14.

[13] 'County Remains Haunted by Spectre of Ghost Estates,' *Leitrim Observer*, 25 Oct 2011.

[14] 'A Pint of Bitterness,' *The Irish Times* 8 August 2009.

[15] McPherson, *The Weir*, 3.

[16] *ibid.*, 3.

[17] *ibid.*, 45.

[18] *ibid.*, 49.

[19] *ibid.*, 19.

[20] *ibid.*, 45.

[21] Cian Molloy, *The Story of the Irish Pub* (Dublin: Liffey, 2002): 91.

[22] McPherson, *The Weir*, 49.

[23] *ibid.*, 19.

[24] *ibid.*, 49.

[25] *ibid.*, 10.

[26] *ibid.*, 13.

[27] *ibid.*, 14.

[28] *ibid.*, 20.

[29] *ibid.*, 22.

[30] *ibid.*, 33.
[31] *ibid.*, 40.
[32] *ibid.*, 49.
[33] *ibid.*, 50.

12 | The Measure of a Pub Spirit in Conor McPherson's *The Weir*

Rhona Trench

If as Kevin C. Kearns wrote in 1996 that the pub is both the 'epicentre' and 'a true microcosm of social life, reflecting the socio-economic ethos of its host community,' then the rural pub presented in *The Weir* (1997) enables, creates and reflects the society that surrounds it. Ondřej Pilný is correct in observing McPherson's dramatic oeuvre as accessible through the real, despite the talk of the supernatural which 'ghosts' McPherson's works. It is with this lens that this essay examines *The Weir*, in an effort to explore the pub space as providing the conditions for storytelling to take place and for issues of subjectivity to emerge. Pilný cites Brian Singleton's comment on *The Seafarer* (2006), which can be extended to all of McPherson's works:

> [T]he plays feature a distinct mixture of comedy and tragedy, concern of the everyday reality of true-to-life characters, and have "the comfortable accessibility and familiarity for a popular audience and more than a hint of the universally tragic to en-sure [their] place in the Irish canon.[1]

Centring on themes of the power of the past in the present, the fragility of human life and isolation, *The Weir* is set in a small bar, part of a house, which is located on a farm in the North West of Ireland. The overall drama leads to the telling of five narratives that are tenuously connected by the characters' loneliness and the figurative ghosts that haunt them. The proprietor, three other local men, and a woman new to the area meet, drink, and unveil their stories. Prior to their recounting of their tales, the banter consists of friendly local talk and gossip that is uneventful in terms of dramatic action in itself.

From the beginning of the play, the 'Celtic Tiger' is referred to – a period well recognized and marked by Ireland's explosion of wealth which began in the mid-1990s and continued for nearly a decade. Low tax rates and tax breaks, the availability of cheap credit and increased inward foreign direct investment led to a growing economy. Further, the influx of returned emigrants, the absence of pressure on its citizens to emigrate and the arrival of diverse immigrants to Ireland's shores meant large population growths. Additionally, the availability of development sites for property building resulted in some making large profits as the values of land and properties soared. The play's characters look introspectively at their place in the world, illustrating how personal projects are formed and how their projects mediate the exercise of systemic constraints and enablements (or not) of the 'Celtic Tiger' economy. Peadar Kirby et al rightly note about the Celtic Tiger period:

> Ireland's contemporary culture is seen as an eloquent expression of new-found confidence where the liberalization of internal markets is matched by the celebration of individual rights and liberties,' with muted attention given to social and cultural changes.[2]

Sara Keating states: 'Late-capitalism Celtic Tiger Ireland was an increasingly individualistic society, where traditional communities had been shattered by urban migration and the swell of social housing on cities' outskirts.'[3]

The disconnection between the values of the 'Celtic Tiger' and tradition is presented at the outset of *The Weir*, not in a way that demonstrates their integration and co-existence, but rather their existence in parallel. From the start, Brendan laments his sisters' visit, whose eyes are firmly fixed on their family land as prospective development. Brendan does not like change, telling Jack: 'No I don't [use the top field much]. Too much trouble driving a herd up. But I know they're looking at it, all they see is new cars for the hubbies, you know?'[4] When Jack suggests that he clears one of the fields for caravans for tourists, Brendan can't bear to imagine how awful the quietness would be after the tourists leave. Finbar too is referred to, before and when he arrives on stage, as the business guru, an auctioneer and hotelier, who is now not in need 'of a few shekels.'[5] Such figures long existed before the 'Celtic Tiger' period, but seemed to proliferate during that period.

Finbar sold Maura Nealon's house to the newcomer, Valerie, and this is the transaction that brings Valerie to Brendan's bar. Finbar takes Valerie for a drink and 'to meet the natives,'[6] a gesture seen to be, in Diarmaid Ferriter's words, 'essential as a means of initiating social contact, especially with strangers.'[7]

Brendan's bar occupies a space somewhere between 'work' and 'home'; indeed the pub's function, according to J. Fiske *et al.*, is to 'mediate their opposition by a complex set of repudiations and incorporations of both.'[8] The pub can operate as a 'home away from home' or as an extension of the workplace, but also contains elements that are opposed to those locations. This essay considers the idea of the pub space in *The Weir* as containing opposing elements of work and home, arguing that the pub operates as a site of in-betweenness, as an existential space that provides the conditions for the intersection of the lives of its characters to populate, live and permeate through narrative and the theatrical form in which they exist. I will explore the formulation of subjectivity via abstract and conceptual means which initially can be accessed through the 'real' but which moves well beyond it as the drama unfolds. This involves theorizing the pub space as a means to show how identity can be explicated through signs and signifiers, including objects, images, social groupings, codes of behaviour and appearance in the play.

Paul Ricoeur's idea of the self is that it is not always immediately transparent to itself nor is it possible to fully master the self. Self-knowledge only comes through our relation to the world and our life with and among others in that world. The pub in *The Weir* is read as the space that mediates the signs, symbols and (con)texts where self-understanding corresponds to the interpretation given to these mediating terms. Ricoeur's notion of the role of narrative as a linguistic construction mediates between the lived time of consciousness and that of physical time which is regulated by the cosmos and measured by human mechanical tracking devices, is evident in the play. Ricoeur correlates 'the activity of telling a story' and the 'temporal character of human experience'[9] as a transcultural form of necessity which produces our narrative identity, considered either at an individual or at a collective level. Stories exist because of their connection and involvement of and with other people, therefore personal and/or communal identity is a narrative identity.[10] Narrative provides coherence and meaning to the flux of events but is never fixed in that it is itself always open to interpretation and/or re-configuring. Narrative is the medium through which the 'inherent temporality of being is expressed,' according to Lois McNay.[11] It shapes identity and is the way in which selfhood is articulated. Both Ricoeur and Lois McNay point out however that narrative mediates the generative configuration, and reconfiguration, of identity.[12] Examining *The Weir* in this context opens up how an excess of subjectivity bleeds outside of the pub space, outside of the narratives recounted and into worlds of 'otherness' in the play.

The role of the pub in Irish theatre has been inextricably linked to other areas of life in plays, particularly related to community life. According to Diane Watson pubs have much to do with habit and repetition: as expressed in the term a 'regular' or a frequent customer. They may offer a sense of continuity, regularity and order that is 'fundamental to [a] sense of place, of time and of security.'[13] Christopher Murray observes that the pub, versions of the pub in sitting rooms or kitchens or a public house in the background has never strayed too far from Irish theatre.[14] The world of alcohol and its main place of consumption (the pub) or alternatives (the kitchen/living room) have featured regularly on the Irish stage: Marina Carr's *Portia Coughlan* (1996), *By the Bog of Cats ...* and *On Raftery's Hill* (2000), Murphy's *A Whistle in the Dark* (1961), *The Gigli Concert* (1983), McPherson's *Rum and Vodka* (1992), *Dublin Carol* (2000), *The Seafarer* (2006) and Martin McDonagh's *The Lonesome West* (1997) to name but a few.

In exploring Irish theatre that can be accessed through the real, an understanding of the representation of the pub is therefore crucial to an understanding of character's relationship with alcohol, with other people and with society, when present in plays. Pilný notes that 'alcohol has been the most prominent false stimulant in which to assuage guilt and unfulfilment culminating the excess, almost parodic imbibing.'[15] Eamonn Jordan notes about *The Weir*: 'The pub functions symbolically as a fantasy and a communal locus, and as a narrative space, where inebriation offers a sense of relaxation and gives a certain type of licence.'[16]

In Ireland, the pub has been seen as a social problem and as an expression of national identity, revealing the role that drinking plays in relation to group/community identity. The fact that the opening stage directions of *The Weir* specify that there are only '*three stools at the counter*' of the bar, '*a small table front with a stool or two*' and in front of the stove '*a low table with small stools and a bigger*

more comfortable chair nearest the fire,'[17] suggests that McPherson
wants to indicate that this bar generally welcomes a small number of
local residents into a 'homely' environment from the surrounding
area. Newcomers are therefore a seasonal intrusion to the place and
even at that, it is implied that there are not many of them. Murray
notes: 'McPherson glories in the pub setting, seeing it as an abode of
camaraderie and good cheer [...]. He works to replicate the
generation of warmth a pub generates so that on stage this feeling
extends to the audience and all share in this sense of bonhomie and
companionship.'[18] I would argue that the pub space is more
challenging than Murray contends and suggest that the 'bonhomie
and companionship' atmosphere of the pub in *The Weir* offers more
than just a site of positive social interaction that reaches the
audience. The pub setting is possessed of a suppressed romanticism
and idealism, shaped by broader structural elements such as issues
of culture and gender, that disguises a deep-seated pain, exposing
the fissures of a society dejected by 'Celtic Tiger' values, reaching
beyond its theatrical limits into worlds of 'otherness,' which has
implications for the audience. As Watson notes:

> when individuals enter a particular pub they are purchasing far
> more than a particular product, such as a drink or a meal. They
> are also purchasing an experience or ambience, which is
> associated with desire, and the creation and expression of
> identity and lifestyle. What is important is not so much the
> actual products that are consumed but the meanings attached
> to those products.[19]

Early theatrical representations of the pub as seen in J.M.
Synge's *The Playboy of the Western World* (1907), which opens in
O'Flaherty's *shebeen* or country pub, is the place where the central
dramatic action emerges. Protagonist Christy Mahon announces his
act of parricide to the pub's patrons and so begins the unravelling of
the drama revealing the beliefs and values of the close knit
community in the play. Social relationships in O'Flaherty's pub are
intimately linked to social relationships outside and play a key role
in reinforcing men's position of control and dominance in relation to
women, specifically wives and daughters in the play. In John B.
Keane's *The Field* (1966), Mick Flanagan's bar in the small village of
Carraigthomond in the southwest of Ireland is the setting for a
different kind of local trade and commerce. Maggie Butler comes to
Mick Flanagan asking him to auction her field and a whole host of
'wheeling and dealings' are enacted. The auction is held and its

outcome does not go according to the protagonist's plan, and so begins a series of events which culminate in a murder, revealing the tight-lipped silence of the local community, which consolidates Ireland's rural people with the land. Tom Murphy's *Conversations on a Homecoming* (1985), set entirely in a pub, is the kind of place that has been incorporated into a broader leisure and tourism industry. As the title indicates, the homecoming of returned emigrant, Michael, sets the action in motion, (the action is performed through many dramatic monologues). Michael's arrival home is celebrated by a group of old friends and acquaintances through the consumption of alcohol in their old local pub. Anthony Roche writes of Murphy's connection to traditional folk narrative and his influence on McPherson:

> In placing the oral recital of a folk narrative at centre stage, Murphy is returning Irish drama to its origins. [...] *Bailegangaire* not only recapitulates the process by which storytelling evolved into the drama of the Irish Literary Revival, but also demonstrates the extent to which in postmodern dramaturgy, the phenomenon of storytelling has itself become the action of drama. In turn, storytelling in Murphy's plays feed directly into the work of a younger contemporary like Conor McPherson in *The Weir*.[20]

The significant use of objects and images in the pub in *The Weir*, serve as cultural functions and the ways in which these forms manifest themselves with entirely local and historical meanings such as genealogies, cultural histories and, particularly, dialogues about the importance of local experience in the face of globalism. The stage directions read: '*An old television is mounted up in a corner. There is a small radio on the shelf behind the bar.*'[21] TVs in Irish pubs typically show sport and (depending on the presence of female clientele) soap opera, two categories frequently differentiated along gender lines and which are linked to media industry and audience practices. Although the soap opera has broadened its audience base to men and teenagers, it still predominantly retains a female audience.[22] Irish soaps themselves regularly feature pubs as central locations in their settings such as *Fair City, Ros na Rún* and the popular British soaps aired on Irish television including *Coronation Street, EastEnders* and *Emmerdale* also depict the pub as a core feature of family and community life.[23]

Valerie's entrance into the pub affects all of the male characters' behaviours particularly in terms of the language they use and the narratives they share. This may be because of the fact that the space suggests that only male locals typically frequent the bar and despite the gradual feminization of drinking spaces,[24] which began in the 1990s to include serving teas/coffees, food, wine, and decor now included soft furnishings and refurbished washrooms. This bar has not evolved to match the increasing domestication of pub spaces.[25] Women at this time were now welcomed into bars and the nature of the spaces themselves changed to accommodate this new market.[26] Yet while Valerie is welcomed into the space, there is no wine at hand to meet her request or to accommodate the new market that pubs offered during this time, and at a later stage when Valerie requests the ladies she is told that 'it is busted' and is shepherded to the toilet in the main part of the farmhouse.[27] This suggests that women therefore rarely set foot in the bar and Brendan is obviously in no rush to fix the ladies toilet, as their presence in the pub is few and far between.

Kearns provides a gendered bias view of the pub which initially fits the kind of pub space offered by *The Weir*, observing that the pub has served as a social support mechanism for men: an environment where 'they can openly share personal feelings about domestic life, work, health, finances and phobias.'[28] In the opening of the play, Jack, a bachelor in his 50s, talks to Brendan the bar man, in his 30s, about being single. Inspired by the news that married and successful businessman Finbar will be bringing the newcomer, Valerie, to the pub later that evening, Jack tells him that he will keep pestering him about his single status until he gives marriage some serious thought. Jim is the handyman about the place, and who does odd jobs with and for Jack and often work opportunities come about from casual conversations that take place in the pub. Jack enquires about Jim's mother's well-being, revealing that Jim lives with his mother on a small farm, which is, according to Finbar, not worth much. Jim tells Brendan and Jack, 'Be lucky to get twenty thousand for the place. Sure, where would you be going with that?'[29] In fact as the play's stories unfold, Brendan provides the priest-like role where his pundits confess their private thoughts to him, the character who 'listens to all others' stories but never tells one of his own, [and] is the theatrical binding force of the play and the central representative of its values,' as Nicholas Grene suggests.[30] Indeed the banter becomes more heightened and 'performative' in the company of Valerie, when the other characters at some point or other defer to her for acknowledgement and/or confirmation of their knowledge, humour and wit. On a number of occasions they try to soften the seriousness and/or the horror of some of the content of the narratives prior to her telling her own revelatory story. But as the alcohol flows, this kind of female gender awareness begins to disappear. As the characters start to feel more comfortable with one another, the stories grow increasingly closer to the personal and to the present day of the play. Indeed examined in the pastoral mode Jordan notes that the pub 'provides relatively free-speaking, communal spaces where burdens can be shared, questions asked with concern and personal issues are within the public domain.'[31]

The radio outlined in the stage directions is more than likely a decorative prop in the pub standing in sharp contrast to the face of evolving global technological changes, that emerged in the 1990s beyond the pub and outside of this walled village, of the World Wide Web which caused a continuing revolution in global communications and business practices. It echoes the modern changes displayed in the photograph of the 'newly' erected weir, a 'modern' structure from the early 1950s, which enables water to be transformed and stored as electricity.

The photographs in the play are important signifiers of cultural archive. Photographs in general record a range of occurrences, present information, afford decoration, trigger memory and are a means of communication. They also represent the power of the archive where collections of snapshots in personal and/or community life activate the representation of entire cultural histories, which are also records of social activities and human interconnectivity, effectively acting as a kind of proof of cultural discourse.

The location of the photographs in the context of The Weir is particularly revealing. The stage directions read: 'On the wall, back, are some old black and white photographs: A ruined abbey; people posing near a newly erected ESB weir; a town in an alcove with mountains around it.'[32] The photographs interact with the variety of oral and written (con)texts explored in the play. Roland Barthes wrote about the power of the photograph in Camera Lucida, in which he explicates two major characteristics of a photograph, the studium and the punctum both of which reveal a range of coded information.[33] The studium is the spectator's attraction to the photograph, because of cultural background, interest and curiosity to an image. It represents all that is recognizable in a photographic image, whether it is geographic or cultural. The punctum is the particular element in a photograph that triggers a personal connection with the viewer that is entirely subjective. The punctum is the detail that catches the eye, jogs the memory and arouses compassion, having the power of expansion, while remaining mere detail. Both the studium and punctum operate strategically in McPherson's work, demonstrating how different systems of meaning can parallel one another and at times 'dialogue' with each other.

Ideally, placing an image within a particular context on the wall of the pub activates the operation of community. It is a public photograph that chronicles public life. The interest of one's display of images to locals and anonymous viewers is assumed. Susan Sontag notes that photographs 'are a grammar, they are an ethics of seeing.'[34] It seems that McPherson's description of photographs in the stage directions of *The Weir* are 'originals,' in the sense that they are not represented and replicated in a way that current technology can allow, which would make the originals untraceable.[35] (The irony of course is that the photographs will be doctored by the set designer to look authentically old!) His desire for black and white photographs points to the usual ravaging effects the ills of time can have on paper. This means that the portraits/images are used for specific purposes, retaining their initial context. The seized set of appearances of 'the ruined Abbey' is probably the remains of Jamestown Abbey – a Franciscan friary of the convent of the Friars' Minor from the seventeenth century, of 'the people posing near the ESB weir,' refers to the modern ESB weir at Jamestown built in 1951, which controls the flow of water levels at that part of the river Shannon and which generates electric power, and 'a town in an alcove with mountains around it' which might be Drumshanbo, Co. Leitrim, surrounded by Sliabh an Iarainn which guards the south-eastern shore of Lough Allen, and the Arigna mountains. What the images capture have nothing to do with us, the audience, in terms of the original meaning of the events that surrounded them when they were taken. Instead, the audience will look at them and, based on their own lives, will infer meaning to them. The visual situation of the photographs offers a paradigmatic example of the journeying through narrative boundaries in *The Weir*; narratives reaching out to the possibilities of humankind's interconnectedness and separateness, of inclusiveness and exclusiveness, of individual and collective identity, continually appealing to what might be outside of and beyond the stories suggested within the photo frames.

The fact that the photographs are hung in a pub, notionally in Jamestown, a village which is located outside of Carrick (Carrick-on-Shannon) places before us the significance of how these images are located in a meaningful context that connects with the audience: 'To photograph is to appropriate the thing photographed. It means putting oneself into a certain relation to the world that feels like knowledge, – and therefore like power.'[36] The context of the photographs, more that the images themselves, are part of the overall drama, constructed alongside the stories of the play (largely monologic memories that draw on the non-natural in terms of style and content), placed beside other photographs, some directly referred to in the play's dialogue, others indirectly; constructed in an ongoing flux of words and images. The resulting context replaces the photographs in time – not its own original time for that is impossible – but in narrated dramatic time. This gives the audience the opportunity to put the photographs into the context of experience, of their experiences, and of cultural and social experiences in the overall context of the play.

Ricouer's notion of emplotment is useful here, which is the subjective cognitive process that allows the audience to follow a story. If the audience is enticed into entering a narrative (stemming from the photographs and/or the play's monologues) by being provoked and engaged by it, they will care what happens next and will make the story their own. Metaphorically the story has become inhabitable. In an existential sense, the audience imagines themselves as actual participants in the stories that they hear. Ricoeur declares:

> [t]he moment of 'understanding' corresponds dialectically to being in a situation: it is the projection of our ownmost possibilities at the very heart of the situations in which we find ourselves... what must be interpreted in a text is a proposed world which I could inhabit and wherein I could project one of my ownmost possibilities.[37]

The pub space then is intimately linked to the five characters, and provides the conditions for the telling of the monologues to emerge, and this could not have taken place if someone else at any moment had entered the space. The inhabited pub space echoes Martin Heidegger's claim that space is dependent on human beings, recognizing that space has a human character and its role is a condition of human experiences.[38] With this in mind then the order and timing of the monologues, the kind of stories unveiled, the location of the pub, Valerie's presence in the bar and the drink consumed are some of the factors that are dependent on the telling of the particular monologues at that particular time that connects the space to all present in the bar and to the audience.

Sara Keating points out that 'the monologue play [prominent in Irish theatre in the 1990s] in its early incarnations in the work of Conor McPherson [...] is a powerful social statement encapsulated in the single-voice dramatic form.[39] Remembering Jim's strange happenings in his monologue which recount the issue of child abuse by a known paedophile and the dead paedophile's request to dig a grave for him in the grave of a young girl, reflects how McPherson believes that the power of monologue is an appropriate dramatic form for such issues:

> These cases of child abuse were ongoing throughout the Celtic Tiger years, one of the series of scandals referred to by McPherson in explaining how the monologue form enabled Irish narratives to go 'inside' and explore the society's secrets in ways other than the reportage of the media and documentary drama.[40]

The monologue form thus relates to Paul Ricoeur's connection of time to human action and suffering. Only in and through the act of telling a story can this time acquire form and, in so doing, be preserved from disappearing with the transience of time.[41] For example, Valerie's presence in the bar and her monologue goes beyond captivating her pub audience; her tale of events reveal the circumstances surrounding the tragic death of her nine year old daughter that spurred her move away from her husband, from her work and from her home in Dublin. For Ricoeur, narrative registers human time, encoding and preserving the memory of what needs to be remembered so that forgetting would be like a second death for the victims. Valerie's narrative functions in this way. Even though her narrative starts with a 'real event,' it is subject to her resourcefulness of composition which appeals to her ability to tell a 'story.' The way in which her story is told (after hearing three previous accounts that involved strange and non-natural experiences) suggests the dichotomies of presence and absence involved in her storytelling while at the same time overcoming them. The sense of loss or absence of her daughter Niamh by drowning is heightened by her vivid memory of how Niamh looked after the terrible event, 'And I gave her a little hug. She was freezing. And I told her Mammy loved her very much. She just looked asleep but her lips were gone blue and she was dead.'[42]

But before this part of her story is revealed, Valerie's lead in to this loss reveals her daughter's complaints at night-time of hearing and seeing 'people at the window, in the attic, coming up the stairs,'[43] occurrences that have already resonated in the three previous monologues told by Jack, Finbar and Jim respectively. This overlapping of narrative content and experiences demonstrates how narratives are essentially interwoven with other narratives. Ricoeur has pointed out how we are subjects in others' stories, others are subjects in our stories; others are authors of our stories and we are authors of others' stories. Ricoeur believes that it is through our discussions and interactions with others that we facilitate the articulation and direction of our narratives, and they ours. This idea is played out in the telling of stories in the play. Finbar's story moves from one involving strange incidents that he got involved in, which happened to the Walsh family because young Niamh Walsh was doing the Ouija board with her friends and had contacted a spirit 'that was after her,'[44] to his own personal strange experience in his home after helping the Walsh family. He tells his audience how he was having his last cigarette in the sitting room before going to bed and found himself unable to turn around and go up the stairs to bed because of the spiritual presence he felt was on the stairs: 'That was the last fag [cigarette] I ever had,'[45] he announces and after the incident he moved to Carrick. Feeling self-conscious after telling the story, he pre-empts his audience's sceptic responses stating, 'It's only headers like me get a fright like that, ha? Feckin Loola.'[46]

The final part of Valerie's monologue describes how one morning after her daughter's death, when she was in bed the phone rang and she answered it: 'The line was very faint. It was like a crossed line. There were voices but I couldn't hear what they were saying. And then I heard Niamh. She said, 'Mammy?' And I … just said you know, 'Yes.'[47] Valerie's presence is back with her daughter, with her husband, at the aftermath of the drowning event as though it was happening once again, and at the idea that Niamh is somewhere out there, needing her. The responses of her pub audience to her monologue vary from one of distraction to confronting the irrational, rational, denial, belief, disbelief and respect. Jack says: 'You don't think it could have been a dream you were having, no?'[48] Finbar says: 'Sure you were after getting a terrible shock, Valerie.

These things happen. Your ... brain is trying to deal with it, you know?'[49] Brendan announces to all: 'She said she knew what it was.'[50] Valerie's story moves between absence and presence brought about by loss. At the end of the narrative experience, neither definite absence nor definite presence defines the pub space for the audience, only presence in absence and vice versa.

Ricoeur's idea of self-knowledge is brought about by Valerie's (and indeed all of the characters' and the audience's) ability to bring things close to her, what Heidegger terms *de-severance* [Entfernung], which 'amounts to making the farness vanish,'[51] so we can use closeness in order to understand ourselves. In this instance, her daughter's death, the other characters and the audience are intimately connected caused by our relation to her story because of our connection to the world and our life with and among others in the world. While one can say that Valerie uses wine and the company as some of the elements that provide the conditions for her to tell her story, it is clearly not the case that the event that has been disclosed is one of familiarity. Rather it is a space, in its familiarity, that evokes what is uncanny [unheimlich], something deeply disturbing that leads her and her audience into worlds of otherness where 'mythic time runs concurrent with naturalist time,[52] and brings her and us to question our being in the world.

Following Heideigger's insights on the interrelatedness between space and self, in the context of all the stories told in the play, the spaces that the characters shape are dependent on their being-in the world manifested by their narratives. They acknowledge and welcome stories (otherwise no stories would have been told) and through it welcome other stories in turn, opening up possibilities for their story to be realized or inflected differently. Through sharing stories they are co-authors of all narratives told and also through sharing stories about themselves they reveal something about themselves of which they were perhaps unaware. One example is Finbar's declaration about moving to Carrick after the incident: 'Maybe that ... had something to do with it. I don't know.[53] His story reveals what he was like in his early twenties and his story also reveals the unrealized effects of helping Mrs Walsh with her daughter and his actions (driving Niamh with her mother back to their house, phoning the doctor, the priest, smoking his last cigarette, moving out of his home after the incident) and experiences through the course of that strange night.

Given the uncanny events and experiences unveiled in the narratives that have been told throughout the evening in the play, Brendan's final line, 'I don't know where they [the Germans] are from'[54] is more a comment on wondering what life is all about than actually speculating about whether they are Germans or if they are, where in Germany they come from. At that moment when Brendan turns off the lights of the bar Jack, Valerie and Brendan, the last to exit the space, leave the pub and the residue of their narratives behind. The monologues told refer not just to the lived experience of loss, guilt, and at times regret inherent in the stories but to a narrated identity to which the audience has become witness. The audience is left with the characters' 'silhouettes' against the background of the bar decorated with TV, radio and old black and white photographs, in the space that was created by the narratives that lead them (and us) to question their very existence and place in the world.

The Weir begins as a play accessible through the real. But to read it only in this way diminishes the complexity embedded in the power of play particularly through the monologue form and the atmosphere created by and in the pub space. The exchange of memories offered by the stories frees the characters from the past in a way that recalls debt, enabling them to engage in some kind of forgiveness. For Jack, it reminds him of his inability to commit to his girlfriend in the 1960s, and his continual demands for self justice that his conscience calls for; for Valerie, her story frees herself from the obligations of the past and the guilt attached to that past, for constantly reflecting on what might have turned out differently if Niamh was not introduced by her to swimming, for believing in worlds of 'alterity' without having to think that she is 'mad.' All the narrative spaces blur subject and object, presence and absence, visibility and invisibility because of the way in which the characters now live after circumstance-changing events. On the whole, *The Weir* presents sharing stories that move from the real into worlds of otherness, making possible a shared present that moves towards forgiveness that makes possible a new kind of future.

Works Cited

Ang, Ien, *Watching Dallas: Soap Opera and the Melodramatic Imagination* (London: Routledge, 1996).

Barthes, Roland, *Camera Lucida: Reflections on Photography*, Trans. Richard Howard (New York: Hill and Wang, 1981).

Ferriter, Diarmaid, *A Nation of Extremes: The Pioneers in Twentieth-Century Ireland* (Dublin: Irish Academic Press, 1999).

Fiske, J., B. Hodge, & G. Turner, *Myths of Oz: Reading Australian popular culture* (Sydney: Allen & Unwin, 1987).

Grene, Nicholas, 'Ireland in Two Minds: Martin McDonagh and Conor McPherson,' *The Yearbook of English Studies*, 35 (2005): 303.

Heidegger, Martin, *Being and Time*. Trans. E. Robinson and J. Macquarrie (New York: Harper, 1962).

Jordan, Eamonn, 'Pastoral Exhibits: Narrating Authenticities in Conor McPherson's *The Weir*,' *Irish University Review*, 34.2 (Autumn-Winter, 2004): 354.

Kearns, Kevin C., *Dublin pub life and lore: An oral history* (Dublin: Gill and Macmillan, 1996).

Keating, Sara, 'No Politics in Irish Theatre? Hold on a second ...' *The Irish Times* 20 June 11.

Kirby, Peadar, Luke Gibbons, Michael Cronin (eds.), *Reinventing Ireland: Culture, Society and the Global Economy* (London: Pluto Press, 2002).

McNay, Lois, *Gender and Agency: Reconfiguring the subject in feminist and social theory*, (Maiden, Mass: Polity Press, 2000).

McPherson, Conor, *The Weir* in *Plays: Two*, (London: Nick Hern Books, 2004).

Molloy, Cian, *The Story of the Irish Pub: An Intoxicating History of the Licensed Trade in Ireland* (Dublin: Liffey Press, 2002).

Murray, Christopher, 'The Supernatural in Conor McPherson's *The Seafarer* and *The Birds*,' in *The Binding Strength of Irish Studies: Festscrift in Honour of Csilla Bertha and Donald E. Morse*, eds. Marianna Gula, Mária Kurdi and István D. Rácz (Debrecen: Debrecen University Press, 2011): 66-77.

Pilny, Ondřej, 'Mercy on the Misfit: Continuity and Transformation in the Plays of Conor McPherson,' *The Binding Strength of Irish Studies: Festscrift in Honour of Csilla Bertha and Donald E. Morse*, eds. Marianna Gula, Mária Kurdi and István D. Rácz (Debrecen: Debrecen University Press, 2011): 87-94.

Ricoeur, Paul, *Hermeneutics and the Human Sciences*, ed. and trans. by John B Thompson (Cambridge: The Cambridge University Press, 1981).

---, *Time and Narrative*, Volume 1. Trans. by Kathleen McLaughlin and David Pellauer (Chicago: The University of Chicago Press, 1984).

Roche, Anthony, *Contemporary Irish Theatre, Second Edition* (Basingstoke: Palgrave Macmillan, 2009).

Sontag, Susan, *On Photography* (New York: Picador, 1977).

Watson, Diane, 'Historical Contexts and Sociological Continuities,' (eds.), Tony Bennett and Diane Watson, *Understanding Everyday Life* (UK: Blackwell Publishing, 2002).

Website www.gaa.ie

[1] Ondřej Pilny, 'Mercy on the Misfit: Continuity and Transformation in the Plays of Conor McPherson,' in *The Binding Strength of Irish Studies: Festscrift in Honour of Csilla Bertha and Donald E. Morse*, eds. Marianna Gula, Mária Kurdi and István D. Rácz (Debrecen: Debrecen University Press, 2011): 87-94, 88.

[2] Peadar Kirby, Luke Gibbons, Michael Cronin (eds.), *Reinventing Ireland: Culture, Society and the Global Economy* (London: Pluto Press, 2002): 7.

[3] Sara Keating, 'No Politics in Irish Theatre? Hold on a second ...' *The Irish Times*, 20 June 11.

[4] Conor McPherson, *The Weir in Plays: Two* (London: Nick Hern Books, 2004): 15.

[5] McPherson, *The Weir*, 23.

[6] *ibid.*, 16.

[7] Diarmaid Ferriter, *A Nation of Extremes: The Pioneers in Twentieth-Century Ireland* (Dublin: Irish Academic Press, 1999):205.

[8] J. Fiske, B. Hodge, & G. Turner, *Myths of Oz: Reading Australian popular culture* (Sydney: Allen & Unwin, 1987): 5.

[9] Paul Ricoeur, *Time and Narrative*, Volume 1. Trans. by Kathleen McLaughlin and David Pellauer (Chicago: The University of Chicago Press, 1984): 52.

[10] Ricoeur, *Time and Narrative*, 52.

[11] Lois McNay, *Gender and Agency: Reconfiguring the subject in feminist and social theory* (Maiden, Mass: Polity Press, 2000): 85.

[12] See Lois McNay, *Gender and Agency*: 74-116, and Paul Ricoeur, *Hermeneutics and the Human Sciences*: 274-296.

[13] Diane Watson, 'Historical Contexts and Sociological Continuities' in *Understanding Everyday Life*, (eds.), Tony Bennett and Diane Watson (UK: Blackwell Publishing, 2002): 188-9.

[14] See Christopher Murray, 'The Supernatural in Conor McPherson's *The Seafarer* and *The Birds*,' in *The Binding Strength of Irish Studies: Festscrift in Honour of Csilla Bertha and Donald E. Morse*, eds. Marianna Gula, Mária Kurdi and István D. Rácz (Hungary: Debrecen University Press, 2011): 67.

[15] Ondřej Pilny, 'Mercy on the Misfit,': 87-94, 88.

[16] Eamonn, Jordan, 'Pastoral Exhibits: Narrating Authenticities in Conor McPherson's *The Weir*,' *Irish University Review*, 34.2, (Autumn-Winter, 2004):351-368, 354.

[17] McPherson, *The Weir*, 13.

[18] Murray, 'The Supernatural in Conor McPherson's *The Seafarer* and *The Birds*,': 66-77, 67.

[19] Watson, 'Historical Contexts and Sociological Continuities,' 207.

[20] Anthony Roche, *Contemporary Irish Theatre, Second Edition* (Basingstoke: Palgrave Macmillan, 2009): 110.

[21] McPherson, *The Weir*, 13.

22 Ien Ang, *Watching Dallas: Soap Opera and the Melodramatic Imagination* (London: Routledge, 1996): 121.

23 However, it would be fair to surmise that this pub would be more inclined to show GAA (a community based organization) football matches if anything, given the privileging of the rural and the local over the urban in the play as well as the strong links between the pub and masculinity. That is not to say that women do not attend or watch GAA football matches but that attendances at GAA matches are still dominated by men. See www.gaa.ie [Accessed 28/06/11]

24 Sybil Taylor notes that women in the 1980s in Ireland were confined to the snug or the lounge part of the pub where a 'pint' would never be on offer to them, only a glass, as a pint was regarded as 'unfeminine.' See *The Life and Lore of Ireland Through its Pubs* (Harmondsworth: Penguin, 1983): 23.

25 See Cian Molloy, *The Story of the Irish Pub: An Intoxicating History of the Licensed Trade in Ireland* (Dublin: Liffey, 2002): 80-83.

26 Molloy, *The Story of the Irish Pub*, 80.

27 McPherson, *The Weir*, 52.

28 Kevin C. Kearns, *Dublin pub life and lore: An oral history* (Dublin: Gill and Macmillan, 1996): 3.

29 McPherson, *The Weir*, 21.

30 Nicholas Grene, 'Ireland in Two Minds: Martin McDonagh and Conor McPherson,' *The Yearbook of English Studies*, 35 (2005): 298-311: 303.

31 Jordan, 'Pastoral Exhibits,' 356.

32 McPherson, *The Weir*, 13.

33 Roland, Barthes, *Camera Lucida: Reflections on Photography*, Trans. Richard Howard (New York: Hill and Wang, 1981): 23-27.

34 Susan Sontag, *On Photography* (New York: Picador, 1977): 3.

35 The programme 'photoshop' can transpose, fade, crop, reduce, highlight and/or superimpose objects and particular images in a photograph in various ways. Also the ways in which images are arranged can influence how the viewer sees the photos.

36 Sontag, *On Photography*, 4.

37 Ricoeur, *Hermeneutics and the Human Sciences*, 142-143.

38 Martin Heidegger, *Being and Time*. Trans. E. Robinson and J. Macquarrie, (New York: Harper, 1962):135-148.

39 Sara Keating, *The Irish Times*.

40 Roche, *Contemporary Irish Theatre*,227.

41 Ricoeur, *Time and Narrative*, 95-120.

42 McPherson, *The Weir*, 59.

43 *ibid.*, 58.

44 *ibid.*, 41.

45 *ibid.*, 44.

46 *ibid.*, 45.

47 *ibid.*, 59.

48 *ibid.*, 60.
49 *ibid.*, 60.
50 *ibid.*, 60.
51 Martin Heidegger, *Being and Time*, 139.
52 Jordan, 'Pastoral Exhibits,' 355.
53 *The Weir*, 44.
54 *ibid.*, 74.

13 | 'Stumbling around in the light': Conor McPherson's partial eclipse.

Ashley Taggart

'I was one of those guys who stumbled around in the dark for a long time. Not that I'm stumbling around in the light now.'
Conor McPherson Interview: Jan 13 2008 *Chicago Tribune*

Just over half an hour into his 2009 feature film, *The Eclipse*, occurs a scene where the protagonist of the piece, Michael Farr, a woodwork teacher who has volunteered his services as a driver during the Cobh literary festival, is driving one of the guest writers – Lena Morelle – back to her house. She has had a difficult day and has drunk too much wine, but as they drive through the dusk, along a cliff-top road, she suddenly becomes aware of the beauty unfolding in front of her, the luminous, heavy clouds, and the shimmer of evening light on the water. She asks Michael if it would be ok if they stopped. He agrees. They get out of the car, and Lena strides away, merely a silhouette now, over the grass towards the edge of the cliff. Michael becomes increasingly disconcerted, worried that in her slightly inebriated state, and in the murk, she might fall.

> **MICHAEL:** Be careful there, Miss Morelle. Be careful there, Lena. Be careful – don't – you don't want to get too close to the edge, Lena – careful . (Michael rushes after her, gesturing for her to return. But it is so dark he fails to see a hole in front of him, and with a roar, he disappears into it.)
> **LENA:** (Turning back, and rushing to his aid) Oh my God! Oh my God! (she reaches him) Oh my God – are you all right? (she laughs.) Oh my God! Are you alright? (she reaches out her hand to help him up)
> **MICHAEL:** (groaning) Jesus Christ!

LENA: Are you ok?
MICHAEL: I think so ...
LENA: Nothing broken?
MICHAEL: (*groans*)
LENA: Oh my God!

Fade up soundtrack – Kyrie Eleison. The two of them hobble to a bench, and sit silently looking out over the sea in the gathering darkness. CUT TO – shot of a full moon, which is now visible.

In some ways, this little scene – darkly comic in multiple senses of the word – is an aside from the main thrust of the plot, which centres on Michael's grief for his dead wife, and an unfolding, messily unfulfilled love triangle between himself, Lena, and Nicholas Holden, another guest writer at the festival. Yet, for anyone who has read any of the interviews given by McPherson over the last decade, it is hard not to sense a deeper resonance.

Challenged by journalists over his predilection for the supernatural, his ongoing fascination with ghosts, vampires and the paranormal, McPherson propounds a theory which serves to situate him within a cultural and historical tradition. He makes the case that these are *Irish* preoccupations, not merely personal ones.

In a UCD *Connections* interview with Dave Fanning, he couches this in terms of 'the beyond,' adding,

> My theory about the Irish psyche, is that Ireland, being the most Western point of Europe beside the Atlantic ocean – for thousands and thousands of years, nobody knew, in Europe, perhaps, that there was anything else beyond that ... we were the place that was 'right beside the beyond,' and I think, somehow we internalized that in quite an anxious way.[1]

He reiterates this a year later – extending it into an explanation of superstition:

> I have a theory about Ireland, being at the edge of Europe,' says the playwright and filmmaker in a telephone interview. 'For 1,000 years, people didn't know what was beyond. But we thought about it – a lot. And that 'beyond' became internalized in our psyche. And then Catholicism took hold – and it was a superstitious religion with ghostly imagery. There's something in our culture that makes us connect with that.'[2]

One of McPherson's consistent talents is to explore such monolithic themes with a light touch. Later, when Lena and Michael talk about what happened, it is the absurdity of the situation that comes to the fore.

> **LENA:** (laughs) I was just thinking about when you fell in that hole – you completely disappeared. (*Laughs*) I'm sorry.
> **MICHAEL:** I'm glad somebody's amused, I nearly broke me fuckin' arse.

Watching Lena and Michael blundering around in the gloom, peering out over the sea, in their own slightly farcical version of 'right beside the beyond' seems like a dramatization of this notional confrontation with the unknown. And, sure enough, the voice of reason – in this case, Michael – urging caution, fearful of an accident, is the voice that is suddenly reduced to inarticulate groans by an ironic pratfall. The message is unambiguous. Faced with the ineffable, our faculty of reason will always show a comic deficit.

Watching the scene, this point comes across clearly, but it is only by transcribing the dialogue that another element, also alluded to by McPherson in his interviews, emerges. In the space of a few moments 'God' is invoked five times, and 'Christ' once, whilst in his soundtrack McPherson chooses to fade up a 'Kyrie Eleison' on the final moments: 'Lord, have mercy.' It seems that human beings, confronted with 'the beyond,' cannot help but revert to their 'superstitious religion,' in extremis, and in the absence of anything else.

The scene is concluded with a shot of the full moon – given the title of the film, surely McPherson's way of underscoring the significance of this little episode, letting the audience know that, slight though it seems, it is freighted with meaning. This is one of only two occasions in the film where he chooses to drop in an image of the moon, the other being about half an hour later when Michael is secreted up in his attic, trying to write, trying to express what he is going through. In frustration, he scores out what he has written, and looks up to see a photograph of his dead wife. Cut to a shot of the full moon. The reason this is an important juncture is that, over the past few days, Michael, whether he wants to admit it or not, has been growing closer to Lena. This is the crucial emotional journey in the film – Michael's journey, away from his dead wife, and towards Lena.

But Michael's transition is a difficult one, fraught with fears and anxieties. At one point, in a confessional moment in Lena's house, just before the arrival of a very drunk Nicholas, he discusses one of the most poignant: the fear that you will forget the person you loved.

> **MICHAEL:** ... you're terrified of forgetting that person. Even the pain – you're afraid that if you let go ...
> **LENA:** You'll lose them.

Watching the unfolding story of *The Eclipse*, however, this seems far from likely. All of the central characters are haunted. Michael by his dead wife, and by his father-in-law Malachy, Malachy by the loss of his daughter, Nicholas by the memory of his one-night-stand with Lena and Lena by the ghost of a girl she saw in Italy, and by the memories of her son who has just left home. Indeed, throughout the film, the absent and the dead seem to superimpose themselves upon the present and the living.

When it opened, the film was generally well received. But it is fair to say it was always dogged by the issue of genre, to the extent that, early on, some potential backers turned down the opportunity to invest in it. Is this a ghost story containing a love story, or a love story which happens to contain some ghosts? McPherson himself has described the film in terms of a 'melding of genres.' It is notable that Billy Roche's original piece, *Table Manners*, on which the film is (very loosely) based, eschews all supernatural elements.

McPherson in his dual role of co-writer/director refuses to be bound by genre conventions – indeed wants to challenge them, and put the audience on the 'back-foot' from the outset. Take the opening sequence. In film, these few minutes are typically used to announce key themes, point us towards the rules of *this* particular game, invoke images that will frame the narrative to come. And here, what do we have? The initial shot is of an 18th century painting, a landscape, somewhat grimy and discoloured, but containing a seated figure who, looking down on the river valley below, seems to be painting it. Then we dissolve to a close-up of the man which reveals a quill pen in his hand. He is, we can now see, a writer, not a painter. We dissolve to another painting of the same era showing figures standing in a half-lit rural setting. Once more the overall impression of murk is enhanced by the oxidized paint, and the 'craquelure' of the varnish – so much so, that we can barely make out their faces. Then dissolve to yet another contemporaneous landscape, this time depicting three figures dwarfed by the countryside and the sky. Now when we cut in, we can discern that they are in fact two men and a woman.

Certainly, you might think, a strange, almost perverse, certainly anachronistic way to open a film set in modern Ireland, and, although there are elements which foreshadow the ensuing plot –

the writer observed, the potential triangle of two men and a woman, the visual emphasis on dusk, shadow, chiaroscuro – it deliberately undermines any expectation we may have of what is to come. The burning question is: why is this sequence here?

Even when the camera finally moves away from the bucolic world depicted on the canvas into 'real life,' what we are then given is an image which also seems to be from another era – a close-up of a taper lighting a candle. All of this creates a slightly uncomfortable feeling. It is as if we have fallen into another time – are somehow watching the 'wrong' film. This sense of discomfort sits well with McPherson's paranormal ambitions for the rest of the piece – priming us for the fact that, in the world he is about to depict, time will not flow smoothly, but turn back on itself, the temporal plane will reveal holes and gaps, ruptures, lacunae. After all, what is a ghost but a person who has somehow fallen out of their time, into ours? What is grieving but the intrusive irruption of the past into the present?

Here, it is only, finally, when the camera pans back from the candle to reveal the woman lighting it, and the contemporary dining room in which it is sitting, that we can, in any way, begin to get our bearings as an audience. Even then, to push home the point, McPherson chooses to end this opening montage with a time-lapse shot of guests arriving (materializing) as if from nowhere, into the room.

There are at least two other occasions in the film where we seem to experience a precipitous 'drop' into another time. One occurs shortly after Michael has taken Lena home and gently put her to sleep on the sofa. We then follow Nicholas in a montage that shows him bedding one of the hotel maids (all the while checking his mobile phone for messages from Lena). Abruptly, we cut to a shot of a bouquet of flowers by a window. A woman in period costume enters the frame, we follow her and pan back, revealing the servants kitchen, as she brings a taper to light a lamp. This is clearly a reprise of the opening sequence, but this time, we are not instantly 'restored' to the present, but instead follow her with steady-cam down a dark hallway and up into the ground floor of a stately home – it appears that, here , we are truly in the past. The illusion is only, belatedly, broken when she enters through double doors to reveal the Cobh 'writer's dinner' in full swing.

The third and final 'drop' happens after Lena and Michael have visited the ruined Abbey, and are clearly becoming more intimate –

we see them on the lawn of a stately home, with 'servants' in period livery bringing them drinks.

In each case the sudden temporal shift causes momentary disorientation in the viewer and a heightened awareness that the surface of the story (with its neatly chronological unfolding) is itself an artifice, created on the page and in the editing suite. In this disturbed world temporal 'slippage' can occur in many ways – so that, for example, Michael can be haunted by the ghost of someone (Malachy) who hasn't even the decency to be dead yet.

As if to embody the point visually, we see Michael slipping and falling on several occasions. The first, as mentioned, on the cliff. The second when he marches into Malachy's room in the old people's home, determined to confront him at last, slips in a pool of blood and shockingly crashes to the ground.

> **MICHAEL**: Jesus Christ! (*looks about him in horror, and at the blood on his hands*). (*Fade up choral soundtrack – 'Agnus Dei'*)

We, like Michael, are made to feel in these instances that we have somehow 'disappeared into a hole' in our understanding. Events seem to fly in the face of any attempt to reason them away. Tellingly (in one of the few moments in the film where we feel ourselves being led by the nose) Lena's response to seeing the ghost of a little girl is to study 'theoretical physics' –presumably to try and gain some kind of understanding of a subject which also defies everyday logic – where a particle can be in two spaces at the one time, and where space and time resolve into a continuum. McPherson notes:

> Like most of us, I find that life is a supernatural experience. We live in a mysterious environment that we don't understand. We are told that the universe is infinite. Time is relative. If you speed up, time slows down. Those things are bewildering.[3]

The film is full of examples of people being in the right place at the wrong time and vice versa. Michael is meant to pick up Lena at the train station and misses her. He also misses Nicholas Holden, who is, typically, furious. It is probably no coincidence here that the word 'eclipse' is taken from the Greek, meaning 'fail to appear.'

On the other hand, Malachy, who should be safely ensconced in a home, repeatedly 'appears' as a malign apparition in Michael's house, just as Michael unintentionally terrifies Lena, by suddenly appearing in her house with a welcome hamper. Later, after Michael has returned home late from driving her, he discovers that his son has 'disappeared,' and goes in frantic search of him. If the temporal plane is disrupted here, so too is the spatial, with various forms of dislocation wreaking havoc on the character's lives. Consequently everyone ends up leaving phone messages – Nicholas (increasingly needy) for Lena; Malachy for Michael, and finally (movingly) Lena for Michael – after she has returned to London and persuaded him to let her see his writing.

> **LENA:** (*on phone message in Michael's car*) Thanks for your stories – they're great ... and I hope you don't mind but I showed them to my friend Maurice Bowman, at a dinner-party I had here the other night, ... he publishes mystery ... supernatural stuff ... he really liked them, they really are beautifully written ... and I thought, if you ever wanted me to put you in contact ... If you're ever coming to London ... I'd love to, I'd love to meet up again. I hope everything is going well for you, and you're not being too harassed by – by life ... call me.

And of course, a phone message is itself a kind of ghostly manifestation – an 'absent presence' with a claim on our attention and our time.

The sense of dislocation and disorientation is pervasive. So, for instance, Lena complains bitterly about her accommodation ('Where have they put me?') which even requires a ferry journey to the festival venue, whilst, in a telling scene at the ruined Abbey, Michael and Lena discuss the future and the past in terms that conflate spatial and temporal distance, the living and the dead, and the restlessness of the human spirit.

> **LENA:** Do you ever imagine your name on a gravestone.
> **MICHAEL:** I don't have to imagine – my parents are buried here. (*speaking of his parents*).
> She was crazy about him, but he was always looking over the next hill, you know?
> **LENA:** (*pensive*) Mmmm.
> **MICHAEL:** You were about to say men are always looking over the next hill.
> **LENA:** No, no ... I was going to ask you if this is the place your wife was buried, and then I thought it might be too personal.
> **MICHAEL:** No ... she's ah, she's somewhere else. (*pause*)
> Have you never come close to tying the knot yourself?
> **LENA:** No, no, I'm a complete disaster ... Not that I haven't had a few offers.
> **MICHAEL:** I'm sure you have.
> (*Sudden thunder and heavy downfall of rain – as they flee for cover, we see his wife's grave. Michael has lied.*)

McPherson conjures up, in just a few lines, a topography of desire and loss, where both craving and mourning are visualized as, respectively, 'over the next hill,' or 'somewhere else.' It is clear too that he chose the location of the film – Cobh – because, in addition to the looming presence of St Colman's Cathedral, it offered opportunities to see the characters ascending and descending stairs, steps, hills, as the narrative line dictates. He has cited *The Exorcist* (1973) as a major influence – another film which deploys the vertical plane to great effect. To take just two of many examples, when Lena finally tells him about her encounter with a ghost, she and Michael are walking down a long flight of steps heading underground, from sunlight into shade (quite literally). And in perhaps his most nightmarish vision of Malachy (in the cupboard) the older man tries to haul Michael downwards into the darkness.

But looked at from another angle, Michael Farr is already dead – his name already carved on the headstone. This name is also a pointer – Michael is in some senses 'far gone' from life – psychologically inhabiting the world of the shades, unable to let go of his wife's presence. It is becoming clear by this point in the film that Lena's function is to bring him back – to return this particular Orpheus from the underworld. Even so, at this stage he cannot quite bear to have Lena and Eleanor (notice that his wife's name 'contains' Lena's) knowingly inhabit the same space/time – he cannot quite face up to the fact that he is 'moving on' from his grief.

During the entire course of the film the themes of haunting and writing interweave and feed one another. So, the scene above, touching on Michael's dead wife, is cued up by a discussion about his writing.

> **LENA:** Tell me Michael, what do you write?
> **MICHAEL:** I don't write, I'm a wood work teacher.
> **LENA:** Someone was telling me you write.
> **MICHAEL:** Who?
> **LENA:** It was just someone, earlier.
> **MICHAEL:** I used to mess around a bit when I was younger – like a lot of people ... No I don't write.
> **LENA:** What did you write then, stories?
> **MICHAEL:** Yeah.

When Nicholas ('the ego has landed') Holden, finally manages to meet up with Lena – he speaks to her about their previous entanglement in supernatural terms. She is already wary, having listened to the obsessive messages from him on her phone. For

Nicholas, the 'afterlife' of their brief affair has permeated his entire being and, specifically, his writing.

> **LENA:** 'I've just been listening to all of your messages ...
> **NICHOLAS:** 'I'm haunted by that night – you should see the shit I've been writing since that night... I mean, it made me question what I've been doing all my life....I'm a fake, a miserable fake, and the dishonesty has to end. I'm going to tell my wife I don't really love her – and you're to blame ...
> **LENA:** We don't really know each other.
> **NICHOLAS:** ... Past lives, we've been here before. You brought out a gentleness in me that I thought was dead, gone.'

In some ways, Nicholas is the photographic negative of Michael. Where Nicholas tries to sell Lena the impression of a fake resurrection, a false rebirth, and lay it at her door, Michael almost unwittingly edges towards the real thing. So desperate is Nicholas for connection with Lena that he even, spuriously, appeals to the notion of 'past lives' in an effort to bind her to him – cynically tapping into another kind of temporal 'overlay' for his own ends.

McPherson hints at this antithetical relationship between the two men in some of the interviews he has given: 'Nicolas is running away from his wife. Michael is trying to find his wife. She is gone forever, of course. In a funny way, they are joined up like that. But they are going in opposite directions. It is kind of funny.'[4]

Although the film is about universal themes – loss, redemption – it is also, crucially, about writers and, I would contend, about the act of writing itself. After all, the three central figures are writers, even though Michael is reluctant to admit as much, and all three of them are haunted, even tormented by the need to express what they are feeling in words. The essential mysteriousness of the process of writing – the fact that it originates outside of our conscious rational control, is something McPherson has discussed over the years in terms which resonate strongly with some of the key themes in *The Eclipse*. McPherson contends that plays come 'very much from the unconscious for me': adding, 'I describe it as coming from the body and your brain is catching up.' Writing is not, for him, a matter of choice. 'If I wasn't plagued by needing to write things,' he muses, 'that would perhaps be a blessing.'[5]

Occasionally he even extends the analogy, making explicit the (for him) 'paranormal' basis of the act of writing:

> It's like getting rid of demons, like an exorcism of what's been preoccupying you for a long time...[6]

Here, the urge to write, and the consequent 'images in (my) brain' have become a form of possession. At this juncture, McPherson's predilection for the occult, and some of his more extreme statements, 'Life is a supernatural experience'[7] and, 'All of life is a paranormal experience,'[8] perhaps become more comprehensible.

Over and over again, McPherson discusses the unconscious, re: creativity, in terms which explicitly echo his attitude to 'the unknown,' 'the supernatural.' Certainly, he exhibits a heightened awareness of internal division (between the conscious and the unconscious mind, the brain and the body, 'appetites' and 'thoughts') which mirrors a perceived *external* division between the knowable and the unknowable in the world at large. For instance:

> ... human beings are animals: 90% of our behaviour is animal behaviour, and we've just got this 10% veneer, the semblance of civilized, rational choice. Our thoughts are always trailing around after our appetites, justifying them with language: it's tragic and it's hilarious.[9]

Put like this, you could almost say the conscious mind, the linguistic mind, resembles one of McPherson's ghosts, appearing hopelessly out of its time, as a *post hoc* manifestation of the ego, desperate to make sense of circumstances it can barely comprehend. Thoughts 'trail around after appetites,' like a love-sick soul (like Nicholas after Lena, or Michael after Eleanor).

Let's look briefly at Lena's description of the mental disjuncture that occurs at the instant of seeing a ghost. She is giving a public reading from her work – a book which (as if to underline the fact that this film is *about writing*) is itself entitled *The Eclipse*. On separate occasions we see Michael, and then Nicholas, clutching a copy.

> When you see a ghost, something very interesting happens Your brain splits in two – one side of you is rejecting what you are seeing because it doesn't tally with our ordinary idea of reality, and the other side is screaming that this is for real. In that moment reality itself is collapsed and reconfigured in a way that changes you profoundly, although at the time you're not aware of it.

The encounter precipitates a painful sense of fracture, of the breakdown of unitary conscious awareness, when 'reality itself is collapsed and reconfigured in a way that changes you profoundly, although at the time you're not aware of it.' In a neat, reflexive *coup*, this latter phrase encapsulates the entire narrative arc of the very film we are watching at the moment we hear it. In the course of *The Eclipse* (the film, that is) Michael's reality is 'collapsed and reconfigured' by the visitations and nightmares he experiences, and for him too, personal awareness lags some way behind unfolding events.

Incidentally, McPherson's powerful sense of internal schism, the 'dis-integrated self' is a major factor in his love of Beckett's work: 'I believe that his plays will continue to echo through time because he managed to articulate a feeling as opposed to an idea. And that feeling is the unique human predicament of being alive and conscious.'[10]

Notably, for him in this respect, feelings are 'opposed to' ideas. Beckett is praised for the attempt to convey the self in tatters.[11] As he says of *Waiting for Godot* later in the same article, 'There is no resolution in the traditional sense. But it's really a revolutionary play because it takes the human mind itself as its subject matter and brilliantly dramatizes it by splitting it in two... It presents the anxious, modern, divided self.'[12]

As for *Endgame* – the play McPherson directed on film – he describes it as not only an 'apocalyptic vision,' but as yet another 'moving picture of the human mind.' In the UCD interview, he brings up Beckett as a playwright who utilized extreme situations as a way to illuminate deep-seated antitheses in our being: 'The end of the world is such an interesting place to put characters – a lot of Beckett's plays seem to be about the end of the world – it pares everything down to the bone – it is people at their most animalistic – and also at their most human, ironically.'[13]

Oddly, it transpires that some of the most recent scientific attempts to understand 'the predicament of being alive and conscious' depend entirely on *theatrical* models. So Beckett's (and McPherson's) attempt to convey the fundamental experience of consciousness by means of theatre turns out to be strangely apt. Bernard J. Baars notes the so called 'Global Workspace Theory' begins from an experimental demonstration of the constraints upon consciousness. In this model the brain is envisaged as a stage, where the (severely curtailed) conscious mind is like a spotlight which can illuminate just a little of the circumambient darkness.[14]

A theatre combines a corral of (very limited) events taking place on stage in front of a vast audience, just as consciousness involves limited information that can create access to a vast number of unconscious sources of knowledge. Baars goes beyond advancing the theatrical analogy as one hypothesis amongst many, to boldly state that 'All of our unified models of mental functioning today are theatre metaphors; it is essentially all we have.'[15]

Our outer senses, inner senses and ideas all jostle and compete for access to the 'stage' of working memory, with its spotlight of consciousness, which is under voluntary control. The 'action' on the stage is then performed in front of a vast unconscious 'audience' of disposition, memory, inference and learned skills.

There is no space here to tease out the intriguing implications for theatre practice of this complex, subtle, model of mind – except to point to the fact that McPherson's 'right beside the beyond' and his (Beckettian) use of darkness, silhouette, the poorly seen and the half-visualized has a fascinating theoretical corollary.

Sufficient to say the writerly focus of *The Eclipse* extends into its filmic style – containing many scenes where the darkness appears to emanate from Michael (as indeed may his nightmarish 'visions') and where wide-shots are consistently used to imply that the characters are dwarfed by forces they cannot even begin to intuit. This is surely in keeping with both the ostensible theme of a man haunted by grief, and the implied one – the occult workings of the creative mind.

Looking back over this brief analysis of *The Eclipse*, we can now go some way to explaining McPherson's choice of shooting style, the inclusion throughout of looming unknowns, the largely religious soundtrack and focus on liminal scenes (clifftops, graveyards, windows and doors) even the love-triangle of writers, and the unusual 'melding' of horror and naturalism. These stylistic choices are all congruent with a work which projects supernatural mysteries onto creative ones.

And yet that bizarre series of landscape paintings at the opening still jars, its relevance uncertain, until the author reveals, in interview, that his next writing project immediately following this film, is to be ... a costume drama: 'I've started writing a new play – a period play – set in the 1830s in Ireland.'[16] And looking back to the very first shot – the very first landscape painting, in the film, it becomes clear that it is actually, if you look very carefully, the depiction not just of a river, but of a weir. Consistent to the end, and in a last piece of temporal sleight-of-hand, McPherson has secreted his own authorial past and future in the fine grain of his latest work.

Works Cited

Baars, Bernard J., 'Global Workspace Theory, A Rigorous Scientific Theory of Consciousness,'*Journal of Consciousness Studies*, 4.4, 1996: 292- 309.

Jones, Chris, 'Conor McPherson: The agony of conscious souls',http://leisureblogs.chicagotribune.com/the_theater_loop/20 08/01/conor-mcpherson.html [Accessed 10/1/2012]

Costa, Maddy, an interview with McPherson, Conor, 'Human beings are animals,' in *The Guardian*, *ttp://www.guardian.co.uk/stage/2006/sep/13/theatre4*

Fine, Marshall, an interview with Conor McPherson, 'Conor McPherson goes out on the edge with 'The Eclipse' http://hollywoodandfine.com/interviews/?p=675 [Accessed 10/1/2012]

Fanning, Dave, an interview with Conor McPherson, UCD *Connections*, November 2009, See http://www.youtube.com/watch?v=HwzUHtwgcbA

---

[1] Dave Fanning in an interview with Conor Mcpherson, UCD *Connections*, November 2009, Part 6 (Parts 1-7) See http://www.youtube.com/watch?v=HwzUHtwgcbA

[2] Marshall Fine, an interview with Conor McPherson, 'Conor McPherson goes out on the edge with 'The Eclipse' http://hollywoodandfine.com/-interviews/?p=675 [Accessed 10/1/2012]

[3] Movieweb.net interview, 'Ciaran Hinds and Conor McPherson Join Forces for *The Eclipse*' http://www.movieweb.com/news/exclusive-ciaran-hinds-and-conor-mcpherson-join-forces-for-the-eclipse [Accessed 10/1/2012]

[4] Movieweb.net interview, 'Ciaran Hinds and Conor McPherson Join Forces for *The Eclipse*'

[5] Maddy Costa, an Interview with Conor McPherson 'Human beings are animals,' in *The Guardian* *http://www.guardian.co.uk/stage/2006/sep/13/theatre4*

[6] Dave Fanning in an interview with Conor Mcpherson, Part 4.

[7] Interview: Extras, *Eclipse* DVD

[8] Interview Mar 25 2010 Lori Lander Murphy

[9] Maddy Costa, an Interview with Conor McPherson

[10] Maddy Costa, an Interview with Conor McPherson

[11] Witness, too, Nicholas' hilariously sophistical response to Lena's accusation: 'You told me that night that you and your wife were separated". To which he replies, "I've never been more separated than I was that night.'

[12] Maddy Costa, an Interview with Conor McPherson

---

[13] Dave Fanning in an interview with Conor Mcpherson Part 3

[14] See Bernard J. Baars, 'Global Workspace Theory, A Rigorous Scientific Theory of Consciousness,'*Journal of Consciousness Studies*, 4.4, 1996: 292- 309.

[15] *Baars,* 301.

[16] Dave Fanning in an interview with Conor McPherson, Part 6

14 | The Supernatural in Conor McPherson's *The Seafarer* and *The Birds* *

Christopher Murray

> I look down towards his feet, but that's a fable,
> If that thou be'st a devil, I cannot kill thee.
> --Shakespeare, *Othello* (5.2.287-88)

It may be considered inappropriate to begin an essay on McPherson with a reference to Shakespeare, and yet we are now being schooled to consider Shakespeare as interacting with the Irish writer.[1] Moreover, McPherson is a subtle writer to whom intertextuality is meat and drink. Arguably it is thus perfectly in order to take our position here from Othello's comment on Iago, the 'demi-devil' who has ensnared Othello's soul and body, if we are to inspect McPherson's concept of evil. This is the subject here.

Othello inspects Iago's feet to check if they are cloven in traditional style and then dismisses the notion and the semiotics: 'but that's a fable.' The ambiguity of 'fable' is significant. It can mean a false account in the way 'myth' is often employed, or it can denote 'story' qua narrative. Clearly, a story can be true (as in 'what's the story?,' asking for news, a factual account of experience) and in that

---

* A version of this article 'The Supernatural in Conor McPherson's *The Seafarer* and *The Birds*,' was first published in *The Binding Strength of Irish Studies. Festschrift in Honour of Csilla Bertha and Donald E. Morse*, eds. Marianna Gula, Mária Kurdi, István D. Rácz (Debrecen: Debrecen University Press, 2011): 66-77.

context story carries responsibility: there is no licence to mislead. It can be claimed as axiomatic in literary discourse that *fabula* is the basis of all western literature: from Homer's *Iliad* on, stories are to be read analogically as moral metaphors of the human condition. Roy Foster extends the claim by insisting that Irish history itself is a 'story' with the form and trappings of fiction: 'the formal modes of the *Bildungsroman*, ghost story, deliverance tale, family romance, all [...] have lent motifs to the ways Irish history has been told.'[2] Presumably, Foster accepts that such 'stories' as history adduces are attempts at truth-telling rather than the contrary. Consequently folklore, a specialized genre of Irish culture, may likewise be seen as forms of story (in oral form), usually archetypal and therefore international in currency, with a strong basis on truth. The devil, it may be said, holds a firm place in folklore. Othello is confused on this point when he dismisses the validity of fable when, earlier in the play, he had already outlined how he had won Desdemona's love by tales of wonder: tales so extravagant and fabulous that her father could only conceive of their effect as witchcraft. But this is what plays do with any audience: cast a spell so that the fabulous is believed. Othello's tragedy derives from his ignorance on this point. McPherson knows it so well that in play after play he tells what Yeats called 'an old wives' tale' in order to hold an audience spellbound while he relays an affecting truth.[3]

McPherson thinks allusively and analogically. He knows that ghost stories are and are not hokum: that they both hold the audience rapt – of *The Weir* (1997) for example – and at the same time offer entrance to the dark world of the Jungian unconscious and its disguised truths. 'For as long as I can remember I've always had an interest in Irish folklore.'[4] He built *The Weir* from bits and scraps of stories heard second-hand from his grandfather in Co. Leitrim. His practice, he has said in interview, is to write incrementally, seeing a story 'like a film' in which he tries to get the characters talking, saying 'something believable. [...] What they are talking about is moving from detail to detail, so I like those details to come organically.'[5] Tactfully, the emphasis is on simplicity, on making something that will entertain and in this process, 'when it is all mounted up, it is a barrage of experience.'[6] That seems to be the goal; to create unpretentiously and in a form not of ideas but of an absorbing story in which playing, playacting, and gamesmanship of various kinds offer actors and audience a shared world where make-believe is humanized and shades over into the uncanny. 'It just shows you that great theatre can come from anywhere. You just have to have heart.'7 This is a new departure in Irish drama, far less intense than Tom Murphy, far less implicated with poetic finesse than Brian Friel; perhaps only Enda Walsh among the new generation of dramatists shares McPherson's unusual combination of populism and pure theatricality, and Walsh seems closer in style to the absurdists (Genet in particular) of an earlier generation.

In line with McPherson's intense interest in play and playfulness, the card-game in *The Seafarer* (2006) forms the core of a shared experience where drink flows liberally and a good time is – up to a point – had by all. And as Pinter might say, that 'point' marks the reason the play was written in the first place. The point of *The Seafarer*, as I hope to show, is that good fellowship or ordinary humanity is more powerful in its frailty than the terrible representative of the forces of evil. To this end McPherson makes the setting approximate a pub: '*the grim living area of a* house' in Dublin that '*has morphed into a kind of bar in its appearance.*' The stage direction goes on: '*Those who live or pass through here are so immersed in pub culture that many artefacts in the room are originally from bars.*'8 We are returned to the setting of *The Weir*, a setting vital in every sense to McPherson's work. (There could be no *Dublin Carol* (2000) without a public house in the background any more than there could be a *Christmas Carol* [1843] without a ghost: both texts are haunted.) Yet McPherson's use of the pub as setting differs sharply from the traditional conventions on the Irish stage. In Synge's *Playboy of the Western World* (1907), which was the original play-in-a-pub, the setting was very rough, untidy, and, apart from the presence of Pegeen, Hogarthian in its satiric potential. The rake who makes his progress through this setting ultimately shows up its owners and clientele as corrupt and hypocritical. McPherson has no such moral ambition. On the contrary, he glories in the pub setting, seeing it as the abode of camaraderie and good cheer: the globalized Irish pub, in fact, much loved by the advertising industry. Yet this comparison may be misleading. The end of advertising is to sell a product, a particular brand. Although he does not despise the techniques of advertising, which have to be slick visually if they are to be efficient, McPherson's use of the Irish pub as setting is rather more subtle. He works to replicate the generation of warmth a pub (or more accurately the ideal pub) generates so that on stage this feeling extends to the audience and all share in this sense of bonhomie and companionship. The style of realism employed, never breaking the fourth wall and never overtly declaring a purpose, creates an environment within which all participants are democratized. What we witness here is the subversion of the kind of realism inaugurated by Gorky's *The Lower Depths* (1902).

For all this emphasis on pub culture and realism McPherson's work is surprisingly layered with the supernatural. *The Seafarer* goes further into what might be called 'iceman' territory than do McPherson's previous plays. The original iceman, in O'Neill's 1946 Pulitzer-prize winner *The Iceman Cometh*, is death. The inescapable reality of death and the challenge it issues to a delinquent man form O'Neill's central theme. Famously, in interview at the time of the première of his play O'Neill expanded his theme into a critique of the American pursuit of material success; America had sold its soul for profit. O'Neill's title parodied the description of the sudden 'coming of the Savior' to the wise and foolish virgins in the Bible, 'But at midnight there was a cry made, Behold the bridegroom cometh, catching the foolish ones off-guard and dooming them to destruction. Thus O'Neill's parodic saviour of the down-and-outs in a New York pub was "a messiah of death".'[9] O'Neill's pessimism led him to insist that hope is delusory. McPherson, on the other hand, is no pessimist. His Hickey figure, Mr Lockhart, while possessing the power to destroy is outwitted by the weak. This too is a spiritual statement.

In the published text of *The Seafarer* McPherson supplies a subtitle for act 1, *The Devil at Binn Eadair*. The description refers to the stranger at the Christmas card game, Mr Lockhart. *Binn Eadair* is the Gaelic name for Howth, north of Dublin city. In a note in the text on the setting, it is clear the play is actually set in Baldoyle, some way off but with a view of Howth Head, which 'Due to its prominence [...] has long been the focus of myths and legends.'[10] Mr Lockhart, although English, is referred to as staying at Howth so that he can be associated if not with ancient Irish legends then at least with folktales featuring the devil who joins a game of cards in search of a soul to take back to hell. As one folklorist testifies: 'The Devil is an important character, if not the leading one, in over thirty international tales told in Ireland.'[11] There is a whole section on 'the cardplayer with a cloven hoof,' in which 'some men, who are playing cards, are joined by a stranger; a card falls, and the player from whom it has fallen notices, when he tries to pick it up, that the stranger has cloven hooves.'[12] What happens next varies, but in some stories a priest is sent for and in the ensuing battle the devil is routed, in others the death of one card player (the subject of the story) occurs soon after the discovery. It may be said that the association of the devil with card playing, as with whiskey, derived from deep-rooted suspicion of pastimes which threatened the fulfilment of Christian duties within a believing community. Consequently, such stories were fundamentally cautionary tales. No less than forty-eight variants of the devil-as card-player legend exist, and in each there are five stages: meeting the devil; the game; the sighting of the cloven foot; the devil's departure; the effect of the incident on the house and those present.[13] McPherson is not too concerned about the morphology. In *The Seafarer* he skips the most dramatic moment of the story, the discovery of the cloven hoof. This is an inspired decision, partly because the cloven hoof would carry little impact for today's audience and mainly because in the play Mr Lockhart's identity remains a secret between him, Sharky, and eventually the audience. This sharing of vital information is a crucial factor in the feel-good effect of the play's ending.

In characterizing Sharky as the eponymous Seafarer McPherson deftly moves back in time to weave in a completely different source for the dramatic action, the tenth-century Anglo-Saxon poem 'The Seafarer,' a first-person narrative of a sailor's allegorical calling:

> ... my troubled home
> On many a ship has been the heaving waves,
> Where grim night-watch has often been my lot
> At the ship's prow as it beat past the cliffs.
> Oppressed by cold my feet were bound by frost
> In icy bonds, while worries simmered hot
> About my heart, and hunger from within
> Tore the sea-weary spirit ...[14]

McPherson quotes a few lines preceding these as epigraph to his text of the play. He would have been familiar with the Anglo-Saxon original from his study of English for his BA degree at University College Dublin. (As will be shown below, the play is also enriched by his knowledge of Christopher Marlowe's *Doctor Faustus* (c.1592).) The original Seafarer is a Christian archetype, his seafaring a symbol of the hard and lonely journey the individual must make toward salvation; he becomes McPherson's twenty-first-century Irish Sharky, former sailor, recently chauffeur, an eternal drifter who 'has a recklessness in his heart which is the undoing and ruination of his whole life.'[15] The situation McPherson creates focuses on the fate of this unpromising figure. The time chosen might have been

Hallowe'en or any other turning point in the old Celtic calendar but is in fact the great Christian moment, the eve of Christmas. The season gives warrant to alcoholic indulgence, which both establishes the mood of the play and, as stated already, involves the audience in empathy. But the alcoholic Sharky is not drinking, which isolates him and highlights his struggle to find a new life. During his time at home he cares for his older and recently blinded brother Richard, who plays irascible Hamm to his patient Clov. Thus the play astonishingly shifts its paradigm from Christian homiletic to high-modernist absurdist discourse.

When Mr Lockhart arrives towards the end of act 1 for the card game he is sharply distinguished from the rough company and surroundings by his tailoring; '*He is well-dressed with a camel hair Crombie overcoat, a silk scarf, a fine trilby hat and an expensive-looking suit. He looks like a wealthy businessman and bon viveur.*'[16] So should debt collectors always appear. In spite of this apparent class distinction, however, he is warmly welcomed into the gathering. He hides under cover of this hospitality until he can reveal himself privately to his victim: 'I'm the son of the morning, Sharky. I'm the snake in the garden. I've come here for your soul this Christmas.'[17] At this point, the pub-like atmosphere receives a chilling reduction.

The context of this situation, though secular, is nevertheless superficially religious. On the stairway down which Mr Lockhart arrives and by which he eventually leaves, is a small red lamp beneath an oleograph of the Sacred Heart of Jesus, a very common icon in Irish homes up to the 1960s and 1970s but rarely seen nowadays. In the play the red light flickers uncertainly at times and is set to rights by a slight tap from Sharky, a little piece of stage trickery (from Sean O'Casey's *Juno and the Paycock*) that amusingly draws attention to the divine presence and its unsteady influence. Here McPherson's attitude to moribund Irish Catholicism is interesting. He sees something 'very beautiful' in its doctrine of forgiveness and redemption while also ruefully recognizing this attitude as 'kind of the culture of the hangover.'[18] It is the Catholicism, he says, which makes his plays Irish, especially the notion of 'the spiritual world somehow being more real than the material world.'[19] Elsewhere McPherson says: 'I think that Christianity (and particularly Catholicism) took root so well in Ireland because we are a superstitious race. Our superstition is embedded in ancient knowledge and rituals which echo dimly through time but always catch our ear.'[20] It could be Yeats speaking. (Is there a medium in the house?)

The social context, however, is unusual so far as folktales are concerned. In the traditional devil-as-card-player tale the location tends to be higher-class. In no fewer than eighteen variants the setting is a Big House, representative of the landed class.[21] The most infamous of these was the Hellfire Club on the Dublin-Wicklow border, from which McPherson drew inspiration:

> I first heard the story of the Hellfire Club as a young boy. This story concerns an eighteenth century ruin in the Wicklow mountains where young landowning aristocrats would carouse and gamble. One stormy night, the Hellfire members were having a game of poker [*sic*] at their remote den when a stranger arrived at the door asking shelter. The stranger was brought inside and invited to join the card-players.[22]

This version continues in the usual detail, and when the stranger's cloven hoofs are discovered he 'disappeared in a thunderclap – for he was really the devil.' McPherson confesses that though 'intriguing' the story was 'always [...] mildly disappointing' to him because 'it seemed to end just as the scene was set.'[23] Clearly, the final stages of the story, the devil's disappearance and the effects on the household, offered McPherson the most interest and together formed the challenge of the play he was to write.

He is too shrewd a writer to plunge headfirst into an Irish folktale along the lines of an Abbey playwright from the 1950s, Michael J. Molloy for example. I would argue that Beckett's *Endgame*, instead, gave him the hint he needed to convert the folktale into a contemporary exploration of the nature of good and evil in entertaining style. He had directed *Endgame* for Michael Colgan's season of Beckett productions at the Gate theatre, Dublin, in 1999, and later directed the film version. 'I just wanted to make sure it was funny because, if it was funny, it could be understood. It's a comedy, a bittersweet comedy.'[24] Reference has already been made to the resemblance between the blind Richard and his brother Sharky who serves him, and Beckett's blind Hamm and his servant (possibly his son) Clov. This is a start. But for McPherson there is more to *Endgame* than brotherly love-hate. He sees Beckett turning here 'to an examination of human morals' and sees *Endgame* 'as a moving picture of the human mind—only this time [as distinct from what happens in *Waiting for Godot*] it's what happens in the mind when we think about other human beings. The characters are racked with notions of responsibility and our desire to be free of it.'[25] Set in a basement resembling the bunker in which *Endgame* is played out, *The Seafarer* transforms a traditional Irish folktale into an accessible and compassionate fable about human survival.

It is time now to focus on the theme of evil addressed in the play. In Christian doctrine, evil began with Lucifer's revolt in heaven. In Milton's *Paradise Lost* God says of Lucifer: 'I made him just and right, / Sufficient to have stood, though free to fall,'[26] implying that God himself created the possibility of evil, which he foreknew. When Milton's Satan (that is, the fallen Lucifer) sees God's new creatures Adam and Eve in their terrestrial paradise he is overcome by dismay, remorse, and despair, leading him to cry out: 'Which[ever] way I fly is Hell; myself am Hell' and since in revenge against God he dedicates himself to evil by wrecking the happy state of humanity: 'Evil, be thou my good.'[27] When Mr Lockhart speaks alone a second time with Sharky, during time out in the card game, he describes hell to him in terms that seem to coincide with Milton's as a state of exclusion from the joys of human companionship, a profound loneliness and 'self-loathing' born of the knowledge that 'there truly is no one to love you,' not even God himself.[28] Hell is to be 'locked in a space that's smaller than a coffin. And lying a thousand miles down, under the bed of a vast, icy, pitch-black sea' unable to die.[29] It is the original Seafarer's worst nightmare, from which he is saved by his steadfast faith in God. McPherson's notion of evil in the modern world is more persuasive than that of Terry Eagleton in his recent book on the subject. To the latter evil is 'supremely pointless. Anything as humdrum as a purpose would tarnish its lethal purity.'[30] Rather, he argues, 'It involves a megalomaniac overvaluing of the self, and an equally pathological devaluing of it.'[31] He distinguishes evil (rare) from wickedness (common enough) and finds it difficult to believe that evil *per se* actually exists, since it is 'an extremely powerful argument against the existence of God.'[32] Moreover, hell is a place of obscene enjoyment and he is inclined 'to believe that the devil is a Frenchman.'[33] Can he have been misled by Shaw's hell scene in *Man and Superman* (1903)?

McPherson's play finds its resolution by an altogether different metaphysic than Eagleton's. It can be taken for granted that McPherson's characters are all 'wicked' to a man (there are no women in the play, and when mentioned they are trouble-makers): this is a play about sinners, but lovable sinners who share friendship within that happy metaphor addressed earlier as the Irish pub culture. No evil exists among these brothers and friends. There is no Stanley Kowalski at this poker night, and so no need to depend on the kindness of strangers. Indeed, it is the stranger who is evil, that is, bringing extreme ill-will to bear on others, specifically on Sharky. It is significant that Mr Lockhart hates music and cannot abide a 'sing-along' in a pub.[34] Act 2 of the text is subtitled *Music in the Sun*, which relates to the major speech Mr Lockhart makes to Sharky indicating its association with heaven: 'At a certain point each day, music plays. It seems to emanate from the very sun itself. Not so much a tune as a heartbreakingly beautiful vibration in the sunlight shining on and through all the souls. It's so moving you wonder how you could ever have doubted anything.'[35] To him now all music is 'just ugly noise,'[36] whereas to the foolish Ivan, the play's antihero, such a thing is inconceivable and to Sharky the gift in the post of compact discs of music is a powerful sign of hope. All literature from Plato to Thomas Mann has made music vital to the health of the soul. To Shakespeare, 'The man that hath no music in himself, / Nor is not moved with concord of sweet sounds, / Is fit for treasons, stratagems, and spoils, / [...] Let no such man be trusted.'[37] Consequently, his hatred of music marks the inhumanity of Mr Lockhart and the necessity that he be defeated and driven off.

Here the card game is decisive, but it is the gormless Ivan's role in the final hand that delivers the surprise coup de grace. It is, of course, also a barefaced coup de théâtre. The purblind Ivan, Richard's helper in reading the cards, finally finds his lost spectacles and discovers that he and Richard have the winning hand after all. The cheater is thus cheated by the fool. This too in Shakespearean, where from *Much Ado about Nothing* to *King Lear* wisdom is often given to fools while kings and governors fail to see the obvious. Against all the rules of the bigger game, the battle between good and evil, Ivan wins the day. In folklore the devil may be driven off but he is never outwitted. In the only other modern Irish version of this story, Benedict Kiely's novel *The Cards of the Gambler* (1953) the protagonist tries hard to beat the devil but in the end must die.

The originality of *The Seafarer* lies in the working out of the paradox that in spiritual matters the loser wins. McPherson's idea is rooted in St Augustine concerning the human longing for eternity: 'we are part of eternity, we have lost and won the battle.'[38] This idea can only be theatrically convincing if the characters on stage, apart from Mr Lockhart, are all in their different way losers and the audience is drawn to their side to glory in the victory of the feeble.

The metaphysic is summed up in the comment: 'Once the show starts, you have to keep the love flowing.'[39] The effect of the devil's defeat, as he goes off, is boldly signified by the coming back on of the lamp under the Sacred Heart picture and the communication of the sense that all may yet be well. Richard, ignorant, of course, of the real nature of Sharky's release, urges him to 'buck up,' adding 'Do you hear me? We all know you're an alcoholic and your life is in tatters and you're an awful fucking gobshite. We know all that. But you know what? You're alive, aren't you? (*Beat.*) Aren't you?.'[40] And as a new dawn breaks on this particular Christmas Day, Ivan puts on some music while the sunlight begins to pour in.

The Birds

Something inherent in the denouement of *The Seafarer,* which played at the Abbey Theatre from 26 April to 7 June 2008 before touring to Galway, Cork, and Letterkenny, may have led McPherson to attempt an adaptation of Daphne du Maurier's short story 'The Birds' for the Dublin Theatre Festival in 2009, and to follow that with an adaptation of Billy Roche's story 'Table Manners' as a television play, *Eclipse,* (2009) (screened 17 March 2010 by RTE), which he co-wrote and directed. Each of these adaptations suggests that McPherson is moving closer to an exploration of evil via stories of the paranormal. It needs to be emphasized that Billy Roche's original story, published in the collection *Tales from Rainwater Pond* (2006), has no supernatural features whereas *Eclipse,* which deals with a man's trauma following the death of his wife, includes her ghost and some Gothic horrors. In McPherson's adaptation it is as if the central character, Michael Carr, is himself 'eclipsed' in an uncanny way from the sustaining power of love.

On the face of it, *The Birds*, directed by McPherson for its premiere at the Gate Theatre on 29 September 2009, is a puzzling experiment. Du Maurier's story, first published in 1952, gains its effect mainly from the sharp discrepancy between the specific realism of hero Nat Hocken's Robinson-Crusoe-like practicality and the birds' inexplicable attack on his house, family, and property. The fable has a rationality which McPherson turns into a post-apocalyptic nightmare. Du Maurier is at pains to locate the 'madness' which seizes the birds on a specific day, 3 December, in a literal 'cold war' atmosphere of unnaturally bitter weather.[41] The seagulls sit on the sea in huge numbers 'like a mighty fleet at anchor, waiting on the tide,'[42] or rising like airplanes 'spreading out in huge formation across the sky'[43] before making for 'their target,'[44] when 'with each dive, they became bolder.'[45] Much emphasis is placed on the complacency of the population. Nat Hocken alone is quick enough to literally put his house in order to withstand the siege, so that he can say proudly to his wife: 'we're snug and tight, like an air-raid shelter.'[46] At first the national radio broadcasts soothing advice to all (British) citizens but after a time the radio falls silent and Nat realizes 'we've got to depend upon ourselves.'[47] The story becomes one of individual human survival against invasion from the air. At its end, the siege continues, with Nat wondering in awe at 'this instinct to destroy mankind with all the deft precision of machines.'[48] McPherson radically changed this 1950s existentialism to something much more vague, nightmarish, and postmodern.

McPherson's Nat is no Robinson Crusoe. He is not even a Hemingwayesque shadow of Crusoe, the dogged monarch of all he surveys. He is a man on the run from life. He takes shelter in an abandoned house with a woman (Diane) he met on the road and together they try to survive against inner as much as outer onslaughts that are psychological and metaphysical rather than realistic. This play is a new departure for McPherson. He moves from the playfulness and pub culture underpinning *The Seafarer* to a strange, entirely serious and rather Gothic exploration of evil. It is as if, brooding again on Mr Lockhart's speech on loss of God in act 2 of *The Seafarer* McPherson had been moved to venture further, to bring together his thoughts on breakdown, failure, self-love and dread without the support and comfort of a social community; to consider as it were Clov's afterlife had he indeed left the managed interior of *Endgame* for the terrible world outside, only to discover ... what? That he was wrong in declaring '[t]here's no more nature'?.[49] That, in fact, nature was all too much in evidence, taking its revenge in some terrible way? Perhaps. But certainly, so far as du Maurier's fable is concerned, McPherson decided to dramatize not so much the urgency of the situation of invasion as the horror of tragic upheaval and human ultimacy.

Side-stepping Alfred Hitchcock's 1963 film version in *The Birds* (screenplay by Evan Hunter), which merely sensationalized the meaninglessness of the upheaval in nature by representing the birds apocalyptically 'as a perverse ode to woman's sexual glamour,'[50] McPherson addressed the fable metaphysically. He prefaces the typescript of *The Birds*[51] with two epigraphs, one classical, the other biblical. These quotations serve to frame the play in religious terms.

The first epigraph reads: 'I am the eye with which the Universe / Beholds itself, and knows it is divine,' and is derived from Shelley's short poem 'Song of Apollo' (1820) in which the god debates with Pan and asserts his supremacy as daily bringer of light and harmony to the earth.[52] As in Greek tragedy, Apollo is celebrated in Shelley's poem as the opponent of Dionysus, albeit in the debased form of Pan. Well in advance of Nietzsche Shelley understood the birth of tragedy and its roots in a specific dialectic. Order and harmony are fundamental to the universe and any denial admits the Dionysian chaos. Paradoxically, for the artistic form and beauty of tragedy both Apollo and his counterpart are necessary, which is why audiences vicariously enjoy the spectacle of suffering (evil) on a stage. In the lyric form, which 'Song of Apollo' takes, this paradox is not present; but it is in Shelley's *Prometheus Unbound*. The lyric rests content with its participation in Shelley's 'Defence of Poetry' – i.e. generically the literary arts – as socially indispensable. McPherson's other epigraph is from Genesis 2: 16-17 and reads:

> Then the Lord God placed the man in the Garden of Eden to cultivate it and guard it. He said to him, 'You may eat the fruit of any tree in the garden except the tree that gives knowledge of what is good and what is bad. You must not eat that fruit of that tree; if you do, you will die the same day.[53]

Thus we are presented with two voices of divinity, one asserting the god Apollo's gift to mankind in the form of self-recognition, the other offering a qualification upon human freedom, backed up by a stern warning in the case of non-compliance. The Old Testament quotation emphasizes the consequence of transgression and implies that some forms of knowledge are poison. It would appear that McPherson does not wish to privilege one epigraph over the other. When we put the two together they form a dialogue on universal law. It is at once the law of the ecosystem and the moral law. The du Maurier story is reinterpreted as 'hell,' a representation of what happens after humanity abandons Apollo's way / God's law. It is not the birds who are to blame, for they are only symptoms of upheaval, but (inclusively) mankind. The epigraph from Genesis reinforces this interpretation, formulating the traditional suspicion of science (*scientia*, knowledge) widely invoked in English Renaissance drama. Thus that ambivalent fable, Marlowe's *Doctor Faustus* unites the Greek and the Christian warning in its concluding, moralistic speech after the devils have dragged Faustus into the hell-mouth:

> Cut is the branch that might have grown full straight,
> And burned is Apollo's laurel bough,
> That sometime [once] grew within this learned man.
> Faustus is gone. Regard his hellish fall.[54]

Marlowe, it is thought, was himself atheistic and used the stage to mock the Christian belief in hell. But his ambivalent ending of the Faust story survives to suggest that God and Lucifer (who comes on stage at one point) are mirror images of order: Lucifer's victory is God's justice. The theatre exploits such contradictions by use of 'delight': whatever happens the audience is amused. McPherson builds on these anomalies.

McPherson's *The Birds* portrays in expressionistic style a world without God, where all laws break down without a known cause. There are three characters in the play (a fourth, Mr Tierney, makes a brief entrance motivated by loneliness, leaves, and is later reported dead). Besides Nat, these are Diane and the much younger Julia. Each comes from a broken home; they meet by chance as strangers. It is as if they had strayed into this temporary shelter from Cormac McCarthy's *The Road* (2006). Nat is the weakest of the three. He is married but separated or divorced, with a teenage daughter somewhere. He may have a history of mental illness; there is some mention of enforced hospitalization. Diane is a novelist who keeps a diary, the entries for which the audience hears as voice-over. It is clear she is manipulative, wanting to dominate relationships, control Nat by plying him with a mixture of whiskey and pills, and to get rid of Julia, who rivals her in the sexual contest for Nat. Between them these three create a kind of functional family, very temporary and destructive. Surprisingly, because she seems at first the stereotypical Hollywood teenage slut, Julia carries the theme of the play: 'People still love each other. We all need to take responsibility!'[55]

McPherson is concerned with two questions in the play: what is the role of consciousness in the presence of evil? And what is the responsibility of the artist in the face of ultimate moral breakdown? There are not many laughs to be elicited from such questions; it has to be accepted that *The Birds* is an unusual departure. Referring to the Genesis narrative McPherson comments; 'I wonder if the fruit they [Adam and Eve] are forbidden to taste represents self-consciousness. [...] As soon as we acquired intelligence we became different from all the other animals and found ourselves in the unique predicament of understanding our own mortality.' He goes on: 'We have been separate from the rest of nature ever since, unreconciled with the mystery of God – or the mystery of creation, if you like.'[56] Nat knows that all three in the ad-hoc family should care for each other under the new conditions: 'This is the new way of living. Right? I mean, we're here.'[57] He is aware and yet he opts out through his drinking. On the other hand, if Diane is Eve to Nat's Adam it is her sub-conscious we hear in the voice-overs relating entries in her diary. As she is a writer we have to decide whether what we hear is true or invented. She welcomes Satanic knowledge deemed necessary for her art. McPherson questions whether art needs to be sterile and amoral in this way.

In the final scenes of *The Birds* Nat comes to see that it is time to go. The birds have got in upstairs and are hatching a new generation of marauders: 'We have to ... find somewhere else.'[58] In her mind Diane gives the leaving a literary spin, 'Today we leave and wander into the wilderness,'[59] echoing Milton's last lines in *Paradise Lost* where Adam and Eve 'with wandering steps and slow, / Through Eden took their solitary way.'[60] They go, the archetypes, to renew human history. Tentatively, McPherson suggests some form of re-start as always a possibility. Diane deliberately leaves behind her in the diary her inmost thoughts, from which we hear one final voice-over. She who is too old to give birth herself has killed off the young girl who was pregnant. Knowledge and pain, she decides, go hand in hand. 'What if we are the only life anywhere in the vastness of time [*sic*] that can actually think, and knows that it exists, and knows that it will die? What if we are the only part of the universe that actually knows itself?.'[61] There's still time and hope for the audience. What they have seen is just a fable. Like the birds in action, it is very much 'in your face,' more devilish by far than *The Seafarer*, which, after all, was advertised in its 2009 revival in Dublin as 'laugh-out-loud funny.'

Works Cited

Abrams, M. H., ed. *The Norton Anthology of English Literature*. Vols. 1-2. 5th ed. (New York: Norton, 1986).

Beckett, Samuel. *The Complete Dramatic Works* (London: Faber, 1990).

Bogard, Travis. *Contour in Time: The Plays of Eugene O'Neill* (New York: Oxford UP, 1972).

Clare, Janet, and Stephen O'Neill. 'Introduction. Interpreting Shakespeare in Ireland.' *Shakespeare and the Irish Writer*. Ed. Janet Clare and Stephen O'Neill (Dublin: UCD Press, 2010) 1-23.

Du Maurier, Daphne. 'The Birds.' *The Apple Tree: A Short Novel and Some Short Stories* (London: Gollancz, 1952) 85-123.

Eagleton, Terry. *On Evil* (New Haven and London: Yale UP, 2010).

Ferguson, Margaret, Mary Jo Salter, and Jon Stallworthy, eds. *The Norton Anthology of Poetry*. 4th ed. (New York: Norton, 1996).

Foster, R. F., *The Irish Story: Telling Tales and Making it up in Ireland* (London: Lane / Penguin, 2001).

Harrington, John P., ed. *Modern and Contemporary Irish Drama*. 2nd ed. (New York: Norton, 2009).

Kiely, Benedict. *The Cards of the Gambler* [1953]. Repr. (Dublin: Millington, 1973).

McPherson, Conor. 'Afterword.' *Plays Two*. (London: Hern, 2004). 207-20.

---, *The Birds*. From the short story by Daphne Du [*sic*] Maurier. Final Draft October 2009. Copy courtesy of Mr McPherson.

---, 'A Note on *Endgame*.' *Beckett on Film: 19 Films x 19 Directors*. Dublin: Blue Angel Films / Tyrone Productions, 2001.

---, 'The Pagan Landscape.' Programme note for *The Seafarer*. Dublin: Abbey Theatre, 2008): 4-5.

---, 'The perfect work is always in the future, like a beautiful dream.' Interview with Hilary Fannin. *The Irish Times* 13 March 2010: 7.

---, 'Telling stories in the dark.' Interview with Victoria White. *The Irish Times* 2 July 1998: 14.

Marlowe, Christopher. *The Complete Plays*. Ed. J.B. Steane (Harmondsworth: Penguin, 1969).

Milton, John. *Paradise Lost*. Abrams Vol. 1. 1446-1590.

Ní Anluain, Eilís. 'The Cardplayers and the Devil (ML 3015): Regional and Social Variation in Ireland.' *Béaloideas: Irish an Chumainn le Béaloideas Éireann* 59 (1991): 45-54.

Nowak, Emil. 'Du Maurier and McPherson in the Hall of Mirrors.' Programme note, *The Birds*. Dublin: Gate Theatre, 29 September 2009.

Ó Súilleabháin, Seán. 'The Devil in Irish Folk Narrative.' *Volksüherlieferung: Festschrift für Kurt Ranke*. Ed. Fritz Harkort, Karel C. Peeters and Robert Wildhaber (Göttingen: Schwartz, 1968): 275-86.

Paglia, Camille. *The Birds* (London: British Film Institute, 1998).

Roche, Billy. *Tales from Rainwater Pond*. (Thomastown, Kilkenny: Pillar, 2006).

Shelley, Percy Bysshe. 'Song of Apollo.' Abrams Vol. 2. 735-36.

Wood, Gerald C. *Imagining Mischief* (Dublin: Liffey, 2003).

Yeats, W.B. *Essays and Introductions* (London and New York: Macmillan, 1961).

---

[1] Janet Clare and Stephen O'Neill, eds., 'Introduction. Interpreting Shakespeare in Ireland.' *Shakespeare and the Irish Writer*. Dublin: UCD Press, 2010: 1-23.

[2] Roy F. Foster, *The Irish Story: Telling Tales and Making it up in Ireland.* London: Lane / Penguin, 2001: 2.

[3] W.B. Yeats, *Essays and Introductions* (London and New York: Macmillan, 1961): 276.

[4] Conor McPherson, 'The Pagan Landscape.' Programme note for *The Seafarer.* Dublin: Abbey Theatre, 2008. 4.

[5] Conor McPherson, cited in Gerald C. Wood, *Imagining Mischief* (Dublin: Liffey, 2003): 123-24.

[6] McPherson cited in *Imagining Mischief*, 124.

[7] McPherson, 'The Pagan Landscape,' 14.

[8] Conor McPherson, *The Seafarer* (London: Nick Hern Books, 2007):3.

[9] Travis Bogard, *Contour in Time: The Plays of Eugene O'Neill* (New York: Oxford UP, 1972): 413.

[10] McPherson, *The Seafarer*, 2.

[11] Seán Ó Súilleabháin, 'The Devil in Irish Folk Narrative.' *Volksüherlieferung: Festschrift für Kurt Ranke.* Ed. Fritz Harkort, Karel C. Peeters and Robert Wildhaber. Göttingen: Schwartz, 1968: 275-86: 275).

[12] Ó Súilleabháin, 'The Devil in Irish Folk Narrative,' 277.

[13] Eilís Ní Anluain, 'The Cardplayers and the Devil (ML 3015): Regional and Social Variation in Ireland.' *Béaloideas: Irish an Chumainn le Béaloideas Éireann* 59 (1991): 45-54: 46.

[14] M.H., Abrams, ed. *The Norton Anthology of English Literature.* Vols. 1-2. 5th ed. New York: Norton, 1986: 10.

[15] McPherson, *The Seafarer,* 69.

[16] *ibid.,* 36.

[17] *ibid.,* 47.

[18] McPherson cited in *Imagining Mischief,* 139.

[19] McPherson cited in *Imagining Mischief,* 140.

[20] McPherson, 'The Pagan Landscape,' 5.

[21] Ní Anluain, 'The Cardplayers and the Devil,' 48.

[22] McPherson, 'The Pagan Landscape,' 5.

[23] *ibid.,* 5.

[24] McPherson, 'The perfect work is always in the future, like a beautiful dream.' Interview with Hilary Fannin. *The Irish Times* 13 March 2010: 7: 31.

[25] John P., Harrington, ed. *Modern and Contemporary Irish Drama.* 2nd ed. (New York: Norton, 2009): 537-38.

[26] John Milton, *Paradise Lost.* Abrams Vol. 1. 1446-1590: (Book 3: lines 98-99).

[27] Milton, *Paradise Lost.* (Book 4: lines 75, 110)

[28] McPherson, *The Seafarer,* 77.

[29] *ibid.,* 77.

30 Terry Eagleton, *On Evil* (New Haven and London: Yale UP, 2010): 84.

31 *ibid.*, 103.

32 *ibid.*, 143.

33 *ibid.*, 93.

34 McPherson, *The Seafarer,* 39.

35 *ibid.*, 78.

36 *ibid.*, 72.

37 William Shakespeare, *The Merchant of Venice*, 5.1.83-88.

38 McPherson, 'The perfect work is always in the future, like a beautiful dream,' 7.

39 McPherson, 'Afterword.' *Plays Two* (London: Hern, 2004):207-220.

40 McPherson, *The Seafarer,* 103.

41 Daphne Du Maurier, 'The Birds.' *The Apple Tree: A Short Novel and Some Short Stories* (London: Gollancz, 1952):5-123, 90.

42 Du Maurier, 'The Birds,' 95.

43 *ibid.*, 100.

44 *ibid.*, 103.

45 *ibid.*, 104.

46 *ibid.*, 106.

47 *ibid.*, 117.

48 *ibid.*, 123.

49 Samuel Beckett, *The Complete Dramatic Works* (London: Faber, 1990): 97.

50 Camille Paglia, *The Birds.* (London: British Film Institute, 1998): 7.

51 *The Birds.* From the short story by Daphne du Maurier. Final Draft October 2009. Copy courtesy of Mr McPherson.

52 M. H., Abrams, ed. *The Norton Anthology of English Literature,* 736.

53 McPherson, *The Birds*, 2.

54 Christopher Marlowe, *The Complete Plays.* Ed. J. B. Steane (Harmondsworth: Penguin, 1969): 339.

55 McPherson, *The Birds*, 64.

56 Emil Nowak, 'Du Maurier and McPherson in the Hall of Mirrors.' Programme note, *The Birds*. Dublin: Gate Theatre, 29 September 2009. Npd.

57 McPherson, *The Birds*, 33.

58 *ibid.*, 69.

59 *ibid.*, 70.

60 John Milton *Paradise Lost,* Book 12, ll. 648-49.

61 McPherson, *The Birds*, 70.

15 | The Gravity of Humour in Samuel Beckett's *Endgame* and Conor McPherson's *The Seafarer**

Eric Weitz

A sense of humour is a curious thing. Not formally admitted to the ranks of the five bodied senses, it is too much a palpable element of human interaction to qualify as a sixth sense. A sense of humour, nevertheless, remains willfully difficult to pin down as a definitively personal circuitry for apprehending the world. Nothing reveals so tellingly who we are than our senses of humour, a concept expressed by psychoanalytic critic Norman Holland: 'In laughing, we suddenly and playfully recreate our identities.'[1] The principle provides for several interesting avenues of consideration, including thought about what the quirks of hilarity say about oneself, one's friends and one's dramatic/literary tastes. There is another worthwhile direction for analytical pursuit, and that is the dramatic sensibility. We sometimes come to know the creative 'identity' of a practitioner, part of which comprises the sense of humour behind, say, a Martin McDonagh play or a Barabbas production. Marina Carr, for the dark inclination behind some of her visions, retains a sly, plainspoken comic voice that defines her creative personality. The collaborative nature of dramatic practice leads to more complex but no less interesting case studies, especially when a practitioner adopts

* An earlier version of this article appears in Rhona Trench (ed.), *Staging Thought: Essays on Irish Theatre, Scholarship and Practice* (Oxford: Peter Lang, 2012).

different positions in the theatre-practice constellation – in this case, screen director and playwright.

On a superficial level, an actor may be capable of inhabiting a playwright's words for some maximum comic effect. Without even addressing the potential for an actor to generate humorous effect through invented business or character choices behind the back of the written text, the word-perfect delivery of dialogue still offers a broad range of comic possibility should a production be so inclined. The director orchestrating a dramatic vision of life, then, discloses something of a comic sensibility in the tuning of that world, through the fashioning, pitch and regulation of its humour.

Conor McPherson, best known as a playwright and director of his own work, has demonstrated a sure grasp of humour's affective nuances in plays like *The Seafarer* (2006). His direction of Samuel Beckett's *Endgame* for the *Beckett on Film* series (2000) throws an alternative light upon his comic sensibilities as apprehended through another writer's text. In this case the other writer is a daunting figure, indeed, with much written by academics, felt by practitioners and presumed by theatre audiences at large about his body of work. Although transposed to a recorded medium, and for most viewings in the DVD age a reduction to the size of a television or computer screen, McPherson's *Endgame* demonstrates a sensibility for humorous effect driven by earnest investment in character and situation rather than bold outline of comic intent. This commitment to the serious core of humorous utterance allows him in *The Seafarer* to bring about a *coup de théâtre* for the first-time viewer.

It is one thing to reach for conventional Beckettian descriptors like 'black humour' and 'comic pathos' when characterizing *Endgame*, quite another to incarnate the words, making conscious decisions about tone, balance and their actual execution. The full sensory impact of a stage world – that parallel universe woven by theatrical materials of words, voices, bodies, space, design materials, etc. – includes the moorings of its humour, which approve or withhold joking permission and colour its comic disposition. For various reasons, it is possible in performance to turn up the comic effect through setting, gesture, intonation and pacing, just as it is possible to suppress it. A playwright or director might want to allow the spectator emotional release or indulgent associations in the former instance, might want to dampen that relief or score dramatic points in the latter. Mel Gussow recalls a conversation in which

Beckett told him that when directing his plays he might come across 'superfluities':

> [Beckett] pointed to *Endgame* as an example: 'Clov climbs up the ladder, looks out, then gets down and forgets to move the ladder. I cut that.' But that was funny [Gussow pointed out]. You cut a laugh? He [Beckett] laughed at the thought.[2]

The director (Beckett) would appear to have cut the playwright's (Beckett's) stage direction from an inner sense of the sequence's momentum. Beckett in conversation with Gussow afforded himself a wave of amusement, perhaps, at the recognition that at other times he had held the opinion during a production of *Endgame* that, 'I would like as much laughter as possible in this play. It is a playful piece.'[3]

On the other hand, just about any dramatic text remains open to comic augmentation, whether via spot emphasis or subtending performance palette. As a candidate for passing comic possibility, consider the following exchange:

> **HAMM:** You don't love me.
> **CLOV:** No.
> **HAMM:** You loved me once.
> **CLOV:** Once!
> **HAMM:** I've made you suffer too much. [*Pause.*] Haven't I?
> **CLOV:** It's not that.
> **HAMM:** [*Shocked.*] I haven't made you suffer too much?[4]

Of the myriad shadings one might imagine, two polar directorial avenues might include pursuing laughter fully and denying it altogether. In the first instance, joking intent might be served through an attempt by the actor playing Hamm to betray an inkling of pride in the concession, 'I've made you suffer too much,' and after a slight pause infusing the 'Haven't I?' with an unseemly quest for validation. The 'shocked' follow-on query might suggest at least a trace of disappointment that he had stopped short of causing excessive suffering. This possible embodiment would be more prone to court laughter, especially if the questions were voiced as side queries bracketed from the main issue and seeming to suspend the weight of the discussion. The two questions might then be taken as laughably anti-sentimental reversals upon the earnest contrition one would usually expect – and not necessarily inappropriate to the antagonistic relationship between Hamm and Clov.

At the other end of the laughter-seriousness seesaw Hamm's questions could be rendered in a spirit of heart-felt remorse, with 'shock' evident in the second one for the recognition of Clov's emotional fortitude in withstanding abusive treatment. This 'serious' embodiment might emphasize something of the unwitting damage we do to one another in the course of a close relationship, suggesting that whatever cruelty has gone between the characters there remains some undeniable bond.

As an example of a fundamental choice that would enhance comic possibility, we might consider a production of *Endgame* directed by Joseph Chaikin in 1979, in which Hamm and Clov were played by Dan Seltzer and Michael Gross, respectively. Jonathan Kalb and Mel Gussow, in their descriptions, would appear to disagree about the suitability and effect of the performances, but they both describe characterizations as clear attempts to increase comic traction. Kalb laments that a vital connection between the characters was denied by exceedingly theatrical choices, Seltzer's Hamm as 'a caricature huckster' and Gross's Clov as 'an explicit imitation of Stan Laurel.'[5] Gussow lauded the performances, highlighting 'Mr Seltzer's voice, which has the timbre of a classical tragedian, and his looks, which are like those of a bearded Old Testament prophet – with a twinkle,' and contrasting them with Gross, 'tall and lean with a look of clownish abashment. His eyes are X's in a cartoon strip. Walking in flopping flapjack boots, he is a cousin to Chaplin.'[6] Turning up the comedy often does serve to lessen the emotional grip; some people would consider it a fair trade while others would not.

It is not in this case necessary to take sides with either predilection – merely to notice how such character choices predispose the entire stage world in ways that supply pervasive comic inflections and deliver unforeseen humorous spins to any given line. Gussow recalls of Seltzer's performance: 'When he announces, "I'm warming up for my last soliloquy," it is as if he is spraying his throat and tuning his tonsils to conquer an obstreperous bit of verse.'[7] Stage humour is inclined to trade upon associations from life outside the theatre, overlaying strips of experience with unlikely behavioural frames. Its other effects notwithstanding, bold characterization is certainly one way to beg the spectator's assistance for heavy comic lifting.

Most productions of *Endgame*, of course, will fall somewhere between the extremes of open-ended comic licence and blanket refusal of laughter. It is no secret Beckett cherishes that charge of amusement at our collective penchant for psychic suffering, as apparently he considered the most important line in the play Nell's, 'Nothing is funnier than unhappiness, I grant you that.'[8] Each director, in league with actors and designers, comes upon a comic tuning for the play, some unknowable mix of response to Beckett's words and a personal sense of humour as material contribution to the affective tissue of performance.

McPherson's thought on Beckett, the comic, and directing *Endgame* seems to launch itself upon the widespread perception that this playwright always promises depressing if not impenetrable viewing: 'Hopefully, the film will demystify Beckett's reputation for being hard going. I just wanted to make sure it was funny, because, if it was funny, it could be understood. It's a comedy, a bittersweet comedy.'[9]

Of utmost interest to the student of comedy is the way in which a stage world introduces itself, as a calibrated context for humorous utterance. Broadness of gesture, ostentatious use of vocal effect and keen attention to the sharpness of reversal (which we sometimes call 'timing') generally signal the kinds of clear comic ascendancy we would associate with farce, panto and many a situation comedy. McPherson's direction declines any such over-determination of genre cueing that would trumpet comic intent. The atmosphere of a world thick with denouement retains buoyancy through measured concretization of the joking intent inherent in Beckett's text.

David Thewlis as Clov more or less follows Beckett's scripted directions for the business of moving the ladder between the two prescribed windows. The playwright calls for the character to take a certain number of steps before he reverses direction and 'goes back for the ladder,' and this happens three times; he then inverts the character's pattern by having him take the ladder with him, then, realizing he doesn't need it to remove the dustbin covers he returns it to the window. The bare bones of this sequence would harbour comic potential, as the character forgets three times to take the ladder with him and has to go back for it, offering possible comic effect in the persistence of forgetting. He establishes the pattern of neglecting to *take* the ladder and buttons it with forgetting to *leave* the ladder (perhaps some of which he chose to cut in one production, as per the anecdote related above by Gussow).

Within the first few moments of a world introduced by a whited-out nowhere seen through what might be an attic window of an old, creaking house, a steady howl of wind outside, these first comic opportunities afforded by Beckett's directions are de-emphasized in

McPherson's reading and Thewlis's portrayal. Clov's reversal of direction is almost automatic, as if he always does it that way – certainly no emphasis upon faulty thought process actively solicits laughter. If Thewlis's lurching, rhythmic gait is at all amusing it is because of its reliable nuisance rather than an attempt at physical comedy, although the actor's scarecrow appearance lends itself to a comic sense of angularity. The 'brief laugh' assigned to Clov when, for example, he looks out the windows is a short wheeze of an utterance, more redolent of private confirmation than sudden amusement and still more habitual than spontaneous. Thewlis discards the sheet covering the bins by holding it for the briefest moment above the floor and then letting it go, as if taking some care as to precisely where on the ground he will discard it. Not a belly laugh, to be sure, but a quirky bit of attention to detail shown in the midst of life's tedious unravelling. McPherson describes just this kind of strangely comic tension between the mundane business of living and the unknowable finitude of existence:

> Beckett's characters are like sitting on the edge of a cliff at a table, and everything's laid out, and the cliff is crumbling and they are going to fall into the sea, but they're actually concerned with using the right fork. It's these silly details that we're all concerned with, when in fact we don't know if there is a God and what will happen when we die.[10]

The sequence introduces a sort of personality for McPherson's take on the humour of the piece, which, although present, is never allowed to take precedence. The performance maintains pace without the artificial intensity that often accompanies stage acting – McPherson notes he attempted to take advantage of the fact that film allowed the actors to speak at normal conversational levels, rather than the boosted volumes required for theatre. These real-life tones of voice as well as the ability to cut quickly from one face to the other allows for a nuance of reaction, which, along with the Dublinesque accents adopted by Thewlis and Michael Gambon as Hamm, supports a subtlety of comic repartée for a double act in closeup (the text's affinity to vaudeville also mentioned in McPherson's comments).

It is worth noting, especially in a discussion of the comic, that in a made-for-film production the fabric of performance remains aloof from the spectator's laughter, which in the theatre would play an active part in the transaction between stage and audience. A film can adopt a performative momentum from which it knows it will not be swayed, and McPherson awards priority to feeling and interaction, out of which humour arises but rarely dominates.

In the 'You don't love me' passage discussed above, Clov responds with a decisive, 'No.' His response to Hamm's, 'You loved me once' comes as a light concession after the briefest reflection, 'Once.' Gambon's Hamm then follows with, 'I've made you suffer too much, haven't I?,' a light-bulb realization accompanied by a slight grin (of triumph that he's guessed right? of satisfaction after all his best efforts?). Clov's, 'It's not that' almost seems to incense Hamm for, 'I haven't made you suffer too much?' Clov says, 'Yes,' and Hamm follows with, 'Ah you gave me a fright,' in apparent relief that the mystery has been cleared up or that all the mistreatment has not gone to waste. In return, Clov asks Hamm, 'Have you bled?' with an impish raise of the eyebrows that withholds complete sympathy. The production's reading of this section allows for a cynical slant on the tit-for-tat humour that remains a common comic trope, albeit without emphasis that might overwhelm the interpersonal grappling that drives it. The dry take on mutual antagonism percolates just below the surface rather than bursting through to distract from the play's larger concerns.

There are, of course, the music-hall inspired exchanges we come to expect from Beckett. Nagg (Charles Simon) seeks to assure his wife from the ashbin next door, 'Our hearing hasn't failed'; Nell (Jean Anderson) responds, 'Our what?' There is no attempt to 'go for' the gag through the facial and vocal emphasis that characterizes broad comic acting, but it's there all the same, given added integrity by the two 90-plus-year-old performers in the roles. Nagg asks, 'Has he changed your sawdust?,' their location in the ashbins turning the query into a casually absurd reference that makes the couple sound more like pet hamsters than, say, grandparents. Nell's disappointed correction, 'It isn't sawdust,' leads to the chastisement, 'Can you not be a little accurate, Nagg?' It is delivered with a timeworn exasperation that evokes a poignancy of feeling between intimates without letting us laugh it away – again, a recognizable behavioural framing that chafes humorously against the bizarre situation. Anderson delivers Beckett's favourite line, 'Nothing is funnier than unhappiness, I grant you that,' as regrettable fact rather than self-reflexive punch line. Any comic effect surely remains understated.

To be sure, Beckett does a fair amount of foundation work for comic potential simply by skewing the context in the direction of the absurd. Many exchanges between Nagg and Nell, as suggested above, might be imported from an elderly couple's after-dinner conversation sitting in favourite living-room chairs or side by side on the back porch. The difference, of course, is that these mundane confidences pass back and forth between two people whose heads emerge from old-fashioned trash bins. They both wear nightcaps and whitened theatrical makeup, but their odd containment does not have entirely commensurate bearing on their thought and mood – it is taken for granted and, though acknowledged, not bemoaned. Nell, unwilling to scratch Nagg's back, advises, 'Rub yourself against the rim.' In this rendering, the camera cuts between talking heads and wider shots that periodically remind us of their incongruous full-bodied circumstances.

The comic strategy of juxtaposing matters of cosmic magnitude with everyday practicality is exemplified in Nagg's lengthy joke about the meticulous tailor, defending his professionalism in working on a man's trousers as the exasperated customer compares the three months he's taken to complete the job with the six days it took God to make the world. McPherson takes a directorial hand in the telling and the timing by jump-cutting angles, finally allowing Nagg to deliver the punch line simply: 'But dear Sir, my dear Sir, look ... at the world ... and look ... at my TROUSERS!' For the first time during the telling of the joke, however, McPherson frames Nagg at the back of the 'stage,' with Hamm in the foreground: Gambon's disdainful facial expression (to a joke Hamm has no doubt heard too many times) tempers whatever amusement the viewer may find in the joke itself.

On the other hand, McPherson's camera angles occasionally serve to enhance comic effect through the use of closeup. When Hamm commands Clov, 'Take me for a little turn,' the camera cuts to Hamm's sock-covered feet kicking heels against the floor with something like childlike glee. What would under other circumstances mean a spin on country roads or even a tour of the grounds amounts to an aborted circumnavigation of the attic, turned into far more of an adventure by McPherson's ability to place the camera close to the armchair-on-wheels with Clov's face right behind Hamm's. Hamm demands to be returned to the exact centre of the room, rejecting Clov's offer to 'go and get the tape' for precise measurement. Thewlis's wide eyes and perfunctory adjustment to the chair – essentially returning to the same position – lead to the blind man's implausible spatial reckoning, 'I feel a little too far to the left.' Sucking on his finger, we get a sense first that Hamm is toying with his attendant, finally sliding into a tone of threat for the last line of the sequence, 'Now I feel a little too far back,' a subtlety of feeling afforded by the close proximity the spectator is allowed through film. Hamm fires over his shoulder at Clov, 'Don't stay there, you give me the shivers,' with an air of undisguised nastiness, to which Clov responds, speaking down and away from Hamm, as if to himself, 'If I could kill him I'd die happy.'

This rocking between lightness and harshness of mood is, perhaps, embedded in Beckett's words, but is modulated by McPherson for a narrower range and richer depth of feeling. An ensuing section approximates a music-hall pattern on the page:

HAMM: Look at the earth.
CLOV: I've looked
HAMM: With the glass?
CLOV: No need of the glass.
HAMM: Look at it with the glass.
CLOV: I'll go and get the glass.
HAMM: No need of the glass!
CLOV: I'm back again, with the glass!

This canter of contrariness and repetition is played at speed, as it would be onstage. Again, it proceeds to downshift into acrimony, the serial alteration between whimsy and harshness a central motion of the stage world, especially as realized through McPherson's direction. A reverse effect sometimes serves to puncture a grave mood: Hamm's weighty concession, 'We're getting on,' is immediately followed by the closeup of the toy dog being plopped onto the banister by Clov and given a few squeaky hops – again a sudden flash of silliness isolated by the camera in a way that isn't possible on the stage.

Hamm appears to sink into a mood of abject despair, asking, 'Do you not think this has gone on long enough?' Clov responds with an emphatic, 'Yes!,' then a wave of confusion crosses his face and he asks, 'What?' This simple exchange, simulating yet another common comic reversal (confident, assertive answer, followed by some diffident or confused opposite) renders the gag in a minor key. Although a pattern that we are used to laughing at, the overall weight of the 'stage world' and the setup based in Hamm's uncharacteristic vulnerability are likely to pull upon any comic effect. It becomes a vital facet of this filmed production's personality that McPherson enables the plethora of comic possibilities while seeing that they never quite eclipse the graver issues at stake.

Sigmund Freud assigns humour (as distinguished from jokes and wit) the explicit task of protecting the emotions, in that, 'the super-ego tries, by means of humour, to console the ego and protect it from suffering.'[11] By way of example, he cites the story about a 'rogue' being led out to execution on a Monday morning and remarking, 'Well, this week's beginning nicely.' One can broadly suppose the incongruously chipper pronouncement as denying mortality the weight of its imminence – the condemned man's life force rallies feeling, mind and body to an act of psychic defiance, even in the shadow of the gallows. In this case Beckett plays the Freudian rogue on our behalf, while McPherson keeps a confident hand on the comic throttle, navigating the experience to keep caprice and bleakness ever in tandem.

In *The Seafarer*, McPherson the playwright demonstrates a skilled grasp of humour's affective dynamics. As structural engineer of this stage world, he supplies a blueprint that uses humour's weight against itself to foresee a clever reversal of feeling. The anchoring of comic possibility in pointed social observation magically alters effect by executing a trick of generic perspective.

Part of how we process a text lies in perceived markers in theme and hue, what they tell us about the kind of world unfolding before us, as well as intertextual expectations they instil. Catherine Belsey, wondering rhetorically why Shakespeare seems to retain a sense of currency all these centuries later, claims that it has to do with his employment of folk tales which enter our little beings from childhood and establish narrative patterns in our receptive apparatus with regard, say, to a story of three brothers or a poor man and his wondrous daughter. McPherson had drawn the premise for *The Seafarer* from local tales of the Hellfire Club in Dublin, where it was held that the devil came to play cards. There are, however, broader narratives about man and the devil – in some the devil ultimately holds all the cards, in others man, through trickery or displays of spiritual valour, escapes to live another day. McPherson exploits the seams and overlaps of such generic materials to shrewd effect, with particular insight as to the slant of humorous radiance.

In *The Seafarer*, McPherson appears to adopt a view of humanity (and Irish humanity, at that) from the underbelly, which would lead us to expect a lesson as strong and unflinching as any morality play. The central character, Sharky, is something of a lost soul whose temper too often gets him into trouble, and who has returned home under vague circumstances. Sharky is trying to give up drink, and we would be trained to expect the sternest of tests at the final hurdle, which will brand him either worthy of redemption or fatally flawed. Sharky surely gets no help from those around him, beginning with his brother, Richard, who cajoles and ridicules him for his abstention. Two other men join in the poker game that becomes the centrepiece of the tale – Ivan, who spends the whole play looking for his specs (an important through line) and dreading having to explain to his wife where he has been all this time; and Nicky, a nice enough guy who can't hold his liquor and has moved in with Sharky's ex.

The key tone of this stage world is that of waste and delusion, embodied by the setting of the 'grim living area of a house in Baldoyle' where a 'scrawny artificial Christmas tree haunts a corner.'[12] Much of the humour written into the play trades on a socio-cultural stereotype of grand-talking, do-nothing camaraderie, held together by the glue of alcohol dependency. Richard in particular is a remarkable stage confection of laziness, eloquence and guile, interested in little more than the connivance of a next drink. He shamelessly exploits the fact that he needs help with everything he does, having rendered himself blind by falling into a skip on Halloween, no doubt in a drunken stupor. At one point, when Sharky leaves the room, Richard and Ivan launch into a comic set piece of emptying their cups of tea (on the carpet, since there's nowhere else to hand) and refilling them with whiskey, urgently draining them despite their bodies' revolts against the deluge, then refilling them so as to present a respectable tableau as Sharky reappears. It's a strip of physical business (prescribed by the stage directions), which combines a panicked urgency often found in farce with childlike desperation. That such frenzied machinations are required to meet a desperate craving for alcohol supplies a broadly comic physical shell with an internal motivation that underscores the abject pathos of these types.

The demon drink is advanced as nothing short of a latter-day tragic flaw, sabotaging the potential for individual realization even as it remains enshrined in the etiquette of a sub-culture's socializing. Its effects upon character and relationship underpin an ambivalent humour in this stage world – what we watch is pathetic, yet we know it so well. One of the play's most poignant comic formulations comes in the form of Ivan's reminiscence about how he received a sudden windfall and gambled, ate and drank himself into the hospital over a three-week period, much of which he can't even remember: 'Do you remember Richard? Best Christmas ever!'[13]

Sharky, at the centre of the stage world, reads as a tragic hero and is delineated as a deeply troubled man. Richard's character summation of Sharky is intended for comic effect in its no-holds-barred truthfulness, but we cannot help but take it as an all too serious assessment: 'he has a recklessness in his heart which is the undoing and ruination of his whole life.'[14]

Sharky rarely makes jokes himself, they happen around him, or, occasionally, *to* him. Before Nicky arrives Sharky describes spotting him driving the car he had given to his ex: 'I *loaned* it to her for the school run, Dick. I didn't ever expect to see that fucker driving around in it! I saw him pulling out of the shops down there in Bayside, and I was walking down to get the bus in the pissing rain! And he was in *my* car!'[15] This reads as an absurdist kind of humour at the expense of the hero, crystallizing a remorseless cosmic cruelty in life after God.

The final character in the mix is Mr. Lockhart, whom Nicky brings to call for a Christmas poker game, and whom we discover is the devil come to settle an old score with Sharky. Lockhart presents himself publicly as a sort of *bon vivant*, mysterious with regard to his personal circumstances, but well up for cards and drink, the only things the men really care about. It is only when left alone with Sharky that he announces his satanic mission, borne ever more forcefully upon a personalized sense of vendetta. Lockhart demonstrates an ability to inflict deep physical pain upon his mortal prey from across the room. With Sharky on the floor and in unbearable physical and psychic agony, Lockhart drills him with the full force of his avenging intention: 'Because we're gonna play for your soul and I'm gonna win and you're coming through the old hole in the wall with me tonight.'[16]

Lockhart later attains the full measure of a contemporary tragic antagonist by describing hell in the most fervently poetic terms we hear all night. He then says, 'Trust you to blow it, Sharky. Trust you. That's how I know you'll be coming with me tonight. I know you'll lose this next hand. Because you always make a pig's mickey of everything [...].'[17] The stage directions instruct: '*Sharky seems to ponder his whole life for a moment, then goes to the bottle of poteen and pours himself a huge measure. He begins to drink it perfunctorily with one hand on his hip ...*'[18] Lockhart continues, 'That's it Sharky, good man. Drink yourself up onto the next shelf in the basement. Drink to where possibility seems endless and your immortality feels strong.' (*Sharky, having drained the glass, joylessly pours another.*) That's it ... Genius! You poor stupid bastard.'[19] A few lines later Lockhart says, 'You nearly made it, Sharky. You were just two drinks away from never again.'[20]

Sharky has failed to show the moral resolve we would normally interpret as worthy of redemption and, in an astutely calibrated production, spectators by this point might think they were watching a play sliding toward a hard-learned lesson at the end of its day. The night wears on, tempers turn nasty, and the table stakes rise beyond all reason, leaving, as expected, one last showdown of a hand. Sharky seems to play with an air of surrender, as if he's decided it's best just to go along quietly to his eternal damnation. With, effectively, his soul in the kitty, they reveal their hands: Ivan, still playing without his glasses, announces four fours, Sharky four eights and Lockhart a winning four tens.

The play seems to be winding down to an inevitable downbeat conclusion, when Ivan suddenly finds his specs and discovers he had misread his hand, which actually contains four aces. This, as one can imagine, considerably affects the outcome of the play and presumably would alter quite substantially the feeling in the room, by which I mean, the theatre. In hypothetical performance, humorous utterances placed in the several pages after this reversal stand to receive a double shot of relief *and* sudden glory – a groundswell of feeling from a genre diametrically opposed to the one previously thought to be in force.

There's further humour about the unseemly affection for alcohol, but it changes perspective. Richard suggests they take in the early mass at the friary, where they might find someone to intervene on Ivan's behalf when he finally shows up at home. Ivan is unconvinced and Richard adds, 'And you know of course that they brew their own ale up there?'[21] The play's joking sentiment seems to have changed from sardonic critique to a semi-appreciation of Richard's irrepressible nature.

Richard has previously turned his uncharitable wit upon his brother: 'It's a well-known fact in this whole area that my brother has that rare gift which is, unfortunately, the opposite to whatever the Midas touch was.'[22] Now he is the first to speak after Lockhart departs: 'Well, that is one maudlin fucker! Talk about a poor loser!,' a certifiable peak audience laugh, if ever there was one, with an element of triumphant feeling unknown earlier in the evening.[23]

Dramatic humour is always in some ways beholden to its context, the prevailing mood within which it is made. The relationship between humour and dramatic context is symbiotic, though, and my point in this case is that the same kinds of jokes take on a different aspect when made in a different kind of play than we thought we were watching a few minutes ago. To drive home the obvious, mood plays an important part in how fully we laugh. With Ivan's reversal many a spectator may ride an unprecedented wave of psychic relief to the end of the play, having been airlifted from the depths of tragic territory to a victory party thrown by the life spirit. In fact, the humour has not moved; the audience have simply been shifted to the other side of the tragedy-comedy divide.

The placement and viability of humour has provided no small point for discussion with regard to both the fictional worlds discussed in this essay – and clearly this is where each individual reader/spectator's internal framing matrix may be put to an interesting litmus test. As director for *Endgame* and writer of *The Seafarer*, Conor McPherson makes palpable the deeper currents of comic and tragic worlds, exploiting the affective ground on either side of the invisible line between them with sense and dexterity. And by toying with the gravity of humour he shows how useful it can be for theatrical projects with more on their minds than mere laughter.

Works cited

Beckett, Samuel, *Endgame* in *The Complete Dramatic Works* (London: Faber and Faber, 1990): 89-134.

---, *Endgame*, DVD. Dir. by Conor McPherson in *Beckett on Film*, Disc 4, Blue Angel Films, 2002.

Bergson, Henri, 'Laughter' (1900) in W. Sypher (ed.), *Comedy* (Baltimore: Johns Hopkins, 1980): 591-90.

Cohn, Ruby, 'Beckett Directs: *Endgame* and *Krapp's Last Tape*' in *On Beckett: Essays and Criticism*, ed. by S.E. Gontarski (New York: Grove, 1986): 291-3.

Freud, Sigmund,' Humour' (1927), in *Art and Literature*, ed. by Albert Dickson (Harmondsworth: Penguin, 1990): 425-33.

Gussow, Mel, *Conversations with and about Beckett* (New York: Grove, 1996).

Holland, Norman, *Laughing: A Psychology of Humor* (Ithaca: Cornell University, 1982).

Kalb, Jonathan, *Beckett in performance* (Cambridge: Cambridge University, 1991).

McPherson, Conor, *The Seafarer* (New York: Dramatists Play Service, 2008).

---, 'Interview' on Beckett on Film website,
   http//www.beckettonfilm.com/ plays/endgame/-
   interview_macphearson.html; [Accessed 21 October 2011]

---

[1] Norman Holland, *Laughing: A Psychology of Humor* (Ithaca: Cornell
   University, 1982): 198.

[2] Mel Gussow, *Conversations with and about Beckett* (New York:
   Grove, 1996): 37.

[3] *ibid.*, 181.

[4] Samuel Beckett, *Endgame* in *The Complete Dramatic Works*
   (London: Faber and Faber, 1990): 101.

[5] Jonathan Kalb, *Beckett in performance* (Cambridge: Cambridge
   University, 1991), this and the preceding phrase from a longer
   description on page 40.

[6] Gussow, *Conversations*, both descriptions, 152-3.

[7] *ibid.*, 152.

[8] Beckett, *Endgame*, 101.

[9] Conor McPherson, 'Interview' on Beckett on Film website,
   http//www.beckettonfilm.com/plays/endgame/interview_macphear
   son.html; [Accessed 21 October 2011]

[10] *ibid.*

[11] Sigmund Freud, 'Humour' (1927), in *Art and Literature,* ed. Albert
   Dickson (Harmondsworth: Penguin, 1990): 433.

[12] Conor McPherson, *The Seafarer* (New York: Dramatists Play Service,
   2008): 7.

[13] *ibid.*, 48.

[14] *ibid.*, 54.

[15] *ibid.*, 26.

[16] *ibid.*, 39.

[17] *ibid.*, 60.

[18] *ibid.*, 60.

[19] *ibid.*, 60.

[20] *ibid.*, 60.

[21] *ibid.*, 76.

[22] *ibid.*, 62.

[23] *ibid.*, 76.

16 | Conor McPherson's *The Seafarer*: Male Pattern Blindness

Audrey McNamara

'Lest man know not/That he on dry land loveliest liveth'[1] is a line from Ezra Pound's translation of the Anglo-Saxon poem that shares its name with *The Seafarer*. It is almost as if Conor McPherson is writing against this particular line throughout his play and giving lie to the fact that there is any easy place to be in life. In actual fact, McPherson's play shows nothing could be further from the truth. All through the play darkness is simmering under the surface. Black humour acts as a buffer against the themes of despair underpinning the discourse. It would seem that should the laughter stop, both the characters and the audience would have to face up to the twisted reality being presented on stage. As Eckart Voigts-Virchow and Mark Schreiber argue: 'McPherson brings to the stage desperate and hopelessly lost male characters in need to share their stories with us, the audience.'[2]

The Abbey Theatre's production of *The Seafarer* in December 2009 is testimony to this. Superbly directed by McPherson himself, the performance of the play expertly exploited every nuance and theme of the text. The superb cast worked in tight harmony both with the themes of the play and with each other. The play is set on the north side of Dublin in Baldoyle on Christmas Eve. It tells the tale of Sharky (Liam Carney), an alcoholic, who is struggling with his recent attempts at sobriety and who has just returned to the city from the countryside under dubious circumstances 'three or four days'[3] before Christmas Eve to look after his recently blinded brother, Richard, (Maeliosa Stafford) who is also an alcoholic. They are joined on stage by Ivan (Don Wycherly) who is Richard's drinking partner. The end of the first act heralds the arrival of Nicky, (Phelim Drew) who is now living with Sharky's wife, and the mysterious Mr Lockhart (Nick Dunning).

It quickly becomes apparent that Lockhart is in fact the Devil and that he has come to take Sharky's soul. IFTA award-winning actor Nick Dunning embraced the character of Lockhart with frightening ease. His English accent pitched against an otherwise very heavily Dublin accented performance created the precise amount of tension, a foreshadowing of the events to follow. Liam Carney displayed an eerily real sense of fear and foreboding, when it dawns on him what is going on.

> **LOCKHART;** I'm the son of the morning, Sharky. I'm the snake in the garden. I've come here for your soul this Christmas and I've been looking for you all fucking day! We made a deal. We played cards for your freedom and you promised me, you promised me, the chance to play you again. So don't start messing me about now. (*Short pause.*) Of course, after you skipped merrily off to some early house in the morning you probably never even thought about it again, did you? Ha? You think I'm just farting around? You think you're better than me? Pig. Well, think again. Because we're gonna play for your soul and I'm gonna win and you're coming through the old hole in the wall with me tonight.[4]

Brian Singleton is correct in describing Lockhart as the stuff of fables, 'a Mephistopheles who unleashes the demons lurking underneath the surface of the other men.'[5] While Lockhart is undoubtedly the devil, his arrival does not indicate the beginning of the other characters' troubles, it merely brings them to light, especially those of Sharky.

In an interview with Maddy Costa, Conor McPherson states that he writes from the standpoint that:

> human beings are animals: 90% of our behaviour is animal behaviour, and we've just got this 10% veneer, the semblance of civilized, rational choice. Our thoughts are always trailing around after our appetites, justifying them with language: it's tragic and it's hilarious. That's the picture I put together in my plays: of the animals who can talk, and think because of that they know everything.[6]

This certainly holds true of *The Seafarer*. Though McPherson does capture the very essence of the feral nature of human beings through his characters in this play, he succeeds in achieving empathy through laughter that softens the harsh reality in the depiction of their squalid lives. The stage directions for the set depict that squalor. McPherson writes that 'the place lacks a woman's touch. It has morphed into a kind of a bar in its appearance.[7] Paul O'Mahoney's set design captured the essence of a male-only environment. Even the Christmas tree looked neglected. As Dominic Dromgoole noted in the programme for the play:

> *The Seafarer*'s immediate image is a Dante-esque circle of hell, filled with a composite of examples of what the modern world would call losers. The blind, the drunk, the unfaithful, the drunk, the cheating, the more drunk, the petty show-offs, the even more drunk, the terrified, and the so drunk it doesn't matter anymore.[8]

The ostensible theme of drink and the characters' dependence on it emphasizes the other problems that stem from that over-dependence. It highlights relationship problems within the group itself. Ivan's marriage problems are dealt with in a liminal space as is Nicky's relationship with Sharky's ex-wife. By placing the male–female relationships outside the stage space itself, McPherson has cleverly drawn attention to the myopic status of the male characters. Richard's blindness is symbolic of his blindness to all things outside his own sphere; he lives within his own head and is basically unconcerned with anything unless it directly affects him. He is also a bully, playing up on his sight loss to elicit sympathy and uses his disability to achieve his own way. In act I, Richard is raucous when it comes to articulating his feelings:

> **RICHARD:** We'll go in a taxi.
> **SHARKY:** Are you coming as well?
> **RICHARD:** Ah, let me out for a bit, for Jaysus' sake, Sharky, we might even get a Christmas pint ...
> **SHARKY:** (*sighing*). Oh ... well, wait now because if ...
> **RICHARD:** No, because we need to get a few bits in as well, Sharky, from the off-licence, in case anyone calls. We'll get a taxi back, because I want to be settled in here now for Christmas Eve ...
> **SHARKY:** Yeah, but wait a minute, because if I have to ...
> **RICHARD:** (*suddenly despairing*). I have so little left to live for!
>
> *Pause*
>
> **IVAN:** (*reassuringly*). Ah now, Richard
> **RICHARD:** What! Yous don't know. Yous don't know.
> **SHARKY:** No we'll all ... we'll go ... we'll get the few bits and ...

> **IVAN:** Sure you'll be grand, you'll have a grand Christmas here
> with Sharky here, and with you and all, and ...[9]

Maeliosa Stafford's Richard plays on the others' inabilities to deal
with emotion in a disturbingly realistic way and they, Ivan and
Sharky, in turn acquiesce just in case they have actually to delve into
any meaningful conversation. Ivan's loss of his glasses is also
symbolic of his myopia towards his own life, but where Richard's
blindness is total and irreversible; there is a chance of redemption
for Ivan, who will see properly again, obviously, when he finds his
glasses, but, metaphorically speaking, whether he takes that chance
to open his eyes to his own situation or not is dependent on how he
deals with his relationship with both Richard and alcohol. Although
Ivan is aware that his own behaviour is at the root of his marital
problems, he tries to justify his own weakness by staying away from
the home situation. Richard feeds into this, telling Ivan, as he
organizes Sharky to get yet another drink for him:

> Now, not to worry Ivan. The woman is being completely
> unreasonable, she'll come round, just you watch. And we'll be
> nice and cosy here now and we'll figure it out.[10]

Here, Richard's motives are twofold. Firstly, he likes to be in
control of Ivan and if they are drinking together it makes using
alcohol more of a social exercise, and secondly, it stops his own
feelings of loneliness. This loneliness is apparent in the way he is
constantly talking about having people around and inviting others
into the house. In his own twisted way he is trying to create a family-
like atmosphere without having the skills to do so. He knows that
there is a lack in his life and he has identified that as the need to be
with others. His problem is he is incapable of having or sustaining a
relationship of any description. Stafford found the necessary pitch
for these complicated and contradictory emotions and sensations.
Eamonn Jordan argues when discussing McPherson's plays:

> Male characters display an absence of awareness, a lack of
> internal composure, an inability to have an inner dialogue,
> rather than an inner monologue. Reflections seem endlessly
> postponed, not because of indifference per se, but because of an
> inability to validate or substantiate.[11]

Not only do they have an inability to have an inner dialogue, they
have problems with an external one as well. Their conversation
always tends towards the general and inevitably focuses on alcohol.
This inability to communicate tells its own story. It is McPherson's

way of, as Voigts-Virchow and Schreiber argue, exploring masculinity in crisis.[12] Ondřej Pilný correctly maintains that:

> ... McPherson presents the audience with an over-the-top version of his customary lost souls, who take the shape of permanently boozing crusties, in order to induce compassion and understanding all the more strongly.[13]

Audiences are drawn into the shambles that passes for their sitting room. It is notable that the room's position is in a basement as it symbolizes the characters' place in life and society. Each one of them is crawling around the bottom of the pile trying to find justification for their miserable lives and each is lacking the vision to do something about it. Each of them, with the exception of Sharky, desperately seeks solace and self validation in alcohol. This prevents them seeing themselves as they really are; males whose only real achievement is the ability to drink until they fall into oblivion. Richard's feeble attempt to elevate his status by referring disparagingly to the 'winos' out in the back lane is not lost on the audience. It is ironic that Richard refers to 'them filthy fucking winos have all puke and piss and everything else all down our step, all up the fucking door out there,'[14] when the audience have been made privy to the state of Richard's own bathroom at the beginning of act I.

> **SHARKY:** (*opens the toilet door*)
> Ah! Richard, who did that all over the floor?
> **RICHARD:** Well I don't know![15]

One of the only main differences between them and the winos is that they have a roof over their head. The similarities are the feral existence they both live. Richard refers to the home as a 'den'.[16] When Ivan tells Sharky that he 'slept on the rug,' Richard replies 'Did you sleep on the floor? Like an animal.'[17] These animal references demonstrate how the physical squalor they live in reflects and depicts the characters' mental squalor. They are completely blind to the farcical nature of their notions. At times Stafford's Richard seems painfully aware of the facade, whereas Wycherly's Ivan remains immune to awareness.

Sharky's character is more complex and Liam Carney captured the essence of that complexity in his performance. Firstly it would seem that, in giving up the drink, Sharky is trying to take control of his life. Yet, nothing could be further from the truth. He gave it up because he was involved in a fight on his first night home and got badly beaten up. This is as far as he seems prepared to go. There is the sense that, while he may still stay sober, the pattern of his life will never change. He lives a 'Ground Hog Day' type of existence. He will always lumber from one crisis to the next and, like the others, will never learn anything from it. Carney's use of the space, his staccato-like movements, tidying up this and that, created a nervous tension that would not allow the audience to relax comfortably into the comedy of the play. Sharky's past becomes the focal point of the play with the arrival of Lockhart. That something sinister was imminent is also flagged when Ivan told the story of Maurice Macken who survived electrocution only to be burned to death in a fire when he arrived home from hospital.[18] A sense of eeriness is created when Ivan turns the tale into a ghost story stating that Macken has been seen 'hanging around at the off-licence serving hatch'[19] at Grainger's pub.

> **RICHARD:** That's bollocks.
> **IVAN:** Yeah, well, apparently he looks really white. He was standing near the hatch. Big Bernard's cousin saw him. Apparently he was just standing there looking out into the car park, like he was waiting on a lift or something.
> **RICHARD:** Go on out of that! What's he waiting on? A few cans? *He laughs*
> **IVAN:** (*to Sharky*) Spooky though, isn't it?[20]

This is one of the few times that Ivan addresses a serious issue. The only other time that Ivan is seen to take any topic seriously is when he talks about his children and how he hates fighting in front of them. Don Wycherley's acrobatics and antics gave a 'comédie in vaudeville' feel to the performance and this whole comedy factor served to relieve the audience of the sense of despair which the *mise-en-scène* was so obviously signalling.

Lockhart's impending arrival is gestured by three loud knocks at the door. This is a play on the biblical reference of the cock crowing three times as Peter denied Jesus Christ. The knock is a harbinger of the turn the play is going to take. Although on this occasion it is the postman with a parcel for Sharky, the tone of the drama takes a seismic shift in the direction of darkness. The subversion of the words of a Christmas song by Richard further emphasizes the change in the atmosphere of the play. The stage directions inform us that 'it is completely dark outside now' as Lockhart and Nicky Giblin arrive. Chris Murray argues:

> It can be taken for granted that McPherson's characters are all 'wicked' to a man [...] this is a play about sinners but loveable sinners who share friendship within that happy metaphor addressed earlier as the Irish pub culture.[21]

While there is some truth in this statement, it would have to be argued that their friendship is superficial and what holds them together is their dependence on alcohol. Even Richard and Sharky's relationship, though brothers, is questionable. The myopia that exists precludes almost any sort of intimate connection. They really know little or nothing about each other's lives and there is no willingness to share confidences. The brothers' myopic view also prevents them from identifying the threat, in the form of Lockhart, which has just walked into the house. The dynamic between Stafford and Carney played out this relationship to the point where reality and fantasy merged. However the foil for this blurring of boundaries was the heightened theatricality of Ivan, Wycherley's comedic creation, who both reminded the audience that this was 'theatre' and that they should respond to it emotionally and passionately with a certain degree of licence, in the way that the story itself takes considerable licence and relies on a considerable suspension of disbelief.

Although Lockhart appears to be in possession of a lot of information, especially about Sharky, he too is myopic in his own way. As he is so intent on getting what he wants, he fails to take into account that it may not turn out as he planned. His mission statement appears to be 'If I can just beat Christmas, I can achieve anything!'[22] His quest to take Sharky's soul is single-minded and determined, so much so, it is as if the card game is just between the two of them. He never took into consideration that somebody other than Sharky could win against him. Ivan, in finding his glasses, introduces a note of hope by discovering that he had read the cards incorrectly, and that, in fact, he and Richard had won the game thereby saving Sharky from Lockhart. While this would appear to be a very warming fact, where good triumphs evil once again, it is frightening to note that they did not even realize they were in the presence of evil or that Sharky actually needed saving. (Of course the audience is on a different page to most of the characters, and therefore celebrate the good fortune.) Lockhart's closing line, when Sharky tells him that he does not want to play any more, can be interpreted as the message the play sets out to deliver. Dunning's delivery of the line was masterful.

LOCKHART: Well you should think about it. Somebody up there likes you, Sharky. You've got it all.[23]

In conclusion, it has to be argued that neither Sharky nor the other characters will take that advice. All the signs are there that will allow change, Ivan finding his glasses, the red votive light under the Sacred Heart picture flickering back into life and Richard's message to Sharky 'You're alive, aren't you?[24] However, the characters are almost completely hemmed into a particular mind-set that will not easily allow for progress. While the dialogue is pithy and extremely funny it cannot alter the fact that an underlying darkness remains. Superb acting in the 2009 production ensured that the audience left with a feel good factor; the comedy of the piece masked the dark underlay that protects against the knowledge that perhaps evil forces really are at work. As Brian Singleton said in his review of the earlier Abbey production of 2008, it is

> proof that the play will remain in the Abbey repertoire for many generations to come; it has the comfortable accessibility and familiarity for a popular audience and more than a hint of the universally tragic to ensure its place in the canon of Irish theatre.[25]

Works Cited

Costa, Maddy, an Interview with Conor McPherson , 'Human beings are animals,' in *The Guardian 13 September 2006,* *http://www.guardian.co.uk/stage/2006/sep/13/theatre4*

Dromgoole, Dominic, *Accidental Truth* in *The Abbey Theatre Programme The Seafarer* 4 December 2009 – 30 January 2010

Jordan, Eamonn, *Dissident Dramaturgies: Contemporary Irish Theatre* (Dublin: Irish Academic Press 2010).

McPherson, Conor, *The Seafarer* London (Nick Hern Books 2007).

Murray, Christopher, 'The Supernatural in Conor McPherson's *The Seafarer* and *The Birds*,' *The Binding Strength of Irish Studies. Festschrift in Honour of Csilla Bertha and Donald E. Morse*, eds. Marianna Gula, Mária Kurdi, István D. Rácz (Debrecen: Debrecen University Press, 2011): 66-77.

Pilný, Ondřej, 'Mercy on the Misfit: Continuity and Transformation in the Plays of Conor McPherson' in *The Binding Strength of Irish Studies. Festschrift in Honour of Csilla Bertha and Donald E. Morse*, eds. Marianna Gula, Mária Kurdi, István D. Rácz (Debrecen: Debrecen University Press, 2011): 87-94.

Pound, Ezra *The Seafarer* in *The Norton Anthology of Poetry Fourth Edition* (WW Norton & Company, Inc USA 1996).

Singleton, Brian, 'Review of The Seafarer', *Irish Theatre Magazine*
www.irishtheatremagazine.ie/Reviews/Current/ The Seafarer
[Accessed 9 July 2011]
Voigts-Virchow, Eckart & Mark Schreiber 'Will the "Wordy Body"
Please Stand Up? The Crisis of Male Impersonation' in *Monological
Drama – Beckett, McPherson, Eno' in Monologues: Theatre,
Performance, Subjectivity*, ed. Claire Wallace (Prague: Litteraria
Pragnesia 2006).

---

1 Ezra Pound *The Seafarer* in *The Norton Anthology of Poetry Fourth
Edition* (WW Norton & Company, Inc USA 1996): 1187.
2 Eckart Voigts-Virchow & Mark Schreiber *'Will the "Wordy Body"
Please Stand Up? The Crisis of Male Impersonation in Monological
Drama – Beckett, McPherson, Eno'* in *Monologues: Theatre,
Performance, Subjectivity*. ed. Claire Wallace (Czech Republic;
Litteraria Pragnesia 2006): 288.
3 Conor McPherson, *The Seafarer* (London: Nick Hern Books, 2007): 8.
4 *ibid.*, 47-8.
5 Brian Singleton, 'Review of The Seafarer', *Irish Theatre Magazine*
www.irishtheatremagazine.ie/Reviews/Current/ The Seafarer
[Accessed 9 July 2011]
6 An Interview With Conor McPherson by Maddy Costa in *The
Guardian*
http://www.guardian.co.uk/stage/2006/sep/13/theatre4
7 McPherson, *The Seafarer*, 3.
8 Dominic Dromgoole *'Accidental Truth'* in *The Abbey Theatre
Programme The Seafarer*, 4 December 2009 – 30 January 2010
9 McPherson, *The Seafarer*, 16-17.
10 *ibid.*, 34.
11 Eamonn Jordan, *Dissident Dramaturgies: Contemporary Irish
Theatre* (Dublin: Irish Academic Press 2010): 222.
12 Eckart Voigts-Virchow & Mark Schreiber , 288.
13 Ondřej Pilný 'Mercy on the Misfit: Continuity and Transformation in
the Plays of Conor McPherson' in *The Binding Strength of Irish
Studies. Festschrift in Honour of Csilla Bertha and Donald E. Morse*,
eds. Marianna Gula, Mária Kurdi, István D. Rácz (Debrecen:
Debrecen University Press, 2011):87-94, 90.
14 McPherson, *The Seafarer*, 31.
15 *ibid.*, 6.
16 *ibid.*, 5.
17 *ibid.*,23.
18 *ibid.*,20.
19 *ibid.*,20.
20 *ibid.*, 20.

[21] Christopher Murray 'The Supernatural in McPherson's *The Seafarer and The Birds,'* in *The Binding Strength of Irish Studies. Festschrift in Honour of Csilla Bertha and Donald E. Morse,* eds. Marianna Gula, Mária Kurdi, István D. Rácz (Debrecen: Debrecen University Press, 2011): 71.

[22] McPherson, *The Seafarer,* 44.

[23] McPherson, *The Seafarer,* 101.

[24] *ibid.,* 103.

[25] Brian Singleton *Irish Theatre Magazine*

17 | Interview with Pál Göttinger[1]

Mária Kurdi

MK: Could you first speak about your career as a director? Is it similar to or different from that of other Hungarian directors?

PG: I completed my studies five years ago, so, including the years at college I have been in this profession for only ten years now. This is not a long period, so I can hardly take a bird's-eye view of my 'career' at this point. Until recently there existed a social ladder within this profession in our country. I encountered just the last remnants of it when leaving college, so I started to climb the ladder by first working as an assistant director in a theatre in the country, then in the capital, and finally I joined a company. But I entered into all this with some delay, since somehow I had the idea that the social ladder did not exist anymore. In the old days (before 1990, the change of régime) once admitted to college one chose the path of acting or directing and knew what to expect in later years. After graduation one had a prospect of employment as either an actor or a director, with the view of a clear-cut future in the profession. Things are fairly different now.

Nowadays there is no sign of the former transparency, and the social ladder has lost its function. Events followed each other in my life quickly and unpredictably. I had some remarkable possibilities but also experienced periods of crisis because of the uncertainties of theatre life in our country and because of working freelance. Since graduation I was engaged in twenty-eight larger or smaller projects as a director, out of which fourteen were premieres filling a whole evening. No doubt, this has been too much. Besides working as a director I am an almost full-time musician, so perhaps my route really differs from that of other young directors. Sometimes I am proud of being able to cope with so much, at other times I fall into despair and feel that it is not possible to do all this on a really high level. I seem to be in great demand. While still at the beginning of my career, I try to look upon the new ventures as part of my probation time, letting those who employ me take the risk. They will not employ me again if they do not want to. Sooner or later I think I will have my place in the system.

For my generation, it was definitely new that during the last year of our studies we were offered the opportunity to do professional practice abroad. In spite of its novelty, somehow it seemed quite natural for us. We thoroughly enjoyed studying abroad, but few of us took full advantage of the opportunity as a source of gaining experience and not as one of making connections only, which many considered highly important. Hungarians are not good at harmonizing these two ambitions with each other. For my part I regard myself as successful in using the opportunity well; I gained access to a great number of good plays, including *The Seafarer* and *Love & Money* by Dennis Kelly which proved to be so important early in my career. Also, I made connections which can be renewed when going to the place again. The Young Vic Genesis Project, of which I am still a member, is a source of considerable help and encouragement. However, since my work and especially the kind of theatre I really like to deal with are linked to text and language, I am determined to work in Hungary despite all the current difficulties and cherish no plans of going back to London.

MK: *The Seafarer* premiered in London, in September 2006. It reached the Hungarian stage in a comparatively short time, in 2008. What explains this speed? Was it its success in London that called the Hungarian theatre people's attention to it?

PG: It was me who had been searching high and low to find a Hungarian theatre that would produce the play before Bárka showed interest in it. I saw the London premiere and read the script itself during my stay in England. I tried to find a theatre and company where they would welcome the McPherson-kind of storytelling on stage. What fuelled me was that I discovered a good amount of tenderness in the text under the obscene jokes and the hardness of the tone. The company of Bárka, headed by its ambitious new director, was just preparing for the new season. Actually, László

Bérczes, who had directed *The Playboy of the Western World* in its new translation a couple of years before in the same theatre, was the person who arranged the acceptance of *The Seafarer* for Bárka.[2] And I can say we managed to find a wonder cast.

MK: How long was *The Seafarer* playing in Bárka Theatre? Were you surprised by the unfailing interest of the audience?

PG: It is still playing, thank God. In Hungary we have a repertoire system, meaning that a performance is put on the programme two or three times a month, and is playing for years. *The Seafarer* has been performed more than fifty times during the last three years. As a matter of fact the success of the play does not surprise me. I was, however, far more surprised by a temporary decrease in the number of spectators during the second year. Fortunately, this did not last long and we tended to have full houses again. I knew that there was no play of a similar artistic approach in the current repertoire of the Hungarian theatres. Therefore I thought that those who come to see it would feel a kind of refreshment not provided by the fashionable works of, say, Martin McDonagh, to name just one author, and would greatly enjoy *The Seafarer*. They would enjoy seeing Zoltán Mucsi play in such a self-forgetting way and enthuse over the survival of Sharky. And they would enjoy the special atmosphere of Christmas in the play. Some of the critics frowned at what, in their view, was the shallowness of the text and the clichés of the story, etc., but we did not allow ourselves to be too much troubled by them. We were convinced that *The Seafarer* is a delight both to watch and to play.

At the same time the performance remained rather unstable, which I do not mind at all, but sometimes this might risk failure. It should be born in mind that for those nurtured on the Hungarian theatre traditions it is difficult to accept the sight of a handful of people sitting around a table as a dramatic scene. In the English-speaking cultures spectators display interest in what the characters say, whereas Hungarian spectators are eager to see what they do. Playing *The Seafarer* involves the risk that after an act in which five characters just keep on sitting around the table the Hungarian spectator might leave with the feeling that nothing has happened. The most difficult part of the whole thing for us lies in making spectators feel that so much happens beyond the level of words. Night by night we have to struggle to achieve this effect. When we succeed, and most of the time we fortunately do, the spectators cry, laugh and applaud frantically at the end. When we don't, well, that comes like a disaster.

MK: Is this the first Irish play you have ever directed, or have you had a part in staging other Irish works too?

PG: I became interested in Irish culture through my love of their music as an enthusiastic singer and whistle-player, and I am proud to say that I set up a band during my secondary school days. I sing and play that instrument even today; part of my income is generated from these activities. With the old band I played live in a new Hungarian production of Brian Friel's *Dancing at Lughnasa*, mounted by Szigligeti Ede Theatre of Szolnok in 2005. As a matter of fact, it was me who devised the music for the production. This had been my connection with Irish drama before *The Seafarer*. Besides, I enjoy reading Irish literature, and have made trips to Dublin a couple of times.

MK: How were you preparing for the job of directing *The Seafarer*; have you, perhaps, read critical reviews of its performances in Ireland and elsewhere?

PG: No, not really. A year before the premiere, during my last year at college, I looked up a lot of the criticism about the drama, but I did not use any of these once we had started to work on the actual production. As a matter of fact, we had to create our own performance. We concentrated on the plot, on the place of love never explicitly stated or shown in the story of a night which unfolds on the stage. We did not borrow from another nation's style of acting or draw from the storehouse of their cultural meanings – neither did we want to have the characters look like Irishmen, or parody the Irish. However, having seen the play in London I was well aware that to find the right actors for the Richard-Sharky-Lockhart trio was the key to a successful production. To my delight, working with the company of Bárka turned out to surpass all my expectations.

MK: When I saw the performance the audience consisted of mainly young people, and there was a long-lasting, standing ovation after the curtain went down. What is it in McPherson's play that mesmerizes the audience, especially young theatre-goers among them, to such an extent?

PG: Young people, myself included, to tell the truth, usually find it very difficult to use 'big' words. It is not at all easy for them to identify with harrowing stories, situations involving severe problems or, God forbid, lofty ideas. The characters of *The Seafarer* are not at all conscious of the fact that highly significant things are happening just to them – they are not moved or inspired to consider the events as dramatic in any sense. When defining the style of the drama for ourselves it was very important to understand that although the characters do not 'know' what is happening they somehow feel it, sense it. This is why, through their superficial (but often very witty) sayings, they start defending themselves. Clearly, it is only their love for each other that can save them from the Devil, yet they would laugh at such a sentimental idea. And so would we, I guess. Young spectators, I suppose, accept the fact that the characters can't be expected to express lofty thoughts in dramatic ways about existential questions. Thus their defensive mechanism becomes switched off and they allow themselves to be influenced by the story. The unexpected catharsis finds them unprepared. The same thing happened to me in London at the end of the performance. Suddenly the spectator manages to realize what it is all about.

MK: Do you know other plays by McPherson, and are you planning to direct one of them in the future?

PG I know most of his plays; besides *The Weir*, *Port Authority* and *Dublin Carol* are my favourites, but these are really unique in terms of their dramaturgy, so I do not know where I could find a place for them with a successful premiere in mind. At the moment I am engaged in other projects ...

MK: Was it difficult to choose the actors for *The Seafarer*, especially for the role of Sharky, Richard and Lockhart? If yes, what was the nature of those difficulties?

PG: In the Hungarian theatre world there is no system of casting which would allow one to search for ever to find the perfect actor for a role. I am not troubled by this at all. I like the idea of companies having a fixed number of members. Sometimes it is necessary to make a compromise with regard not to the quality of acting but, for instance, to the actors' age. In the Bárka version of *The Seafarer* the actors are about ten years younger than the characters they play, because they have proved to be the best choice. Zoltán Mucsi (Richard) is in his early fifties. Our Lockhart is a forty-something robust man, and our Nicky is also a younger man. The rest depended on our professional skills, and we all worked hard. Eventually, our success justified the choices.

MK: Tom Murphy, a great representative of the older generation of contemporary Irish playwriting said about his own drama *Conversations on a Homecoming* in an interview: 'talking about form, I discovered ... that a perfect shape, form, structure for a play is an evening in a pub. ... It is a human situation.'[3] Do you think this bears some relevance to *The Seafarer* as well?

PG: It does, certainly. Although pub talk in Ireland is presumably very different from what it is like in Hungary, their essence may possibly be the same, namely because pub talk can be characterized by superficial exchanges and very serious bits of communication freely alternating with each other. In one moment everyone is pulling everyone else's leg, then, in another the conversation takes a big turn towards very weighty subjects. After a fine talk over some drinks in a pub one might leave with the sense of having made a big trip, having been part of an intellectual *tour-de-force*, and still enjoy oneself in the meantime. This is quite similar to the feelings of a spectator standing up from his/her seat after a really good performance in the theatre.

MK: How were the actors responding to the play, did they find its subject familiar or, perhaps, too strange? Were there debates about the interpretation of certain parts during the rehearsals? What other difficulties occurred?

PG: Not everything went always smoothly, of course. The intertwining of myth and reality was not at all easy to comprehend. In one minute the actors were chatting about the nature of alcoholism, in the other about the concept of redemption – it was difficult to create a balance. They tended to be embarrassed by not knowing the locale; the play contains several references the meaning of which only Dubliners are able to fully grasp. For those living far away it is necessary to have some familiarity with the language and culture of Dublin people. I suppose that when *The Seafarer* is performed in English in an English-speaking country, the audience recognizes the Irish accent immediately and it means something to them. They know how to place it; the first sentence may evoke prejudices but also it brings a lot of information into play. We cannot produce this in Hungary. We cannot imitate the accent, the characteristic use of language, not to speak of identifying the number of allusions. The translator needs to invent a specific language for the occasion, which may be more poetic or more fable-like than the original — Dániel Varró uses this method to render the McDonagh plays for the Hungarian stage. László Upor's translation of *The Seafarer* sounds down-to-earth and foul-mouthed, provoking laughter by its vulgarities.

Once we had come to terms with all these questions, we were free to consider concrete issues of staging: how to play the devil, the drunkard and the delirious person without making them seem parodic. How to see this story, with its absurd turns, as a simple and naturally flowing one, in the way the characters live through it. It was an extremely rewarding job.

MK: What is the place of *The Seafarer* in contemporary world drama? Is there a Hungarian author, in your view, whose work shows affinities with that of McPherson's?

PG: I hear that the play has achieved great international success, which makes me very glad. I do not think I can find any play similar to *The Seafarer* here in Hungary. The general view is that Conor McPherson is too easy-going, superficial. His 'well-made' plays with their transparent structure and plot which make interpretation easy arouse suspicions in Hungarian authors. They prefer plays with a unique form and obscurity of intent, full of secrets and unanswered questions, thus bringing the text closer to literature than to theatre. I have directed such pieces and enjoyed the work, so I do not want to degrade them. *The Seafarer* is really for the stage. Although it seems totally different, on closer inspection I think András Vinnai's work displays some conceptual similarity. Vinnai's scripts are not written as literature but as ones for performance; they are rich in insight into human nature as well as in wry humour.[4] His work is more extreme, daring and unrestrained than McPherson's, whose effects are achieved not by authorial tricks but through turns that come about in the story quite naturally. The tone is gentle even in the McPherson plays with very rough themes. Or at least to the Hungarian ear.

MK: Do you think that it would be worthwhile to discover and produce more of this kind of plays which probe into the hidden layers of personal realities by including elements of myths and legends among their devices?

PG: Yes, definitely. I would be happy to come across more of them, because the brutality of the world is usually presented brutally nowadays, which I cannot agree with as a director. It is quite customary that brutality is portrayed as brutality, failure as failure, and the belief in the supernatural and the primitive as foolish. In most of the texts I read the people governed by an 'inner voice' are shown as schizophrenic or the like. I am uncomfortable with this phenomenon. In my opinion storytelling, especially among adults, is very theatrical, as it carries the potential of making good theatre. Like telling stories over the table in a pub. But we need time to go to pubs and need the presence of a sense of safety and warmth in those pubs, which conditions are not really evident in our time. We are too distracted by other things. Much as I'd like to see the opposite, I do not think there will be a change of playwriting under the influence of *The Seafarer*, it is not likely to create a fashion in our country.

MK: Christopher Murray, a notable expert on Irish drama claims that *The Seafarer* can be seen as having some common features with Eugene O'Neill's *The Iceman Cometh*. The figure similar to Hickey in the American drama is Mr. Lockhart, who possesses destructive powers too, yet proves incapable of winning. Eventually, he is outwitted by the collective of those weaker than him.[5] How do you respond to this view?

PG: I think that Lockhart's failure is comic, therefore people come to like him. It may sound strange, but this is the reaction we detected among the Hungarian audience. They see a lonely poseur in him, who tries to compensate for this by showing off his darkness of being and terrible secrets. In truth, however, like a stray dog he is eager to escape from the outside to enjoy the warmth of the inside where people are sitting together. It is Christmas, not his day. He is a stranger in a bad mood, who would like to indulge in drinking and talking with the others instead of going home. One option is that he has mercy for Sharky. The other is that someone from above intervenes and rearranges the position of the cards. Either way, this tired man, who goes away empty-handed, does not at all look like Satan.

It is great to notice that even younger members of the audience get nearer to him. Artúr Kálid is an excellent actor, who plays Lockhart with a lot of empathy and understanding.

For us it is new to see that the devil can be helpless against love, even if its light is only flickering. It is a refreshing idea.

MK: Do you view the play as a parable?

PG: No, not really, thank God. It is not a didactic script, in my interpretation, and our performance does not at all wish to teach.

MK: Can you use the experiences gained from your direction of *The Seafarer* in your work in general? What are you currently working on?

PG: The basic skill of my work is the ability to defend all those involved in a performance with equally convincing force. I should be able to justify fully all their moments and sentences on the stage, especially those which are flawed. When there are more than two people on stage, each of them has his/her own story pace, they tend to decode different signals from what is going on and absorb those into the world of their own thoughts. This will affect their deeds and the performance itself eventually. Working on *The Seafarer* is a good example to demonstrate this process. Putting each moment of the incessant quarrels into shape is, in fact, a huge exercise in empathy.

The Bárka performance of *The Seafarer* came into being at the outset of my career, and helps shape my professional identity. I had the opportunity to work with great actors on a great story which unfolds from an embarrassingly quotidian situation involving very small people. I could join the company of Bárka Theatre and meet colleagues I am still working with. All this is due to *The Seafarer*. It made us learn to speak the same language, which has resulted in long-term friendships and alliances. Next I will direct another Irish play, *Freefall* by Michael West. Its protagonist, who is predictably and unavoidably falling towards death will be played by the one-time Mr Lockhart. And the devilish character, who is coming to disinfect the cellar covered with the fungus of memories, despair and repressions, will be played by the one-time Sharky. After all, there is much to say for a permanent company. I am looking forward to the new job immensely.

Works Cited

Kurdi, Mária, 'An Interview with Tom Murphy' *Irish Studies Review* 12.2 (August 2004): 233-240.

Murray, Christopher, 'The Supernatural in Conor McPherson's *The Seafarer* and *The Birds*,' *The Binding Strength of Irish Studies. Festschrift in Honour of Csilla Bertha and Donald E. Morse*, eds. Marianna Gula, Mária Kurdi, István D. Rácz (Debrecen: Debrecen University Press, 2011): 66-77.

---

[1] Pál Göttinger is director of the first Hungarian production of Conor McPherson's *The Seafarer* in Bárka Theatre, Budapest.

[2] The Bárka Theatre's production of the new Hungarian *Playboy* was running for two seasons with considerable success. Most reviewers emphasized the efforts of the company to achieve a complex aesthetic effect through the application of an innovative stage symbolism.

[3] Mária Kurdi, 'An Interview with Tom Murphy' *Irish Studies Review*, 12.2 (August 2004): 237.

[4] András Vinnai wrote the script for the play *Rattledanddisappeared*, inspired by *The Trial*, the well-known novel of Franz Kafka. It was produced by Katona József Theatre, Budapest, and, due to its international success, it was invited to feature in the Dublin Theatre Festival 2006.

[5] See Christopher Murray, 'The Supernatural in Conor McPherson's *The Seafarer* and *The Birds*,' *The Binding Strength of Irish Studies. Festschrift in Honour of Csilla Bertha and Donald E. Morse*, eds. Marianna Gula, Mária Kurdi, István D. Rácz (Debrecen: Debrecen University Press, 2011): 68.

18 | Para-Normal Views/Para-Gothic Activities in Conor McPherson's *The Veil*

Eamonn Jordan

> The camera shows you exactly what is going on. A film does the dreaming for you. That suits me from time to time, but the magic of a play is that you actively are dreaming. At every point you are being reminded of its artificiality, that these people are pretending, but what's so interesting is there's almost an ancient telepathy between the audience. It's like a church service, where the story unfolds before us. It's dark, you have to strain to suspend disbelief, but the effort you make pulls you into a deeper trance.[1]

Rending the Veil

Conor McPherson's first Gothic historical play *The Veil*, which premiered at London's National Theatre's Lyttleton auditorium on 4 October 2011, is clearly one of McPherson's most complex and challenging works to date. In some respects, this work is a reprise of many of the concerns previously articulated across the full body of McPherson's work, namely; what is the nature of good and evil, how do characters distinguish between personal and collective responsibilities and in what ways do these characters negotiate with their own inconsistencies, anxieties and fears. To these ends, what determines the varying breaking points of characters and what are the characteristics of agency in the face of overwhelming pressures and crushing odds brought about by natural or economic disasters, psychic or socio-political forces. These recurring questions invite considerations that are ultimately about endurance and the requisites of survival or otherwise for McPherson's characters. In addition, an extra layer is provided by reflections on how the past haunts the present and substantially configures the future, and how memories may be exorcized, ameliorated or accommodated, as when trauma is displaced, dis-recognized or transposed into fantasy it both ghosts and disorientates the immediate present.

The Veil is set in 1822 in Mount Prospect, near Jamestown, Co. Roscommon, Ireland, where the Protestant Ascendancy Lambroke family live. The Big House itself is in disrepair, paint is peeling from the crumbling walls, and as Rae Smith designs it, a large tree seems to be trespassing on the living space. The estate manager Mr Fingal (Peter McDonald) has not been paid for thirteen months, and the two horses that might be put at the visitors' disposal are now lame. The hospitality that the Lambrokes might once have provided is no longer possible, as food and heat are increasingly scarce.

Other indigenous staff members, the housemaid, Clare Wallace (Caoilfhionn Dunne), and the housekeeper Mrs Goulding (Bríd Brennan) do their best to attend to the situation, but cannot keep the realities of the household's existence at bay. The servant and managerially employed Irish characters are despised locally, yet they are in a far better position to survive the economic hardships which are evident all around them. As the play opens, the seventeen year old Hannah Lambroke has gone missing and there is a fear that her 'old complaint' has returned.[2] In the past Hannah has claimed to have heard voices; when she played the piano she could hear someone singing or crying, probably a child. Further, Hannah is haunted by her discovery of the body of her father, Edward, who had committed suicide by hanging himself in the living room from a brace over the fireplace. Hannah was eight or nine years of age at the time. Most recently, she claims that she has heard a man shouting in their home on Sunday evening last, as she sat writing.

On her appearance, Emily Taaffe plays the character of Hannah as if to contradict previous impressions of her, as she is determined, perceptive and far more assertive and less vulnerable than one might have been enticed to assume. In order to stave off financial ruin, the family is depending on the marriage of Hannah to the Marquis of Newbury, eldest son of Lord Ashby, whose seat is outside of Northampton, England. (The Marquis has already made the Duke of Wellborough's widow pregnant, but both she and the child died prior to childbirth, freeing him from any paternal obligations.) Hannah knows that her potential groom does not love her and, indeed, she is unnerved by his 'alarming moral disarray.'[3] There is a suspicion that it is Lord Ashby and not the son that seems more interested in Hannah. For her mother, Madeleine (Fenella Woolgar), Hannah has little choice, as waiting for 'some outcast to be dispatched from a dissolute estate in the north' or marrying in the locality one of the sons of Colonel Bennett are no better options.[4] Hannah sees her ordeal as if she is being sold into a hellish existence and that she has been un-housed, effectively 'put' out or evicted by her mother.[5]

However, if Hannah is forced to marry, she expresses the wish to face the ordeal alone and intends to punish her mother, by leaving behind Madeleine and her great grandmother, Maria also called Grandie (Ursula Jones), who suffers with Alzheimer's Disease. Marriage functions as a metaphor perhaps for the pressure on a woman to marry against her will under these particular socio-economic circumstances and it also serves as an expression of women's symbolic and material exchange value within a patriarchal economy.[6] Additionally, Mrs Goulding wants Hannah taken away because ... 'The glow that comes off Hannah will bring her good luck there. Here it will only darken all her evenings. The fairies are jealous of her.'[7] That sort of twisted logic, like that of both imperialism and the patriarchal economy are held to task throughout the work.[8]

The defrocked Anglican priest Reverend Berkeley (Jim Norton) and his philosopher travelling companion, Charles Audelle (Adrian Schiller) arrive at Mount Prospect, intent on escorting Hannah to England. Their arrival brings more than is initially bargained for. During early exchanges Hannah confronts Audelle about accusations of plagiarism made against his work. He admits to the unacknowledged influence of German idealists on his writing, which he picked up when he visited Tübingen and Jena universities.[9] Hannah also confronts the practices of philosophers, asking, 'you do not tire of ... inventing worlds where nobody lives?'[10] A capacity to engage philosophically with some conviction is but one part of the complexity of Hannah's character which Emily Taaffe addresses with great assurance. Additionally, it is Hannah's passion when arguing with her mother, her ongoing vulnerability, and her alertness to the supernatural that need to be consistently foregrounded by Taaffe's performance.

Ireland itself seems to be the perfect domain for Audelle to test his skills as a sensate. Initially it is Berkeley's belief that the ghost of

Hannah's father haunts the living space, something that Audelle is also happy to promote, having felt some sort of presence himself.

> **BERKELEY:** The spirit realm flows through this place like a river! It always has! This is the very place that piqued my interest in everything that even led to my downfall and my disgrace, but I don't regret it. Not for a second. Audelle is sensate. And he can feel it. I know him. And I know he can barely keep his mind together, so strong is its current.[11]

For Audelle,

> An elemental darkness is already inside each of us, how we explain it to ourselves is for each of us to bear. Anyone with a gift such as Hannah's is like a beacon in the dark.[12]

In addition, her father-in-law to be, Lord Ashby mentions in his letter his special regard for Hannah, which Berkeley construes to be her 'unique aspect,' and 'something *elemental*,' which is based on 'her unique atunement.'[13] Berkeley believes that Hannah 'hears echoes of the past none else hears.'[14] Like the meddling, destructive, faux-idealist Gregers Werle in Henrik Ibsen's *The Wild Duck* (1884), the tinkering, visionary and farcical certainties of Berkeley are bound to prove problematic. Norton excels in maintaining that deluded, over-confident fixation that leaves his Berkeley comfortable and assured in the later attempts to summon the dead through prayer. Berkeley's predilection for the otherworldly and less conventional belief systems is the reason for his defrocking. (Indeed, the Bishop of Solsbury, who will perform Hannah's marriage ceremony, is the one who instigated such a move.) Hannah, to all of the men in a variety of ways, is seen as a force to repel the darkness. That is why they all wish to (dis)possess her. This aspect and their need to exchange her between themselves are confidently challenged by the play's dramaturgy.[15]

Hannah tells the tale of a man, so drunk that he fell 'asleep under the bushes out by a country road.'[16] He was taken to see the King of the Fairies and begged for drink. When he awoke there were three full bottles of poitín by his side. After a week's drinking, he went home. His child was gone; he had bartered the thing he valued most for drink and now in his child's cot, there is a changeling. If there is a localized promotion of the supernatural and if the visitors project their fantasies onto others and the local environment, there is an even more intricate complication then introduced, because what is happening on the ground close by, so to speak, has a huge influence on all of the characters in this play. Nearby, children are dying from illnesses like scarlet fever, tenants are unable to pay rents, and there is a degree of political agitation rising against landlords. Because of the economic hardships all round, those who are surviving or subsisting are effectively the living dead, so haggard and decimated are their bodies.

Equally, if tenants are not paying rents to their landlord elites, such as the Lambrokes, then the Lambrokes are in no position to pay their staff. In that way the circularity of money links in with the circularity of time. The Lambrokes are reliant on Colonel Bennett to extend credit to them, but even he is going to have to reduce rents by half in order to avoid mass evictions. More soldiers are moving into Queensfort, public works are in the offing, and everyone is endeavouring to hang on in there till the next crop. That said, Fingal does point out that the Colonel is addicted to the acquisition of property. Indeed, all this emphasis on landlords, property acquisition, a fixation on money, extensions of credit, bankruptcy, and people living beyond their means points also towards the contemporary.

So, set in a place in decline, with concerns about marriage and the future, with an acceptance of dead figures haunting the present, with fears around fairies with the threat of madness, this play's *mise-en-scène* evokes Big House Gothic sensibilities.[17] Jerrold E. Hogle notes that 'gothic fictions generally play with and oscillate between the earthly laws of conventional reality and the possibilities of the supernatural.'[18] Hogle goes on to distinguish between 'terror gothic' and 'horror gothic' (Ann Radcliffe's distinction). The former, 'holds characters and readers mostly in anxious suspense about threats to life, safety, and sanity [which are] kept largely out of sight or in the shadows or suggestions from a hidden past, while the latter 'confronts the principal characters with the gross violence of physical or psychological dissolution, explicitly shattering the assumed norms (including the repressions) of everyday life with wildly shocking, and even revolting, consequences.'[19]

There are two levels of unconsciousness, within the Gothic which Hogle notes, the one that is normally associated with individual repression, and the second, a socio/political unconscious, where 'deep-seated social and historical dilemmas, often of many types at once', become more 'fearsome' the more they are 'covered up' and 'fundamental rather than symbolic resolution is what should be desired' when encountering them.[20] W.J. McCormack's observations on the Gothic novel are especially interesting: he notes how 'the sublime and asymmetrical character of gothic architecture, transformed into verbal intricacy, convoluted plot, emotional intensity – and all overlaid with the implications of supernatural agency – lies behind the literary experiment.'[21] (Rae Smith's design uses roman design features in contrast.)

The Gothic novel 'endlessly exposed the violence and corruption that lay behind authority, ancient authority for the most part: in this sense it was a subversive force in the eighteenth century and the period following the French Revolution,' McCormack suggests.[22] Equally McCormack identifies an 'underlying concern for linkage and continuity, especially for the transmission of property at a time of repeated assaults on the traditional basis of English society,'[23] and such a concern is central to this drama. But unlike its English counterpart, Irish Gothic writing seemingly 'is remarkably explicit in the way that it demonstrates its attachment to history and politics.'[24] Such meetings of public and private, the real and Gothic, and the historic and the contemporary give rise to the great complexities of this Gothic-inspired play.

Prayer seems to be one of the answers to the chaos and disharmony palpable in the world of the play. So when Berkeley leads the others in prayer, his invocation of the dead is a seminal moment in performance, as there is a strong sense of some sort of rupture or psychic disturbance. There is a loud noise that unnerves them all and the moment is staged so as to exacerbate the fear, as if the dead may be in communion with the living.

On this defining moment the play script suggests that 'There is a sudden deafening bang like a gunshot over their heads. It seems to blow the room apart with its sonic impact. Their drinks go flying, cups are dropped. Each instinctively cries out and cowers.'[25] This sensational moment is a challenge for the superb scenography of Rae Smith, Paul Arditti's sound and Neil Austin's lighting designs.[26] Sound, candlelight, shadow play and the positioning of the actors on stage create memorable moments in performance.[27] There is a demented, delusional quality to the acting of Norton, a despairing self-deception pivotal to Schiller's Audelle, and a superb unnerving vulnerability and susceptibility to Taaffe's Hannah during the moments leading up to the thunderclap. The impact is almost one of real unnerving intensity in performance, one which is not mawkish or self-indulgent as the suspension of disbelief seems well earned.[28]

On the 'suspension of disbelief,' a concept coined by the Romantic poet Samuel Taylor Coleridge, McPherson notes:

It's a phrase we take for granted now, but Coleridge 'uses a double negative where a simple positive ("belief") might have done, but somehow this doesn't quite capture the strange trance we are willing to enter when we watch a play.[29]

Again this comment brings one back to the one at the start of this article. McPherson adds:

Coleridge had a great mind and was immersed in the intellectual debates of his time. He was an advocate of German transcendental philosophy, which began with Immanuel Kant (1724-1804). Kant maintained that because we have only five senses, what we know of the world is essentially limited. Our eyes perceive only a narrow band of the spectrum of light; our ears only a narrow frequency range, so we are cut off from the whole of reality – ignorant of how the world really appears.[30]

During this vital performance moment, then, there is direct evidence that McPherson as both writer and director is endeavouring to find ways of extending the spectrum of light, of broadening the frequency, range of the ears, and of heightening the senses of the work, or at least providing the illusion of that. There is real evidence of the quality and precision that McPherson, as director, does so well. In performance, while the loud thunderclap did have an impact, this crucial happening is not quite as sensational or as disconcerting, as one might have imagined it to be. However, the knock on the door that soon follows this incident extends the implications of this stunning performance moment as reports indicate that local living quarters have collapsed; these are owned by the Lambroke family and are home to the destitute of Jamestown, leading to many being dead, and more trapped in the rubble, including numerous children.

Such a coincidental collapse of the building symbolizes the fundamental impact of British and Anglo-Irish landlord classes in general, whose lifestyles are funded by exorbitant rents, and effectively ensure the staggering poverty that the Irish tenant farming classes and the destitute experience.[31] Hannah connects both the collapse of the housing and the summoning of the dead and is distressed by the implications of such a connection. Audelle especially annoys her because of his disregard for the lives of others, as he is more concerned with what has transpired, what he has witnessed. Once these two crucial moments are passed, Hannah is now even more alert to her own demons and dysfunctionality. Appearing normal is taking its toll, for she knows, 'there is something real, separate from me – (*Short pause.*) and I know it's waiting for me, calling for me to do what my father did. It knows how tired I am. It knows how old being so exhausted and lonely can make you feel.'[32]

Mirror Kings and a Queen's Tomb

The consuming of laudanum by both Hannah and Audelle at the end of the first act leaves the spectator with certain intensities and mysteries in the air, but probably one does not have a real sense as to what direction the work may go. Act two opens with Audelle and Hannah just back from their visit to the Queen's tomb, during which Hannah hallucinates that there is a couple sheltering in the tomb, but really it is their own corpses which have walked out. Berkeley regards the tomb as a place of 'dark enchantment,' and Audelle tells of laying his hands on the prehistoric stones and how they 'induced a sense of connectedness to the mysterious ancestors of this place,' something he had not previously experienced.[33] Hannah is less committed to self-revelation and is pushed by Berkeley to reflect on how her father still lives in her mind. Proposals as to how the dead exist in some other dimension are made. In this three-way exchange, Audelle and Berkeley are in a way wanting to influence Hannah immensely. In performance, Taaffe responds to their pressure with a mixture of assertiveness, hesitation and confusion but also with an open vulnerability, driven by some need to make sense of her paranormal experiences and to push back psychic boundaries. She also demonstrates that she is in dread of her future.

Hannah's talent, for Audelle, is that it is 'simply consciousness itself. That's right. And so profound is your talent in this case, so acute its perceptiveness, you are capable of beholding not just what is here in this moment, but what is beyond and before time.'[34] If Hannah can uncover the divine within, then her fears of ghosts and haunting will pass and Berkeley suggests a séance so all those that haunt her can also find that inner light. Hannah is pressured by these men to release fear, and to forgive herself in order to set in motion a freedom that will enable her.[35] With Audelle and Hannah consuming more laudanum and also brandy, Berkeley continues with his séance. Again this proves to be another crucial moment of the performance. Furniture moves overhead, Hannah starts to sing, searches for a child the others cannot see, then, uncannily, a small child with long blond hair stands staring at Audelle. Grandie witnesses the event, and she mocks him, hits Audelle with a stick, and terrifies him. Indeed Grandie is the silent witness almost throughout the work and Jones's stage presence ensures that it is another haunting of sorts.

In response to the child's appearance Hannah also believes that she is witnessing her future, her perishing in childbirth, and her leaving behind a child to survive alone. Eternity for her will be spent wandering and looking for a child she cannot trace. However, Audelle admits that the child Hannah sees is not her future but is in fact the ghost of his own dead child. Audelle then becomes the second male suicide in the house, and the gunshot offstage during performance made many reflexively jump, given its loudness and its unexpectedness. (He had of course made previous attempts on his own life.)

Mrs Goulding, who is present on special family occasions, was once affectionately called by all in the household their 'maid mother,'[36] according to Berkeley. Mrs Goulding knocks her own kind, declaring:

> The ingratitude of the wretches who skulk about this island?
> Who are these people? The wildness in them. And the badness
> in them. They are only filthy tinkers the half of them.[37]

She also comments negatively on people hoarding supplies when given to them and remarks that the locals are also 'in league with the devil the half of them.'[38] Brennan's convincing performance captures in part the indigenous internalization of imperial values. She is not alone. Fingal expresses a similar outlook:

> **FINGAL**: They say such is the lot of the poor.
> **MADELEINE**: To suffer the rich.
> **FINGAL**: They suffer themselves. They should better
> themselves.[39]

Fingal is an especially interesting figure, enamoured with Madeleine, and admits to having been the one who stood on watch for Edward, during his mad episodes. Fingal works without pay, and feels that it is his role to confront Audelle for giving Hannah the laudanum. The beating he doles out to James Furay, a relative innocent, is appalling, and fundamentally undermines any idea of the native under imperialism as simply a hapless victim. There is only something insubstantial to be said of victims needing to pass on their victimhood, which is indeed complicated by the fact that it is

Hannah who goes to help James and to bathe his wounds. Fingal persists with the belief that the discipline shown in the violence perpetrated on James is an expression of his loyalty to the household, his faithfulness to Madeleine. Fingal, in his own words, is 'neither one thing nor the other anymore.'[40] Indeed, Fingal wants a revolt of sorts, or at least promises that he will no longer 'walk out of this house, ignorant of the forces that keep me perpetually on my knees!'[41] It is a striking statement in the context of a play performed at the British National Theatre about the history between Ireland and Britain and so soon after the British Queen's symbolically significant visit to Ireland in 2011. (Ironically perhaps, Audelle dies using Fingal's misplaced gun.)

Interestingly, the word 'veil' is used in association with Daniel O'Connell, a figure who shaped political change in terms of Catholic Emancipation – Mrs Goulding reports the line 'it will take a strong draught to blow back the veil of confusion,' from an O'Connell speech at Loughferry.[42] W.J. McCormack notes that Daniel O'Connell was a major *bête noire* of the Anglo-Irish ascendency, 'a countryman, hard-headed and roughly spoken, scion of a tribe who had thrived in the demanding conditions of Penal Ireland. Although he was a landowner and a barrister, O'Connell was regarded by his Protestant counterparts as an upstart and a vulgarian.'[43] McCormack continues, after the failure of the 1798 rebellion, the Catholic masses were without leadership and demoralized, but 'O'Connell had energy and organizing genius, and he worked for forty years to create an articulate public opinion in Ireland, representing the Catholic majority rather than the Protestant establishment.'[44] O'Connell's voice of protest helped define the future of Ireland, and he, like the other indigenous characters who die in the building collapse, haunts this work.

There is note of a bridge 'half destroyed by so-called revolutionaries,'[45] in the words of Berkeley. Berkeley further notes how, 'Desperate men and women suddenly descended upon our coach. So numerous were the pale hands outstretched towards us, it was only later I understood that an insensible infant thrust before me by a cadaverous wild-eyed woman must surely have been deceased.'[46] And although Audelle is the figure most likely to romanticize the nation, that capacity is quickly challenged by his observations that 'a crowd of haggard-looking men and women turned to look at me with such alien ferocity.'[47] In many ways the play itself is a form of 'alien ferocity,' a form of playing with the traditional tropes associated with Gothic Big House novels in particular, and then turns many of them on their heads. The Colonel has been shooting at intruders a previous evening. The play asks the question as to who the intruder truly is.

In some ways towards the end the drama's focus shifts from daughter to mother. Madeleine's guilt over her husband's death is increasingly palpable. She did nothing to protect the unnerved Edward, as she was enraged by him, saying all the things that she thought of him and when he went out of the house distressed, she did not pursue him, knowing full well that he should not be left alone. Madeleine apportions her lack of compassionate action to 'anger and evil.'[48] Berkeley believes that Madeleine has the 'darkest instinct for second sight.'[49] However, Madeleine criticizes Berkeley's emotive disposition, stating that she believes him 'like a man with an infant's toy box in his head.'[50]

Woolgar's performance as Madeleine is remarkable at this late stage in particular. Until now she has been very deliberate and focused in her actions, and steered the other characters around her consistent with her status. Here at this point something else shines through, which in some ways prepares one for the lingering kiss between Madeleine and Fingal. This kiss can be taken to mean many things, but the idea that it is symbolic of some form of resolution between the Irish and the Anglo-Irish, between those from different classes or between genders would be a false one. It is a lengthy kiss, the stillness is held for a protracted time, and remains like an image from a painting that lingers in the imagination. Hoggle draws on Julia Kristeva's theory of the abject in relation to the Gothic, and suggests that

> the repressed, archaic, and thus deeply unconscious Feminine is a fundamental level of being to which most Gothic finally refers, often in displacements of it that seem to be old patriarchal structures, and all the blurred oppositions that are abjected onto monsters or spectres by Gothic characters face their ultimate dissolution into primal chaos as they approach this feminized nadir that is both the ultimate Other and the basically groundless ground of the self.'[51]

If there is a 'primal chaos', even a primal, cyclical destructiveness evident in failures of characters, ghosts and the collapse of the buildings, there is also something more positive, in the form of defiance and resilience in the form of those who display resoluteness and conviction.

An Encore of Ghost Estates/A Celtic High

In terms of a myth of origins, during the first act Grandie tells a story of St. Patrick, in which he is a gold prospector rather than the religious visionary and leader, and it is a story that highlights issues of foreignness and the taking of local material resources and also the dispossessing of pagan belief systems amongst indigenous peoples. Later in the published text she has a second narrative about money and profit again. In this narrative when someone looks into the face of the King with mirror's eyes, they see only themselves. This King has told her a story about gentle people who existed before St. Patrick's arrival. They were hunters and fishermen. The arrival of farmers brought the arrival of a different God.

What is striking is the sensibility of living off the land, living close to nature, but most of all living in a world free from a profit-driven economic system. The fact that this second speech was eliminated during the rehearsal process is especially interesting, and perhaps it indicates that McPherson was concerned that the play was trying to do too much. By cutting this speech, he probably felt less is more in this instance, and simply that there is not much merit in just hammering home a point of view. The editing back of this final story hinders a more direct relationship to the contemporary situation, but its absence does not take away too much from the overall sensibility of the play. The work's main intention is to capture a world on the cusp of difference, leaving characters traumatized by transitions and by fundamental changes in their circumstances. It is with this contemporary connection in mind that I wish to conclude.

In some insightful interviews prior to the play opening in London McPherson attempts to open things up: 'There was a big economic crash following the Napoleonic wars. So a place like Ireland, which was very poor, was just on the floor.'[52] In an interview with Liz Hoggard he adds to this point by stating that in addition to the famine and the poverty, this 'was a moment when he believes human beings became deluded about their own importance.'[53] McPherson explains it thus: 'The German philosopher Hegel thought we'd reached the end of history, everything was completed, so the German state represented the perfect state, and Lutheran Christianity was the perfect spiritual fulfilment.'[54]

In other comments McPherson steers his reflections in another direction. In an interview with Liz Hoggard he notes that he:

> started making notes [for the play] in late 2008 as Ireland had suddenly started to be in bad trouble. We had been through such a strange journey in the sense that we were poor, then we were told we were one of the richest nations in the world, then suddenly we were in the hands of the IMF [International Monetary Fund]. For the first time, I realized the public can share a dysfunctional psyche, and that psyche can be generational. The Irish Famine is only five generations ago. I began to realize the mess we'd got ourselves into must have come from some tremendous trauma. For the first time, I accepted I am Irish – up till then I'd always felt European or a citizen of the world.[55]

McPherson remarks further:

> When I look at what's happened to Ireland, I think: where did this awful dysfunction in our psyche come from that we've destroyed our own country? On one level you can say it's just post-colonial corruption and mismanagement. On another level, it's like an echo of a long, violent trauma. For hundreds of years, to be Irish and Catholic meant your life was just shit. You were not allowed to go to school, you were not allowed to own land, you didn't have any rights. If people suddenly get that power back, of course they fuck it up.[56]

'We never felt we owned our country, it was all: "Get what you can cos it'll be gone soon." I could see we'd done it to ourselves,' he adds.[57] In an interview with Caroline McGinn, McPherson acknowledges that he had 'always mistakenly felt that I was just a person, tuned into something more cosmic. But you realize you're down in the mud with the same ideas as everyone else.'[58] The fact that most reviewers failed to pick up on the play's contemporary perspective is especially interesting, with the exception of Michael Billington, even after McPherson's numerous interviews and opinion pieces in advance of the play's opening.[59]

This play then marks a fixation on land, property, investment, borrowings and speculation, which for some proves positive and for others disastrous. (The ghosts of Edward and Audelle's child suggest the impact of other types of lack of emotional investment, loss and absence on a psyche.) The indigenous Irish are effectively excluded from these transactions. Equally, the collapse of the rented housing nearby symbolizes rupture and chaos, which may be an Act of God or an act of mankind, in terms of poor construction? The Colonel, the character who does not appear, profits from the failure of those around him to maintain cash flow – the invisible, but not absent landlord and speculator, and he keeps Mrs Goulding and James on.

In the 1820s land ownership for the indigenous population was almost impossible, indeed as it was for many generations of people until the 1990s, but by that stage almost everyone had become obsessed with ownership, and not just the native Irish living in Ireland. There was naive belief in the certainty of order, of trusting markets more generally to regulate and not to be driven by chaos. Key then to the Celtic Tiger period was a myth of alchemy, and with its failure to transmute base metal into gold and a myth of difference, that history would not see a repeat of boom/burst model associated with bubble markets.

Yes, there is personal responsibility, but what is not fully recognized, is the innate instinct of those who fell foul of the marketing of property and role of government, regulation, banking, developers and estate agents in creating a frenzied, Ponzi scheme. From a left wing point of view, it is easy to tease out how ideology structures consciousness and constructs and maintains inequality in socio-political dynamics, and also how citizens are manipulated by language, values, rituals, media and governance, etc. That desire to own one's home was prompted in part by huge rents for accommodation, and in part by general everyday ideologically-shaped opinion in the media and in casual conversation, meaning that people as part of a herd effectively purchased homes at grossly inflated prices, and borrowed accordingly up to 110% of the then market value of the house or apartment. (The application of poor stress testing and the need for banks to increase profitability meant the exponential expansion of loan books held by banks and other lending institutions.) The Irish state in many respects was the property market's biggest cheerleader. Tax rates, borrowing and investment incentives incited many less than calculated transactions. It must be stressed that not everyone was a speculator, as many just wanted simply to get onto the 'housing ladder'. It was all about the now, the longer you waited the more it cost. (Currently, for anyone who purchased a home after 2000/1, they are now in negative equity eleven years on, having previously seen significant value in paper gains until 2006. The nearer the home purchase to 2006 means the bigger the percent of negative equity.)

Many people invested locally and many others overseas. People did boast about property portfolios, the joys and benefits of speculation, taking certain degrees of false assurance from governments, from the willingness of banks to lend based on proper valuations, from international markets who were lending to the Irish lenders and from upward trends in property prices internationally. (The conditions for other bubbles internationally were ignored and dismissed, with the uniqueness of the Irish situation stressed.)

The prime lending problem in America and the collapse of Lehman Brothers did lead to one sort of rupture, the over borrowing by many European governments and excessive lending by a significant number of banks across the continent led to another, but for a country like Ireland with its open economy and its specific vulnerability to international economic conditions, the period of plenty (but not, it must be noted, a period marked by a greater distribution of wealth) has been followed by a period of great recession and austerity. The Celtic Tiger period was an abnormal set of conditions and circumstances in many respects, there was a huge feel good factor, and people did lose the run of themselves, with a range of extravagances. Property speculation was not just confined to the upper and middle classes; equally some members of the working classes also found in property investment the first real potential opportunity in generations to move beyond subsistence living. (Non-Irish nationals were also active in such investments.)

The traditional deficit or subsistence model of living for the majority of Ireland's citizens meant that many did not cope well with extra resources, within a model of relative plenty. Having more did not bring general satiation. Today, indebtedness, negative equity and bankruptcy haunt this current Irish society, as well as, of course, national indebtedness, in such a way that the legacy of the boom and bust cycle will be carried by a number of generations to follow. The country went from a position of almost full employment to almost fifteen percent unemployment, close but not quite back to the rates of seventeen percent plus of the late 1980s. Cheap credit drove most of the extravagance.

The financial bailout from the Troika comprising International Monetary Fund (IMF), European Central Bank (ECB) and the European Commission (EC), led effectively to the loss of Ireland's economic sovereignty and the austerity guidelines set down by the Troika suggest as much, as the nation is rescued from its immature recklessness, its significant decisions are now centralized not in London as it was historically, but in Brussels.[60] (So there is a deep irony in Audelle's comment, 'Well, I have no doubt, in the future, the

Irishman will be beholden to no one and walk amid the spirit of his age with pride,' has proven to be an unfortunate assessment.)

While the play somewhat distances itself from the traumas of the current reality, it does not slip into victim mode. Instead it suggests that things are cyclical; a different social order over-extended itself and as a consequence had to make hard choices. Therefore one could say that what is pivotal in performance is not the tragic-comedy mode one gets in Chekhov's plays about social decay and rupture, but instead one experiences a celebration, if one can call it that, of resoluteness and pragmatism, which Madeleine and the other characters show in the face of chaos. And in some ways, the elimination of Grandie's final narrative mentioned earlier, which is effectively a more sentimental take on the world, leaves the world of the play in a harder, resolute and less victimizing space. It is McPherson's greatness as a writer to recognize the chaos, maintain high levels of empathy, but also to insist on resoluteness and not despair at moments of great change.

In performance the complexity of *The Veil* is apparent, the intricate connections are so well established by the staging and by the play's rhythm that owe much to the dramaturgical sensibility of Chekhov, where so many of the characters are interconnected or bonded in complex ways. But for that complexity to shine through more thoroughly, the complex rhythms of the piece I had imagined them to be from my reading of the play in advance of seeing the production were not fully apparent in the slightly up-tempo performance. (Maybe if I had not read the piece in advance, I may have thought differently.) That was my only real quibble with this outstanding National Theatre production. (The production was not helped by the two insightful but predominantly historically focused program notes on Ireland's history during the 1820s and German Idealism, the former by Fergal Keane and the latter by Dermot Moran.)

TBC?

Ireland is a complex presence within the play's *mise-en-scène*. On the one hand, it is, in the words of Berkeley, a romanticized repository of 'beauty and wildness'; and, on the other, it is a place of Gothic marginality, where ghosts are active, where it seems as if there is a validation of nature over culture, the supernatural over politics. The Irish characters' obsessions with land, insurrection, alcohol, gambling, fairies and ghosts may be regarded as a negative self-defining feature, but what McPherson does is to unravel these stories of addiction, fairies and dead babies in particular, not by placing them only as some form of social superstition, but more as ways of making some sense of addiction as self-destruction, the supernatural as doom and chaos, where babies go missing or simply die all too easily.

Like the father in the story who exchanges his child with the fairies for drink, Madeleine facilitates the marital exchange of her daughter in order to stave off financial meltdown. In the world of the characters there is a fundamental fear of doom, chaos and the absence of order. Madeleine, in response to the collapse of the local housing, explains how she cried at her own 'powerlessness and selfishness seeing how they had lived and died!'[61] This seems to be the crux of the play: an awareness of a lack of empathy, and the absence of a social duty of care, and it symbolizes the acts of some landlords and developers in building housing that is not fit for purpose, whether it is housing left unfinished, built on flood plains or with inadequate fire safety. (The Irish government's poor regulative systems are equally indicted.)

Equally, the work is also about the powerlessness, a lack of agency, even for social elites to intervene against chaotic forces beyond themselves. However, there is hope in Hannah's compulsion to defend figures like James, for whom she has feelings of love, against the likes of Fingal. Her sentiment rings through, even if she cannot match it with substantive action. And if Hannah does leave to marry, with Berkeley, Madeleine and Grandie now to follow, Clare also departs Ireland for Canada under a different set of circumstances. Clare agrees to marry Fingal, knowing his weaknesses, but also realizing it is the best option for her and for them as a couple.

Wallace is a solid and alert character, making the most of the dire circumstances, and, as Dunne plays her, she has the tenacities and convictions and the energy of someone likely to succeed, as many of the Irish Diaspora did when they emigrated throughout the world, particularly from the early nineteenth century forward, before and after the Great Famine. In that, it is not so much that Clare knows her place and stabilizes that reality, but that she has the discernment to make substantial calculations without being conniving or selling herself short. Emigration is again unfortunately the safety valve for a new generation, as it is for Wallace and Fingal, and of course Hannah. Indeed there is a formidable matriarchal dividend evident towards the play's end, where the focus is less on the patriarchal economy and more on the male attrition and on female agency. Audelle seeks out the darkness and the divine in others, but both are a projection of his own inner struggles. It is the women, in their different ways, who display the necessary resoluteness to go on, as do Fingal and Berkeley in their different ways.

The rupturing of the veil, of course, has strong Christian connotations of the rending of the veil in the temple to coincide with the death of Jesus Christ. In the Gothic novel more generally, the veil denotes modesty, virginity, concealment, disguise, something that divides or sets apart.[62] Marriage and patriarchal exchange confirms the significance of sex. (Indeed sex is Audelle's downfall in his quest for the sublime.) The veil in this play has more to do with the membrane between life and death, the osmosis between both, and just as importantly how a linear temporality makes way for the circularity of time, making past and present less and less distinguishable, leading to a rupturing of the irrational from within to the without, and from the without to the within. It is not death or the hold of the past over the present which is unveiled; it is instead tenacity, in the face of rupture. It is a looking behind the veil to the absence in the Mirror King's eyes, to embrace the natural and the supernatural.[63] For generations the wealthy were destined to these contagious cycles of gains and losses, exuberance, over-extension, loss and then asset stripping. The relatively impoverished Irish, once they moved beyond subsistence living, were effectively just as prone to these economic cycles, under capitalism/globalization, of growth and abrupt capitulation, and the future predicted by the play was the Celtic Tiger period. The cyclicality of history is no sensational Gothic fantasy or hoax, but a brutal recurrence in large measure. Clearly, this production at the National Theatre London heralds the first great post-Celtic Tiger play.

Works Cited

Billington, Michael, Review of *The Veil*, *The Guardian*, 5 October, http://www.guardian.co.uk/stage/2011/oct/05/the-veil-review [Accessed 3/11/11]

Costa, Maddy, in an interview with Conor McPherson, 'Human beings are animals,' *The Guardian*, Wednesday 13 September 2006. http://www.guardian.co.uk/stage/2006/sep/13/theatre4 [Accessed 4/1/12]

---, in an interview with Conor McPherson, 'Conor McPherson: drawing on supernatural resources,' *The Guardian*, 28 September, 2011, http://www.guardian.co.uk/stage/2011/sep/28/conor-mcpherson-interview [Accessed 4/1/12]

Hoggard, Liz, in an interview with Conor McPherson, 'Conor McPherson knows what women want,' *London Evening Standard*, 13 Sep 2011, http://www.thisislondon.co.uk/theatre/article-23986309-conor-mcpherson-knows-what-women-want.do [Accessed 3/11/11]

Hogle, Jerrold E., (ed.), 'Introduction', in *The Cambridge Companion to Gothic Fiction*. (Cambridge: Cambridge University Press, 2002).

Hughes, Clair, 'Death of the House: Molly Keane and the Anglo-Irish Gothic Novel' in *Troubled Histories, Troubled Fictions: Twentieth-Century Anglo-Irish Prose,* Theo D'haen and José Lanters (eds.) (Amsterdam: Atlanta, Ga.: Rodopi, 1995):119-128.

Kosofsky Sedgwick, Eve, 'The Character in the Veil: Imagery of the Surface in the Gothic,' *PMLA*, 96.2 (Mar., 1981): 255-270, http://www.jstor.org/stable/10.2307/461992 [Accessed 5/3/2102]

Mc Cormack, W.J., *Sheridan Le Fanu and Victorian Ireland*. (Oxford: Clarendon Press, 1980).

---, 'Introduction to Irish Gothic and After', *The Field Day Anthology of Irish Writing Volume II*, ed. Seamus Deane. (Derry: Field Day Publication, 1991):831-854.

McGinn, Caroline, in an interview with Conor McPherson, *Time Out*, 26 Sep 2011, http://www.timeout.com/london/theatre/-article/2782/interview-conor-mcpherson [Accessed 3/11/11]

McPherson, Conor, *The Veil* (London: Nick Hern Books, 2011).

---, '*The Veil* at the National Theatre: A journey into the unknown,' *Daily Telegraph*, 27 Sep 2011, http://www.telegraph.co.uk/culture/theatre/theatre-features/8792604/The-Veil-at-the-National-Theatre-A-journey-into-the-unknown.html [Accessed 3/11/11]

---

[1] Liz Hoggard, 'Conor McPherson knows what women want,' *London Evening Standard*, 13 Sep 2011, http://www.thisislondon.co.uk/-theatre/article-23986309-conor-mcpherson-knows-what-women-want.do [Accessed 3/11/11]

[2] Conor McPherson, *The Veil* (London: Nick Hern Books, 2011): 18.

[3] *ibid.*, 35.

[4] *ibid.*, 35.

[5] *ibid.*, 37-8.

[6] Further, and more substantially, marriage also captures in a complicated if elusive fashion the compulsory political union between Ireland and Britain, based on the Act of Union (1800), which created the United Kingdom of Britain and Ireland. In more traditional work it is the forced or arranged marriage of an

indigenous Irish woman with a colonial male that symbolically suggests false communion, through the deployment of a myth of reciprocity that is often central to imperialist projects. Here, Hannah is Irish born, but of Protestant Ascendancy stock, and is obliged to marry an Englishman and her future is to live with him not in Ireland but in England.

7 McPherson, *The Veil*, 51.

8 In the interview with Hoggard, McPherson notes that fairies are 'the rationalization of very deep folkloric, ancient respect for the mystery of nature and the universe and everything we cannot know.' See 'Conor McPherson knows what women want.'

9 He also found inspiration in the German transcendental philosophy of the early 19th century. "It's so out there. The idea that human beings are the part of God that is awakening and coming to know he is God, it's crazy stuff." See Maddy Costa 'Conor McPherson: drawing on supernatural resources,' *The Guardian*, Wednesday 28 September, 2011, http://www.guardian.co.uk/stage/2011/sep/28/conor-mcpherson-interview [Accessed 4/1/12]

10 McPherson, *The Veil*, 32.

11 *ibid.*, 92.

12 *ibid.*, 52.

13 *ibid.*, 50.

14 *ibid.*, 50.

15 Madeleine is also susceptible to the otherworldly, as she has seen a ghost in London, that of a young man, who had been murdered in the room.

16 McPherson, *The Veil*, 55.

17 Clair Hughes notes 'The biggest Big House in Irish Big House literature must be the Majestic Hotel of J.G. Farrell's novel *Troubles* (1970), which is set in 1919, adding, 'In its dying moments – true to type – the hotel becomes a towering inferno,' and the fire reflects the fundamental decay and collapse of the Protestant Ascendancy class, and the hotel. See 'Death of the House: Molly Keane and the Anglo-Irish Gothic Novel' in *Troubled Histories, Troubled Fictions: Twentieth-Century Anglo-Irish Prose,* Theo D'haen and José Lanters (eds.) (Amsterdam: Atlanta, Ga.: Rodopi, 1995). (119-128):120.

18 Jerrold E. Hogle, (ed.), 'Introduction', in *The Cambridge Companion to Gothic Fiction* (Cambridge: Cambridge University Press, 2002): 2.

19 *ibid.*, 3.

20 *ibid.*, 3.

21 W.J. McCormack 'Introduction to The Irish Gothic and After' in *The Field Day Anthology of Irish Writing Volume II*, ed. Seamus Deane (Derry: Field Day Publication, 1991), (831-854):831.

22 *ibid.*, 831.

[23] *ibid.*, 831.

[24] *ibid.*, 833.

[25] McPherson, *The Veil*, ibid., 59.

[26] The poster for *The Veil* is inspired by the late 19th century Danish painting by Vilhelm Hammershøi called 'Interior,' photo by Dean Rogers, and designed by Charlotte Wilkinson. Indeed both the production's mysterious sensibility and colour palette, takes inspiration from Hammershøi's, muted use of colour.

[27] See Helen Warner's wonderful production photographs of *The Veil* at http://www.nationaltheatre.org.uk/?lid=66093 [Accessed 6/1/12]

[28] See Conor McPherson, '*The Veil* at the National Theatre: A journey into the unknown,' Daily Telegraph, 27 Sep 2011, http://www.telegraph.co.uk/culture/theatre/theatre-features/8792604/The-Veil-at-the-National-Theatre-A-journey-into-the-unknown.html [Accessed 3/11/11]

[29] McPherson, '*The Veil* at the National Theatre: A journey into the unknown.'

[30] McPherson, '*The Veil* at the National Theatre: A journey into the unknown.'

[31] Additionally, the horrific realities of the Irish famine to come in the 1840s haunt this McPherson play in a similar way to that of the 'sweet smell' of a potentially failed potato crop that is in the air in Brian Friel's *Translations* (1980).

[32] McPherson, *The Veil*, 66.

[33] *ibid.*, 69.

[34] *ibid.*, 72.

[35] Maddy Costa notes: 'Currently, he says, he writes from the standpoint that "human beings are animals: 90% of our behaviour is animal behaviour, and we've just got this 10% veneer, the semblance of civilised, rational choice. Our thoughts are always trailing around after our appetites, justifying them with language: it's tragic and it's hilarious. That's the picture I put together in my plays: of the animals who can talk, and think because of that they know everything.' See 'Human beings are animals,' *The Guardian*, 13 September 2006, http://www.guardian.co.uk/stage/2006/sep/13/theatre4 [Accessed 4/1/12]

[36] McPherson, *The Veil*, 24.

[37] *ibid.*, 50-1.

[38] *ibid.*, 51.

[39] *ibid.*, 89.

[40] *ibid.*, 40.

[41] *ibid.*, 109.

[42] *ibid.*, 37.

43 W.J. McCormack, *Sheridan Le Fanu and Victorian Ireland* (Oxford: Clarendon Press, 1980):11.

44 *ibid.*, p.12.

45 McPherson, *The Veil*, 26.

46 *ibid.*, 27.

47 *ibid.*, 44.

48 McPherson, *The Veil*, 95.

49 *ibid.*, 94.

50 *ibid.*, 93.

51 Hogle, 'Introduction', in *The Cambridge Companion to Gothic Fiction*:11.

52 Costa, 'Conor McPherson: drawing on supernatural resources,'

53 Hoggard, 'Conor McPherson knows what women want.'

54 *ibid.*

55 *ibid.*

56 Costa 'Conor McPherson: drawing on supernatural resources.'

57 Caroline McGinn, 'Interview', an interview with Conor McPherson, *Time Out*, 26 Sep 2011, http://www.timeout.com/london/theatre/article/2782/interview-conor-mcpherson [Accessed 3/11/11]

58 McGinn, 'Interview.'

59 See Michael Billington, Review in *The Guardian*, 5 October, http://www.guardian.co.uk/stage/2011/oct/05/the-veil-review [Accessed 3/11/11]

60 The promise of a legacy that has such short-lived changes for the Boyle family in Sean O'Casey's *Juno and the Paycock* (1924) seems a pertinent point of comparison. Believing that they have come into money, the Boyle family surrounds themselves with the trappings of the middle classes, such as material objects which are at odds with their tenement surroundings. Captain Boyle's expression of bourgeois values and sentiments and new found interest in Consols says as much again. But what enters the tenement space are the realities of communal bonds, the ineptitude of the legal profession (or ruling classes) to deal with Boyle's uncle's will or in Bentham's case to take responsibility for Mary's pregnancy, and the realities of a civil war tear asunder the family environment as Johnny Boyle is taken away to be killed for his part in the ambushing of a neighbour. The lack of loyalty to friends and neighbours and borrowing on the promise of money to come have a great deal to say to both the current economic realities and to McPherson's play more generally.

61 *ibid.*, 94.

62 Eve Kosofsky Sedgwick notes 'The veil itself, however, is also suffused with sexuality. This is true partly because of the other, apparently opposite set of meanings it hides: the veil that conceals and inhibits sexuality comes by the same gesture to represent it, both as a

metonym of the thing covered and as a metaphor for the system of prohibitions by which sexual desire is enhanced and specified. Like virginity, the veil that symbolizes virginity in a girl or a nun has a strong erotic savor of its own, and characters in Gothic novels fall in love as much with women's veils as with women'. See 'The Character in the Veil: Imagery of the Surface in the Gothic,' *PMLA*, 96.2 (Mar., 1981): 255-270, p256. http://www.jstor.org/stable/10.2307/461992 (Accessed 5/3/12).

[63] The influence of James Joyce's *Finnegans Wake* is significant, in that, as McPherson notes, 'The premise of the book is that it's a family asleep and dreaming,' and he adds: 'What appealed was Joyce's representation of the timelessness of dreaming: years can go by in a dream, all time is eternity. I wanted to create a play in which time was crashing in on itself, so that what people might think is an echo of the past is in fact a premonition of the future.' See Costa, 'Conor McPherson: drawing on supernatural resources.'

19 | Interview with Conor McPherson

Noelia Ruiz

Foreword

Having read and watched the majority of Conor McPherson's previous interviews, it was my firm intention to avoid asking him the same questions about his life. His relationship with alcohol in particular, seems to recur in every single newspaper, book and video account I have come across. In that respect, I also wanted to allow for a different and valuable experience; the chance to talk more about his work as a director in theatre, the differences between writing for the stage and writing for the screen, and his international reception. The reason for this approach was primarily to explore Conor's work in a different light, especially as a playwright that directs his own plays.

I met Conor McPherson one bright summer morning at the beginning of June in the Royal Marine Hotel in Dun Laoghaire. Conor has a calm and pleasant manner, and speaks in a soft voice, although he is firm in what he believes. He is a very intelligent and articulate person, which might be an obvious statement given that he is a playwright. However, sometimes we forget to acknowledge the obvious.

We started talking about his artistic drive. In his interview with Dave Fanning, for UCD's *Connections* magazine launch night[1] on 3 November 2009, Conor said that he never wanted to be a playwright but a musician. This came about when he was around ten years old. One Christmas Day, when they were showing all The Beatles films on TV, Conor decided he had to get a guitar. After finishing school at sixteen, Conor did not want to go to university; he just wanted to play music. His parents convinced him to go to college with the argument that he would have plenty of free time to play music, so he applied to study Arts in UCD. Unsure of what subjects to choose, Conor applied the typical pragmatic reasoning for that age. Thus, he chose English so he could read books; Psychology because he thought he would be looking at rats in a box; and Philosophy because he believed it was going to be really easy to think about 'what is nothing.'

As it turns out, in the mysterious ways of life, these random choices would quickly define and inform his career as a playwright and director. By the end of his second year in college Conor wrote his first one act play, which he describes as having just 'popped out.' To add a score to the music of chance, when he approached Dramsoc with *Rum and Vodka* their only concern was who was going to be the director. There and then Conor decided it was going to be himself. Thus, the playwright-director was born.

NR: You never intended to be a playwright.

Conor McPherson: No, I suppose not. I wanted to play music really. But I suppose that artistic drive, even though it's quite reckless, was there. But that's youth as well. It's ignorance, which is bliss; it's a great place to be, where you have no fear of the consequences for your life. But it's like a lottery for everybody who has that drive, very many don't manage to make a living out of it. But without me really consciously trying to create that, it just happened. Which is the way it should be. It shouldn't be that conscious. Even the first ten years of my life as a professional playwright I was completely unconscious in that I had no insight into myself or the world. I realized that when I was being interviewed for a show called *The South Bank Show* in London. It was a comprehensive hour-long programme so they were asking me quite in-depth questions about my work and I realized in that moment that I sort of knew nothing about it or where it came from. That was quite shocking at the time and forced me in a way to move into another phase – of much more conscious work, but you can't help feeling nostalgic for all the time that you never really thought about it at all, you just did it.

NR: It's like an impulse.

CMP: Yes, like a biological impulse. A hunger.

NR: You studied philosophy and it seems from other interviews that it had a great influence in your work. Do you think the stage is a perfect place to posit philosophical questions, understanding philosophy as a reflection of the world we live in?

CMP: (*Silence*) Yeah (*hesitantly*). It depends what you are interested in. For me the theatre is a very mysterious place which has something to do with human consciousness and our ability to create our world, which is what all of us do every day. We all create a world within our own mind which we think makes sense. It includes our own personal history as well as our intentions for the future. But it is all an illusion. It is an essential illusion because the world has to mean something to us otherwise we cannot live. Once I heard someone describing depression as the inability to create the illusion of meaning. And I think the theatre distils that capacity in a very pure way because as a group, collectively, in the dark, we all collude in suspending our disbelief together, willingly, to allow an illusion to unfold before us. In theatre you have to concentrate quite hard to maintain the illusion, but that collective effort deepens the experience and takes us into a kind of a trance. And when that happens I think it really concentrates the theatre's peculiar brand of magic which reflects the magic of being alive, the magic of being conscious, the mystery and the miracle of that, the complete unknown aspect of all of that which is so necessary to live our lives. If you can get everything flowing right in the theatre, and sometimes you can't do it for a whole play but you might get a good twenty minutes, that is a very successful evening in the theatre for me, and it can stay with people for the rest of their lives.

If there are any questions I am asking they are really about getting into the everyday hustle and bustle of life and take a moment – it's almost a religious thing – to consider the great mystery that we live in and that we know nothing about. Even though life is very painful a lot of the time for many people, being here is something that at least for a little while you can feel good about and share it? So those are the questions that are usually underneath my work in some way. But really on the surface it has nothing to do with any of that, it's just normal people doing normal stuff because it is normal life, which is underpinned by the mystery. So you have to present normal life in some way and then somehow pull the rug under normal life and allow the mystery in.

NR: Is this why in many of your plays you use the supernatural as an element?

CMP: The more we learn from science the more mysterious everything becomes, the more we find out the more questions arise about why everything is the way it is. To me that is a very consistent feeling, it is very present all the time: the mystery of time and space, and the mystery of infinity and the mystery of actually being aware, of being conscious of it; how you are a human being, an animal that can actually understand that you are in a mystery. To me it's a supernatural experience. I don't see any line between the natural and the supernatural. To me nature is a mystery, completely, and that's what we live in. To me that's life, so when I write anything its borders have to be those borders otherwise the story makes no sense to me.

You are trying to address timelessness, you are trying to escape the boundary of time. When you introduce phenomena which are unfettered it frees the mind and it's the ultimate freedom because you want to be able for the human mind to commune with the eternal. To me that is such a desirable thing to be able to do. We can only really do it in death of course, but then the problem is that we probably just cease to exist and we don't have a clue, so we have to die in ignorance and that's it. But at least while we are here we can create the illusion of something else. And illusions can be beautiful. And beauty has its own sense of truthfulness.

Sometimes I think it is also a longing for the human spirit and for all human beings, just in a very Freudian way, to return to the great mother or father, to be taken into the arms of the universe and eternity and cradled, and even if that is in death. So sometimes my plays suggest the longing to somehow reach towards the eternal mother or father.

I suppose that being brought up in Ireland the majority of people of my generation would have been brought up as Roman Catholics, and perhaps when you grow older you question that or move away from it, but it's still somehow in your DNA to consider stories which are powerful enough to contain all of these concepts. The stories in the Bible are fantastic because they really do contain them in such a creative way, like the story of Jesus Christ and that little holy family, and how Jesus died, even if he was God, he died. In someway it is sort of the perfect melding of the infinite and the painfully finite. Even those two words 'God Died' are such a powerful resonant image, so even if you don't believe in any of those concepts they do allow you to reflect on things in a different way.

NR: In relation to this, I also find the setting of Christmas Eve very interesting in your plays. Why is that?

CMP: Anyone who is brought up as a Christian probably still feels the sense of possibility of Christmas Eve. Christmas day is probably less important, but Christmas Eve has always had that magic. I suppose what Christmas has managed to do is to take a very pagan festival, which is marking the end of the worst of the winter, to survive it and then celebrate you are going to be moving into the spring. It is a wonderful festival that really says something about the human condition, especially the feeling of the longest night along with the idea that a baby is born who somehow unifies the family and unifies the world; it's such a powerful message. So it is lovely to place people that are having difficult lives and look at them on Christmas Eve and then suggest all of these things. It's a very magical thing and especially in the theatre because of the idea of community where you have everybody helping to create the illusion. It really gives people an experience when it is good.

NR: How would you explain creativity?

CMP: There is this idea that an artist is visited by 'the muse' from time to time. Billy Roche believes that if you are writing something that you are really tuned into, even if it is just for a few minutes, whatever you write has the real burn of lived experience. And whenever you see that piece of writing performed onstage, even years later, it still has that moment intact and you know something is happening in the audience at that point. It's a moment of inspiration.

Nobody knows where that comes from and that is why you have to be very patient with your work. Tom Murphy, the playwright, says that writing, perhaps playwriting most of all, teaches you real humility because you'll find that often you can't do it, you are not able to do it. And every time you do it you are always starting again, and you are thus constantly reminded that you know nothing; and your past work can't help you. You can't go back to that, you can't relive your own life. And you walk away from your desk feeling you are a failure, that it is over, you can't ever do this again. But then it's only when you have done that and you'll be doing something else, making a cup of tea or going for a walk and feeling quite dejected or whatever, that something might pop into your head: and that little thing that comes from nowhere is the way forward. But in order to reach that place, Tom Murphy says you have to go through the acceptance that you are utterly unable to do your work. And that is real humility because you realize you are nothing, you have no power. It's a real humiliation and you have to go through that. It constantly beats you down. I find that if I'm writing a first draft of a play you have to allow spaces where you can just live your life, otherwise your work is far too contrived because you are consciously moving from A to B to C, whereas there should be little moments of surprise all the time. That is how a play has a chance of staying ahead of the audience and it must always stay ahead of the audience. Everything that happens every three pages or so must be something that they could never quite see coming. Even if it is just very subtle, it doesn't have to be amazingly mind-bending, but as long as you're staying ahead of the audience, it's working. But I find the only way to do that is to be able to come and go from the work quite a lot, so when you come back you have something. You've got to build it very carefully like that. In some existential way you have to feel like a piece of shit. There is no other way to face your work properly. If it's really easy you suspect it's probably quite shallow.

NR: Why do you direct your own plays?

CMP: At the beginning it was out of necessity, but then as time went by I just realized I like it because it is very efficient in the sense that I can try things out and change the play very quickly. When you are working with a director it just slows all that down because you got another voice in the mix, questioning why you are going to change something when you just might want to cut it or do something else completely. But, particularly, when you are working with actors and you see a moment and you go 'Oh, I see the way through here, we don't need any of this,' very quickly you can change it and that's very inspiring. That's how I finish a play and I need that direct access to the actors, I can't have someone in the way saying 'Let's talk about this.' I don't want to have to talk about it. I just want to be able to do it. And the director of course needs to feel they are directing the play, I mean they don't want to feel like this person (i.e. the writer) is just completely taking over the process. And they are right.

NR: Is it hard to see how a director puts his/her own stamp on your work?

CMP: Every time a play script is done it should be different. I have worked with some really good directors. One of the best directors I worked with was Ian Rickson who directed *The Weir* for the first time and that was a wonderful experience. He was totally open to having the writer as part of the process. And I have worked with other very good directors with plays that I've directed before, directors who are open to me changing the play again if necessary, who allow me to go on that journey. Those are the directors I work with the best.

NR: When you did *The Seafarer* in The Abbey it was directed by Jimmy Fay. Did you collaborate with him? Were you in the rehearsal room?

CMP: Initially I wanted to stay out of it because I had directed the play a number of times already so I just wanted to allow it to happen. But then I ended up being involved with it because Jimmy wanted me to come in. Of course I started changing the play! And then when The Abbey brought it back for a second run in 2009 Jimmy was unavailable so they just asked if I would do it, so we did it again and we changed it again even with the same cast. I never stop writing a play if I am directing it. I keep reshaping it round the particular actors I'm working with.

NR: How do you start the rehearsal process? Do you start by sitting around a table, talking about the ideas in the play, doing a reading, analysing the characters?

CMP: I find that it depends. Usually when I am directing a play for the first time we might sit around the table for one or two days but I am very impatient, I want to get away from the table and start to explore, to get the play into three dimensions because then I can start to see the characters moving through the space and hear them.

Once that happens the play can develop and that's what I want to do.

NR: Some directors require the actors to learn the lines before the first day of rehearsal, do you do that or do they learn the lines throughout the process?

CMP: They usually learn them throughout the process. Some people are very quick, some are slower but usually by about the third week I really want them to know the lines for the most part. I don't mind if they want to hold the script for certain bits, but you can't direct a play when they are reading. But I wouldn't require them to learn the lines before we start the process because I know the play is going to change and that's not fair because they might have learnt lots of stuff that is not going to be in the play anymore.

NR: Do you ask them to improvise around the characters?

CMP: Usually what we try to do it's to get into great detail rather than improvise. We try to underpin everything that's happening with tremendous amount of detail so nothing is glossed over, even things that seem inconsequential, like somebody wiping a table. In a sense we spend a long time digging under everything rather than improvising. Not all actors are comfortable with improvisation, some people are very good at it, some people hate it, some people can't think of anything to do or say, and I don't think it should be even expected that actors should have to improvise.

NR: Sorry, I should have clarified what I mean by improvisation. Some directors are very clear in the definition or idea they have of characters, and they instruct the actors in a way that dictates to them which direction to go. Other directors allow the actors more freedom to explore their characters (it might be through movement, through voice, etc.) and bring out an angle to those characters, even a personality that perhaps the director didn't foresee when reading the play but that might be more interesting.

CMP: Well that is a big part of going into the detail. I am fully aware that is not me that has to go onstage and perform it, and if they are doing something that doesn't feel right to them there is a reason for that; I am trying to get them as close to the character as possible. So sometimes I rewrite and change the way the character speaks to suit the actor so that when they are onstage they are utterly open, so there are no doubts and the audience can be taken by the power and authority of the performances. That's usually what I'm trying to get to, and that's why I rewrite a lot to help the actor by shifting things into a way that suits them. So then if we do the play another time say with a different cast, I'll change it again.

NR: That's very interesting because very few playwrights would do that nowadays and in that sense I wonder if in the process of writing a play the lines in the play are not fixed then the rest of the theatrical elements such as music, set design, costume, etc. aren't either?

CMP: Everything changes because when you are writing it you are trying to see it. But then when you start to do it of course it's nothing like you thought it was going to be, and when people start speaking and all these different actors come into these roles everything is altered. But that's a great relief because finally the play is showing me what it is.

NR: So it comes quite clearly that when you write a play, it is not fixed in any way?

CMP: No. And that's another reason why I tend not to get involved with many productions of my plays because if I were to do that I'd want to change everything. So it is better to just not get involved as productions go on in different places.

NR: I am asking because in other interviews sometimes it comes across that your aim to direct your plays comes out from a need to control the artistic product, or being precious about it. Whereas now that I am talking to you it seems obvious that directing your plays is not only your way of finishing the play before the first opening, but also it is in a constant process of evolution to suit a context, to suit a time and a moment, rather than to control it, rather than saying that you don't want to see someone else taking it over.

CMP: Basically you could spend the rest of your life in rehearsal rooms when you should be writing something else, so that's what it is really. Ultimately directing plays is emotionally a huge thing to do, it's a big journey so you need to be able to pull away from that and for one year or two years not be involved in directing anything. And then usually by the end of that time you are ready to go back and you want to do it again. You need serious time to do both if you are writing and directing.

NR: Do you use any specific technique to direct the actors or do you just trust that they know what they are doing?

CMP: Good actors are easy to direct, it's that simple, because they have so many gears. The first thing I'd say is that acting is a mystery in the sense that somebody says something and you believe it, and the next person says it and instinctively as a human being who knows what's real and what's not real, you just don't buy it. And we call that acting 'wooden.' What is it that is making it wooden? Who can say? We don't know. We just don't believe that person – and any human being can spot wooden acting. The really good actors have a direct route from their brain to their mouth and to their appearance, straight into a kind of truthfulness. And when they speak it is utterly convincing. What you need is as much of that as possible and as many of those actors as possible. If you find that your entire cast are like that, you know everything is going to be fine.

A lot of what a director does is sometimes more a kind of coaching than directing and good actors want you to do that. You are like a football coach, you are trying to get them ready for the game, the big game, so it's a very holistic approach, you don't only just help them to understand the play, to understand what they are trying to do; you are trying to help them as people, to make them feel comfortable when they walk out on stage. My most emotionally open and enthusiastic relationships are with the people I am working with. Because for me the line between my work and my life and my inner self is ... there is no line, it is me. So on every level you try to be there for that person. I'm not saying I always succeed however!

NR: So do you cast your actors?

CMP: Yes.

NR: How do you cast them?

CMP: Usually there are certain actors you return to because they have very good instinct for your work so you might just decide to offer them a part because you had them in mind when you were writing, and others you audition, you give them the script to read and you try to see if they are good.

NR: You work a lot internationally, especially in the UK and the US. Is there a difference culturally in working with Irish actors, British actors or American actors?

CMP: There are differences. Britain has an incredible tradition of theatre and of theatre training, so you would find actors there that are very fit, they are very experienced, very developed, their theatre muscle is very strong. And that is not just on an acting level, they also need to be physically strong because they have to be able to do the play every night, you must be able to hear them at the back of the theatre – all of that is really important.

Because of the lack of subsidies for theatre in the United States there are often a lot of people competing for not that much work, and they do an unbelievable amount of preparation. Anyone who comes in for an audition in New York usually knows the lines and they would probably even have gone to an accent coach for a couple of sessions. So when they come in they are utterly prepared.

But in terms of cultural differences, let's say with an Irish play, perhaps what they struggle to realize is the sense of pessimism of an Irish person. They often find that dysfunctional and frightening in a way. Whereas an Irish audience sees something happening and they just get it: 'This guy is a loser.' In America the actors are much more inclined to go 'Why doesn't he tell his wife he loves her?' Whereas an Irish person would go, 'He just can't tell his wife he loves her.' They just get it. Perhaps in America they have a strong, positive outlook on life, so they have to work their way into the brokenness of certain Irish characters. In Britain, they understand the Irish psyche as we are much closer neighbours.

Ireland is a small place. It is very hard for an actor here to make a living. Even the really good ones sometimes struggle to find work and that's very tough. It's hard here. Small country, small population, small theatre market, and yet we always seem to have interesting work being generated here.

NR: What about in terms of audience reception in different countries? In the video available in The Abbey's youtube channel[2] before opening *The Seafarer* in April 2008 you said you were very excited about opening in Dublin because you felt that although audiences in London and Broadway enjoyed the play, it would really go under the skin of audiences here.

CMP: Well, Irish people know the characters. The minute they walk onstage they know who they are. And so many people say to you 'That's exactly like my dad or my brother or my uncle or whoever.' That's why you get a lot of laughter in those productions. Something I noticed over the years is that laughter in the theatre is quite complex. People laugh because they think something is funny, that's one way of laughing. Another way of laughing is that the audience are communicating with each other and with the performers – who they know can hear them – simply out of recognition, and it's a way of saying 'We all share this little thing.' I remember there was a line in *Shining City*, which is not a particularly funny line nor was it supposed to be, when the character John is running late. He comes onto the stage and says 'God the parking around here is horrendous, isn't it?.' In London nobody laughed. In Ireland they just burst out laughing and you wonder why, but it's because they just connected in that moment and they liked it.

NR: You directed Samuel Beckett's *Endgame*, Eugene O'Brien's *Eden* and Billy Roche's play *Poor Beast in the Rain*. Where does that necessity of directing someone else's work come from?

CMP: I haven't done it very often. They have to be plays that I can really relate to. You have to be inspired by the world of the play so you know you can go there with those characters and live in that world, and question it and have answers. It's a lovely feeling when it is not your play, when you are just purely being a director. With *Endgame* I learnt so much, it's kind of a perfect play. It's not the kind of way I could ever write, it's beyond me, but structurally it's just absolutely brilliant and brave, beautiful and moving. Eugene's play *Eden* is so emotional, I just loved that. And I really think it spoke to something that was going on in Ireland at that time, during the Celtic Tiger, which was a massive explosion of change and of confidence in Ireland. I think there was a suspicion that the good times weren't 'real.' And that turned out to be true. In that play, like a lot of the plays at the time which were monologues, it was almost like the suspicion was so great that the stories became very private. It was almost like eavesdropping, and very powerful because of that. And that is what people needed. They needed to get right inside other people at that time because that's where the truth was. The truth wasn't around us in wider society. I've heard it said 'Oh, nobody dramatized the Celtic Tiger.' I'd say, no, they did, they dramatized what it felt like to be so alienated from what was going on, and that's why I think there were so many monologues at that time. And I think that time will reveal that. A play like *Eden* is really spot on. I didn't know that at the time, I just thought it was a good play, but the more I look back I see it was the perfect play for its time and what was interesting about it was its unexpected success. They did it in The Peacock, then they had to bring it back for another entire run, but the demand for tickets was so great they had to transfer it up into The Abbey, then it went on tour, then it went to London, then they brought it back to the Abbey again. And it's just a two-hander with a man and a woman talking to the audience about their marriage! But the hunger for that was massive. So that was an interesting time. And then Billy Roche's play I directed, *Poor Beast in the Rain*, it's again so emotional, so sad and moving. It was lovely to go there with the actors and allow all that to be released so you can watch bits of it and cry. It's great, I love that.

NR: Moving onto another topic, are there any directors, playwrights or people who have had a major impact on you and your work, an influence?

CMP: Regarding directors I'm not really that sure who has influenced me. The work of the best theatre directors is often invisible in a sense. The play just hits you and you don't notice the 'directing.' Regarding playwrights, if you look at someone like Samuel Beckett you think 'Ok, he wasn't just a mischievous, groundbreaking, playwright but he was an amazing writer, full stop,' the writing is just fantastic, it's like poetry. Like James Joyce, the power of his talent is inspiring and daunting at the same time. As a writer you look at that work and realize very quickly, 'Oh God, I'm just nowhere compared to this.' Then you can also look at someone like Chekhov and you go, 'What is this about?' People make these incredible emotional outbursts and there is something so courageous about that, and you go 'I'd love to have that kind of courage.' In terms of Irish writers you have to admire someone like Brian Friel, he is always able to tie up his plays into such an appetizing package for an audience. He can say exactly what he wants to say and make it very entertaining, that's a really rare talent. But then you look at someone like Tom Murphy and it's almost like he doesn't give a shit if the audience are entertained or not, it's like 'This is what I'm doing, and that's it. If you don't get it, then it's not for you.' And that's incredibly powerful and inspiring. I admire many playwrights, in fact I admire any playwright that manages to do it, but there are people that you look at like Caryl Churchill, incredibly brave, doing her own thing, almost like she doesn't care what happens. And I am not that brave, I've often been like 'I really hope the audience are going to like this' because I really want them to connect with it and feel something. But there are other playwrights that go 'Well, this is what I'm doing, the audience might like it or not.' Maybe that's where I'll end up eventually. I hope so.

NR: You've directed and co-written the film *The Eclipse* with Billy Roche. How was the experience of co-writing a script?

CMP: It was beautiful, a profound experience, one of the lovely working experiences of my life, I'm very proud of that time. It is lovely because writing is really alienating because you are constantly out of the world. I mean, you are in the world, of course, but then from time to time you have to step back, distil it, present it, so it's really a horrible experience in a way. But working with someone with whom you are sharing that space is a lovely thing to do. What's so clever about Billy's work and his story which was based on that script was that what it presented seemed so ordinary: ordinary people doing ordinary things. And yet the depth beneath it will keep you going all day long. It took us five years to make that film and I never felt that there was any shortage of energy because I always felt that there was something beneath it that was very sustaining. So it was great to feel that way because you often might not feel it with your own work. You are driven a lot by anxiety. You kind of go, 'Is this going to be good? Oh God it's going to be terrible,' that's the drive. But to be driven by something that you feel 'I totally believe in this person's vision,' it's a lovely place to be, it's a relief.

NR: Is it very different to write for the screen than for the stage?

CMP: Yes, because you don't have to write as much dialogue. On stage, with the very traditional kind of plays that I do – and they are very traditional – everybody has to be talking or nothing is happening really. I usually try to create space where people are doing stuff without talking in the theatre, but on film you can have ten minutes where nobody speaks. You are just showing scenes that are moving the story along and that's a lovely way to tell a story. I love that.

NR: You said in an interview once that your monologues are quite cinematic because you create those images for the audience through the words.

CMP: Well, that's it, a monologue is very efficient. You can flow, you can compress time beautifully, you can speed time up, you can slow it down very easily. You can jump right through a story in a way that a naturalistic presentation onstage can't. When people come in to a room, they are in a room and they are not going to leave until the conversation has taken place. But with the monologue you can skip all that very quickly and slow down when you get to the bit that you want to describe. So the narrator is the camera and the music.

NR: Is it very different to direct actors in theatre and in cinema?

CMP: Yes, completely different. On film you only need little bits of things, little bits of truth and sometimes they can happen by accident but you have it forever, whereas in theatre rehearsals you are doing the same thing every day, every day, every day. You have to keep doing it over and over and over so that it gets deeper and deeper and deeper, so by the time they go onstage they have utter confidence and belief and a flow of truth in what they're doing; and it has to be built to last. They have to be like athletes being trained for an event. So it's a very different thing. When you are making a film, once you shoot something you move on, you don't even have time to think about it the next day. You know you have it and you get back to it in the editing process. Then editing film is where you can have a great time, playing around with the whole story, which gives you a refreshing freedom.

And also – you were asking about improvisation – on film the script is suggesting that certain things happen, but mostly I really want the actors just to do what feels right to them. If you did that in the theatre it would all fall apart, because if someone decides on a certain night 'Oh, I'm just going to do something different' everyone else is like 'What the fuck is happening?' But you can do it on film.

NR: You mention the role of accidents in cinema. What about the role of accidents in the rehearsal room?

CMP: They happen there too and they are great, and you keep it if it's really good. Someone says something totally wrong, but you can go, 'Let's keep that,' because although it makes no sense there is something great about it, something striking about it and you keep it. You realize it does make sense because it has the feeling of reality, and reality is a bit like that, people do things that nobody understands and you move along.

NR: What's your relationship with critics?

CMP: I don't have a relationship with them really. I don't read reviews until well after the event of an opening, if at all. While failure is important and inevitable you don't need critics to tell you that. You know yourself if you haven't managed to achieve what you set out to do. When you have a success you don't learn anything. Success is a great relief and it's good to know you can continue to make a living. But when something isn't well received it's still a very interesting place to be. It can be confusing and painful in the moment but it reminds you that you are not as clever as you think you are. A failure inspires you by challenging you to believe in your work and in yourself. You need that fire in your belly, and you need that self-belief because no one else is going to give it to you.

---

[1] See http://www.youtube.com/watch?v=HwzUHtwgcbA 30/06/2011
[2] See http://www.youtube.com/user/AbbeyTheatre#p/u/17/-sz25qS-zWs8 [06/07/2011]

Biographical Notes

Lilian Chambers has had a life-long passion for theatre. She was awarded an M.A. in Drama Studies from University College Dublin and is a founding director of Carysfort Press. She co-edited *Theatre Talk – Voices of Irish Theatre Practitioners* and *The Theatre of Martin McDonagh – A World of Savage Stories*. She has been a member of the Friends Council of the Dublin Theatre Festival since its inception.

Susanne Colleary was awarded a PhD in 2010, writing on Stand-Up Comedy and Performance. Susanne works as a tutor for the School of English, Drama and Film at UCD and works as an Assistant Lecturer at the Sligo Institute of Technology. Susanne has published articles on the stand up performance works of Tommy Tiernan and Maeve Higgins. She is the founder of the Óg Youth Theatre in Sligo, and has worked as an actor/director and writer at amateur, student and professional levels. Most recently Susanne directed a series of 'video diaries' film shorts commissioned by Sligo VEC in 2009.

Lisa Fitzpatrick is Lecturer in Drama at the School of Creative Arts in the University of Ulster. She studied in Dublin at Trinity and UCD, and completed her Ph.D. at the Graduate Centre for Study of Drama in Toronto. She has published on contemporary Irish theatre, women's writing, Canadian theatre and post-conflict theatre and her current work is on sexual violence in performance. Carysfort Press published her edited collection *Performing Violence in Contemporary Ireland* in 2009 and in 2012 will publish her collection on *Performing Feminisms in Contemporary Ireland*.

Eamonn Jordan is Lecturer in Drama Studies at the School of English, Drama and Film, University College Dublin. His book *The Feast of Famine: The Plays of Frank McGuinness* (1997) is the first full-length study on McGuinness's work. In 2000, he edited *Theatre Stuff: Critical Essays on Contemporary Irish Theatre*. More recently, he co-edited with Lilian Chambers *The Theatre of Martin McDonagh: A World of Savage Stories* (2006). His book *Dissident Dramaturgies: Contemporary Irish Theatre* was published in 2010 by Irish Academic Press.

Sara Keating writes about theatre and cultural affairs for *The Irish Times*. She received her PhD from Trinity College Dublin and teaches courses on Irish theatre at Trinity College Dublin, University College Dublin and New York University.

Kevin Kerrane is Professor of English at the University of Delaware, where his work ranges from the history of journalism, including documentary film, to Irish literature and drama. He is the co-editor (with Ben Yagoda) of *The Art of Fact: A Historical Anthology of Literary Journalism*, and the author of *Dollar Sign on the Muscle: The World of Baseball Scouting*. His essays have appeared in *Irish Review, New Hibernia Review, Sports Illustrated*, and on-line at *salon.com*. He recently edited another Carysfort Press collection of essays: *Wexford as the World:The Achievement of Billy Roche* (2012).

Mária Kurdi is professor in the Institute of English Studies at the University of Pécs, Hungary. Her main fields of research are modern Irish theatre and drama as well as English-speaking drama in general. Her publications include three books on contemporary Irish drama, a collection of interviews with Irish playwrights, an anthology of excerpts from critical essays for the study of Irish literature, and several articles in journals and scholarly volumes. She is editor and co-editor of books and journal issues containing essays on modern Irish literature, Irish and international drama. In April 2011 she hosted the 6th Conference of ISTR.

Audrey McNamara has an MA in Anglo-Irish Literature and is currently working on the final part of her PhD on the drama of Bernard Shaw. Audrey is a tutor in UCD, teaching both English Literature and Drama modules. During the summer months she is

Director of Studies for an English language school. Her main project recently has been the organizing of a Bernard Shaw conference in UCD June (2012) with the backing of the Humanities Institute of Ireland and the International Shaw Society.

P.J. Mathews completed his doctoral research at Trinity College Dublin and joined the University College of Dublin's School of English, Drama and Film in 2004. Prior to that he lectured at St Patrick's College, Dublin City University (2001-2004) and Trinity College Dublin (1999-2001). He was Director of the Parnell Summer School from 2002-05 and was appointed Naughton Fellow and Visiting Associate Professor of English at the University of Notre Dame for 2007-08. He is author of *Revival: The Abbey Theatre, Sinn Féin, the Gaelic League and the Co-operative Movement* (2003) and editor *of The Cambridge Companion to J.M. Synge* (2009) and *New Voices in Irish Criticism* (2000).

Christopher Murray is Emeritus Professor of Drama and Theatre History in the School of English and Drama, University College Dublin. A former editor of *Irish University Review* (1986-1997) and chair (2000-2003) of the International Association for the Study of Irish Literatures (IASIL), he is author of *Twentieth-Century Irish Drama: Mirror Up to Nation* (1997) and *Sean O'Casey Writer at Work: A Biography* (2004), and has edited *Brian Friel: Essays, Diaries, Interviews 1964-1999* (1999) and the RTE Thomas Davis Lectures for Samuel Beckett's centenary, *Beckett at 100, The Centenary Essays* (2006). He is editor of *'Alive in Time': The Enduring Drama of Tom Murphy: New Essays* (Carysfort Press).

Emilie Pine lectures in modern drama at University College Dublin. She has published widely on Irish cultural studies, most recently *The Politics of Irish Memory: Performing Remembrance in Contemporary Irish Culture* (Palgrave, 2011).

Anthony Roche is an Associate Professor in the School of English, Drama and Film in University College Dublin. He has published widely on twentieth and twenty-first century Irish drama and theatre. Recent publications include *The Cambridge Companion to Brian Friel* (2006) and *Contemporary Irish Drama: Second Edition* (Palgrave Macmillan, 2009). His *Brian Friel: Theatre and*

Politics (Palgrave Macmillan, 2011) will be published in paperback in 2012; and Carysfort Press will publish his *Synge and the Making of Modern Irish Drama* in 2012.

Noelia Ruiz is a PhD Researcher in the Drama Studies Centre in University College Dublin, and the focus of her research is Contemporary Theatre and Performance Creative Processes. In March 2010 she was awarded an artistic residency in MAKE, a residential laboratory in Ireland. In June 2010 she was also part of Project Brand New Generation. In 2010, she directed the interactive multilingual theatre piece *The Cappuccino Culture* in the ABSOLUT Fringe Festival. In 2011 she performed and wrote *Better Loved From Afar*, a work which explores the relationship between photography, narrative and performance in documentary form around the subject of the Irish Diaspora in Argentina.

Carmen Szabo is a Lecturer in Theatre at the University of Sheffield. She has published extensively on Irish contemporary theatre, Shakespeare in performance and physical approaches to text. Her main research interests include game and play theories in contemporary actor training and political performance in Eastern Europe. She is also a translator, focusing on translation of contemporary Romanian plays into English. She published in 2007 *'Clearing the Ground' – the Field Day Theatre Company and the Creation of Irish Identities* (Cambridge: Cambridge Scholars Press) and a book on Barabbas Theatre Company (Carysfort Press) is forthcoming in 2012.

Ashley Taggart directs the IES Abroad programme in Dublin. He has written short films – the most recent screened in the Chicago Film Festival and the Cork Film Festival, and in 2009 was a winner of the P.J. O'Connor radio drama awards. His PhD is on the influence of evolutionary theory on modern drama. He is currently working on a book about Neuroscience and Literature.

Rhona Trench is former Programme Chair and Lecturer in Performing Arts at Institute of Technology Sligo. She is the Vice President of the Irish Society for Theatre Research. In 2010 she published the first monograph on the work of Marina Carr titled *Bloody Living: The Loss of Selfhood in the Plays of Marina Carr* (Peter Lang) and is editor of *Staging Thought: Essays on Irish*

Theatre, Scholarship and Practice (Oxford: Peter Lang, 2012). Her current research interests are theatre and performance processes and practices, with particular emphasis on Blue Raincoat Theatre Company, Sligo. She has published a number of articles on this company already.

Clare Wallace is Associate Professor and lectures at the Department of Anglophone Literatures and Cultures at Charles University in Prague. She is author of *Suspect Cultures: Narrative, Identity and Citation in 1990s New Drama* (2007) and is editor of *Monologues: Theatre, Performance, Subjectivity* (2006) and *Stewart Parker Television Plays* (2008). Co-edited books include, *Giacomo Joyce: Envoys of the Other* with Louis Armand (2002), *Global Ireland: Irish Literatures for the New Millennium* with Ondřej Pilný (2006) and *Stewart Parker Dramatis Personae and Other Writings* (2008) and *Cosmotopia: Transnational Identities in David Greig's Theatre* with Anja Müller (2011). She has contributed essays to *The Theatre of Marina Carr: "Before rules was made"* (2003), *Engaging Modernity* (2003), *Extending the Code: New Forms of Dramatic and Theatrical Expression CDE11* (2003) *Beyond Borders: IASIL Essays on Modern Irish Writing* (2004) and *Irish Literature Since 1990: Diverse Voices* (2009), *The Methuen Drama Guide to Contemporary Irish Playwrights* (2010) and *The Methuen Drama Guide to Contemporary British Playwrights* (2011).

Kevin Wallace is lecturer in Twentieth Century Irish Literature at the Institute of Art Design and Technology, Dun Laoghaire. He completed his PhD in University College Dublin's school of English Drama and Film with a thesis examining the work of playwrights Marina Carr and Sarah Kane. His current research interests include twentieth century literature and drama, and contemporary British and Irish theatre.

Ian R. Walsh is a graduate of University College Dublin where he completed his doctoral research and now teaches there in the School of English, Drama and Film. He has contributed articles to *Irish University Review* and to *Voicing Dissent: New Perspectives in Irish Criticism* and his book *Experimental Irish Theatre, after W.B Yeats* was published by Palgrave Macmillan in 2012. Ian also works as a theatre reviewer for RTE Radio 1's *Arena* and as a director of

Theatre and Opera; his most recent production was of Mozart's *The Magic Flute* for the DLR Glasthule Opera Festival in June 2011.

Eric Weitz is Assistant Professor and Head of Drama at Trinity College Dublin, lecturing in Acting, Comedy and other subjects. He is author of *The Cambridge Introduction to Comedy*, editor of *The Power of Laughter: Comedy and Contemporary Irish Theatre*, and has contributed to a number of collections and journals.

Performances and Bibliography

First Performances

Taking Stock (1989), *Michelle Pfeiffer* (1990) and *Scenes Federal* (1991) were all premiered at University College Dublin's Dramsoc.[1]

Rum and Vodka, Dramsoc, University College Dublin, 27 November 1992, and was first professionally performed in August 1994 in The International Bar, Dublin.

Radio Play, The International Bar, Dublin, Fly By Night Theatre Company, 17 August 1992.

A Light in the Window of Industry, The International Bar, Fly By Night Theatre Company, 3 August 1993.

Inventing Fortune's Wheel, The Firken Crane Centre, Shandon, Cork, 3 March 1994, having been given previously a one off performance on 12 February 1992 in Dramsoc.

The Stars Lose Their Glory, The International Bar, Fly By Night Theatre Company, 1 August 1994.

The Good Thief (First performed under the title *The Light of Jesus*) 18 April 1994 City Arts Centre, Dublin produced by Fly by Night Theatre Company, later in October 1994 as part of the Dublin Theatre Festival.

This Lime Tree Bower, Crypt Arts Centre, co-produced by Íomhá Ildánach/Fly by Night Theatre Company, 26 September 1995, subsequently performed at the Bush Theatre, London, 3 July 1996.

St. Nicholas, The Bush Theatre, London, 19 February 1997.

The Weir, Royal Court Theatre Upstairs, London, 4 July 1997.

Dublin Carol, Royal Court Theatre Downstairs, 7 January 2000.

Port Authority, New Ambassadors, London, 22 February 2001. (It was produced by Dublin's Gate Theatre, and transferred to Dublin 24 April 2001.)

Come on Over, Gate Theatre, Dublin, 27 September 2001.

Shining City, Royal Court Theatre Downstairs, 9 June 2004 and at the Gate Theatre, Dublin, 28 September 2004.

The Seafarer, National Theatre, London, Cottesloe auditorium, 28 September 2006.
The Birds, Gate Theatre, Dublin, 25 September 2009.
The Veil, National Theatre, London, Lyttleton auditorium, 4 October 2011.

Films[2]

I Went Down, 1997. Treasure Films, BBC Films, Bord Scannán na hÉireann, Radio-Telefís Éireann, Euskal Media. Written by Conor McPherson. Directed by Paddy Breathnach.
Saltwater, 2000. Treasure Films, Bord Scannán na hÉireann, BBC Films, Radio-Telefís Éireann, Alta Films, Dyehouse. Written and directed by Conor McPherson.
Endgame, 2000. Blue Angel Films, Tyrone Productions, Radio-Telefís Éireann, Channel Four, Bord Scannán na hÉireann, Channel 4 International. Written by Samuel Beckett. Directed by Conor McPherson.
The Actors, 2003. FilmFour, Company of Wolves, Miramax Films, Senator Film Produktion GmbH, Bord Scannán na hÉireann, Four Provinces Films, Section 481. Written and directed by Conor McPherson.
The Eclipse, 2009. Treasure Films, Broadcasting Commission of Ireland, Bord Scannán na hÉireann, Radio-Telefís Éireann, Submarine. Screenplay by Conor McPherson and Billy Roche, and is based on a short story by Billy Roche. Directed by Conor McPherson.

Published Plays and Screenplays

This Lime Tree Bower: Three Plays [*Rum and Vodka*; *The Good Thief*; *This Lime Tree Bower*] (Dublin: New Island Books; London: Nick Hern Books, in association with the Bush Theatre, 1996)
I Went Down: The Shooting Script (London: Nick Hern Books, 1997)
St. Nicholas and *The Weir: Two Plays* (Dublin: New Island Books; London: Nick Hern Books, in association with the Bush Theatre, 1997)
St. Nicholas and *The Weir: Two Plays* (Dublin: New Island Books; London: Nick Hern Books, in association with the Bush Theatre, 1997).
Rum and Vodka, The Good Thief, This Lime Tree Bower & *St. Nicholas*, in *Four Plays* (London: Nick Hern Books, 1999)
The Weir and Other Plays, (New York: Theater Communications Group, 1999)
Saltwater, NHB Shooting Script Series (London: Nick Hern Books, 2001)

The Actors, NHB Shooting Script Series (London: Nick Hern Books, 2003).
The Weir in *Plays: Two* (London: Nick Hern Books, 2004)
Port Authority in *Plays: Two* (London: Nick Hern Books, 2004)
Dublin Carol in *Plays: Two* (London: Nick Hern Books, 2004)
Come on Over in *Plays: Two* (London: Nick Hern Books, 2004)
Shining City (London: Nick Hern Books, 2004)
The Seafarer (London: Nick Hern Books, 2007)
The Seafarer (New York: Dramatists Play Service, 2008)
The Birds. Unpublished Manuscript Final Draft October 2009. (Copy courtesy of Conor McPherson.)
The Veil (London: Nick Hern Books, 2011)

Bibliography

Csencsitz, Cassandra, 'Conor McPherson Lifts the Veil,' *American Theatre*, 24, (2007) 36-83.

Cummings, Scott T., 'Homo Fabulator: The Narrative Imperative in Conor McPherson's Plays.' *Theatre Stuff: Critical Essays on Contemporary Irish Theatre*, ed. Eamonn Jordan (Dublin: Carysfort, 2000): 303-312.

Fricker, Karen, 'Same Old Show: The Performance of Masculinity in Conor McPherson's *Port Authority* and Mark O'Rowe's *Made in China*,' *The Irish Review* 29 (Autumn 2002): 84-94.

Grene, Nicholas, 'Stories in Shallow Space: Port Authority,' *Irish Review* 29 (Autumn 2002): 70-83.

---, 'Ireland in Two Minds: Martin McDonagh and Conor McPherson,' *The Yearbook of English Studies*, 35, (2005): 298-311.

Hughes, Declan, 'Who The Hell Do We Still Think We Are? Reflections on Irish Theatre and Identity in *Theatre Stuff: Critical Essays on Contemporary Irish Theatre,* ed. Eamonn Jordan (Dublin: Carysfort Press, 2000).

Jordan, Eamonn, 'Look Who's Talking Too: The Narrative Myth of Naïve Duplicity,' in Wallace, ed, *Monologues: Theatre, Performance, Subjectivity* (Litteraria Pragenzia: Prague, 2006), 125-156.

---, 'Pastoral Exhibits: Narrating Authenticities in Conor McPherson's *The Weir*,' *Irish University Press*, 34 (2004): 351-368.

Kerrane, Kevin, 'The Structural Elegance of Conor McPherson's *The Weir*', *New Hibernia Review*, 10.4 (2006): 105-121.

Lonergan, Patrick, *Theatre and Globalization: Irish Drama in the Celtic Tiger Era* (Palgrave, 2009).

Mathews, P.J., 'In Praise of "Hibernocentricism": Republicanism, Globalization and Irish Culture,' *The Republic*, 4 (2005): 5-14.

Pilny, Ondřej. 'Mercy on the Misfit: Continuity and Transformation in the Plays of Conor McPherson,' *The Binding Strength of Irish Studies: Festscrift in Honour of Csilla Bertha and Donald E. Morse,* eds. Marianna Gula, Mária Kurdi and István D. Rácz, (Hungary: Debrecen University Press, 2011): 87-94.

Roche, Anthony, *Contemporary Irish Theatre, Second Edition*, (Basingstoke: Palgrave Macmillan, 2009).

Singleton, Brian, 'Am I Talking to Myself? Men, Masculinities and the Monologue in Contemporary Irish Theatre' in Clare Wallace ed. *Monologues: Theatre, Performance, Subjectivity* (Litteraria Pragenzia: Prague, 2006), 260-77.

Voigts-Virchow, Eckart & Mark Schreiber 'Will the "Wordy Body" Please Stand Up? The Crisis of Male Impersonation in Monological Drama – Beckett, McPherson, Eno' in *Monologues: Theatre, Performance, Subjectivity*, ed. Claire Wallace (Prague: Litteraria Pragensia 2006).

Wallace, Clare, 'Monologue Theatre, Solo Performance and Self as Spectacle,' in *Monologues: Theatre, Performance, Subjectivity*, ed. Clare Wallace (Prague: Litteraria Pragensia, 2006): 1-16.

---, *Suspect Cultures: Narrative, Identity and Citation in 1990s New Drama* (Prague: Litteraria Pragensia, 2006).

---, 'Conor McPherson, *'The Methuen Drama Guide to Contemporary Irish Playwrights*, ed. Martin Middeke and Peter Paul Schnierer (London: Methuen, 2010): 271-289.

Wood, Gerald C., *Conor McPherson: Imagining Mischief* (Dublin: Liffey 2003).

Newspaper Articles, Features and Interviews

Adams, Tim, an interview with Conor McPherson, 'So There's These Three Irishmen...,' *The Observer*, 4 February, 2001.

Bragg, Melvyn, *South Bank Show*. Special episode on Conor McPherson, London Weekend Television, May 18 2003.

Costa, Maddy, an interview with Conor McPherson, 'Human beings are animals,' *The Guardian*, 13 September 2006, http://www.guardian.co.uk/stage/2006/sep/13/theatre4 [Accessed 4/1/12]

Costa, Maddy, an interview with Conor McPherson, 'Conor McPherson: drawing on supernatural resources,' *The Guardian*, 28 September, 2011, http://www.guardian.co.uk/stage/2011/-sep/28/conor-mcpherson-interview [Accessed 4/1/12]

Donaldson, Sarah, an interview with Conor McPherson, *Telegraph*, 17 May 2003, <http://www.telegraph.co.uk/culture/film/3594723/film-makers-on-film-conor-mcpherson.html>

Fannin, Hilary, an interview with Conor McPherson, 'The perfect work is always in the future, like a beautiful dream.' *The Irish Times*, 13 March 2010: 7.

Fanning, Dave, an interview with Conor McPherson, UCD *Connections*, November 2009, See http://www.youtube.com/watch?v=HwzUHtwgcbA

Fine, Marshall, an interview with Conor McPherson, 'Conor McPherson goes out on the edge with 'The Eclipse' http://hollywoodandfine.com/interviews/?p=675 [Accessed 10/1/2012]

McGinn, Caroline, 'Interview', an interview with Conor McPherson, *Time Out*, Sep 26 2011, http://www.timeout.com/london/theatre/article/2782/interview-conor-mcpherson [Accessed 3/11/11]

McPherson, Conor, 'Film or theatre, which is better? Conor McPherson, director of *The Actors*, says it's all in the performance', *The Guardian*, Friday 2 May 2003, http://www.guardian.co.uk/culture/2003/may/02/artsfeatures [Accessed 11/1/12]

---,'A Note on *Endgame.' Beckett on Film: 19 Films x 19 Directors*. Dublin: Blue Angel Films / Tyrone Productions, 2001.

---, 'Interview' on Beckett on Film website, http//www.beckettonfilm.com/plays/endgame/interview_macphearson.html

---,'Chronicles of the Human Heart,' *The Guardian*, Wednesday 1 March, 2006.

Vincent, Sally, an interview with Conor McPherson and Dylan Moran, 'Funny, peculiar,' *The Guardian*, Saturday 13 July, 2002.

White, Victoria, an interview with Conor McPherson 'Telling stories in the dark.' *The Irish Times* 2 July 1998: 14.

---

[1] See Irish Playography. http://www.irishplayography.com/-person.aspx?personid=341 [Accessed 6/1/12]

[2] See *Film Index International*.http://fii.chadwyck.co.uk/film/search [Accessed 6/3/2012]

Index

A

Abbey Theatre (*see also* Peacock Theatre), 3, 15, 25, 79, 114, 206, 211-12, 231, 238, 239
Act of Union (1800), 153, 269
Adams, Tim, 58, 127, 134-35
Anderson, Jean, 221
Arditti, Paul, 256
Ascendancy class, 252, 270
Atlantic Theater Company, 2, 19
Austin, Neil, 256

B

Barabbas Theatre Company, 215, 294
Bárka Theatre, Budapest, 15, 242-46, 249-50
Barry, Sebastian
    The Pride of Parnell Street, 33, 40, 41
Barthes, Roland, 139, 172, 178, 181
Beckett, Samuel, 2, 14, 24, 45, 47, 75, 111-12, 128, 138, 140, 193, 203, 210-11, 213, 215-24, 228-29, 239, 286, 287, 293, 298, 300-301
    Endgame, 2, 14, 112, 128, 193, 203, 207, 211, 215-19, 228-29, 286, 298, 301
    Ohio Impromptu, 45
    Waiting for Godot, 140, 193, 203
Belsey , Catherine, 224
Bergson, Henri, 228
Big House novel, 261
Billington, Michael, 58, 92, 100-101, 263, 268, 272
Biltmore Theater, New York, 89
Birthistle, Eva, 120
Black Humour, 86-87
Brantley, Ben, 78, 84, 86-88, 138, 147
Breathnach, Paddy, 9, 103, 111, 124, 298
Brennan, Bríd, 44, 57-58, 252, 259
Broadway, 2, 19, 286
Brooks, Peter, 130, 134-35
Bush Theatre, 1-2, 29-30, 45, 77, 86-87, 297-98
Byrne, Antoine, 9, 104

C

Caffrey, Peter, 9, 104
Caine, Michael, 10, 131-32
Carney, Liam, 15, 231-32, 235,
    237
Carr, Marina, 44, 57-58, 168,
    206, 215, 294-95
    On Raftery's Hill, 168
    Portia Coughlan, 168
Catholicism, 46, 93-94, 97, 99,
    184, 202
Celtic Tiger, 12, 14, 16, 32, 46,
    151, 153-61, 166, 169, 175,
    264-65, 268, 286, 299
Chaikin, Joseph, 218
Chekhov, Anton, 8, 266, 287
Chicago, 36, 179-80, 183, 294
Churchill, Caryl, 288
City Arts Centre, Dublin, 18, 23,
    64, 297
Coleridge, Samuel Taylor, 127,
    257
Colgan, Michael, 2, 128, 132,
    203
Comedy, 78, 86, 87, 88, 228,
    291, 295
Comic, 77, 82
Costa, Maddy, 195, 232, 238,
    239, 268, 270-73, 300
Cox, Brian, 1, 77-78, 116, 122,
    126, 144
Crypt Arts Centre, Dublin, 1,
    69, 297
Cummings, Scott T., 47, 49, 57-
    59, 74, 82, 86-87, 147-48,
    162, 299
Cusack, Sinead, 2

D

de Buitléar, Cian, 118

Dickens, Charles
    A Christmas Carol, 137, 140,
        146-47
Dolan, Jill, 7, 67-68, 71, 74-75
Donaldson, Sarah, 19, 86-87
Drew, Phelim, 15, 232
Dromgoole, Dominic, 233, 238-
    39
du Maurier, Daphne
    Birds, The (Short Story), 2,
        13, 179-80, 197, 206-13,
        238, 240, 250, 298-99
Dublin City, 160
Dunne, Caoilfhionn, 252
Dunning, Nick, 15, 232, 237
Dyer, Richard, 94, 100-101

E

Eagleton, Terry, 204, 211, 213
Entropy, 78, 86-88

F

Fairies (See also Supernatural),
    254
Farrell , Colin, 110, 270
Fay, Jimmy, 19, 281
Ferriter, Diarmaid, 167, 179-80
Fiennes, Ralph, 110
Fly By Night Theatre Company,
    1, 22-23, 297
Foster, Roy, 198, 211-12
Freud, Sigmund, 224, 228-29
Fricker, Karen, 100, 299
Friel, Brian, 111
    Faith Healer, 24, 114
    Freedom of the City, The, 22

    Philadelphia, Here I Come!,
        109, 111-12
    Translations, 153-54, 271

Yalta Game, The, 2
Fuchs, Elinor, 11, 139, 147
  Death of Character, The,
    139, 147-49

G

Gambon, Michael, 133, 220-22
Gate Theatre (Dublin), 2, 23,
  25, 72, 89, 203, 206, 211,
  213, 297-98
Geis, Deborah, 45, 57-58
Gender, 179-80
Genette, Gerard, 129, 134
German Idealism, 266
Ghost Estates, 12, 154
Ghost stories, 13, 62, 96, 99,
  137, 198
Gleeson, Brendan, 9, 19, 104,
  110-12, 119
Gothic, 16, 206-207, 251, 255-
  56, 261, 266, 268-73
Göttinger, Pál, 15, 241, 250
Greek tragedy, 208
Grene, Nicholas, 99-100, 102,
  147-48, 171, 179, 181, 299
Gussow, Mel, 216-19, 228-29
Guthrie Theater, Minneapolis,
  2

H

Hammershøi, Vilhelm, 271
Heidegger, Martin, 174, 177,
  179, 181-82
Hely, Kevin, 23
Hitchcock, Alfred, 207
  Birds, The, 2, 13, 179-80, 197,
    206-211, 213, 238, 240,
    250, 298-99
Hoggard , Liz, 262-63, 269

Hogle, Jerrold E., 255, 269-70,
  272
Holland, Norman, 215, 229
Hughes, Declan, 31, 40
Humour, 215, 228-29
Hutcheon, Linda, 58

I

Ibsen, Henrik
  Wild Duck, The, 254
International Bar, 18, 23, 297
Ionesco, Eugène, 86
Irish Diaspora, 267, 294
Irish folklore, 198

J

Jameson, Fredric, 57, 130, 133,
  135
Jim Sheridan, 111
Jones, Ursula, 253
Jordan, Neil, 2, 27, 129, 131
  White Horses, 2
Joyce, James
  Finnegans Wake, 273

K

Kalb, Jonathan, 218, 229
Kane, Sarah, 43, 76, 89, 101,
  295
  4.48 Psychosis, 89, 100-101
Kant, Immanuel, 257
Keane, John B.
  Field, The, 169, 269-70
Kearney, Richard, 97-98, 100,
  102
  On Stories, 97, 100, 102
Kinlan, Laurence, 116, 123
Kirby, Peadar, 166, 179-80
Kosofsky Sedgwick, Eve, 269,
  272

L

LaBute, Neil, 43
Laughter, 228, 295
Lothe, Jakob, 131, 134-35
Lyotard, Jean-François, 46-48,
    57-58

M

Marlowe, Christopher, 201,
    208, 209, 211, 213
Masculinity/Masculinities, 89,
    94, 100-101, 108, 299
McCarthy, Cormac
    Road, The, 209
McCormack, W.J., 255-56, 260,
    270, 272
McDonagh, Martin, 19, 110-11,
    128, 147-48, 161-62, 168, 179,
    181, 215, 243, 247, 291, 292,
    299
    In Bruges, 19, 110-12
    Lonesome West, The, 168
McDonald, Peter, 9, 23, 104,
    111, 119, 252
McElhatton, Michael, 19, 104,
    119
McGinn, Caroline, 263, 269,
    272, 301
McGuinness, Frank, 19, 45, 75,
    292
McPherson, Conor, *passim*
    *A Light in the Window of
        Industry*, 18, 297
    Actors, The, 3, 10-11, 13, 19,
        78, 86-87, 127, 129, 131-
        34, 298-99, 301
    Birds, The, 2, 14, 207, 213
    Come on Over, 2, 7, 297, 299

Dublin Carol, 1, 7, 11, 19, 32,
    36-43, 111, 137-38, 140-49,
    168, 199, 245, 297, 299
Eclipse, The, 3, 14, 107, 183,
    186, 191-95, 206, 288,
    298, 301
Endgame (Beckett on Film),
    2, 14, 112, 128, 193, 203,
    207, 211, 215-19, 228-29,
    286, 298, 301
Good Thief, The (formerly
    titled *The Light of Jesus*),
    5-8, 18, 27-31, 39, 43, 57-
    58, 61-62, 64, 66-67, 73,
    75, 103, 297-98
I Went Down, 3, 9, 28, 103-
    104, 107-12, 119, 124, 298
Inventing Fortune's Wheel,
    18, 297
Michelle Pfeiffer, 18, 22, 297
Port Authority, 2, 6, 7, 31,
    34-35, 41-44, 54, 56, 90,
    95, 96, 99-102, 107, 111,
    114, 127, 245, 297, 299
Radio Play, 18, 297
Rum and Vodka, 5-7, 18-19,
    23, 29-35, 39, 41, 43, 61-
    62, 65-66, 72, 75, 90, 95,
    99, 168, 276, 297-98
Saltwater, 3, 10, 27, 107, 112-
    26, 298
Scenes Federal, 18, 297
Seafarer, The, 2-3, 7, 14-15,
    18-19, 32, 36, 39, 41, 43,
    58, 90, 93, 95-102, 107,
    111, 138, 165, 168, 179-80,
    197, 199-207, 210-16, 224,
    228-33, 238-50, 281, 286,
    298-99

Shining City, 1-2, 7-9, 19, 24-25, 32, 36-43, 89-101, 107, 148, 286, 297, 299

St. Nicholas, 1, 6-7, 19, 25, 29, 43-45, 49-51, 58, 77-86, 98-101, 137, 297, 298

Stars Lose Their Glory, The, 18, 297

Taking Stock, 18, 297

This Lime Tree Bower, 1, 3, 5, 7, 10, 19, 22, 24, 26, 29-33, 36, 39, 41-45, 51, 54-56, 61, 66, 69-76, 101, 107, 113-14, 120, 122-27, 297-98

Veil, The, 2, 7, 13, 16-18, 147-49, 251-52, 266-73, 298-99

Weir, The, 1-3, 6-7, 12-13, 17-18, 29, 43-45, 57-63, 72-75, 90, 93, 95, 99, 101, 107, 125, 127-28, 137, 147-48, 151-56, 161-62, 165-73, 178-82, 198-99, 245, 281, 297-99

Milton, John
Paradise Lost, 204, 210,-213

Monologue, 40-44, 46, 48, 56-58, 86-87, 114, 147-48, 300

Moran, Dylan, 10, 131, 134, 301

Moroney, Mic, 84, 86, 88

Moxley, Gina, 119

Mullen, Conor, 120

Murphy, Tom, 19, 24, 45, 168, 170, 195, 199, 246, 250, 279, 288, 293
Bailegangaire, 170
Conversations on a Homecoming, 170, 246
Gigli Concert, The, 24, 168

mysterium, 11, 137-42, 145-46

N

Narrative *see also* storytelling, 40, 41, 48, 51, 57, 58, 59, 74, 86, 87, 89, 94, 97, 98, 127, 129, 130, 134, 135, 147, 148, 162, 167, 179, 180, 181, 211, 212, 294, 299, 300

National Theatre, London, 2, 251, 260, 266, 268, 269, 271, 298
Cottesloe, 2, 298
Lyttleton, 2, 251, 298

Newton, Adam Zachary, 48, 59

Norton , Jim, 2, 210-13, 238-39, 253-56

O

O'Boyle , Caroline, 117

O'Brien, Eugene
Eden, 3, 24, 114, 125, 208, 210, 286

O'Casey, Sean
Juno and the Paycock, 202, 272

O'Connor , Coilin, 22

O'Mahoney, Paul, 15, 233

O'Neill , Nuala, 121

O'Neill, Eugene
Iceman Cometh, The, 16, 200, 248

O'Rourke , David, 117

O'Rowe, Mark, 7, 19, 24, 33, 41, 43, 76, 100-101, 114, 299
Intermission, 19, 33, 41
Terminus, 7

P

Paglia, Camille, 211, 213

Pierce, Nev, 78, 87

Pilný, Ondřej, 165, 168, 235, 238-39, 295
Plague Monkeys, The, 123, 126
Postdramatic Theatre, 74
Pound, Ezra, 231, 239
Primary Stages (New York), 19, 69, 78

Q

Quinn, Aidan, 3

R

Ravenhill, Mark, 43, 76
Rickson, Ian, 1, 19, 281
Ricoeur, Paul, 13, 167, 174-81
Roche, Billy, 3, 13, 45, 186, 206, 279, 286-88, 292, 298
   'Table Manners', 13, 186, 206
   Poor Beast in the Rain, 3, 286-87
   Tales from Rainwater Pond, 206, 211
Royal Court, 1- 2, 23, 25, 37, 61, 89, 100-101, 141, 144, 151, 297

S

Schiller, Adrian, 253
Scorsese, Martin
   King of Comedy, The, 7, 19, 78, 86, 87
Shakespeare, William
   Hamlet, 11, 132, 137
   Othello, 197
   Richard III, 10, 131-34
Shelley, Percy Bysshe
   'Song of Apollo', 208, 211
   Prometheus Unbound, 208
Simon, Charles, 221

Singleton , Brian, 41, 46, 58-59, 148, 165, 232, 238-40
Smith, Rae, 1, 141, 252, 256
Sontag, Susan, 173, 181
Spallen, Abbie
   Pumpgirl, 114
Spelman, Valerie, 23, 120
Spielberg, Steven, 128
Stafford, Maeliosa, 15, 231, 234
Stewart Parker Award, 1
Storytelling, 22-23, 45, 49-50, 53-54, 78, 84, 97-98, 127, 129, 131, 134, 154, 156, 159, 165, 170, 175, 242, 248
Supernatural (The), 179-80, 197, 238, 240, 250
Synge, J.M.
   Riders to the Sea, 152-53, 157, 160
   Shadow of the Glen, The, 156, 162

T

Taylor, Paul, 77, 87
Thewlis, David, 219, 220, 222
Tony Awards, 2, 19
Troika, comprising International Monetary Fund (IMF), European Commission (EC), European Central Bank (ECB), 16, 265
Truffaut, François, 114

U

University College Dublin Dramsoc, 1, 18, 21-22, 276, 297
UCD, 1, 4, 10, 21, 23-26, 29, 120, 127, 184, 193, 195, 201,

210-211, 275, 291-95, 297, 301
Upor, László, 15, 247
Utilitarianism, 5, 25, 29-30

V

Violence, 61, 291

W

Walpole, Robert, 9, 103, 124
Walsh, Enda, 24, 33, 43, 199

West, Michael
  Freefall, 249
Wilmot, David, 9, 19, 104
Wood, Gerald C., 29-30, 47, 57, 58, 114, 119, 123, 125-26, 212
Woolgar, Fenella, 253, 261
Wycherly, Don, 15, 24, 231, 235

Y

Young Vic Genesis Project, 242

Carysfort Press was formed in the summer of 1998. It receives annual funding from the Arts Council.

The directors believe that drama is playing an ever-increasing role in today's society and that enjoyment of the theatre, both professional and amateur, currently plays a central part in Irish culture.

The Press aims to produce high quality publications which, though written and/or edited by academics, will be made accessible to a general readership. The organisation would also like to provide a forum for critical thinking in the Arts in Ireland, again keeping the needs and interests of the general public in view.

The company publishes contemporary Irish writing for and about the theatre.

Editorial and publishing inquiries to:
Carysfort Press Ltd.,
58 Woodfield,
Scholarstown Road,
Rathfarnham,
Dublin 16,
Republic of Ireland.

T (353 1) 493 7383
F (353 1) 406 9815
E: info@carysfortpress.com
www.carysfortpress.com

HOW TO ORDER

TRADE ORDERS DIRECTLY TO:
Irish Book Distribution
Unit 12, North Park, North Road,
Finglas, Dublin 11.

T: (353 1) 8239580
F: (353 1) 8239599
E: mary@argosybooks.ie
www.argosybooks.ie

INDIVIDUAL ORDERS DIRECTLY TO:
eprint Ltd.
35 Coolmine Industrial Estate,
Blanchardstown, Dublin 15.
T: (353 1) 827 8860
F: (353 1) 827 8804 Order online @
E: books@eprint.ie
www.eprint.ie

FOR SALES IN NORTH AMERICA AND CANADA:
Dufour Editions Inc.,
124 Byers Road,
PO Box 7,
Chester Springs,
PA 19425,
USA

T: 1-610-458-5005
F: 1-610-458-7103

The Story of Barabbas, The Company

Carmen Szabo

Acclaimed by audiences and critics alike for their highly innovative, adventurous and entertaining theatre, Barabbas The Company have created playful, intelligent and dynamic productions for over 17 years. Breaking the mould of Irish theatrical tradition and moving away from a text dominated theatre, Barabbas The Company's productions have established an instantly recognizable performance style influenced by the theatre of clown, circus, mime, puppetry, object manipulation and commedia dell'arte. This is the story of a unique company within the framework of Irish theatre, discussing the influences that shape their performances and establish their position within the history and development of contemporary Irish theatre. This book addresses the overwhelming necessity to reconsider Irish theatre history and to explore, in a language accessible to a wide range of readers, the issues of physicality and movement based theatre in Ireland.

ISBN: 978-1-904505-59-4   €25

Irish Drama: Local and Global Perspectives

Edited by Nicholas Grene and Patrick Lonergan

Since the late 1970s there has been a marked internationalization of Irish drama, with individual plays, playwrights, and theatrical companies establishing newly global reputations. This book reflects upon these developments, drawing together leading scholars and playwrights to consider the consequences that arise when Irish theatre travels abroad.

Contributors: Chris Morash, Martine Pelletier, José Lanters, Richard Cave, James Moran, Werner Huber, Rhona Trench, Christopher Murray, Ursula Rani Sarma, Jesse Weaver, Enda Walsh, Elizabeth Kuti

ISBN: 978-1-904505-63-1   €20

What Shakespeare Stole From Rome

Brian Arkins

What Shakespeare Stole From Rome analyses the multiple ways Shakespeare used material from Roman history and Latin poetry in his plays and poems. From the history of the Roman Republic to the tragedies of Seneca; from the Comedies of Platus to Ovid's poetry; this enlightening book examines the important influence of Rome and Greece on Shakespeare's work.

ISBN: 978-1-904505-58-7   €20

Polite Forms

Harry White

Polite Forms is a sequence of poems that meditates on family life. These poems remember and reimagine scenes from childhood and adolescence through the formal composure of the sonnet, so that the uniformity of this framing device promotes a tension as between a neatly arranged album of photographs and the chaos and flow of experience itself. Throughout the collection there is a constant preoccupation with the difference between actual remembrance and the illumination or meaning which poetry can afford. Some of the poems 'rewind the tapes of childhood' across two or three generations, and all of them are akin to pictures at an exhibition which survey individual impressions of childhood and parenthood in a thematically continuous series of portraits drawn from life.

Harry White was born in Dublin in 1958. He is Professor of Music at University College Dublin and widely known for his work in musicology and cultural history. His publications include "Music and the Irish Literary Imagination" (Oxford, 2008), which was awarded the Michael J. Durkan prize of the American Conference for Irish Studies in 2009. "Polite Forms" is his first collection of poems

ISBN: 978-1-904505-55-6   €10

Ibsen and Chekhov on the Irish Stage

Edited by Ros Dixon and Irina Ruppo Malone

Ibsen and Chekhov on the Irish Stage presents articles on the theories of translation and adaptation, new insights on the work of Brian Friel, Frank McGuinness, Thomas Kilroy, and Tom Murphy, historical analyses of theatrical productions during the Irish Revival, interviews with contemporary theatre directors, and a round-table discussion with the playwrights, Michael West and Thomas Kilroy.

Ibsen and Chekhov on the Irish Stage challenges the notion that a country's dramatic tradition develops in cultural isolation. It uncovers connections between past productions of plays by Ibsen and Chekhov and contemporary literary adaptations of their works by Irish playwrights, demonstrating the significance of international influence for the formation of national canon.

Conceived in the spirit of a round-table discussion, *Ibsen and Chekhov on the Irish Stage* is a collective study of the intricacies of trans-cultural migration of dramatic works and a re-examination of Irish theatre history from 1890 to the present day.

ISBN: 978-1-904505-57-0   €20

Tom Swift Selected Plays

With an introduction by Peter Crawley.

The inaugural production of Performance Corporation in 2002 matched Voltaire's withering assault against the doctrine of optimism with a playful aesthetic and endlessly inventive stagecraft.

Each play in this collection was originally staged by the Performance Corporation and though Swift has explored different avenues ever since, such playfulness is a constant. The writing is precise, but leaves room for the discoveries of rehearsals, the flesh of the theatre. All plays are blueprints for performance, but several of these scripts – many of which are site-specific and all of them slyly topical – are documents for something unrepeatable.

ISBN: 978-1-904505-56-3   €20

Synge and His Influences: Centenary Essays from the Synge Summer School

Edited by Patrick Lonergan

The year 2009 was the centenary of the death of John Millington Synge, one of the world's great dramatists. To mark the occasion, this book gathers essays by leading scholars of Irish drama, aiming to explore the writers and movements that shaped Synge, and to consider his enduring legacies. Essays discuss Synge's work in its Irish, European and world contexts – showing his engagement not just with the Irish literary revival but with European politics and culture too. The book also explores Synge's influence on later writers: Irish dramatists such as Brian Friel, Tom Murphy and Marina Carr, as well as international writers like Mustapha Matura and Erisa Kironde. It also considers Synge's place in Ireland today, revealing how *The Playboy of the Western World* has helped to shape Ireland's responses to globalisation and multiculturalism, in celebrated productions by the Abbey Theatre, Druid Theatre, and Pan Pan Theatre Company.

Contributors include Ann Saddlemyer, Ben Levitas, Mary Burke, Paige Reynolds, Eilís Ní Dhuibhne, Mark Phelan, Shaun Richards, Ondřej Pilný, Richard Pine, Alexandra Poulain, Emilie Pine, Melissa Sihra, Sara Keating, Bisi Adigun, Adrian Frazier and Anthony Roche.

ISBN: 978-1-904505-50-1   €20.00

Constellations - The Life and Music of John Buckley

Benjamin Dwyer

Benjamin Dwyer provides a long overdue assessment of one of Ireland's most prolific composers of the last decades. He looks at John Buckley's music in the context of his biography and Irish cultural life. This is no hagiography but a critical assessment of Buckley's work, his roots and aesthetics. While looking closely at several of Buckley's compositions, the book is written in a comprehensible style that makes it easily accessible to anybody interested in Irish musical and cultural history.   *Wolfgang Marx*

As well as providing a very readable and comprehensive study of the life and music of John Buckley, Constellations also offers an up-to-date and informative catalogue of compositions, a complete discography, translations of set texts and the full libretto of his chamber opera, making this book an essential guide for both students and professional scholars alike.

ISBN: 978-1-904505-52-5   €20.00

'Because We Are Poor': Irish Theatre in the 1990s

Victor Merriman

"Victor Merriman's work on Irish theatre is in the vanguard of a whole new paradigm in Irish theatre scholarship, one that is not content to contemplate monuments of past or present achievement, but for which the theatre is a lens that makes visible the hidden malaises in Irish society. That he has been able to do so by focusing on a period when so much else in Irish culture conspired to hide those problems is only testimony to the considerable power of his critical scrutiny." Chris Morash, NUI Maynooth.

ISBN: 978-1-904505-51-8   €20.00

'Buffoonery and Easy Sentiment':
Popular Irish Plays in the Decade Prior to the Opening of The Abbey Theatre

Christopher Fitz-Simon

In this fascinating reappraisal of the non-literary drama of the late 19th - early 20th century, Christopher Fitz-Simon discloses a unique world of plays, players and producers in metropolitan theatres in Ireland and other countries where Ireland was viewed as a source of extraordinary topics at once contemporary and comfortably remote: revolution, eviction, famine, agrarian agitation, political assassination.

The form was the fashionable one of melodrama, yet Irish melodrama was of a particular kind replete with hidden messages, and the language was far more allusive, colourful and entertaining than that of its English equivalent.

ISBN: 978-1-9045505-49-5   €20.00

The Fourth Seamus Heaney Lectures, 'Mirror up to Nature':

Ed. Patrick Burke

What, in particular, is the contemporary usefulness for the building of societies of one of our oldest and culturally valued ideals, that of drama? The Fourth Seamus Heaney Lectures, 'Mirror up to Nature': Drama and Theatre in the Modern World, given at St Patrick's College, Drumcondra, between October 2006 and April 2007, addressed these and related questions. Patrick Mason spoke on the essence of theatre, Thomas Kilroy on Ireland's contribution to the art of theatre, Cecily O'Neill and Jonothan Neelands on the rich potential of drama in the classroom. Brenna Katz Clarke examined the relationship between drama and film, and John Buckley spoke on opera and its history and gave an illuminating account of his own *Words Upon The Window-Pane.*

ISBN 978-1-9045505-48-8   €12

The Theatre of Tom Mac Intyre: 'Strays from the ether'

Eds. Bernadette Sweeney and Marie Kelly

This long overdue anthology captures the soul of Mac Intyre's dramatic canon – its ethereal qualities, its extraordinary diversity, its emphasis on the poetic and on performance – in an extensive range of visual, journalistic and scholarly contributions from writers, theatre practitioners.

ISBN 978-1-904505-46-4 €25

Irish Appropriation Of Greek Tragedy

Brian Arkins

This book presents an analysis of more than 30 plays written by Irish dramatists and poets that are based on the tragedies of Sophocles, Euripides and Aeschylus. These plays proceed from the time of Yeats and Synge through MacNeice and the Longfords on to many of today's leading writers.

ISBN 978-1-904505-47-1 €20

Alive in Time: The Enduring Drama of Tom Murphy

Ed. Christopher Murray

Almost 50 years after he first hit the headlines as Ireland's most challenging playwright, the 'angry young man' of those times Tom Murphy still commands his place at the pinnacle of Irish theatre. Here 17 new essays by prominent critics and academics, with an introduction by Christopher Murray, survey Murphy's dramatic oeuvre in a concerted attempt to define his greatness and enduring appeal, making this book a significant study of a unique genius.

ISBN 978-1-904505-45-7 €25

Performing Violence in Contemporary Ireland

Ed. Lisa Fitzpatrick

This interdisciplinary collection of fifteen new essays by scholars of theatre, Irish studies, music, design and politics explores aspects of the performance of violence in contemporary Ireland. With chapters on the work of playwrights Martin McDonagh, Martin Lynch, Conor McPherson and Gary Mitchell, on Republican commemorations and the 90th anniversary ceremonies for the Battle of the Somme and the Easter Rising, this book aims to contribute to the ongoing international debate on the performance of violence in contemporary societies.

ISBN 978-1-904505-44-0 (2009) €20

Ireland's Economic Crisis - Time to Act. Essays from over 40 leading Irish thinkers at the MacGill Summer School 2009

Eds. Joe Mulholland and Finbarr Bradley

Ireland's economic crisis requires a radical transformation in policymaking. In this volume, political, industrial, academic, trade union and business leaders and commentators tell the story of the Irish economy and its rise and fall. Contributions at Glenties range from policy, vision and context to practical suggestions on how the country can emerge from its crisis.

ISBN 978-1-904505-43-3 (2009) €20

Deviant Acts: Essays on Queer Performance

Ed. David Cregan

This book contains an exciting collection of essays focusing on a variety of alternative performances happening in contemporary Ireland. While it highlights the particular representations of gay and lesbian identity it also brings to light how diversity has always been a part of Irish culture and is, in fact, shaping what it means to be Irish today.

ISBN 978-1-904505-42-6 (2009) €20

Seán Keating in Context: Responses to Culture and Politics in Post-Civil War Ireland

Compiled, edited and introduced by Éimear O'Connor

Irish artist Seán Keating has been judged by his critics as the personification of old-fashioned traditionalist values. This book presents a different view. The story reveals Keating's early determination to attain government support for the visual arts. It also illustrates his socialist leanings, his disappointment with capitalism, and his attitude to cultural snobbery, to art critics, and to the Academy. Given the national and global circumstances nowadays, Keating's critical and wry observations are prophetic – and highly amusing.

ISBN 978-1-904505-41-9 €25

Dialogue of the Ancients of Ireland: A new translation of Acallam na Senorach

Translated with introduction and notes by Maurice Harmon

One of Ireland's greatest collections of stories and poems, The Dialogue of the Ancients of Ireland is a new translation by Maurice Harmon of the 12th century *Acallam na Senorach*. Retold in a refreshing modern idiom, the *Dialogue* is an extraordinary account of journeys to the four provinces by St. Patrick and the pagan Cailte, one of the surviving Fian. Within the frame story are over 200 other stories reflecting many genres – wonder tales, sea journeys, romances, stories of revenge, tales of monsters and magic. The poems are equally varied – lyrics, nature poems, eulogies, prophecies, laments, genealogical poems. After the *Tain Bo Cuailnge*, the *Acallam* is the largest surviving prose work in Old and Middle Irish.

ISBN: 978-1-904505-39-6 (2009) €20

Literary and Cultural Relations between Ireland and Hungary and Central and Eastern Europe

Ed. Maria Kurdi

This lively, informative and incisive collection of essays sheds fascinating new light on the literary interrelations between Ireland, Hungary, Poland, Romania and the Czech Republic. It charts a hitherto under-explored history of the reception of modern Irish culture in Central and Eastern Europe and also investigates how key authors have been translated, performed and adapted. The revealing explorations undertaken in this volume of a wide array of Irish dramatic and literary texts, ranging from *Gulliver's Travels* to *Translations* and *The Pillowman*, tease out the subtly altered nuances that they acquire in a Central European context.

ISBN: 978-1-904505-40-2 (2009)   €20

Plays and Controversies: Abbey Theatre Diaries 2000-2005

Ben Barnes

In diaries covering the period of his artistic directorship of the Abbey, Ben Barnes offers a frank, honest, and probing account of a much commented upon and controversial period in the history of the national theatre. These diaries also provide fascinating personal insights into the day-to- day pressures, joys, and frustrations of running one of Ireland's most iconic institutions.

ISBN: 978-1-904505-38-9 (2008)   €20

Interactions: Dublin Theatre Festival 1957-2007. Irish Theatrical Diaspora Series: 3

Eds. Nicholas Grene and Patrick Lonergan with Lilian Chambers

For over 50 years the Dublin Theatre Festival has been one of Ireland's most important cultural events, bringing countless new Irish plays to the world stage, while introducing Irish audiences to the most important international theatre companies and artists. Interactions explores and celebrates the achievements of the renowned Festival since 1957 and includes specially commissioned memoirs from past organizers, offering a unique perspective on the controversies and successes that have marked the event's history. An especially valuable feature of the volume, also, is a complete listing of the shows that have appeared at the Festival from 1957 to 2008.

ISBN: 978-1-904505-36-5   €20

The Informer: A play by Tom Murphy based on the novel by Liam O'Flaherty

The Informer, Tom Murphy's stage adaptation of Liam O'Flaherty's novel, was produced in the 1981 Dublin Theatre Festival, directed by the playwright himself, with Liam Neeson in the leading role. The central subject of the play is the quest of a character at the point of emotional and moral breakdown for some source of meaning or identity. In the case of Gypo Nolan, the informer of the title, this involves a nightmarish progress through a Dublin underworld in which he changes from a Judas figure to a scapegoat surrogate for Jesus, taking upon himself the sins of the world. A cinematic style, with flash-back and intercut scenes, is used rather than a conventional theatrical structure to catch the fevered and phantasmagoric progression of Gypo's mind. The language, characteristically for Murphy, mixes graphically colloquial Dublin slang with the haunted intricacies of the central character groping for the meaning of his own actions. The dynamic rhythm of the action builds towards an inevitable but theatrically satisfying tragic catastrophe. ' [The Informer] is, in many ways closer to being an original Murphy play than it is to O'Flaherty...' Fintan O'Toole.

ISBN: 978-1-904505-37-2 (2008) €10

Shifting Scenes: Irish theatre-going 1955-1985

Eds. Nicholas Grene and Chris Morash

Transcript of conversations with John Devitt, academic and reviewer, about his lifelong passion for the theatre. A fascinating and entertaining insight into Dublin theatre over the course of thirty years provided by Devitt's vivid reminiscences and astute observations.

ISBN: 978-1-904505-33-4 (2008) €10

Irish Literature: Feminist Perspectives

Eds. Patricia Coughlan and Tina O'Toole

The collection discusses texts from the early 18th century to the present. A central theme of the book is the need to renegotiate the relations of feminism with nationalism and to transact the potential contest of these two important narratives, each possessing powerful emancipatory force. Irish Literature: Feminist Perspectives contributes incisively to contemporary debates about Irish culture, gender and ideology.

ISBN: 978-1-904505-35-8 (2008) €20

Silenced Voices: Hungarian Plays from Transylvania

Selected and translated by Csilla Bertha and Donald E. Morse

The five plays are wonderfully theatrical, moving fluidly from absurdism to tragedy, and from satire to the darkly comic. Donald Morse and Csilla Bertha's translations capture these qualities perfectly, giving voice to the 'forgotten playwrights of Central Europe'. They also deeply enrich our understanding of the relationship between art, ethics, and politics in Europe.

ISBN: 978-1-904505-34-1 (2008) €20

A Hazardous Melody of Being:
Seóirse Bodley's Song Cycles on the poems of Micheal O'Siadhail

Ed. Lorraine Byrne Bodley

This apograph is the first publication of Bodley's O'Siadhail song cycles and is the first book to explore the composer's lyrical modernity from a number of perspectives. Lorraine Byrne Bodley's insightful introduction describes in detail the development and essence of Bodley's musical thinking, the European influences he absorbed which linger in these cycles, and the importance of his work as a composer of the Irish art song.

ISBN: 978-1-904505-31-0 (2008)   €25

Irish Theatre in England: Irish Theatrical Diaspora Series: 2

Eds. Richard Cave and Ben Levitas

Irish theatre in England has frequently illustrated the complex relations between two distinct cultures. How English reviewers and audiences interpret Irish plays is often decidedly different from how the plays were read in performance in Ireland. How certain Irish performers have chosen to be understood in Dublin is not necessarily how audiences in London have perceived their constructed stage personae. Though a collection by diverse authors, the twelve essays in this volume investigate these issues from a variety of perspectives that together chart the trajectory of Irish performance in England from the mid-nineteenth century till today.

ISBN: 978-1-904505-26-6 (2007)   €20

Goethe and Anna Amalia: A Forbidden Love?

Ettore Ghibellino, Trans. Dan Farrelly

In this study Ghibellino sets out to show that the platonic relationship between Goethe and Charlotte von Stein – lady-in-waiting to Anna Amalia, the Dowager Duchess of Weimar – was used as part of a cover-up for Goethe's intense and prolonged love relationship with the Duchess Anna Amalia herself. The book attempts to uncover a hitherto closely-kept state secret. Readers convinced by the evidence supporting Ghibellino's hypothesis will see in it one of the very great love stories in European history – to rank with that of Dante and Beatrice, and Petrarch and Laura.

ISBN: 978-1-904505-24-2   €20

Ireland on Stage: Beckett and After

Eds. Hiroko Mikami, Minako Okamuro, Naoko Yagi

The collection focuses primarily on Irish playwrights and their work, both in text and on the stage during the latter half of the twentieth century. The central figure is Samuel Beckett, but the contributors freely draw on Beckett and his work provides a springboard to discuss contemporary playwrights such as Brian Friel, Frank McGuinness, Marina Carr and Conor McPherson amongst others. Contributors include: Anthony Roche, Hiroko Mikami, Naoko Yagi, Cathy Leeney, Joseph Long, Noreem Doody, Minako Okamuro, Christopher Murray, Futoshi Sakauchi and Declan Kiberd

ISBN: 978-1-904505-23-5 (2007) €20

'Echoes Down the Corridor': Irish Theatre - Past, Present and Future

Eds. Patrick Lonergan and Riana O'Dwyer

This collection of fourteen new essays explores Irish theatre from exciting new perspectives. How has Irish theatre been received internationally - and, as the country becomes more multicultural, how will international theatre influence the development of drama in Ireland? These and many other important questions.

ISBN: 978-1-904505-25-9 (2007) €20

Musics of Belonging: The Poetry of Micheal O'Siadhail

Eds. Marc Caball & David F. Ford

An overall account is given of O'Siadhail's life, his work and the reception of his poetry so far. There are close readings of some poems, analyses of his artistry in matching diverse content with both classical and innovative forms, and studies of recurrent themes such as love, death, language, music, and the shifts of modern life.

ISBN: 978-1-904505-22-8 (2007) €25 (Paperback)
ISBN: 978-1-904505-21-1 (2007) €50 (Casebound)

Modern Death: The End of Civilization

Carl-Henning Wijkmark. Trans: Dan Farrelly

Modern Death is written in the form of a symposium, in which a government agency brings together a group of experts to discuss a strategy for dealing with an ageing population.

The speakers take up the thread of the ongoing debates about care for the aged and about euthanasia. In dark satirical mode the author shows what grim developments are possible. The theme of a 'final solution' is mentioned, though the connection with Hitler is explicitly denied. The most inhuman crimes against human dignity are discussed in the symposium as if they were a necessary condition of future progress.

The fiercely ironical treatment of the material tears off the thin veil that disguises the specious arguments and insidious expressions of concern for the well-being of the younger generation. Though the text was written nearly thirty years ago, the play has a terrifyingly modern relevance.

ISBN: 978 1 904505 28 0 (2007)   €8

Brian Friel's Dramatic Artistry: 'The Work has Value'

Eds. Donald E. Morse, Csilla Bertha and Maria Kurdi

Brian Friel's Dramatic Artistry presents a refreshingly broad range of voices: new work from some of the leading English-speaking authorities on Friel, and fascinating essays from scholars in Germany, Italy, Portugal, and Hungary. This book will deepen our knowledge and enjoyment of Friel's work.

ISBN: 978-1-904505-17-4 (2006)   €25

The Theatre of Martin McDonagh: 'A World of Savage Stories'

Eds. Lilian Chambers and Eamonn Jordan

The book is a vital response to the many challenges set by McDonagh for those involved in the production and reception of his work. Critics and commentators from around the world offer a diverse range of often provocative approaches. What is not surprising is the focus and commitment of the engagement, given the controversial and stimulating nature of the work.

ISBN: 978-1-904505-19-8 (2006)   €30

Edna O'Brien: New Critical Perspectives

Eds. Kathryn Laing, Sinead Mooney and Maureen O'Connor

The essays collected here illustrate some of the range, complexity, and interest of Edna O'Brien as a fiction writer and dramatist. They will contribute to a broader appreciation of her work and to an evolution of new critical approaches, as well as igniting more interest in the many unexplored areas of her considerable oeuvre.

ISBN: 978-1-904505-20-4 (2006)   €20

Irish Theatre on Tour

Eds. Nicholas Grene and Chris Morash

'Touring has been at the strategic heart of Druid's artistic policy since the early eighties. Everyone has the right to see professional theatre in their own communities. Irish theatre on tour is a crucial part of Irish theatre as a whole'. Garry Hynes

ISBN 978-1-904505-13-6 (2005) €20

Poems 2000-2005 by Hugh Maxton

Poems 2000-2005 is a transitional collection written while the author – also known to be W.J. Mc Cormack, literary historian – was in the process of moving back from London to settle in rural Ireland.

ISBN 978-1-904505-12-9 (2005) €10

Synge: A Celebration

Ed. Colm Tóibín

A collection of essays by some of Ireland's most creative writers on the work of John Millington Synge, featuring Sebastian Barry, Marina Carr, Anthony Cronin, Roddy Doyle, Anne Enright, Hugo Hamilton, Joseph O'Connor, Mary O'Malley, Fintan O'Toole, Colm Toibin, Vincent Woods.

ISBN 978-1-904505-14-3 (2005) €15

East of Eden: New Romanian Plays

Ed. Andrei Marinescu

Four of the most promising Romanian playwrights, young and very young, are in this collection, each one with a specific way of seeing the Romanian reality, each one with a style of communicating an articulated artistic vision of the society we are living in. Ion Caramitru, General Director Romanian National Theatre Bucharest.
ISBN 978-1-904505-15-0 (2005) €10

George Fitzmaurice: 'Wild in His Own Way', Biography of an Irish Playwright

Fiona Brennan

'Fiona Brennan's introduction to his considerable output allows us a much greater appreciation and understanding of Fitzmaurice, the one remaining under-celebrated genius of twentieth-century Irish drama'. Conall Morrison

ISBN 978-1-904505-16-7 (2005) €20

Out of History: Essays on the Writings of Sebastian Barry

Ed. Christina Hunt Mahony

The essays address Barry's engagement with the contemporary cultural debate in Ireland and also with issues that inform postcolonial critical theory. The range and selection of contributors has ensured a high level of critical expression and an insightful assessment of Barry and his works.

ISBN: 978-1-904505-18-1 (2005) €20

Three Congregational Masses

Seoirse Bodley

'From the simpler congregational settings in the Mass of Peace and the Mass of Joy to the richer textures of the Mass of Glory, they are immediately attractive and accessible, and with a distinctively Irish melodic quality.' Barra Boydell

ISBN: 978-1-904505-11-2 (2005) €15

Georg Büchner's Woyzeck,

A new translation by Dan Farrelly

The most up-to-date German scholarship of Thomas Michael Mayer and Burghard Dedner has finally made it possible to establish an authentic sequence of scenes. The wide-spread view that this play is a prime example of loose, open theatre is no longer sustainable. Directors and teachers are challenged to "read it again".

ISBN: 978-1-904505-02-0 (2004) €10

Playboys of the Western World: Production Histories

Ed. Adrian Frazier

'The book is remarkably well-focused: half is a series of production histories of Playboy performances through the twentieth century in the UK, Northern Ireland, the USA, and Ireland. The remainder focuses on one contemporary performance, that of Druid Theatre, as directed by Garry Hynes. The various contemporary social issues that are addressed in relation to Synge's play and this performance of it give the volume an additional interest: it shows how the arts matter.' Kevin Barry

ISBN: 978-1-904505-06-8 (2004) €20

The Power of Laughter: Comedy and Contemporary Irish Theatre

Ed. Eric Weitz

The collection draws on a wide range of perspectives and voices including critics, playwrights, directors and performers. The result is a series of fascinating and provocative debates about the myriad functions of comedy in contemporary Irish theatre. Anna McMullan

As Stan Laurel said, 'it takes only an onion to cry. Peel it and weep. Comedy is harder'. 'These essays listen to the power of laughter. They hear the tough heart of Irish theatre – hard and wicked and funny'. Frank McGuinness

ISBN: 978-1-904505-05-1 (2004) €20

Sacred Play: Soul-Journeys in contemporary Irish Theatre

Anne F. O'Reilly

'Theatre as a space or container for sacred play allows audiences to glimpse mystery and to experience transformation. This book charts how Irish playwrights negotiate the labyrinth of the Irish soul and shows how their plays contribute to a poetics of Irish culture that enables a new imagining. Playwrights discussed are: McGuinness, Murphy, Friel, Le Marquand Hartigan, Burke Brogan, Harding, Meehan, Carr, Parker, Devlin, and Barry.'

ISBN: 978-1-904505-07-5 (2004) €20

The Irish Harp Book

Sheila Larchet Cuthbert

This is a facsimile of the edition originally published by Mercier Press in 1993. There is a new preface by Sheila Larchet Cuthbert, and the biographical material has been updated. It is a collection of studies and exercises for the use of teachers and pupils of the Irish harp.

ISBN: 978-1-904505-08-2 (2004) €35

The Drunkard

Tom Murphy

'The Drunkard is a wonderfully eloquent play. Murphy's ear is finely attuned to the glories and absurdities of melodramatic exclamation, and even while he is wringing out its ludicrous overstatement, he is also making it sing.' The Irish Times

ISBN: 978-1-90 05-09-9 (2004) €10

Goethe: Musical Poet, Musical Catalyst

Ed. Lorraine Byrne

'Goethe was interested in, and acutely aware of, the place of music in human experience generally - and of its particular role in modern culture. Moreover, his own literary work - especially the poetry and Faust - inspired some of the major composers of the European tradition to produce some of their finest works.' Martin Swales

ISBN: 978-1-9045-10-5 (2004) €25

The Theatre of Marina Carr: "Before rules was made"

Eds. Anna McMullan & Cathy Leeney

As the first published collection of articles on the theatre of Marina Carr, this volume explores the world of Carr's theatrical imagination, the place of her plays in contemporary theatre in Ireland and abroad and the significance of her highly individual voice.

ISBN: 978-0-9534257-7-8 (2003) €20

Critical Moments: Fintan O'Toole on Modern Irish Theatre

Eds. Julia Furay & Redmond O'Hanlon

This new book on the work of Fintan O'Toole, the internationally acclaimed theatre critic and cultural commentator, offers percussive analyses and assessments of the major plays and playwrights in the canon of modern Irish theatre. Fearless and provocative in his judgements, O'Toole is essential reading for anyone interested in criticism or in the current state of Irish theatre.

ISBN: 978-1-904505-03-7 (2003) €20

Goethe and Schubert: Across the Divide

Eds. Lorraine Byrne & Dan Farrelly

Proceedings of the International Conference, 'Goethe and Schubert in Perspective and Performance', Trinity College Dublin, 2003. This volume includes essays by leading scholars – Barkhoff, Boyle, Byrne, Canisius, Dürr, Fischer, Hill, Kramer, Lamport, Lund, Meikle, Newbould, Norman McKay, White, Whitton, Wright, Youens – on Goethe's musicality and his relationship to Schubert; Schubert's contribution to sacred music and the Lied and his setting of Goethe's Singspiel, Claudine. A companion volume of this Singspiel (with piano reduction and English translation) is also available.

ISBN: 978-1-904505-04-4 (2003) €25

Goethe's Singspiel, 'Claudine von Villa Bella'

Set by Franz Schubert

Goethe's Singspiel in three acts was set to music by Schubert in 1815. Only Act One of Schuberts's Claudine score is extant. The present volume makes Act One available for performance in English and German. It comprises both a piano reduction by Lorraine Byrne of the original Schubert orchestral score and a bilingual text translated for the modern stage by Dan Farrelly. This is a tale, wittily told, of lovers and vagabonds, romance, reconciliation, and resolution of family conflict.

ISBN: 978-0-9544290-0-3 (2002) €14

Theatre of Sound, Radio and the Dramatic Imagination

Dermot Rattigan

An innovative study of the challenges that radio drama poses to the creative imagination of the writer, the production team, and the listener.
"A remarkably fine study of radio drama – everywhere informed by the writer's professional experience of such drama in the making…A new theoretical and analytical approach – informative, illuminating and at all times readable." Richard Allen Cave

ISBN: 978- 0-9534-257-5-4 (2002) €20

Talking about Tom Murphy

Ed. Nicholas Grene

Talking About Tom Murphy is shaped around the six plays in the landmark Abbey Theatre Murphy Season of 2001, assembling some of the best-known commentators on his work: Fintan O'Toole, Chris Morash, Lionel Pilkington, Alexandra Poulain, Shaun Richards, Nicholas Grene and Declan Kiberd.

ISBN: 978-0-9534-257-9-2 (2002) €12

Hamlet: The Shakespearean Director

Mike Wilcock

"This study of the Shakespearean director as viewed through various interpretations of HAMLET is a welcome addition to our understanding of how essential it is for a director to have a clear vision of a great play. It is an important study from which all of us who love Shakespeare and who understand the importance of continuing contemporary exploration may gain new insights." From the Foreword, by Joe Dowling, Artistic Director, The Guthrie Theater, Minneapolis, MN

ISBN: 978-1-904505-00-6 (2002) €20

The Theatre of Frank Mc Guinness: Stages of Mutability

Ed. Helen Lojek

The first edited collection of essays about internationally renowned Irish playwright Frank McGuinness focuses on both performance and text. Interpreters come to diverse conclusions, creating a vigorous dialogue that enriches understanding and reflects a strong consensus about the value of McGuinness's complex work.

ISBN: 978-1904505-01-3. (2002) €20

Theatre Talk: Voices of Irish Theatre Practitioners

Eds Lilian Chambers, Ger Fitzgibbon and Eamonn Jordan

"This book is the right approach - asking practitioners what they feel." Sebastian Barry, Playwright "... an invaluable and informative collection of interviews with those who make and shape the landscape of Irish Theatre." Ben Barnes, Artistic Director of the Abbey Theatre

ISBN: 978-0-9534-257-6-1 (2001) €20

In Search of the South African Iphigenie

Erika von Wietersheim and Dan Farrelly

Discussions of Goethe's "Iphigenie auf Tauris" (Under the Curse) as relevant to women's issues in modern South Africa: women in family and public life; the force of women's spirituality; experience of personal relationships; attitudes to parents and ancestors; involvement with religion.

ISBN: 978-0-9534257-8-5 (2001) €10

'The Starving' and 'October Song':

Two contemporary Irish plays by Andrew Hinds

The Starving, set during and after the siege of Derry in 1689, is a moving and engrossing drama of the emotional journey of two men.

October Song, a superbly written family drama set in real time in pre-ceasefire Derry.

ISBN: 978-0-9534-257-4-7 (2001) €10

Seen and Heard: Six new plays by Irish women

Ed. Cathy Leeney

A rich and funny, moving and theatrically exciting collection of plays by Mary Elizabeth Burke-Kennedy, Síofra Campbell, Emma Donoghue, Anne Le Marquand Hartigan, Michelle Read and Dolores Walshe.

ISBN: 978-0-9534-257-3-0 (2001)   €20

Theatre Stuff: Critical essays on contemporary Irish theatre

Ed. Eamonn Jordan

Best selling essays on the successes and debates of contemporary Irish theatre at home and abroad. Contributors include: Thomas Kilroy, Declan Hughes, Anna McMullan, Declan Kiberd, Deirdre Mulrooney, Fintan O'Toole, Christopher Murray, Caoimhe McAvinchey and Terry Eagleton.

ISBN: 978-0-9534-2571-1-6 (2000)   €20

Under the Curse. Goethe's "Iphigenie Auf Tauris", A New Version

Dan Farrelly

The Greek myth of Iphigenie grappling with the curse on the house of Atreus is brought vividly to life. This version is currently being used in Johannesburg to explore problems of ancestry, religion, and Black African women's spirituality.

ISBN: 978-09534-257-8-5 (2000)   €10

Urfaust, A New Version of Goethe's early "Faust" in Brechtian Mode

Dan Farrelly

This version is based on Brecht's irreverent and daring re-interpretation of the German classic. "Urfaust is a kind of well-spring for German theatre… The love-story is the most daring and the most profound in German dramatic literature." Brecht

ISBN: 978-0-9534-257-0-9 (1998)   €10